The Place of the Dead
Death and Remembrance in Late Medieval and Early Modern Europe

This volume of essays represents the first comprehensive treatment of a very significant component of the societies of late medieval and early modern Europe: the dead. It argues that to contemporaries the 'placing' of the dead, in physical, spiritual and social terms, was a vitally important exercise, and one which often involved conflict and complex negotiation.

The contributions range widely geographically, from Scotland to Transylvania, and address a spectrum of themes: attitudes towards the corpse, patterns of burial, forms of commemoration, the treatment of dead infants, the nature of the afterlife, and ghosts. Individually the essays help to illuminate several current historiographical concerns: the significance of the Black Death, the impact of the Protestant and Catholic Reformations, and interactions between 'elite' and 'popular' culture. Collectively, by exploring the social and cultural meanings of attitudes towards the dead, they provide genuinely original insight into the way these past societies understood themselves.

BRUCE GORDON is Lecturer in History and Associate Director of the Reformation Studies Institute, University of St Andrews. He is the author of *Clerical Discipline and the Rural Reformation* (1992) and editor of *Protestant History and Identity in Sixteenth-Century Europe* (1996).

PETER MARSHALL is Lecturer in History, University of Warwick. He is the author of *The Catholic Priesthood and the English Reformation* (1994) and editor of *The Impact of the English Reformation, 1500–1640* (1997).

The Place of the Dead
Death and Remembrance in Late Medieval and Early Modern Europe

Edited by Bruce Gordon
and Peter Marshall

 CAMBRIDGE
UNIVERSITY PRESS

GT
3242
.P53
2000

PUBLISHED BY THE PRESS SYNDICATE OF THE UNIVERSITY OF CAMBRIDGE
The Pitt Building, Trumpington Street, Cambridge CB2 1RP, United Kingdom

CAMBRIDGE UNIVERSITY PRESS
The Edinburgh Building, Cambridge CB2 2RU, UK   http://www.cup.cam.ac.uk
40 West 20th Street, New York, NY 10011–4211, USA   http://www.cup.org
10 Stamford Road, Oakleigh, Melbourne 3166, Australia

First published 2000

Printed in the United Kingdom at the University Press, Cambridge

Typeset in Garamond 11/13pt   CE

A catalogue record for this book is available from the British Library

Library of Congress cataloguing in publication data

The place of the dead: death and remembrance in late medieval and early modern
Europe / edited by Bruce Gordon and Peter Marshall.
    p.   cm.
ISBN 0 521 64256 6 (hardback)
1. Funeral rites and ceremonies – Europe – History. 2. Dead. 3. Europe – Religious life
and customs. I. Gordon, Bruce, 1962– . II. Marshall, Peter, 1964– .
GT3242.P53   1999
393′.094– dc21   99–20482 CIP

ISBN 0 521 64256 6 hardback
ISBN 0 521 64518 2 paperback

For Charlotte and Catherine
our new daughters

Contents

Illustrations

Notes on contributors

JAMES M. BOYDEN is Associate Professor of History at Tulane University, New Orleans. He is the author of *The Courtier and the King: Ruy Gomez de Silva, Philip II, and the Court of Spain* (1995) and is currently researching cultural changes in early modern Iberia stemming from the experience of overseas empire.

CLIVE BURGESS teaches in the History department at University College London. He has written extensively on the religious culture of late medieval England. He is editing *The Pre-Reformation Records of All Saints' Bristol* (vol. I, 1995).

NANCY CACIOLA is Assistant Professor of History at the University of California, San Diego. She was awarded the 1996 Van Courtlandt Elliot Prize from the Medieval Academy of America for an article on revenants. Her current project is a monograph on feminine sanctity, demonic possession and the discernment of spirits in the later Middle Ages.

SAMUEL K. COHN Jr is Professor of Medieval History at the University of Glasgow. His most recent book is *Florence and the Mountains: the Formation of a Regional State from the Black Death to the Medici*. He is currently working on a monograph entitled *Disease, Society and Culture: the Black Death in Comparative Perspective*.

WILL COSTER is Senior Lecturer in History at De Montford University, Bedford. His research interests are in the early modern family, popular religion and community. He is the author of *Kinship and Inheritance in Early Modern England: Three Yorkshire parishes* and a forthcoming study of baptism and spiritual kinship.

BRUCE GORDON is Lecturer in Modern History at the University of St Andrews and Associate Director of the St Andrews Reformation Studies Institute. He is the author of *Clerical Discipline and the Rural Reformation* (1992) and editor of *Protestant History and Identity in Sixteenth-Century Europe* (2 vols., 1996). He is currently writing a book on Zwingli.

VANESSA HARDING is Senior Lecturer in History at Birkbeck College, London. She has published widely on the history of London, including trade, marketing and topological development, and is currently working on the history of death and burial in early modern London and Paris.

J. S. W. HELT is Assistant Professor at the University of Michigan-Flint. He has written on early modern England and is completing a monograph entitled *Purgatory, Polity and Piety in Sixteenth-Century England*.

PETER MARSHALL is Lecturer in History at the University of Warwick. He is author of *The Catholic Priesthood and the English Reformation* (1994) and editor of *The Impact of the English Reformation, 1500–1640* (1997). He is currently writing a monograph to be called *Belief, Society, and the Dead in Reformation England*.

GRAEME MURDOCK is Lecturer in Modern History at the University of Birmingham. He has published articles on the Reformation in Eastern Europe and is preparing a monograph on the Hungarian Reformation. His research interests are in aspects of Calvinism in early modern Europe.

PENNY ROBERTS is Lecturer in the Department of History at the University of Warwick. She is author of *A City in Conflict: Troyes during the French Wars of Religion* (1996) and joint editor of two volumes of essays: *Fear in Early Modern Society* (1997) and *The Massacre in History* (1999). She has also published a number of research articles and essays on the social and religious history of early modern France.

PHILIP M. SOERGEL is Associate Professor at Arizona State University, Tempe. He is the author of *Wondrous in His Saints: Counter-Reformation Propaganda in Bavaria* (1993). He is currently completing a study of the use of prodigies and natural wonders among sixteenth-century Lutherans.

ANDREW SPICER teaches at Stonyhurst College and is Honorary Research Fellow at the University of Aberdeen. He is the author of *The French-speaking Reformed Community and their Church in Southampton, 1567–c. 1620* (1998). He is currently researching the impact of the Reformation upon church architecture, and is editing a volume entitled *Society and Culture in the Huguenot World, c. 1559–1685*.

LARISSA JULIET TAYLOR is Chair and Associate Professor of History at Colby College. She is the author of *Soldiers of Christ: Preaching in Late Medieval and Reformation France* (1992), which received the John Nicholas Brown Prize of the Medieval Academy of America. She has recently completed *Heresy and Orthodoxy in Sixteenth-Century Paris: François Picart and the Beginnings of the Catholic Reformation in France* (1999). She is Book Review Editor of the *Sixteenth Century Journal*.

Preface

This volume was conceived in the late summer of 1996 when the editors discovered they had a mutual (historical) interest in ghosts, and decided to investigate the prospects for a volume examining the ways in which the dead remained integral to the communities of late medieval and early modern Europe. We then pursued electronically scholars on both sides of the Atlantic, putting this matter before them and inviting them to consider the issues relative to their own areas of research. We are delighted that so many of our invitations were accepted, and grateful for the encouragement and helpful comments from those who were unable, for various reasons, to write for this book. William Davies at Cambridge University Press was supportive from the start and offered sage advice for which we offer our heartfelt thanks. The positive criticism and suggestions provided by the readers for the Press gave us much food for thought, and we have endeavoured to address their concerns. Various friends read the text in its entirety or in part and we gratefully acknowledge their gifts of time and energy: Rona Johnston Gordon, Andrew Pettegree, Paul Nelles, Julia Smith. Elaine Fulton cheerfully and accurately re-typed a manuscript when software problems emerged at the last moment. Dr Julian Crowe of the St Andrews University Computing Service dealt benevolently with the technical limitations of one editor, while Tim Lockley and Sarah Richardson similarly came to the rescue of the other in Warwick. Through their various efforts each of these people has made a significant contribution to the final result.

1 Introduction: placing the dead in late medieval and early modern Europe

Bruce Gordon and Peter Marshall

Like the poor, the dead are always with us. Even in this increasingly postmodern world it can confidently be asserted of all human societies that the endless loss of their members to the ravages of death is not a cultural construction but a biologically determined fact. Nonetheless, as a social or historical category 'the dead' can only be approached through the expressed and recorded memories, hopes and fears of the living.[1] Throughout history, it has proved virtually impossible for the living simply to ignore the dead. At the most basic level, if only to guard against disease and contamination, their physical remains must be disposed of. Moreover, even beyond an initial period of grief and bereavement, the emotional bonds which link the survivors to the deceased have usually demanded some form of symbolic commemoration, as well as a belief in the continued existence of the dead in some afterlife place or state. If societies are to continue to function, the dead must, in a variety of senses, be put in their place. Over the last twenty years or so the social history of death, a once neglected field, has begun to interest historians, particularly for the late medieval and early modern periods. To date, however, relatively little of this scholarship has attempted to examine in any comprehensive way the role and status of the dead after the process of dying was completed.[2] This lacuna is a significant one. An obvious

---

[1] See the epigrammatic opening of J.-C. Schmitt's *Ghosts in the Middle Ages: the Living and the Dead in Medieval Society*, tr. T. L. Fagan (Chicago and London, 1998): 'the dead have no existence other than that which the living imagine for them'.

[2] The historiography of this subject is now too vast to deal with comprehensively here, though particular mention should be made of the pioneering (if flawed) work of P. Ariès, *The Hour of our Death*, tr. H. Weaver (London 1981), and also of a number of other French historians who have led the way in this field: P. Chaunu, *La mort à Paris: XVIe, XVIIe et XVIIIe siècles* (Paris, 1978); J. Chiffoleau, *La comptabilité de l'au-delà: les hommes,*

consequence of the punitive mortality regime prevailing in pre-modern Europe was that, relative to our own society, throughout their lives people typically experienced the deaths of far greater numbers of children, kin or acquaintance.[3] In such circumstances the dead were a significant social 'presence', their importance underscored by the fact that so many did not live to share what has been called the 'disengaged social situation' (retirement, withdrawal from fully active social roles) of the dying in the Europe of today.[4]

The purpose of this collection of essays is to explore how groups of people in late medieval and early modern Europe sought to determine what the place of the dead should be, and how they managed to 'place' the dead in physical, spiritual, emotional, social and cultural terms.[5] Presented here is a thematically linked series of case studies from a wide variety of perspectives and directions in which scholars ask broadly similar questions about the societies they study: what was the status of the dead, socially and ontologically? What obligations did the living owe to them, and how in fulfilling those obligations did the living allow the dead to shape patterns of social organisation, and religious and cultural outlooks? In what circumstances did the dead threaten the living, and in

---

la mort et la religion dans la région d'Avignon à la fin du moyen âge (Rome, 1980); M. Vovelle, *La mort et l'Occident de 1300 à nos jours* (Paris, 1983). The social history of death for early modern England is now also fairly generously provided for: C. Gittings, *Death, Burial and the Individual in Early Modern England* (London, 1984); D. Cressy, *Birth, Marriage, and Death: Ritual, Religion, and the Life-cycle in Tudor and Stuart England* (Oxford, 1997); R. Houlbrooke, *Death, Religion, and the Family in England 1480–1750* (Oxford, 1998). Historians who have most explicitly tackled an agenda similar to the one envisaged here have tended to be medievalists. See P. J. Geary, *Living with the Dead in the Middle Ages* (Ithaca and London, 1994); O. G. Oexele, 'Die Gegenwart der Toten', in H. Braet and W. Verbecke (eds.), *Death in the Middle Ages* (Louvain, 1983), pp. 19–77; Schmitt, *Ghosts in the Middle Ages.*

[3] Even outside of crisis years of plague or famine, death rates were strikingly high. In early modern England, for example, they were often three times those of modern developed countries, while average life expectancy was about half: Houlbrooke, *Death, Religion, and the Family,* pp. 7–10.

[4] R. Blauner, 'Death and Social Structure', *Psychiatry* 29 (1966), cited in K. Thomas, *Religion and the Decline of Magic: Studies in Popular Beliefs in Sixteenth- and Seventeenth-Century England* (Harmondsworth, 1973), p. 723.

[5] The collection thus poses a set of questions of the type which have particularly interested social anthropologists. See, for example, J. Goody, *Death, Property, and the Ancestors: a Study of the Mortuary Customs of the Lodagaa of West Africa* (Stanford, CA, 1962); M. Bloch, *Placing the Dead: Tombs, Ancestral Villages and Kinship Organisation in Madagascar* (London, 1971); H. G. Nutini, *Todos Santos in Rural Tlaxcala: a Syncretic, Expressive, and Symbolic Analysis of the Cult of the Dead* (Princeton, NJ, 1988). It may be, however, that the theoretical and interpretative models in these works are too culturally specific to be readily transplanted to the societies of late medieval and early modern Europe.

what ways could the living exploit the dead for their own social and political purposes? If we speak, as perhaps we must, of a 'relationship' between the living and the dead, what, in specific historical contexts, were the parameters of that relationship, its successes and failures, functions and dysfunctions?

In setting out to address these and a good many other questions, the essays in this collection range broadly in their thematic focus, chronology and geographical setting, and they are informed by a variety of methodological and theoretical approaches. Common to them all, however, is the conviction not only that attitudes and behaviour towards the dead represent an important historical theme in their own right, but that 'discourses about the dead' provide particularly poignant and revealing points of entry into how these societies understood themselves, and how they articulated and negotiated religious, social and cultural developments and conflicts.

One of the volume's recurring themes is how the relations of the living with the dead were profoundly embedded in religious cultures, and, further, how those relations were not only shaped by, but themselves helped to shape the processes of religious change. Historians of the late Middle Ages have for some time reflected on A. N. Galpern's striking observation that pre-Reformation Catholicism was in large measure 'a cult of the living in the service of the dead'.[6] The prominence of the dead in late medieval Latin Christianity was pre-eminently the result of the conjunction of two compelling ideas. The first was the gradual evolution and eventual formalisation of the belief that the majority of the faithful dead did not proceed immediately to the beatific vision, but underwent a painful purgation of the debt due for their sins in the intermediary state (and place) of Purgatory.[7] The second was the conviction, predicated upon the theory that all faithful Christians in this world and the next were incorporated in a single 'communion of saints', that the living had the ability (and the duty) to ease the dead's sufferings in Purgatory. Masses, prayers, alms-giving and fasting were all held to be beneficial to

---

[6] A. N. Galpern, 'The Legacy of Late Medieval Religion in Sixteenth-Century Champagne', in C. Trinkaus and H. O. Oberman (eds.), *The Pursuit of Holiness in Late Medieval and Renaissance Religion* (Leiden, 1974), p. 149.

[7] Jacques Le Goff's deservedly influential *The Birth of Purgatory*, tr. A. Goldhammer (Aldershot, 1984) argues that the idea of Purgatory took hold in the late twelfth century. A number of scholars have questioned this chronology, without, however, contesting the importance of the development itself: R. W. Southern, 'Between Heaven and Hell', *Times Literary Supplement* (18 June 1982), pp. 651–2; P. Ariès, 'Le purgatoire et la cosmologie de l'au-delà', *Annales* 38 (1983), pp. 151–7; B. P. McGuire, 'Purgatory, the Communion of Saints, and Medieval Change', *Viator* 20 (1989), pp. 61–84.

the dead, as increasingly in the later Middle Ages were indulgences.[8] As it was virtually universally accepted that it was more efficacious to pray for the dead individually than collectively, the naming of the dead in a liturgical context (*memoria*) played a crucial part in preserving the memory of dead individuals in the minds of the communities charged with praying for them, perhaps also in the formation of medieval consciousness of the past more generally.[9]

However, to characterise the relationship between the living and the dead in late medieval society merely in terms of the former's service of the latter may be to misconstrue the interiority of pre-Reformation religious attitudes. Much of the recent writing on medieval 'popular religion' has emphasised the themes of reciprocity, exchange and mutual gift-giving between the living and the dead.[10] The saints in heaven interceded for the living, as the living interceded for the dead in Purgatory.[11] In praying for the souls of the departed, Christians performed a quintessential good-work for which in due course benefits would accrue to themselves; as Thomas More put it in 1529, when good people give alms to priests to pray for souls, 'then ryseth there myche more good and profyt uppon all sydys'.[12] Moreover, by bestowing benefactions on the community through their

---

[8] The quadripartite schema of intercession was variously attributed to Augustine and Gregory the Great: see S. Powell and A. Fletcher, '"In die Sepulture seu Trigintali": the Late Medieval Funeral and Memorial Sermon', *Leeds Studies in English* 12 (1981), p. 197. On indulgences, see R. W. Schaffern, 'Learned Discussions of Indulgences for the Dead in the Middle Ages', *Church History* 61 (1992), pp. 367–81.

[9] On *memoria*, see Geary, *Living with the Dead*, pp. 87–91; P. J. Geary, *Phantoms of Remembrance: Memory and Oblivion at the End of the First Millennium* (Princeton, NJ, 1994), pp. 15–19, 54, 131; D. L. d'Avray, *Death and the Prince: Memorial Preaching before 1350* (Oxford, 1994), pp. 60, 69–70; Oexele, 'Die Gegenwart der Toten'; K. Schmid and J. Wollasch (eds.), *Memoria. Der geschichtliche Zeugniswert des liturgischen Gedenkens im Mittelalter* (Munich, 1984); J. Wollasch, 'Les moines et la mémoire des morts', in D. Iogna-Prat and J. Ch. Picard (eds.), *Religion et culture autour de l'an mil. Royaume Capétien et Lotharingie* (Paris, 1990), pp. 47–54.

[10] P. J. Geary, 'Exchange and Interaction between the Living and the Dead in Early Medieval Society', in Geary, *Living with the Dead*, pp. 77–94; R. N. Swanson, *Religion and Devotion in Europe c. 1215– c. 1515* (Cambridge, 1995), pp. 212–15; P. Binski, *Medieval Death: Ritual and Representation* (London, 1996), pp. 24–5, 93; Peter Dinzelbacher, *Angst in Mittelalter: Teufel-, Todes- und Gotteserfahrung: Mentalitätsgeschichte und Ikonographie* (Paderborn, 1996); M. Tetel, *Life and Death in Fifteenth-Century Florence* (Durham, NC, 1989); N. Ohler, *Sterben und Tod im Mittelalter* (Munich, 1990); P. Jezler (ed.), *Himmel, Hölle, Fegefeuer. Das Jenseits im Mittelalter* (Exhibition catalogue, Zurich, 1994); A. Borst (ed.), *Tod im Mittelalter* (Constance, 1993); C. Blum, *La représentation de la mort dans la Littérature française de la Renaissance* (Paris, 1989); Chiffoleau, *La Comptabilité*.

[11] On this the most important recent work is André Vauchez, *Sainthood in the Later Middle Ages*, tr. Jean Birrell (Cambridge, 1997).

[12] Thomas More, *The Supplication of Souls*, ed. F. Manley *et al.*, Yale edn of the *Complete Works of St Thomas More*, vol. VII (New Haven and London, 1990), p. 205.

testaments, the dead established a claim on the memory of the living, and, explicitly or implicitly, and in a virtually contractual manner, required the 'counter-gift' of prayers for their souls in Purgatory.

These issues have in recent years been explored in the context of fifteenth-century England, most notably in the writing of Eamon Duffy and Clive Burgess.[13] Burgess's contribution to the present volume elaborates these broad themes within the context of one late medieval English community (All Saints', Bristol), demonstrating how the dead 'perpetuated their identities' through a remarkably successful series of strategies for remembrance, weaving their names and images into the fabric of the liturgy and into the material paraphernalia of parish worship. Perhaps most striking in this account is its emphasis on the corporate and communal character of commemorating the dead. The obligation of remembering extended well beyond the immediate kin-group. The involvement of wider forms of association, particularly confraternities, in the perpetuation of the memory of the dead has also been stressed by historians of late medieval Italy.[14] For the humble this could provide the assurance of a standard of burial and intercessory prayer the immediate family could not guarantee; for those of higher status it could involve the representation of social power. Sharon Strocchia has suggested how the lavish intercession Piero de'Medici arranged for his father (involving some 12,000 masses, at fifty-three different ecclesiastical institutions) was

[13] E. Duffy, *The Stripping of the Altars: Traditional Religion in England 1400–1580* (New Haven and London, 1992), chaps. 9–10; C. Burgess, ' "A Fond Thing Vainly Invented": an Essay on Purgatory and Pious Motive in Later Medieval England', in S. J. Wright (ed.), *Parish, Church and People. Local Studies in Lay Religion, 1350–1750* (London, 1988), pp. 56–84; C. Burgess, 'Late Medieval Wills and Pious Convention: Testamentary Evidence Reconsidered', in M. A. Hicks (ed.), *Profit, Piety and the Professions* (Gloucester, 1990), pp. 14–33; C. Burgess, 'The Benefactions of Mortality: the Lay Response in the Late Medieval Parish', in D. M. Smith (ed.), *Studies in Clergy and Ministry in Medieval England* (Borthwick Studies in History, 1, 1991), pp. 65–86. See also C. Burgess and B. Kümin, 'Penitential Bequests and Parish Regimes in Late Medieval England', *Journal of Ecclesiastical History* 44 (1993), pp. 610–30; V. Bainbridge, 'The Medieval Way of Death: Commemoration and the Afterlife in Pre-Reformation Cambridgeshire', in M. Wilks (ed.), *Prophecy and Eschatology*, Studies in Church History Subsidia, 10 (Oxford, 1994), pp. 183–204; A. D. Brown, *Popular Piety in Late Medieval England: the Diocese of Salisbury 1250–1550* (Oxford, 1995), chap. 4; B. Kümin, *The Shaping of a Community: the Rise and Reformation of the English Parish, c. 1400–1560* (Aldershot, 1996), pp. 109–20.

[14] J. Henderson, 'Religious Confraternities and Death in Early Renaissance Florence', in P. Denley and C. Elam (eds.), *Florence and Italy: Renaissance Studies in Honour of Nicolai Rubinstein* (London, 1988), pp. 383–94; J. R. Banker, *Death in the Community. Memorialisation and Confraternities in an Italian Commune in the Late Middle Ages* (Athens, GA and London, 1988); Sharon T. Strocchia, *Death and Ritual in Renaissance Florence* (Baltimore and London, 1992).

the primary means whereby Piero 'helped multiply the family's capital as institutional patrons'.[15] The chapter in this book by Samuel Cohn addresses similar issues about the scope and meaning of commemoration in the late Middle Ages. In this case, a comparison of wills from Florence and the Flemish cloth town of Douai is used to explore the nature of that emergent 'individualism' which a number of historians, from Burckhardt through Huizinga to Chiffoleau and Ariès, have seen reflected in the death-culture of late medieval Europe. While Cohn detects in the aftermath of the Black Death a distinct movement towards the 'individuation' of graves and burial places, he finds in Florence (*pace* Burckhardt) a growing tendency to associate the individual with the ancestral lineage, and in Douai an impulse to commemorate the deceased within the context of the family, which is far from the 'narcissism and egoism of a "fragile" urban bourgeoisie stripped from its familial moorings' evoked by Huizinga.

An awareness of the extensiveness of reciprocity and exchanges between the living and the dead has encouraged some historians to portray the dead as integral to contemporary constructions of community, to locate the dead within the very demographic structures of late medieval society. Thus for Natalie Zemon Davis (borrowing and building upon a suggestion of André Varagnac) the dead in traditional Catholic societies should be regarded as forming an 'age-group', with distinct rights and responsibilities *vis-à-vis* their 'younger' living contemporaries.[16] In John Bossy's view, envisaging the dead as an age-group meant that 'relations with the living could be put on a manageable collective footing'.[17] These insights have done much to further a sophisticated and empathetic reading of the social and cultural nexuses of pre-Reformation religion, but such neat classifications can rest uneasily upon a functional view of the place of the dead in late medieval society in which the departed are too comfortably subsumed into a self-regulating ecosystem of mortality and social stability.

---

[15] Strocchia, *Death and Ritual*, p. 183.
[16] N. Z. Davis, 'Some Tasks and Themes in the Study of Popular Religion', in Trinkaus and Oberman, *The Pursuit of Holiness*, pp. 327–8. See also her 'Ghosts, Kin and Progeny: Some Features of Family Life in Early Modern France', *Daedalus* 106 (2) (1977), pp. 87–114. The concept of the dead as an 'age group' has subsequently been deployed by R. Muchembled, *Popular and Elite Culture in France 1400–1750*, tr. L. Cochrane (Baton Rouge and London, 1985), p. 55; R. Dinn, 'Death and Rebirth in Late Medieval Bury St Edmunds', in S. Bassett (ed.), *Death in Towns: Urban Responses to the Dying and the Dead, 100–1600* (Leicester, 1992), p. 161; Geary, *Living with the Dead*, p. 36; N. Caciola, 'Wraiths, Revenants and Ritual in Medieval Culture', *Past and Present* 152 (1996), p. 7.
[17] J. Bossy, *Christianity in the West, 1400–1700* (Oxford, 1985), p. 30.

In fact, as some of the essays in this collection make clear, attitudes and practices pertaining to the dead could be marked by profound ambivalence, reflecting an awareness that the interests of the living and the dead were not always as convergent as the model of reciprocity in prayer and intercession might imply. The dead might be hostile to the living; the living fearful of, or indifferent to, the dead. Moreover, late medieval perceptions of the status and place of the dead were by no means univocal; officially sanctioned exchanges with the dead operated alongside and within a 'black-market' of popular customs and beliefs. In contrast to the authorised teaching that the souls of the dead proceeded immediately to a particular judgement by God and were assigned forthwith to Heaven, Hell or Purgatory, it seems to have been widely believed across Europe in the Middle Ages (and for much longer) that for a period after death the dead remained in the vicinity of their bodies, liable to haunt the locations they had inhabited and the persons they had known when alive.[18] This constituted a dangerously liminal time when the dead might seek to seize companions from the world of the living to accompany them into the abodes of the deceased. The survivors were wise to take precautions against the possibility of revenants, opening windows in the death-room to allow the soul to escape, washing the corpse to enable the dead to rest easily in the grave, or pouring water behind the coffin to create a barrier to their return. The most dangerous among potential revenants, like suicides and criminals, were sometimes buried face-down, at cross-roads, or with a stake through the corpse, or their bodies were thrown into the river.[19]

Underpinning such beliefs and practices were anxieties about negotiating and even identifying the boundary between life and death itself, reminding us that the categories of 'the living' and 'the dead' are themselves less fixed and more fluid than we are accustomed to expect. The attribution of some degree of sentience or 'life-force' to the corpses of the recently deceased was a very long-standing popular intuition, informing, for example, both Ruth Richardson's work on anatomy in Georgian Britain and Nancy Caciola's recent discussion of wraiths and

---

[18] Davis, 'Some Tasks and Themes', p. 333; Muchembled, *Popular and Elite Culture*, p. 64.

[19] Davis, 'Ghosts, Kin and Progeny', p. 94; R. W. Scribner, 'The Impact of the Reformation on Daily Life', in M. H. Appelt (ed.), *Mensch und Objekt im Mittelalter und in der frühen Neuzeit* (Vienna, 1990); R. W. Scribner, 'Elements of Popular Belief', in T. Brady, H. O. Oberman and J. D. Tracey (eds.), *Handbook of European History 1400–1600: Late Middle Ages, Renaissance and Reformation*, vol. I: *Structures and Assertions* (Leiden, 1994), pp. 237–8; P. Barber, *Vampires, Burial, and Death: Folklore and Reality* (New Haven and London, 1988), *passim*.

revenants in medieval culture.[20] Caciola's contribution to the present volume, an analysis of late medieval understandings of the meaning of possession, suggests how the explanation found convincing in a number of Swiss and Italian urban communities (namely, that the spirits of the dead could take hold of the bodies of the living) reflected 'an intimate, immanent and amoral view of the supernatural', in which the dead remained far more tightly bound to the material world than they did in the eschatologies of the theologians. These spirits could be threatening and vengeful. For many late medieval Christians the desire to commemorate the dead and the need to propitiate them went pretty much hand in hand. Philippe Ariès's contention that after the adoption of intramural burial in the early Middle Ages, 'the dead completely ceased to inspire fear' is as implausible as Sir James Frazer's imperious claim that the fear of the spirits of the dead was a virtually universal feature of pre-modern and primitive societies, and a primary influence on the development of all religious thought.[21]

Attitudes towards the dead in this period were often complex, if not contradictory, stemming from the confluence of a number of factors: official doctrine about the afterlife, folkloric ghost beliefs, natural affection for the deceased, horror of the corpse, the obligation to remember and the impulse to forget.[22] Yet it is fundamental to remember that the ties between living and dead were not merely cultural and emotional ones; they were also necessarily economic, involving the disposition of property and the dedication of resources to the demands of intercession and commemoration. Over the generations, the effect was a cumulative one, leading some historians of later medieval Europe to speak of an unbearable weight of obligations, the over-burdening of the living by the dead.[23] Unsurprisingly, at times the living could show themselves inattentive to the declared wishes of the dead: bequests might remain unfulfilled, chantries unfounded and annual commemorations of the dead (particu-

---

[20] R. Richardson, *Death, Dissection and the Destitute* (London, 1987), chap. 1: 'The Corpse and Popular Culture'; Caciola, 'Wraiths, Revenants and Ritual'.

[21] Ariès, *Hour of our Death*, p. 36; J. G. Frazer, *The Fear of the Dead in Primitive Religion* (3 vols., London, 1933–6), esp. I, pp. 10–11; III, p. 311. See also the emphasis on a 'universal fear of the dead' in E. Canetti, *Crowds and Power*, tr. C. Stewart (Harmondsworth, 1973), pp. 305–17.

[22] For the range of emotions evoked by the spectacle of the dead body, see Vanessa Harding's chapter below. The view that, paradoxically, the prime purpose of commemoration was to enable the living to forget the dead is a recurrent theme of Schmitt, *Ghosts in the Middle Ages*, pp. 5, 9, 35, 200.

[23] C. Platt, *King Death: the Black Death and its Aftermath in Late-Medieval England* (London, 1996), pp. 105–7; Swanson, *Religion and Devotion*, pp. 233–4.

larly the long-dead) might be amalgamated or abandoned.[24] In late medieval devotional literature one counterpoint to the expressions of piety towards the dead is what Margaret Aston has described as 'the proverbial friendlessness of the dead', the often-expressed fear that executors would prove untrustworthy, that those who ought to remember would be liable to forget.[25]

If the dead placed burdens on the living which the latter were sometimes unwilling to fulfil, can one then argue (somewhat against the tide of recent scholarship stressing the popularity and adaptability of late medieval Catholicism) that a growing resentment of such burdens helps to explain the sixteenth-century revolt against the Church? Quite apart from Luther's original protest against the abuse of indulgences, the propaganda of the early Reformation was eloquent on this score, simultaneously accusing the Catholic clergy of *Totenfresserei* (feeding upon the dead) and arguing the social injustice of endowing intercessions for the dead, which took their rightful property from widows and children, and from the poor.[26] In lands where the Reformation took hold, the place of the dead had to be fundamentally reviewed and renegotiated, and many of the chapters in this collection address themselves to one aspect or other of this momentous social and theological realignment.

It has become something of a truism to state that the Reformation fractured the community of the living and the dead; that it cast out the dead from the society of the living and abolished the dead's status as an 'age-group'.[27] Certainly, it would be difficult to overstate the importance,

---

[24] A. Kreider, *English Chantries: the Road to Dissolution* (Cambridge, MA, 1979), pp. 87–9; M. Hicks, 'Chantries, Obits and Almshouses: the Hungerford Foundations 1325–1478', in C. Barron and C. Harper-Bill (eds.), *The Church in Pre-Reformation Society* (Woodbridge, 1985), pp. 123–42; C. J. Somerville, *The Secularisation of Early Modern England: from Religious Culture to Religious Faith* (Oxford, 1992), p. 77; Brown, *Popular Piety*, pp. 96–7, 110, 168, 226–7.

[25] M. Aston, 'Death', in R. Horrox (ed.), *Fifteenth-Century Attitudes: Perceptions of Society in Late Medieval England* (Cambridge, 1994), pp. 213–15; Duffy, *Stripping of the Altars*, pp. 349–52; C. Gittings, 'Urban Funerals in Late Medieval and Reformation England', in Bassett, *Death in Towns*, p. 176; C. Daniell, *Death and Burial in Medieval England, 1066–1550* (London and New York,1997), p. 41.

[26] S. Ozment, *The Reformation in the Cities* (New Haven and London, 1975), pp. 111–16; H. Latimer, *Sermons and Remains*, ed. G. E. Corrie, Parker Society (Cambridge, 1845), pp. 238, 363. See also L. P. Buck, 'The Reformation, Purgatory, and Perpetual Rents in the Revolt of 1525 at Frankfurt am Main', in K. C. Sessions and P. N. Bebb (eds.), *Pietas et Societas: New Trends in Reformation Social History* (Kirksville, MO, 1985), pp. 23–33.

[27] Davis, 'Some Tasks and Themes', p. 330; Duffy, *Stripping of the Altars*, pp. 474–5, 494–5; C. Richmond, 'The English Gentry and Religion, c. 1500', in C. Harper-Bill (ed.), *Religious Belief and Ecclesiastical Careers in Late Medieval England* (Woodbridge, 1991), pp. 143–4; S. C. Karant-Nunn, *The Reformation of Ritual: an Interpretation of*

in terms of formal theology, liturgy, ecclesiastical structures and ritual practice of the abrogation of Purgatory and the repudiation of any form of intercession for the dead. Peter Marshall's chapter, for example, argues that English Protestants' aversion to the Catholic 'geography' of the afterlife in the late sixteenth and early seventeenth centuries may have played a significant role in the formation of more recognisably 'modern' constructions of life after death in general. The claim is also sometimes made that an important result of the abolition of Purgatory and prayer for the dead in Protestant states was a kind of 'secularisation', or at least 'naturalisation' of the memory of the dead. Those facing death displayed an increasing concern with the reputation and 'fame' they would leave behind them, while the survivors were encouraged to contemplate the deceased as exemplifications of virtue and achievement, rather than as persons with whom any kind of relationship could be maintained.[28]

In seeking comparisons between the place of the dead in pre-Reformation Catholic and post-Reformation Protestant cultures it is probably wise, however, to attempt to avoid juxtaposing sets of neatly contrasting paradigms, to present static 'before' and 'after' snapshots of a series of processes that were in reality dynamic, evolutionary and thoroughly untidy. We should note here the arresting observation of Bob Scribner that relations with the dead touched a 'neuralgic point for early modern official Protestantism'; that well into the twentieth century there survived 'a thick sub-stratum of Protestant popular belief about spirits, ghosts, poltergeists, restless souls'.[29] Despite the repeated insistence of Protestant theologians that there could be no commerce and exchange between the quick and the dead, that the living could do nothing to alter the condition of the deceased, and that the dead had no knowledge of the affairs of the living, a recognition of the reciprocal bonds between present and past generations was too deep-rooted in popular consciousness to be easily eradicated. Jacob Helt's chapter, an analysis of the patterns of gift-giving in women's wills in Elizabethan Essex, suggests how the designation of

---

Early Modern Germany (London, 1997), p. 178. Cressy, *Birth, Marriage, and Death*, p. 396 goes so far as to say the effect of eliminating Purgatory was to 'sever the relationship between the dead and the living'.

[28] Gittings, *Death, Burial and the Individual*, pp. 144–9; R. Rex, 'Monumental Brasses and the Reformation', *Transactions of the Monumental Brass Society* 14 (5) (1990), pp. 376–94.

[29] B. Scribner, 'Introduction', in Scribner and T. Johnson (eds.), *Popular Religion in Germany and Central Europe, 1400–1800* (Basingstoke, 1996), p. 10. See also J. Beyer, 'A Lübeck Prophet in Local and Lutheran Context', in *ibid.*, pp. 172–5, and for comparable arguments for early modern England, Thomas, *Religion and the Decline of Magic*, chap. 19; R. Hutton, 'The English Reformation and the Evidence of Folklore', *Past and Present* 148 (1995), pp. 89–116.

'rememberers' through the gendered social networks that women had belonged to in life served to sustain 'a sense of spiritual and material affinity between the dead and the living community' despite the theological revolution which had anathematised prayer for the dead. Bruce Gordon's examination of ghosts in the Swiss context discusses how apparitions remained an integral part of the Protestant spiritual landscape for both reformers and the common folk. Although the notion of ghosts as the dead returning from Purgatory could not be sustained, in their approaches to pastoral care, Protestant writers remained deeply influenced by the medieval culture of death and intercession. The intense interest among Protestants in angels represented the deeper need of the reformers to reclaim aspects of medieval religion in another form. Here the Reformation did not merely act attritionally upon stubborn and intractable 'popular' attitudes about the dead; to some extent at least it reacted with the concerns of the people to forge acceptable solutions to perplexing pastoral problems. Will Coster's chapter on the changing meanings of the term 'chrisom child' in Reformation England is another case in point. The mutations of this expression, originally applied to infants dying after baptism, to cover all dead infants and, latterly, those dying unbaptised, seems to represent a fusion of the baptismal theology of the reformers with the psychological needs of bereaved parents.

In much of Europe a complicating factor in the Protestant reordering of relations with the dead was the fact that links with past (Catholic) generations were both physically and symbolically preserved at the heart of urban and rural communities by the tombs and burial places that pervaded parish churches and by the graveyards that enveloped them. Recent work on the removal of cemeteries to new extramural sites in a number of sixteenth-century German Lutheran cities has seen the process as indicative of the desire of Protestant authorities to effect 'a thoroughgoing separation between living and dead'.[30] Yet well into the seventeenth century such literal relocations of the place of the dead could meet opposition from Lutheran parishioners.[31] The issue of physical proximity between the living and the dead was resonant outside Germany, as is shown in the contributions here by Penny Roberts and Andrew Spicer. Roberts's account of burial disputes in Reformation France shows that Huguenots were often keen to be buried with their Catholic ancestors,

---

[30] Karant-Nunn, *Reformation of Ritual*, pp. 178–9, 187; C. Koslofsky, 'Death and Ritual in Reformation Germany' (University of Michigan PhD thesis, 1994), chap. 3, and his forthcoming monograph, *The Reformation of the Dead*. Dr Koslofsky had hoped to contribute to the current volume; unfortunately circumstances conspired to prevent this.

[31] Beyer, 'A Lübeck Prophet', pp. 170–1.

and to take their place within the 'geography and social hierarchy of sacred burial space'. Their demands for separate burial sites came slowly, and were probably largely prompted by the ferocious determination of Catholics to keep their burial places free of heretical contamination. Spicer's discussion of kirk-burial in early modern Scotland (where the ecclesiastical authorities were bitterly opposed to the practice as a derogation of true worship and a prop to superstition) reveals an intriguing process of negotiation between the demands of doctrinal probity and the aspirations of lay elites. Through the construction of collateral burial aisles lairds and nobles were able to continue to express symbolic solidarity with their ancestors, as well as to assert their own elevated social importance. In early modern Paris, as Vanessa Harding's contribution reveals, the impulses behind choice of burial location were probably similar. The desire to be buried near a member of the family or *lignage* was prevalent, suggestive both of a claim to social status and of a continuing attribution of personal identity to the corpses rotting in the ground.

As these examples suggest, Protestant and Catholic responses to the dead in early modern Europe could show remarkable points of similarity, in spite of radically opposing theories of salvation, death rituals and views of the afterlife. In particular, commentators from very different confessional standpoints displayed a willingness both to draw imperative moral messages from the condition of the dead and the manner and timing of their passing, and to employ (or exploit?) the dead and the occasions of their commemoration in pursuit of religious or political objectives. This theme is developed in several of the chapters below. In James Boyden's treatment of the death and afterlife of Don Rodrigo Calderón we have a striking example of how it could all go very wrong. The carefully choreographed execution was intended by the government of Philip IV as a public demonstration of its distance from a political culture perceived as execrably corrupt. Calderón's conversion, his devotion to Teresa of Avila and his conduct at the moment of execution, however, served to place his death in another sphere of meaning which clearly had a deeper hold on the Spanish imagination – the good Catholic death. Boyden demonstrates how the death and execution of one person could be read in contrasting ways; even ritualised deaths retained an unstable character, foiling human attempts to control their import.[32] Exemplary deaths of a different sort are involved in Philip

---

[32] The manner of dying and deportment on the death-bed invited equally didactic constructions in contemporary Protestant societies. See R. Houlbrooke, 'The Puritan Death-Bed, *c.* 1560–*c.* 1660', in C. Durston and J. Eales (eds.), *The Culture of English Puritanism,*

Soergel's discussion of the 'reading' of the corpses of deformed infants in Lutheran Germany. In turning to monstrous births as evidence for divine disapprobation of contemporary mores, Lutheran pamphleteers displayed an attitude that had much in common with the traditional Catholic tendency to extract messages from the miraculously preserved bodies of saints and other disruptions of the accustomed order of nature. Parallels in the ways reformers and counter-reformers could make capital out of the dead are perhaps most marked in the uses they made of an instrument of commemoration that was common to both of them throughout the early modern period, the funeral sermon.[33] This theme is developed in the chapters by Larissa Taylor and Graeme Murdock. Taylor's account of Catholic funeral sermons during the French Wars of Religion reveals how they might frequently become the occasion for unabashed religious propaganda, the castigation of heretics and the urging of Catholics to hold fast in a militant defence of the faith. In the very different, but equally unstable conditions of mid-seventeenth-century Transylvania, Murdock describes how the sermons delivered at the funerals of Reformed princes and their counsellors construed their deaths as signals of impending doom and judgement against the principality, and issued calls to collective repentance and emulation of these (idealised) godly rulers.

Such a picture of a complex layering and interweaving of continuities and discontinuities and of subtle long-term negotiations of change makes it increasingly difficult to issue simplistic generalisations about the impact of the religious reformations of the sixteenth and seventeenth centuries on the social significance of the dead in European communities. The issue is further complicated by the suggestion in some recent work of marked regional differences in attitudes towards the dead, both before

---

1560–1700 (Basingstoke, 1996), pp. 122–44; M. C. Cross, 'The Third Earl of Huntingdon's Death-bed: a Calvinist Example of the *Ars Moriendi*', *Northern History* 21 (1985), pp. 80–107; L. M. Beier, 'The Good Death in Seventeenth-Century England', in R. Houlbrooke (ed.), *Death, Ritual and Bereavement* (London and New York, 1989), pp. 43–61.

33   Protestant scruples about funeral sermons as a relic of popish intercessory practices seem to have been fairly rapidly overcome across Europe as preachers became attuned to the advantages of a captive audience, and the poignancy of the theme of mortality for framing calls to repentence and right living. See F. B. Tromly, ' "According to Sounde Religion": the Elizabethan Controversy over the Funeral Sermon', *Journal of Medieval and Renaissance Studies* 13 (1983), pp. 293–312; P. Collinson, ' "A Magazine of Religious Patterns": an Erasmian Topic transposed in English Protestantism', in idem, *Godly People: Essays on English Protestantism and Puritanism* (London, 1983), pp. 499–525; Karant-Nunn, *Reformation of Ritual*, pp. 156–62; on opposition to funeral sermons among the Swiss reformers, however, see Martin Illi, *Wohin die Toten gehen. Begräbnis und Kirchhof in der vorindustriellen Stadt* (Zurich, 1992).

and after the Reformation period.[34] Thus, while historians of late medieval England have seen popular awareness of Purgatory and its place in the penitential cycle as a crucial determinant of piety, it has been asserted that Purgatory failed to capture the popular imagination in France until the middle of the seventeenth century.[35] Carlos Eire regards the sums spent on the dead in the later sixteenth century as evidence of a uniquely Spanish preoccupation with post-mortem ritual and intercession, even within the remaining Catholic world.[36] Henry Kamen, on the other hand, remarks upon 'the impressive absence of Purgatory' in rural Catalonia before the mid-seventeenth century, and contrasts 'the haunting presence of the purgatorial dead' in the religious outlook of northern Europe with a more muted version in the south.[37] It has been further suggested that devotion to the dead was particularly characteristic of 'the entire Atlantic fringe from Galicia, through Brittany, Ireland, and England', areas where Catholicism can be portrayed as having 'received most reinforcement from pre-Christian religious beliefs'.[38] The essays in this volume provide a great deal of further nuancing and shading of the national and regional distinctiveness of mortuary and memorial cultures in late medieval and early modern Europe, and inevitably they serve to problematise some issues even as they clarify and resolve others. They make a collectively telling argument for the view that 'the social significance of death is constructed with great variety and complexity within different cultural contexts'.[39]

Yet whatever the cultural traditions and political and socio-economic structures of the societies in which they lived, every man and woman in this

---

[34] Though note the suggestion of Samuel Cohn in his chapter below that traditional historiographies have misconstrued the differences in the commemorative cultures of late medieval Flanders and Tuscany.

[35] See works by Burgess and Duffy cited in note 13 above. Ariès, *Hour of our Death*, pp. 153, 201, 306, 463. For evidence of marked regional disparities within England in the patterns of intercessory foundations, see Kreider, *English Chantries*, pp. 15–19, 90–1; R. Whiting, 'Local Responses to the Henrician Reformation', in D. MacCulloch (ed.), *The Reign of Henry VIII: Politics, Policy and Piety* (Basingstoke, 1995), pp. 214, 220.

[36] C. Eire, *From Madrid to Purgatory: the Art and Craft of Dying in Sixteenth-Century Spain* (Cambridge, 1995), p. 529.

[37] H. Kamen, *The Phoenix and the Flame: Catalonia and the Counter-Reformation* (New Haven and London, 1993), pp. 12, 168–9, 195. Note here also Paul Binski's obervation that in the late Middle Ages Northern Europe had a 'far more pronounced culture of the macabre' than did Italy: *Medieval Death*, p. 122.

[38] V. Turner, 'Death and the Dead in the Pilgrimage Process', in F. E. Reynolds and E. H. Waugh (eds.), *Religious Encounters with Death: Insights from History and Anthropology of Religions* (Pennsylvania and London, 1977), p. 35, citing W. A. Christian, *Person and God in a Spanish Valley* (New York and London, 1972), p. 94.

[39] Caciola, 'Wraiths, Revenants and Ritual', p. 7.

period knew he or she would one day die, a common denominator of palpable, but nonetheless profound significance. That death came indiscriminately for all, from prince to peasant, was a widely disseminated theme, celebrated in the iconography of the 'dance of death', and the *memento mori* message of funeral sermons, tomb imagery and inscriptions. The treatment of the dead was a powerfully poignant theme across Europe because of this universal relevance, and because of its ability to connect the private and the public, to evoke an affinity between the individual experience of memory and loss, and its significance for the community, Church or state. The placing of the dead in late medieval and early modern societies was thus integral to both daily life and the sweep of broader historical movements. The late medieval and early modern worlds had an especial concern with the past. The widespread concern for reform of the Church following the Great Schism led many to reflect upon a better age, when things had been purer. Late medieval concepts of reform were derived from the idea of restoration, a return to the past. History was integral to Renaissance thought, as humanists sought to recapture the genius of classical cultures in order to revivify the languid societies in which they found themselves. The reformations of the sixteenth century, Protestant and Catholic, self-consciously moulded the past in order to make sense of the present. Concern with the place of the dead bespeaks a fundamental need to relate past and present, whether in kinship or the continuity of the Church. English Protestant theologians of the later sixteenth and early seventeenth centuries were generally prepared to answer in the affirmative the question of whether 'our fathers living in popish superstitions might be saved'. In doing so, they addressed sympathetically an issue of considerable pastoral sensitivity as well as making the point, against charges of 'novelty', that the doctrine and practices of the Protestant churches were not completely without historical roots.[40] Many of the essays in this volume demonstrate that there were impulses in the religious cultures which ran deeper than confessional divides. Catholics (pre-Reformation and Tridentine) and Protestants alike wrestled with many of the same questions. Perhaps the most profound question of all was that of how the community should understand and articulate its relationship with those who had gone before it. Their answers to that question reveal much about how pre-industrial European peoples understood themselves.

---

[40] R. Hooker, 'A Learned Discourse of Justification', in *Of the Laws of Ecclesiastical Polity*, ed. C. Morris (2 vols., London, 1907), I, p. 39; A. Milton, *Catholic and Reformed: the Roman and Protestant Churches in English Protestant Thought 1600–1640* (Cambridge, 1995), pp. 285–95.

The theme of 'the place of the dead' is a highly multivalent one, and provides a means of gaining new and unexpected access to a wide range of themes and problems current in a number of apparently discrete historiographies. Yet this is far from implying that we can approach it merely as a shorthand method of expressing and exposing fixed and underlying societal 'structures'. The contributions to this book make clear that in the societies under consideration, the cultural significance of the dead was never a 'given', something taken for granted and unimpeachable. Rather it was the product of a matrix of social, religious and economic relations that had to be enacted and articulated anew with each generation that passed away. That most reflective and past-minded of activities, the remembrance and commemoration of the dead, is in every age a remarkably contemporary testimony.

2 The place of the dead in Flanders and Tuscany: towards a comparative history of the Black Death

Samuel K. Cohn Jr

Two works of history continue to lurk behind the study of fourteenth- and fifteenth-century Western European culture – Jacob Burckhardt's *The Civilisation of the Renaissance in Italy*, first published in German in 1861, and Johann Huizinga's *The Waning of the Middle Ages*, published in Dutch in 1919. The first gave 'the Renaissance' its ideal-typical features, while the second denied them. Burckhardt drew sharp lines between the 'civilisation of the Renaissance' and the medieval past, associating the new era with secularisation, 'unbridled individualism', 'fame and glory', religious indifference, and modernity. According to him, the struggle between the popes and the Hohenstaufen emperors left Italy in a political condition which distinguished it 'from other countries of the West', allowing it to free itself from feudal monarchy and 'the unity of empire'.[1]

By contrast, Huizinga saw a deeper underlying cultural reality beneath the new learning, the intense zeal for 'inner and outward discovery' and a new 'sense of the love of life':[2] 'Living emotion stiffens amid the abused imagery of skeletons and worms.'[3] Even for the small elite of 'humanist scholars' Huizinga claimed Burckhardt's sweeping generalisations were exaggerated: 'With the humanists optimism is still tempered by ancient contempt, both Christian and Stoic, for the world.'[4]

---

[1] J. Burckhardt, *The Civilisation of the Renaissance in Italy*, tr. S. Middlemore (London, 1878), p. 4.

[2] See A. Tenenti, *Il senso della morte e l'amore della vita nel Rinascimento (Francia e Italia)* (Turin, 1957).

[3] J. Huizinga, *The Waning of the Middle Ages: a Study of the Forms of Life, Thought and Art in France and the Netherlands in the Dawn of the Renaissance*, tr. H. Hopman (London, 1924). There is also a new translation, *The Autumn of the Middle Ages*, tr. R. Payton and U. Mammitzsch (Chicago, 1996). The 1924 translation is quoted in this chapter.

[4] *Ibid.*, p. 32.

The note of despair and profound dejection is predominantly sounded not by ascetic monks, but by the court poets and the chroniclers–laymen, living in aristocratic circles and amid aristocratic ideas. They were incapable of finding consolation or hope in the spectacle of universal misery and decay, and could only bewail the decline of the world and despair of justice and of peace.[5]

While sections of Burckhardt's classic – 'Religion and Morality' – have not stood well the test of time, the cornerstones of his thesis – Renaissance individualism, secularisation and a new zeal for 'fame and glory' – continue to shape interpretation of the Italian Renaissance from its tombs to its economic structure.[6] Even within the history of religion and piety a Burckhardtian streak seeps through. Although historians such as P. O. Kristeller long ago debunked Burckhardt's belief that the humanists were godless free thinkers,[7] he also showed that fifteenth-century Italian obsessions over individual 'fame and glory' in the terrestrial domain had their counterpart in the celestial: at no other time in the history of philosophy was so much attention given to the problem of the immortality of the individual's soul.[8] Similarly, other historians[9] have argued that by the fifteenth century piety in Italy had shifted away from the old

---

[5]   *Ibid.*, pp. 32–3.

[6]   In speaking of mid-fifteenth-century Italy, E. Panofsky, *Tomb Sculpture: Four Lectures on its Changing Aspects from Ancient Egypt to Bernini*, ed. H. W. Janson (New York, 1964), pp. 67–9, concludes: 'And it is precisely in its attitude toward the dead that the new epoch most vigorously asserted its "modernity" . . . Here we have indeed a complete reversal of the medieval attitude. Glorification of intellectual achievements and academic honors has taken the place of pious expectations for the future of the soul.' On economics and the building industry, see R. A. Goldthwaite, *The Building of Renaissance Florence: an Economic and Social History* (Baltimore, 1980), p. 111: 'The spirit of individualism that Burckhardt made so central to our appreciation of the Renaissance nowhere expressed itself with greater emphasis than in buildings, and this was no less true in bourgeois Florence than in the courts of the princes and condottieri of northern Italy.' See also Cohn, 'Burckhardt Revisited from Social History', in A. Brown (ed.), *Language and Images of Renaissance Italy*, (Oxford, 1995), pp. 217–34.

[7]   See P. Kristeller, *The Philosophy of Marsilio Ficino*, tr. V. Conant (New York, 1943).

[8]   P. Kristeller, 'The Immortality of the Soul', in M. Mooney (ed.), *Renaissance Thought and its Sources* (New York, 1979), pp. 181–196: 'the cult of fame was linked with the belief in the dignity of man and certainly with the pervasive individualism of the period, a phenomenon admirably described by Burckhardt and after misunderstood by its critics' (p. 183).

[9]   D. Herlihy, *Medieval and Renaissance Pistoia: the Social History of an Italian Town, 1200–1430* (New Haven, 1967); M. Becker, 'Aspects of Lay Piety in Early Renaissance Florence', in C. Trinkaus and H. O. Oberman (eds.), *The Pursuit of Holiness in Late Medieval and Renaissance Religion* (Leiden, 1974), pp. 177–99; G. Brucker, *Renaissance Florence* (2nd edn, Berkeley, 1983), pp. 172–212; R. Brentano, 'Death in Gualdo Tadino and in Rome', *Studia Gratiana* 19 (1976), pp. 79–100.

asceticism and reliance upon earlier monastic foundations towards a 'Civic Christianity' – a more secular ideal of charity aimed at relieving human misery in the present world and of glorifying divine majesty with lavish new liturgical displays, vestments, paintings, buildings and ecclesiastical ornamentation.[10]

At the same time, historians of fourteenth- and fifteenth-century France have mostly followed in the footsteps of Huizinga, interpreting the literature and images of the later Middle Ages as an anti-Renaissance – a period of cultural atrophy coloured by despair. For them the innovative centuries were the thirteenth and the eighteenth. What lay between was a long period of human fragility, filled with physical as well as psychological misery, angst, guilt, fear and an overwhelming sense of apocalyptical doom. With Jean Delumeau such notions crossed the borders of France: 'Since the fourteenth century, plagues, famines, revolts, the advance of the Turks added their traumatic effects to a Christian culture which felt itself under siege.'[11] Under a thin veneer of Renaissance optimism, prophecies of doom and despair, the coming of the apocalypse and of the Antichrist flourished throughout the Italian peninsula, giving rise to a new 'sentiment of the end of the world' which penetrated all levels of society.[12]

More nuanced has been the dialectical approach of Jacques Chiffoleau, who has argued that urbanisation, commercialisation and migration uprooted the individual from families, neighbours and lineages, particularly in cities, as early as the thirteenth century.[13] Following Philippe Ariès, Chiffoleau read from the last wills and testaments of Avignon and its region a new individualism expressed in a new sense of death – death as 'one's own death' – that extended from the thirteenth to the sixteenth century.[14] Marked by solitude, melancholy and angst, this individualism was hardly that of Burckhardt's and instead reaffirmed Huizinga's general

---

[10] Herlihy, *Medieval and Renaissance Pistoia*, pp. 241–58.

[11] J. Delumeau, *La peur en Occident (XIVe–XVIIIe siècles): une cité assiégée* (Paris, 1978), p. 507.

[12] Delumeau, *La peur*, pp. 287 and 508; J. Delumeau, *Le péché et la peur: la culpabilisation en Occident (XIIIe–XVIIIe siècles)* (Paris, 1983), p. 277. See also his *Rassurer et protéger: le sentiment de sécurité dans l'Occident d'autrefois* (Paris, 1989).

[13] J. Chiffoleau, *La comptabilité de l'au-delà: les hommes, la mort et la religion dans la région d'Avignon à la fin du moyen âge* (Rome, 1980); J. Chiffoleau, 'Perché cambia la morte nella regione d'Avignon alla fine del Medioevo', *Quaderni Storici* 17 (1982), pp. 449–65; J. Chiffoleau, 'Analyse d'un rituel flamboyant: Paris mai–août 1412', in Chiffoleau, L. Martines and A. Paravicini Bagliani (eds.), *Riti e rituali nelle società medievali* (Spoleto, 1994), pp. 214–46.

[14] P. Ariès, *Western Attitudes toward Death from the Middle Ages to the Present*, tr. P. Ranum (Baltimore, 1974); P. Ariès, *The Hour of our Death*, tr. H. Weaver (New York, 1981), pp. 95–293.

view of the psychological malaise of the fifteenth century.[15] According to Chiffoleau, the loss of family and ties to the ancestors led to new levels of fear feeding the growth in the territory of Purgatory and with it the need for ever-increasing numbers of masses and intercessors for the soul.[16] Further, individuals compensated for this loss by staging 'flamboyant' and 'profoundly narcissistic' funerals.

Other historians studying different parts of France and Flanders, where custom and law differed greatly from the Roman-law south, have nonetheless followed the broad outlines of Chiffoleau's arguments. According to Jean Pierre Deregnaucourt, 'the disturbances of war, famine, and plague', as in Avignon, 'traumatised' the region of Douai (Flanders), leading to increased solitude and what Chiffoleau first labelled as the 'Great Melancholy'. 'The abandonment of the ancestors' meant that the Douaisiens also became 'uprooted', as seen in the decline of burials in ancestral graves. In unison with Chiffoleau, Deregnaucourt concludes: 'The flamboyance of funerary masses [was] their only compensation.'[17]

Following Ariès, Chiffoleau and Jacques Le Goff, Michel Lauwers has gone further. From a study of death rituals in the region of Liège, he has seen the emergence of the testament in the late twelfth century as the instrument of liberation from the grip of the ancestors and of the formation of a new individualism: again, Ariès's 'de la mort de soi'. According to Lauwers, not only in Liège but throughout Western Europe, the growth of towns, commercial exchange and heightened levels of migration ended the veneration of the ancestors for all but those on the fringes of rural society.[18]

The role of the Black Death of 1348 further separates these two radically different views of the cultural and psychological histories of the

---

[15] One exception to this rule may be Marvin Becker, 'Individualism in the Early Italian Renaissance: Burden and Blessing', *Studies in the Renaissance* 19 (1972), pp. 273–97, who stressed the angst and trauma that the Renaissance splintering of old solidarities imposed on the bourgeois of northern Italian city-states, but unlike Chiffoleau and other recent French historians, Becker stressed the positive consequences of this psychological condition for the efflorescence of Renaissance culture and creativity.

[16] Chiffoleau, *La comptabilité*, pp. 205ff.

[17] J.-P. Deregnaucourt, 'L'élection de sépulture d'après les testaments douaisiens (1295–1500)', *Revue du Nord* 65 (1983), pp. 343–52; J.-P. Deregnaucourt, 'Autour de la mort à Douai: attitudes, pratiques et croyances, 1250–1500' (2 vols., Université Charles de Gaulle, Lille, 1993, Alain Derville). See also M.-T. Lorcin, *Vivre et mourir en Lyonnais a la fin du moyen âge* (Paris, 1981); M.-T. Lorcin, 'Clauses religieuses dans les testaments du plat pays lyonnais aux XIVe et XVe siècles', *Moyen âge* 78 (1972), pp. 287–323, who interprets the pious portions of the Lyonnaise testaments from the late thirteenth to the fifteenth century in much the same fashion.

[18] Michel Lauwers, *La mémoire des ancêtres, le souci des morts: morts, rites et société au moyen âge* (Paris, 1997), pp. 499–500. See also Chiffoleau, *La comptabilité*, p. 207, who argues much the same, entitling one section of this book 'La fin des ancêtres', pp. 153–212.

later Middle Ages. Curiously, neither Burckhardt nor Huizinga gave the Black Death and its demographic consequences across Europe much of a hearing. Indeed, neither 'plague' nor 'Black Death' even appears in Burckhardt's *Civilization*, whose chronology extended without significant fissures from the mid-thirteenth to the mid-sixteenth centuries and depended on political forces – the struggle between Empire and Papacy – rather than on demography or economy.

However, those who have taken up Burckhardt's mantle in recent years have stressed the crucial importance of the Black Death in separating the Middle Ages from the Renaissance. For Richard Goldthwaite, the new dynamic economies of Italy and the consumer societies that resulted depended on the more equitable distribution of income wrought by the demographic changes of the Black Death.[19] For David Herlihy, the consequences of the Black Death, not only for Italy, but across Europe, were more monumental. It changed the demographic system from a pre-modern one based on Malthusian positive checks – war, famine, plague – to a modern one which turned on preventive checks – later ages at marriage, increased celibacy and conscious family planning. Further, the Black Death stood behind the making of modern Europe from its vernacular culture to its capitalist system of interconnected technological progress.[20]

On the other hand, historians of late medieval and early modern France have denied the Black Death's seminal role in transforming the west. For them, the great motors of change in the march to 'modernity' came either in the thirteenth or the eighteenth century. Despite the fact that all of his evidence for the city of Avignon and most for the region as a whole comes after the Black Death of 1348, Chiffoleau nonetheless insisted that new levels of fear, trauma, narcissism, flamboyance, 'Christianisation' and death as 'one's own death' resulted from thirteenth-century developments that broke the hold of feudal society and its lineage structures of demography and mentality. The Black Death only accentuated a process already well underway.[21] For Ariès, the plague is hardly mentioned in his sweeping six-centuries-long investigation of death and western mentality. Renaissance individualism was only a pale reflection of the individualism of the chivalric period, and death as 'one's own death'

---

[19] Goldthwaite, *The Building of Renaissance Florence*, esp. pp. 40–1; R. A. Goldthwaite, *Wealth and the Demand for Art in Italy 1300–1600* (Baltimore, 1993).

[20] D. Herlihy, *The Black Death and the Transformation of the West*, ed. S. Cohn (Cambridge, MA, 1997). See also his *Medieval and Renaissance Pistoia*.

[21] Such a chronology had, moreover, already been sketched out in Emile Mâle's study of death and burial tombs: *L'art religieux de la fin du moyen âge en France* (2nd edn, Paris, 1925), pp. 391–437.

arose sometime in the twelfth century. Again, Michel Lauwers has gone the furthest: urbanisation and the supposed demise of the ancestors' hold over burial, mourning and notions of the family had been completed by the thirteenth century. The Black Death was not even needed to hurry along a process set in motion by an earlier, more creative age. By contrast, Jean Delumeau has emphasised post-plague developments – the Schism of the Church in the later fourteenth century and the invasions of the Turks in the fifteenth and sixteenth centuries – to explain a new European-wide mentality of fear, anxiety and trauma.

Yet, despite these two seminal and starkly conflicting views of the formation of modern Europe, few have juxtaposed Burckhardt and Huizinga, and fewer still, the historiographical traditions they engendered.[22] Do they arise from the proclivities of individual historians or even cultural nationalism as can be seen in the brilliant interpretations of Emile Mâle?[23] After all, ever since Voltaire, the great centuries for the French were the thirteenth and the eighteenth, while for Italy, its crowning moment was the Renaissance. Or, were there fundamental differences in the cultural realities of these two geographic settings? Despite common levels of mortality across wide swaths of Europe, did different places experience differently the plagues and their after-shocks? For some time, historians of political and social structures have seen that the plague had vastly different, even contradictory, consequences for village life, land tenure and inheritance across Europe, especially when comparing Western Europe and lands east of the Elbe.[24] Can a similar approach be taken with the cultural history of post-plague Europe?

To begin such a comparative history, I have studied one set of documents – last wills and testaments – for two areas of Europe. The first – Tuscany

---

[22] On comparisons between Huizinga and Burckhardt, see Eugenio Garin's introduction to the Italian edition of Huizinga, *Autunno del Medio Evo* (Florence, 1961), pp. vii–xxxi; and the brief remarks in Wallace F. Ferguson, *The Renaissance in Historical Thought: Five Centuries of Interpretation* (Cambridge, MA, 1948), p. 373; Haskell, *History and its Images: Art and the Interpretation of the Past* (New Haven, 1993), pp. 482–3; Becker's introduction to the second volume of *Florence in Transition: Studies in the Rise of the Territorial State* (Baltimore, 1968), pp. 3–6 and P. Burke, *Culture and Society in Renaissance Italy 1420–1540* (New York, 1972), p. 192. See most recently David Shaw, 'Huizinga's Timeliness', *History & Theory* 27 (2) (1998), pp. 245–58, esp. pp. 247 and 254. I know of no works that compare the subsequent historiographies.

[23] Mâle, *L'art religieux*, pp. 404–5.

[24] See T. Aston and C. Philpin (eds.), *The Brenner Debate: Agrarian Class Structure and Economic Development in Pre-industrial Europe* (Cambridge, 1985), but recognition of the different social consequences for forced labour, east and west, go back well before Brenner's article of 1976.

and Umbria with a particular attention to Florence – was according to Burckhardt 'the most important workshop of the Italian and indeed of the modern European spirit';[25] the second – northern France or Flanders – was the heartland of Huizinga's fifteenth-century 'cultural atrophy'. Here, the cloth town of Douai, among the first rank of northern cities in the early fourteenth century, has preserved a remarkable collection of last wills and testaments. Although smaller than Florence,[26] Douai's economy and society, based principally on the wool trade before the Black Death, resembled Florence's. Moreover, similar to Florence, it experienced economic decline through the fourteenth century. Its decline was even steeper than Florence's, and by the fifteenth century Douai was classed among the third rank of European cities.[27] But, like in Florence, Douai's economy became less dependent on wool and diversified during the fifteenth century – in Douai's case into linen and the grain trade.[28]

Politically, the two cities were not so different as it might first appear. Both were controlled by merchant oligarchies with some artisan participation, and although the Douaisien aldermen (échevins) were subject to the French crown from 1307 until 1369 and afterwards to the count of Flanders, they retained their rights to select their aldermen, make and enforce laws and collect taxes[29] much the same as in the nominally independent city-state of Florence. The most striking difference between the two cities was in their relations with their surrounding hinterlands. While Florence possessed a territorial state that by the early fifteenth century controlled vast tracts of countryside and towns as large as Arezzo,

---

[25] Burckhardt, *The Civilisation*, p. 70.

[26] Douai's population in the fifteenth century is estimated at between 15,000 and 20,000, while Florence's was around 40,000. For Douai, see A. Derville, 'Le nombre de habitants des villes de l'Artois et de la Flandre Wallone (1300–1450)', *Revue du Nord* 65, (1983), pp. 277–99; M. Howell, *The Marriage Exchange: Property, Social Place, and Gender in Cities of the Low Countries, 1300–1550* (Chicago, 1998), p. 94.

[27] Howell, *The Marriage Exchange*, pp. 72–3. Recent historiography has argued that Douai's decline may not have been as drastic as historians once supposed. See *ibid.*, pp. 177–80. Her conclusions follow the research of Derville.

[28] For the economy and society of Douai before the Black Death, see G. Espinas, *La vie urbaine de Douai au moyen âge* (3 vols., Paris, 1913); G. Dhérent, 'Histoire sociale de la bourgeoisie de Douai, 1280–1350' (2 vols. Thèse d'Ecole des Chartes, 1981, R. Fossier). For the period afterwards, see Howell, *The Marriage Exchange*, pp. 174–95. On Douai and the grain trade, see D. Nicholas, *Medieval Flanders* (London, 1992), pp. 293–5. The same shift from textiles and long-distance exports to grain and regional trade can also be seen at Ghent in the fourteenth and fifteenth-centuries; see D. Nicholas, *The Metamorphosis of a Medieval City: Ghent in the Age of the Arteveldes 1302–1390* (Lincoln, NE, 1987).

[29] Howell, *The Marriage Exchange*, p. 75.

Pisa and Pistoia, political control and economic influence in Douai was restricted much more narrowly to its own city walls.

What makes a comparison of Florence and Douai so attractive is the survival for both of large numbers of last wills and testaments that reach back to the thirteenth century and that reflect spiritual and material horizons for those beneath the highest echelons of feudal and merchant society. For Spain and Italy numerous city archives provide the means for collecting large numbers of testaments before the Black Death.[30] By contrast, collections of significant numbers of testaments before the Black Death or even before the fifteenth century, which focus on those who were neither clergy nor noblemen, are much harder to find for cities north of the Alps. The Roman-law south of France is better supplied than the north, but even here pre-plague testaments in places such as Foréz, Lyon and Avignon are more common for the countryside than for the cities.[31]

Douai is an exception[32] but comparison between it and central Italy must heed differences in the customs, drafting and preservation of testaments in the two regions. For Italy, notarial tradition and Roman law were strong, while for Douai it was not essential, and the survival of notarial registers does not antedate the fifteenth century.[33] Here, as in other nearby cities,[34] the city's aldermen drew up, witnessed and authorized marriage contracts, testaments and many other contracts with parchments called *chirographes*.[35] Those who came before the aldermen to have their

---

[30] For Catalonia and Genoa large numbers of testaments survive even as far back as the twelfth century, see R. Burns, *Jews in the Notarial Culture: Latinate Wills in Mediterranean Spain, 1250–1350* (Berkeley, 1996); S. Epstein, *Wills and Wealth in Medieval Genoa, 1150–1250* (Cambridge, MA, 1984).

[31] See Chiffoleau, *La comptabilité*; Lorcin, *Vivre et mourir en Lyonnais*; Lorcin, 'Clauses religieuses', and *Testaments Foréziens, 1305–1316*, ed. M. Gonon (1951). Besançon is another Burgundian town where large numbers of late medieval testaments have survived; see U. Robert, *Testaments de l'officialité de Besançon 1265–1500*, vol. I: *1265–1400* (Paris, 1902).

[32] Douai is an exception more because of recent events than because of its late medieval past. While Douai has preserved the remarkable number of 35,000 parchment contracts or chirographs from the thirteenth to the sixteenth centuries, neighbouring Tournai had preserved 600,000 for the same period until the Germans bombed the city in May 1940; see H. Platelle, 'Chirographes de Tournai retrouvés dans un fonds de la Bibliothèque de Valenciennes', *Revue du Nord* 44 (1962), pp. 191–200; R. Jacob, *Les époux, le seigneur et la cité: coutume et pratiques matrimoniales des bourgeois et paysans de France du Nord au moyen âge* (Brussels, 1990), p. 77.

[33] The earliest notarial register of testaments is Archives Municipales de Douai (hereafter, AMD), FF 444, Registre aux testaments 1415–1428.

[34] See Platelle, 'Chirographes de Tournai'.

[35] See M. Mestayer, 'Testaments douaisiens antérieurs à 1270', *Nos Patois du Nord* 7 (1962), pp. 63–86; 35,000 to 40,000 *acts chirographes* survive from 1225 to the end of the

contracts approved had to be citizens and, as comparisons with the later notarial protocols reveal, those who relied on the échevins' approval were clearly richer and politically more prominent than those whose acts were notarised.[36] Nonetheless, citizenship cut further down the social hierarchy in Douai than it did in fourteenth- and fifteenth-century Florence. As a result, we find early on testaments and other contracts drawn up in Douai before the town's aldermen by bakers, barbers, shearers of cloth,[37] servants[38] and even poor widows whose bequests did not exceed eight *livres* and who possessed no landed property.[39]

By contrast, in Florence as with other cities of central and northern Italy testaments neither had to be 'proved' by the Church nor authorised by city aldermen. Instead, their testaments were more a private affair,[40] witnessed by friends and family and often drawn up in their own homes. The Italian testaments come down to us either in notarial protocols or 'bastardelli' (the notaries' rough drafts) or as individual parchments most often kept by convents or hospitals. The parchment survivals, like the chirographs for the north, tended to preserve the records of more prominent citizens. Yet, despite the differences in the social character of these two forms of the Italian testament, they chart similar trends in burial practices, pious bequests and attitudes towards death over the fourteenth and fifteenth centuries.[41] Deregnaucourt has shown the same for fifteenth-century Douai: while those drafting chirograph testaments were mostly buried within the prestigious space of church buildings and those from the notaries' registers in church cemeteries, the trends in burial practices, funerals and masses were over time much the same for both.[42]

---

sixteenth century. On the 'technique' of the chirograph, see Deregnaucourt, 'Autour de la mort à Douai', p. 55; Jacob, *Les époux*, pp. 78–9.

[36] The earliest register of notarised wills appeared in 1415; AMD, FF 444, Registre aux testaments 1415–1428.

[37] See the list of occupations for testators in Deregnaucourt, 'Autour de la mort à Douai', pp. 10–19.

[38] E. Kittell, 'Testaments of Two Cities: a Comparative Analysis of the Wills of Medieval Genoa and Douai', *European Review of History* 5 (1998), p. 58; AMD, FF 862, 1328.iv.

[39] Kittell, 'Testaments of Two Cities', p. 59. See also Jacob, *Les époux*, p. 81, who finds that the marriage contracts of Douai approved by the city aldermen included all occupational groups, even day labourers.

[40] Kittell, 'Testaments of Two Cities', esp. pp. 74–9. See also Jacob, *Les époux*, p. 105, on the private–public contrast between notarised contracts in the south of France and those approved by aldermen in cities in the north.

[41] On the social differences between testaments that survive in protocols as opposed to parchment collections in Tuscany and Umbria, see Cohn, *The Cult of Remembrance and the Black Death: Six Renaissance Cities in Central Italy* (Baltimore, 1992), pp. 289–94.

[42] Deregnaucourt, 'L'élection de sépulture', pp. 351–2.

For charting changes in mentality the testament certainly does not reveal all. Testators may have made prior arrangements through *inter vivos* contracts or more likely through oral agreements with spouses, neighbours or clerics.[43] The absence of post-mortem masses, the 'election' of a place of burial, or arrangements for a funeral procession in a testament did not necessarily mean that the testator was indifferent to these matters. Nonetheless, a remarkable uniformity can be seen in testators' attention to them from the late thirteenth to the fifteenth century. In Douai,[44] London,[45] Tuscany and Umbria[46] less than half of the testators specified their desired place of burial before the first quarter of the fourteenth century, and for most regions, the percentage remained low until after the Black Death.[47] In Douai, the election of graves lagged behind London and the cities of central Italy; the first testator to 'elect' his grave here does not appear until 1295,[48] and for the period 1301 to 1338 less than 20 per cent (ten out of fifty-five) specified even the church or cemetery where they wished to be interred.[49] However, by the end of the fourteenth century, the election of graves had increased significantly across central Italy,[50] in London, as well as in Douai.[51] For Tuscan and Umbrian towns the proportion had climbed to over 90 per cent, while for Douai in the year of its most serious plague, 1400, it had risen to 56 per cent (forty-three out of seventy-seven testaments).[52]

---

[43] See the critical remarks of C. Burgess, 'Late Medieval Wills and Pious Convention: Testamentary Evidence Reconsidered', in M. A. Hicks (ed.), *Profit, Piety and the Professions in Later Medieval England* (Gloucester, 1990), pp. 14–33.

[44] Deregnaucourt, 'L'élection de sépulture', p. 345. Unfortunately, Chiffoleau, *La comptabilité*, does not provide information on those testators who gave no indication of their burial choices.

[45] Based on my calculations from the Court of Husting, *Calendar of Wills: Court of Husting, London, AD 1258–AD 1688: the Archives of the Corporation of the City of London at the Guidhall*, ed. R. Sharpe, pt 1: 1258–1358 (London, 1889). Although the editor does not explain his principles of abridgement, it is clear from comparing the calendar testaments with the originals that he included all materials relating to burial choices.

[46] Cohn, *The Cult of Remembrance*, pp. 128–9.

[47] This was not always the case with the wills of the elite; see *Testamenta Eboracensa or Wills Registered at York*, ed. J. Raine, Surtees Society, 4 (London, 1836).

[48] Deregnaucourt, 'L'élection de sépulture', p. 343; AMD, FF 861.

[49] These fifty-five testaments run from July 1301 to May 1338, AMD, FF 862. Perhaps significantly, eight of the ten who specified the place of burial chose sites outside their parish communities with either the Dominicans or the Franciscans. Those who made no such specification most likely were buried in their parish cemetery.

[50] See Cohn, *The Cult of Remembrance*, pp. 128–9.

[51] See AMD, FF 868, comprising seventy-eight testaments, all from the plague year of 1400.

[52] The percentage must have declined slightly afterwards; Deregnaucourt, 'L'élection de sépulture', p. 345, calculates that 72 per cent of those writing chirograph wills elected their own burials. Unfortunately, he groups together all the burial choices before 1400.

Even rarer in early wills before the Black Death was any mention of specific markers, burial monuments or descriptions of where in church-yards or in church fabrics the testator's body was to lie. The evidence from archaeology corroborates the impression given by the lack of specificity in testaments: in the twelfth and thirteenth centuries the bodies of the laity as well as most clerics were placed in mass and undifferentiated graves.[53] In Florence, although those choosing their place of burial rose from less than a quarter in the earliest wills to 1275, to three-quarters by the time of the Black Death, they rarely specified more than the church, and more precise instructions do not appear until the 1320s. Before the Black Death only 15 per cent of testators specified more precisely their final resting place, and only by 1400 did more than half make such specifications. But such levels of precision were precocious and remarkably high compared with other Tuscan and Umbrian cities.[54] And for other areas where such statistics have been compiled, it was less than in central Italy. For the diocesan Exchequer Court of York less than 15 per cent of testators from 1389 to 1475 specified their place of burial beyond simply naming the church.[55]

In Florence, these specific instructions for burial before the Black Death pertained almost exclusively to the wealthy and often involved either the construction 'de nuovo' of a family burial chapel and vault or the conversion of an existing chapel into the testator's own burial complex. Such was the testament of Albizius son of the deceased Nardus of the Genti family who elected his burial in the Dominican church of Santa Maria Novella 'opposite the chapel of All Saints, situated in the bell tower of this church'. He further specified that his body was to lie just outside the portal (a prestigious place of burial in churches throughout Europe[56]), where the friars were to construct a 'beautiful sepulchre' and other ornamentations. The existing altar of the chapel of All Saints was to be adorned with panel paintings, vestments for the officiating priests, altarcloths, a chalice and other decorative 'necessities'. For these expenses, along with the stipend to employ a friar to celebrate masses, the testator bequeathed the large sum (by early fourteenth-century standards) of 160 florins.[57]

Unlike in late medieval London or Douai, where chapel constructions

---

[53] Lauwers, *La mémoire des ancêtres*, pp. 148–52.

[54] Cohn, *The Cult of Remembrance*, pp. 138–9.

[55] C. Daniell, *Death and Burial in Medieval England, 1066–1550* (London and New York, 1997), pp. 97–102, tallies 701 requests of 4,700 wills for burials near altars, chancels and choirs. Perhaps there were other means of specifying graves in these testaments which he fails to disclose. In addition, he does not analyse his figures over time.

[56] See Chiffoleau, *La comptabilité*, p. 170.

[57] Archivio di Stato, Florence (hereafter ASF) Dipl[omatico], S. M. Novella, 1344.iv.6.

were confined to the feudal elite and less than 2 per cent of testators commissioned them or referred to earlier ones that had been built by their predecessors,[58] in Florence and other cities of central Italy, the practice penetrated the middling ranks of society and was even within the reach of artisans and wealthy peasants. A Florentine widow of a notary without a family name in 1369 left sums for a burial tomb and chapel in the church of San Lorenzo.[59] Further down the social scale and with fewer resources, a country cobbler from the Tuscan village of Vinci left only 50 florins to build a chapel and to supply it with a chalice, missal, altarcloth and other ornamentations including an altarpiece to be painted of the Virgin Mary and the saints John the Baptist, Paul, Anthony and Michael the Archangel.[60] Nor was this cobbler necessarily overstepping his bounds. In 1348, an Aretine widow of a weaver sold all her possessions for one pious bequest, the construction of a chapel in her parish.[61] In 1390, the Aretine wife of a beltmaker endowed a chapel to be constructed in the ancient abbey of Santa Fiore.[62] In 1411, a widow of a tanner ordered the construction of a chapel in the Perugian friary of Monte Morciano.[63]

In Tuscany and Umbria as in regions north of the Alps, a burial chapel was not the only means by which a testator might individuate his or her grave beyond the formulaic 'apud ecclesiam'. After 1348, and increasingly after the return of plague in 1363, testators made more specific the topography of their burial grounds. They did so either by designating objects already in place or creating new ones so as to mark the exact place of their burial. Thus, in 1411, a furnace-maker's widow from Pisa insisted that her heirs bury her 'next to the olive trees in the Campo Santo'.[64] Other testators used paintings to specify their place of burial and may have even stimulated demand for local artists after the Black Death.[65] The peasant Nullus f.q. Pepi who lived along the border of the communes of Perugia and Todi used his 1348 testament to commission a *Maiestà* for a mere 10 lire to hang above his grave in the village church of Santa Maria in Castelleone.[66] In the same year, the Perugian Nutius Cioli left 25 lire for a *Maiestà* including the figures of 'Our Lord Jesus Christ

58 Deregnaucourt, 'Autour de la mort à Douai', p. 283.
59 Archivio di San Lorenzo (Florence), no. 809, 1369.xi.3.
60 ASF, Dipl., Arch. Gen., 1416.x.13.
61 ASF, Not[arile]. antecos[iano], no. 20833, n.p. 1348.vii.11.
62 Archivio Capitolare, Arezzo, Testamenta Ser Johanne Cecchi, 3r, 1389.i.6.
63 Archivio di Stato, Perugia [ASPr], Pergamene, Mt. Morciano, no. 335, 1411.vii.29.
64 ASF, Not. antecos., no. 8066, 268r–v, fols. 1410.ii.16.
65 See Cohn, 'Piété et commande d'oeuvres d'art après la peste noire', *Annales: HSS* 51 (1996), pp. 551–73.
66 Archivio di S. Pietro (Perugia), Liber contractuum, no. 495, fols. 203v–204v, 1348.vi.9.

on the Cross, the Glorious Virgin Mary, Saints John and Constantine' to be painted on the wall above his sepulchre. He left other properties to supply a yearly source of oil to keep these figures illuminated for ten years following his death.[67] The Assisian notary Ser Daniel domini Francisci Ciccoli left 100 lire 'or more' for his grave, which he elected 'near the door of the Franciscan church'. To demarcate further his earthly remains he commissioned a painting for that spot (*in dicto pilo*), demanding that 'Our Lord, Jesus Christ' be painted on the cross, with the Virgin 'to the right', Saint John the Evangelist 'to the left' and the Blessed Francis and Mary Magdalene at the foot of the cross.[68]

Across Tuscany and Umbria, the turning point in this attention to precise burial places was the Black Death of 1348 and its return in 1362–3. Perhaps out of fear of mass ignominious burial, testators became less content to leave the places and preparations for their final remains solely to the discretion of executives, confrères, parish priests, or even next of kin. Chroniclers and story-tellers repeated tales of fathers abandoning sons; mothers, daughters; and husbands, wives. Nor did such stories die with the Black Death in 1348. At the end of the century, the story-teller Franco Sacchetti described a testator who demanded that a *staio* of sliced pears be left yearly at a designated place for flies since they were the only ones not to abandon him in his last days of illness.[69]

The contrast between the pre- and post-Black Death wills in Douai is even more striking. In earliest testaments from 1228 to 1366 (185 wills) not a single testator specified a burial place beyond naming either the cemetery or the church. The earliest specific site of a grave demanded by a will in Douai (that I have thus far found) does not come until 1374, when a man 'elected' to be buried in the nave of Saint Pierre de Douai, next to where his wife lay.[70] But by the year of the plague, 1400, matters had changed. Even without the benefit of family chapels that ran through the ranks of bourgeois society in Florence, a third of Douaisien testators (twenty-four out of seventy-seven) and over half of those who named their burial church (twenty-four out of forty-three) now specified their graves by pointing to altars, chapels and sacred images opposite where their bodies were to lie. Usually in conjunction with these sites they also demanded that they be interred next to their deceased mothers, fathers and, above all else, their spouses. Further, they created the specificity of

[67] ASPr, Notarile Bastardello, no. 39, fols. 60v–67v, 1348.vii.1.
[68] *Sacro Convento, Buste, Z*, n. 3 (1363–1543), 1363.
[69] Franco Sacchetti, *Il Trecentonovelle*, ed. Antonio Lanza (Florence, 1984).
[70] AMD, FF 863 1373(4).ii.22.

Plate 2.1   *Burial slab of Robert Braunche between his two wives, 1364, produced in the Low Countries*

their graves by commissioning marble slabs of themselves to lie above their physical remains (see Plate 2.1).[71]

Despite this attention to burial grounds and funerary monuments, a corresponding emphasis cannot be found in the Tuscan, Umbrian or Douaisien wills for specific instructions about funeral processions. For central Italy such detail remained rare and confined mostly to the rich until the Counter Reformation.[72] Allusions to the composition, movements and numbers of candles to be carried in funeral processions remained extremely rare in Tuscan and Umbrian testaments through the fifteenth century, and when Italian notaries alluded to the funeral cortège at all, they hardly described 'flamboyant events' (as Chiffoleau, Deregnaucourt and others have claimed for the north). The notable examples in Tuscany come from Pisa and from its nobility. In comparison with the sixteenth century, these were sparse affairs, at least as far as the testamentary instructions indicate. In 1397 the wife of a Pisan knight (*milites*) from the Lanfranchi family ordered the chaplains of the cathedral to accompany her body to its holy grounds in the Campo Santo. Each was to carry two torches.[73] In 1416 another nobleman from the Ripafratta family failed to specify exactly who was to carry his body to the monastic church of San Paolo in their ancestral village, but insisted that it be accompanied by 'at least' two torches of wax 'and no more'.[74]

In comparison with other Tuscan and Umbrian cities, notarial formulae and practice gave special importance to the funeral in Pisa and Perugia. As early as the 1270s these testaments customarily opened with the choice of burial and the expenses to be paid for wax, masses, meals and clothing for the poor but little else. Usually lumped together with these expenses were additional sums for the poor, either in money, clothing or food, to be doled out on the seventh and thirtieth days after the burial and occasionally on the anniversary so that the exact sums to be spent on the funeral alone cannot be calculated even for these cities. By the last quarter of the fourteenth century, these notarial formulae, in fact, became less precise, increasingly leaving the costs for these last rites to the discretion of spouses, kin and heirs. On the other hand, the records from Siena, Florence and Arezzo throughout the period of my analysis (to 1425) seldom mentioned funeral preparations at all or allocated specific

---

[71] AMD, FF 868 (1400).

[72] See Cohn, *Death and Property in Siena: Strategies for the Afterlife* (Baltimore, 1988), chap. 11.

[73] ASF, Not. ntecos., no. 788, fol. 184r, 1397.i.23.

[74] *Ibid.*, n. 8068, fols. 377v–379r, 1416.v.13.

sums for them. When a will did leave instructions for a funeral procession (usually composed by noblemen), it could not hold a candle to the intricate processions devised even by artisans and peasants in Counter-Reformation Italy.[75] To be sure, the chroniclers do describe the monumental funerals of celebrated statesmen and scholars such as Coluccio Salutati or famous *condottieri* such as John Hawkwood,[76] but it was the commune and not the individual that orchestrated these affairs. The testamentary material in Tuscany and Umbria leaves no traces that urbanisation, migration, war and plagues prompted ordinary citizens to compensate for their loss of kin cohesion with 'flamboyant funerals' as Chiffoleau, Deregnaucourt, Lauwers and others have hypothesised for French-speaking cities north of the Alps.

On the other hand, neither Chiffoleau nor other French historians have provided details of these supposed 'flamboyant funerals' that can in any way match descriptions found for the Counter-Reformation period, especially for the non-elites. Instead, they merely point to increasing numbers of masses and the elaboration in the variety of masses to be sung at different moments after the death of the testator. On this score, Chiffoleau's concrete evidence from the wills at Avignon shows no such break with the thirteenth century as his overarching thesis claims. Instead, the break comes immediately after the Black Death, from the 1360s to the fifteenth century. In Douai, where testaments appear in sufficient numbers before the mid-fourteenth century, providing the basis for a pre- and post-Black Death comparison, the plagues of the late fourteenth and early fifteenth centuries constitute the watershed.[77] Despite a near slavish following of Chiffoleau and the Annalist penchant for stressing 'des mouvements très lents',[78] Deregnaucourt shows a correlation between the plagues and demographic crises of 1380–2, 1400, 1415, 1458 and 1467 and the demand for masses, increases in their prices, and elaboration in their complexity.[79] By the plague of 1400 rich bourgeois of Douai such as

---

[75] See Cohn, *Death and Property*, chap. 11.

[76] See Sharon T. Strocchia, *Death and Ritual in Renaissance Florence* (Baltimore and London, 1992), pp. 79–82, 106–20.

[77] Deregnaucourt, 'Autour de la mort à Douai', pp. 271, 279.

[78] *Ibid.*, p. 391.

[79] Evidence of the plagues of 1348, the 1360s and the mid-1370s is missing for Douai as for several other cities in the Walloon region and southern Brabant; see Gérard Sivéry, 'Le Hainaut et la peste noire', *Société des arts et lettres du Hainault* 79 (1965), pp. 431–44. No testaments survive for the years 1348 to 1350 in the chirographs and only three from Douai's hospitals (see *Inventaire général des chartes, titres et papiers appartenant aux hospices et au bureau de bienfaisance de la ville de Douai*, ed. M. Brassart (Douai, 1839); La bourse commune, no. 1, 1348.ix.28; Fondateur de la table du Saint-Esprit, no. 648, 1350.iv.8;

Jehan de Roquignies called de Fierin demanded vigils and masses on the day of death to be celebrated in all the churches and friaries of Douai as well as offering 100 *sou* worth of wine to all those who carried his body to the grave.[80]

The Tuscan and Umbrian testaments show parallel developments in the demand for masses. For Florence, large numbers with complex cycles are found only after the Black Death and increase in number in the last decades of the fourteenth century. On occasion they appear to have been more 'flamboyant' than any of the examples provided by either Chiffoleau or Deregnaucourt. Such were the 1371 testamentary desires of a Florentine parish priest of Santa Cecilia. First, he required daily masses of the priest who was to officiate in his private chapel. In addition, each year on the feast day of the martyred saints, Tiburtius and Valerianus, the chaplain with six other priests was to celebrate a solemn mass and a divine office followed the next day by an anniversary mass (*unum annuale*) in his chapel with eight other priests, along with a solemn mass with a vigil, an office for the dead and seven low masses (*missas planas*). Each priest was to receive five soldi and one candle. He also left a farm with a cottage and arable lands to a Florentine hospital and required the hospital's director, rector, *conversi* and servants each year on 5 August 'to make a feast and commemoration' for the Blessed Virgin called Santa Maria della Neve at an altar that the testator had previously constructed in the hospital's church. Four priests were to sing one mass for the Virgin (*missa de beata [Virgine]*) and burn two torches containing a pound of wax apiece. On the next day, they were to celebrate an anniversary mass along with five plain masses for the dead and one mass sung over the altar of the Blessed Mary with a vigil and an office for his and his ancestors' souls, this time with six priests to officiate, each receiving five soldi and one candle. Nor did the masses and religious services end here. As long as a certain domina Bilia, the daughter of the former Piero de' Macci, lived, she was

---

Hopital des Wetz ou du béguinage, no. 814, 1349.xi.25 (which is not a testament but a chirograph relating to the execution of a will)). In addition, Dhérent, 'Histoire sociale de la bourgeoisie de Douai', p. 111, finds that the mortality of Douai aldermen was in 1348 to 1350 the same as in non-plague years; only three officers died. From the testamentary evidence 1382 may have been a plague year, but the first major plague in Douai came only in 1400. Not only did the number of testaments soar to its highest point in any one year (seventy-seven), most of which were drafted in August and September, but the following year witnessed the population's recoil in producing the highest number of marriage contracts and *ravestissements*. The same happened after the plague of 1415 but neither Howell nor Jacob mention any such reaction evinced for the marriages after 1348; see Jacob, *Les époux*, pp. 226–7.

80 AMD, FF 868 1400.vi.18, transcribed in Deregnaucourt, 'Autour de la mort à Douai', p. 117.

to have masses sung for this parish priest and his ancestors' souls celebrated on the feast day of the Madonna della Neve on 5 August. In addition, he gave her the *usufructus* to his residence in the parish of Santa Maria in Campo on condition that from the rent she would finance an anniversary mass within the first eight days of each month in the church of Santa Cecilia for his and his ancestors' souls with twelve priests chanting *sub voce* eleven low masses and singing one solemn mass, a vigil, and an office for the dead. Each priest was to receive five soldi and a candle except for the new rector of this parish, who could get 'double payment' – ten soldi and two candles; in addition, two other candles were 'to illuminate the body of Christ' on the altar.[81] Although the barons and counts of Flanders, France and England commanded far more resources than this mere parish priest and asked for far more masses, I have found no examples from the later fourteenth century that compare with its complexity and elaboration of post-mortem masses. Further, by the fifteenth century the numbers of perpetual masses had more than doubled over the previous twenty-five years in Arezzo and Florence, and in Pisa, the numbers had increased by three-and-a-half times.[82] In neither Douai nor Avignon did perpetual masses take off as they did in fifteenth-century Tuscany.[83]

From burial practices, funerals and masses, French historians have argued that the wills confirm Ariès's notion of death as 'one's own death'[84] and express a new 'individualism' as early as the thirteenth century. But their notion of individualism does not conjure the optimism, security and boldness Burckhardt saw for Renaissance Italy. Instead, for Chiffoleau and Deregnaucourt it evoked a new narcissism, egoism and, above all, 'La Grand Mélancolie', where citizens faced death 'uprooted' from former familial solidarities that had cushioned the blows of death in the feudal period.[85]

But, for both the French and the Italian contexts, did these new post-plague burials, funerals and masses actually evoke 'a new individualism' at all, whether with Burckhardtian bravado or northern 'fragility'? First, in the Tuscan and Umbrian contexts, the new attention to individuated graves was a movement towards crypts and monuments for family

---

[81] Archivio di S. Lorenzo, no. 899, 1371.ix.1.

[82] See Cohn, *The Cult of Remembrance*, p. 211.

[83] On perpetual and anniversary masses at Douai, see Deregnaucourt, 'Autour de la mort à Douai', pp. 286–7.

[84] See, for instance, Deregnaucourt, 'Autour de la mort à Douai', p. 90; Chiffoleau, *La comptabilité*, p. 88.

[85] Chiffoleau, *La comptabilité*, p. 207; Deregnaucourt, 'Autour de la mort à Douai,' p. 188.

lineages. By the last years of the fourteenth century these family and ancestral graves began to limit individual burial choices, especially of women testators. Their place of burial had already been 'elected' by an earlier generation of patriarchs who on the heels of the Black Death had begun building crypts for their future lineages. In Italy such lineage graves were not confined to family chapels or to the rich. In Florence from 1400 to 1425, forty-five out of fifty-two or 87 per cent of those who specified their graves beyond simply electing a church or monastery, chose to be buried in ancestral grounds that did not require the testator to build a monumental grave or private burial chapel. While immediately after the plague of 1363[86] these new constructions had comprised nearly 20 per cent of all burial choices, by the early years of the fifteenth century they had slipped to less than 8 per cent.[87]

Moreover, the individuation of graves with works of art – *tabula* or frescoes to be painted above or near the tomb – more often than not was to include depictions of deceased fathers or other ancestors rather than testators alone.[88] And the most commonly ordered decoration was the family coats of arms to be painted, carved, engraved or embroidered on chapel walls, chalices and clerics' vestments. After the second strike of pestilence, even disenfranchised artisans who bore no family names at the time of writing their testaments nonetheless used their testaments to invent new family names and coats of arms, which they ordered to be emblazoned on church objects as simple and as inexpensive as candlestick holders to be positioned near their graves.[89] It was the family and the male line past and future, not the 'deracinated' individual, that Tuscan and Umbrian testators wished to celebrate and have remembered in their last wills and testaments.

In the Italian context, instead of fading to the rural or feudal margins of society as French historians have supposed not only for France but for Western Europe in general, the grip of the ancestors and the solidarity of the male line took hold in the cities rather than in the countryside[90] and with a vigour that penetrated the social ranks of testators from the patriciate to artisans in the wool industry. They further expressed their veneration for their ancestors with their prayers and masses by remem-

---

[86] From 1364 to 1375, thirteen out of seventy burial choices; in 1376 to 1400, fifteen out of eighty-three choices.

[87] Seven of ninety-two choices.

[88] See Cohn, 'Piété et commande d'oeuvres d'art'.

[89] Cohn, *The Cult of Remembrance*, p. 236.

[90] On rural wills in the territory of Florence, see Cohn, 'Piety and Religious Practice in the Rural Dependencies of Renaissance Florence,' *English Historical Review*, forthcoming.

bering the souls of their ancestors – 'suorum antecessorum' – and asking for the redemption of their sins along with those of the testator.

Here, the post-plague changes in mentality of Tuscan and Umbrian cities may have differed from the trends to the north. While Chiffoleau remains vague about the exact timing of testators' 'disengagement from the place where the ancestors rested',[91] Deregnaucourt shows a decline in burial choices in ancestral crypts for fifteenth-century Douai.[92] But was the change so starkly narcissistic as these historians have argued? Were these testators isolated individuals wrought with the angst of solitude, cut from all familial systems of support and security? Instead, the testamentary evidence suggests another scenario. With increasing regularity, husbands and wives in Douai chose to be buried alongside one another and in the 1370s began to commission marble burial slabs representing the conjugal pair. In some cases, husbands even ordered the sculpture of three figures, representing themselves 'lying' between two of their former wives.[93] In other cases, the sculpted group was to be the entire nuclear family 'for their own remembrance and that of their children'.[94] In this case, the burial ground was not even in the more privileged space of a church but instead within the cemetery of the minor friars of Douai, suggesting that such funerary sculpture might have penetrated the lower ranks of the Douaisien bourgeoisie.[95] But this testamentary commission was exceptional; the others were in churches and mostly commemorated the conjugal pair alone.

Curiously, this trend in burial practices correlated with a reverse trend in marriage law and custom that benefited the property rights of the children and the lineage over those of the spouses and in particular those of the widows.[96] But as Martha Howell has shown from the marriage contracts and contemporary literature, this trend away from the 'communal' pact and towards a 'separatist' marriage contract similar to the Italian dowry parallels a trend towards 'romantic love' and the affective ties within marriage as a new partnership.[97] In addition, this northern trend away from the veneration of dead ancestors, at least for Douai, can

---

[91] Chiffoleau, *La comptabilité*, pp. 171, 176.

[92] Deregnaucourt, 'Autour de la mort à Douai', p. 138; Deregnaucourt, 'L'élection de sépulture', pp. 350–1.

[93] See Deregnaucourt, 'Autour de la mort à Douai', p. 142; AMD, FF 863, 1380.xi.8.

[94] AMD, FF 864, 1383.viii.13: 'une lame a pluisses figures pour remenabrance seuls et de leurs enfans.' See also FF 867, 1399.xi.10.

[95] On the different social status of burials within cemeteries and churches, see Deregnaucourt, 'L'élection de sépulture', p. 345.

[96] See Jacob, *Les époux*, pp. 191–207; Howell, *Marriage Exchange*.

[97] Howell, *The Marriage Exchange*, p. 169.

be spotted in another section of the Douaisien wills that historians have yet to quantify or even remark upon. From their earliest examples in the mid-thirteenth century to at least the fifteenth century, testators often began with a formula to explain the reasons for their disposition of property – 'for God and in charity (por Diu et en almosne)' or 'for God and for one's soul'.[98] In the earliest testaments until the 1370s testators rarely went beyond 'for God and in charity', but, on occasion, they extended the formula by enlisting the souls of other relatives, usually starting with their fathers and mothers, occasionally a brother, a sister, even an uncle, and by the early fourteenth century, the souls of their ancestors.[99] Such was the invocation of Ribent de Monsteroed in 1301: 'pour diu et pour l'ame et pour les ames de seu pere et de se mere de ses anchisseurs'.[100] If a testator then went on to demand masses from his religious beneficiaries, he usually required them to pray or say masses for the same souls as the testator listed in his invocation.[101]

For the first part of the batch of chirograph testaments, FF 862, attested between 1301 and 1338 (fifty-five testaments), more than half of those who began their testaments with such invocations linked their own spiritual desires with the souls of their ancestors (ten out of nineteen), and only four recalled the souls of themselves alone; the rest named other deceased relatives – fathers, mothers, uncles, spouses. In one case a woman recalled the soul of her 'baron', perhaps her feudal lord.[102] But after 1348 only one of the fifty-one testators in this batch (to 1366) – a beguine – recalled her ancestors.[103] By the plague of 1400 this picture of ancestral deference had completely vanished: while most now used the formula to name specific relatives, spouses, and even individual friends, not a single testator (out of seventy-seven) recalled the souls of his ancestors;[104] nor have I found any who did so after 1400. Indeed, perhaps reflecting the world invoked by Chiffoleau and Deregnaucourt, these Douaisien bourgeois appear more cut off from their ancestral roots than they had been a century earlier or than their contemporaries in Florence and other early Renaissance northern Italian cities. In 1400, most Douaisiens mentioned their own souls alone or looked back no

---

[98] The first testament to use this formula is AMD, FF 861, 1256.v.20, transcribed in Mestayer, 'Testaments douaisiens,' no. 7, p. 67.

[99] The first testament to enlist the souls of one's ancestors was in 1301.

[100] AMD, FF 862, 1301.viii.

[101] See for instance AMD, FF 862, 1327.v., the testament of Jehan Haus de Cuer.

[102] AMD, FF 862, 1316.iii.6.

[103] AMD, FF 862, 1359.xi.17.

[104] AMD, FF 868.

further than to the souls of their fathers and mothers. Here, the shift seems to have stemmed from the plague years and not to have been a gradual, slow movement, mounting from the thirteenth-century forces of urbanisation as Chiffoleau has claimed (although from the complete absence of wills antedating the Black Death in the city of Avignon).

These post-plague testators, however, do not come across as narcissistic egomaniacs as the French historians have claimed. More often than not in Douai they used their wills to assist the souls of their parents and deceased spouses. In addition, the vast majority of testators in the plague year 1400 (twenty-three of the twenty-four who began their testaments with this formula) used their testaments to benefit the souls of any others whom the testator 'wished to include and to give gifts to' ('et de toutes les ames dont il a intencion de priier et qu'il y volroit accompagnier a avoir après sen déchés les dons et lais qui s'enssievent').[105] Further, the souls of this large group of friends and kin were included when testators asked for prayers or masses for the health of their souls.

This north–south difference before and after the Black Death – the decline in the veneration of the ancestors at Douai; its rise in Florence – cannot be explained simply by pointing vaguely to the forces of urbanisation, commercialisation and migration or by the 'deracinating' forces of the Black Death, wars and famines. Florence, no less than the cities of France and the Low Countries, experienced these same forces and was as seriously hit and probably more so by the fourteenth-century plagues as the 'bonnes villes' of Flanders.[106] Yet in Florence as well as in other major cities of Tuscany and Umbria, they had the very opposite psychological and social consequences as they did in Douai. Burial in lineage vaults increased and spread across social classes, and with increasing regularity these southern testators remembered their dead ancestors with requests for prayers and masses to be sung for these ancestors' souls.

These ties to the ancestors in the celestial realm may have been linked with changes in the social realm of politics and marriage. Anthony Molho has argued that the social structure of Florence's ruling class became more rigid after the Black Death as its members sought to close their ranks and intermarriage within the ruling class tightened.[107] Far from Burckhardt's Renaissance meritocracy, where self-made men such as the *condottiere* Francesco Sforza rose to rule territorial states from low or even illegiti-

---

[105] See for instance AMD, FF 868, 1400.vi.18. In the batch FF 868, twenty-one mentioned no souls at all, and only one mentioned himself and his parents.

[106] Sivéry, 'Le Hainaut et la peste noire'.

[107] A. Molho, *Marriage Alliance in Late Medieval Florence* (Cambridge, MA, 1994).

mate birth, post-plague Florence emerges from Molho's marriage statistics as a closed society with a ruling elite that operated as though it were a social caste. Moreover, despite Richard Goldthwaite's thesis of a Florence formed by a 'dynamic' economy and underscored by Burckhardtian social mobility, his careful study of the syndics of Florence's guild of masons and carpenters shows the opposite – a rigid world of century-long family domination within the crafts of Florence.[108]

On the other hand, the social and political fate of commercial London after the Black Death was just the opposite of Florence's. Here, the Black Death and its accompanying forces favoured the strengthening of 'horizontal ties' at the expense of family lineages.[109] Participation in government and control of guild offices were characterised by 'circulating elites'. Merchant families rarely survived for more than three generations in the male line, and between 1370 and 1500 only one son succeeded his father as a city alderman.[110] To my knowledge, no statistical study comparable to Sylvia Thrupp's exists for Douai or any other late medieval northern French or Flemish city.[111] However, the change of Douai's government from a patriciate based on hereditary office before the Black Death to one of selection afterwards suggests a pattern closer to London's than to Florence's. Even if marriage contracts increasingly benefited the lineage over the conjugal pair, and intermarriage within certain trades may have grown over the fifteenth century, it was not until 1500 that the ruling class of Douai 'lost its amorphous character' and evolved into 'an urban aristocracy made up of men who lived from large-scale commerce, rent, or office'.[112] Further, Robert Jacob concludes that the 'logic' of marriage custom in fourteenth- and fifteenth-century Douai 'engendered great social mobility' and 'a circulation of fortunes and professions', which he sustains with several micro-biographies.[113] The social revolts at

---

[108] Goldthwaite, *The Building of Renaissance Florence*, pp. 272–86.

[109] See Barbara A. Hanawalt, *Growing up in Medieval London: the Experience of Childhood in History* (New York, 1993), p. 132.

[110] See J. A. F. Thomson, *The Transformation of Medieval England, 1370–1529* (London, 1983), p. 50; Sylvia Thrupp, *The Merchant Class of Medieval London* (Chicago, 1948), pp. 363–4.

[111] Despite major social and political upheavals during the second half of the fourteenth century, the social structure of Ghent appears to have remained largely intact; between 1360 and 1385, 650 offices were held by 246 families. Thus, although participation in government sunk much deeper roots in Ghent than in Florence, its governing elites appear not to have circulated with the fluidity found for late medieval London and may have more closely resembled the social structure that lay behind Florence's governance; see Nicholas, *The Metamorphosis of a Medieval City*.

[112] Howell, *The Marriage Exchange*, p. 183.

[113] Jacob, *Les époux*, pp. 94–6.

the end of the thirteenth century and the confiscation of patrician fortunes in the early fourteenth century redistributed wealth and shifted the balance of power, bringing the 'bonnes gens' closer to the common citizen ('commun').[114]

Thus Burckhardtian individualism seems to have been more at work in fifteenth-century cities north of the Alps such as London and Douai than in Renaissance Florence, where by the fifteenth century, instead of the exercise of free choice or the moulding of one's future through 'self-fashioning' the individual (at least as revealed in last testamentary decisions over property and matters of the soul) was more and more ensnared within the previous dictates of the ancestors, which blocked the choice of graves as well as the alienation of landed property. On the other hand, in Douai, 'the testator's capacity remained intact; *retrait lignager* never encumbered the liberty of the contractor'.[115]

Testamentary commissions for works of art bear out the difference. In both Florence and Douai, the Black Death and its aftershocks appear to have stimulated testators to 'individuate' their graves against the threat of mass interment in communal ditches without last rites, proper funerals and subsequent masses to recall their memories and souls. After the second strike of plague in 1363, testamentary commissions for works of art, primarily paintings, in Tuscany and Umbria increased dramatically: by the last quarter of the fourteenth century more than one in every ten testators in Arezzo and Florence left sums to commission paintings, and the number increases still further if family coats of arms and other figures to be engraved on chalices, vestments and candlestick holders are included (see Plate 2.2).[116] But more often than not, these images were to represent and commemorate not the testators themselves alone, but instead these testators' predecessors.

In Douai, the numbers of commissions in testaments also shot up in the last years of the fourteenth and the early fifteenth centuries. While testators in central Italy turned almost exclusively to painting, the bourgeois of Flanders chose funerary sculpture to represent themselves 'lying' on their graves to be remembered before the eyes of kin, neighbours and God. The earliest testamentary commission that I have found or that Deregnaucourt cites from his exhaustive thesis on the last wills of Douai does not appear until 1377, when Margherite de Ghienard chose her place of burial in the nave of the church of Saint Pierre, where 'the

---

[114] *Ibid.*, p. 234.
[115] *Ibid.*, p. 240.
[116] Cohn, 'Piété et commande d'oeuvres d'art', p. 555.

Plate 2.2   *Puccio di Simone, donor painting (detail) from the tryptich of
St Matthew, mid- to late fourteenth century, Florence*

portraits' of herself and her deceased husband had been sculpted lying above their graves.[117] In the 1380s and the 1390s more demands for sculpted burial 'portraits' appear.[118] But it was Douai's major plague in 1400 that provoked the greatest numbers of testators desiring themselves and their spouses to be sculpted in marble for their remembrance.[119] In that year, only one testator commissioned a marble 'portrait' of her mother in addition to herself,[120] and in no case did a Douaisien bourgeois venerate other deceased ancestors through these means. Instead, the artists here were to preserve for posterity the testators themselves with their deceased spouses.

From these testamentary descriptions and against what Emile Mâle has claimed from the rare remains of such northern funerary art, it is clear that Douaisiens wanted more than an idealised type of themselves and their spouse on their burial slabs.[121] All of these commissions refer to their sculpted 'figures' as 'pourtraits'. On occasion, the testator spelled out more emphatically what he or she wanted, specifying that the incumbent figures were to be 'good portraits' with suitable resemblances to themselves. Such was the demand of a parish priest whose testament ordered a slab to be sculpted above his grave, embossed with 'a good portrait of

---

[117] Deregnaucourt, 'Autour de la mort à Douai', p. 142. The earliest material evidence for such funerary effigies of the bourgeoisie in Lille and its environs comes at about the same time, 1368 to 1372; see Hervé Oursel, 'Monuments funéraires des XIIIéme, XIVéme, XVéme et XVIéme siècles à Lille et dans ses environs immédiats', *Revue du Nord* 62 (1980), p. 348.

[118] Deregnaucourt, 'Autour de la mort à Douai', p. 142; and AMD, FF 863, 1380.x.12, 1380.xi.8; FF 864, 1381.xii.12; 1382.vii.1; 1382.ix.8; 1383.viii.13; FF 865, 1386.iii.2; FF 867, 1396.ix.24, 1398.viii.3, 1399.vi.5; 1399.xi.10.

[119] AMD, FF 867, 1399(1400).iii.29; FF 868, 1400.viii.16; 1400.viii.28; 1400.viii.28bis; 1400.viii.31; 1400.ix.1. The early years of the fifteenth century continued to produce such burial requests; see FF 869, 1402.iv.19, 1404.v.9, 1405.ix.6, 1408.vi.7; FF 871, 1415.ix.8, 1418.x.17.

[120] AMD, FF 871, 1400.ix.1.

[121] According to Mâle, *L'art religieux*, pp. 424–6, these effigies were idealised types that did not depict the personal traits of the dead, and were often produced in Parisian workshops and then sent out to the provinces. Nonetheless, the Douaisien testators ordered that they were represented in their own likeness, insisting that their own 'pourtraits' and those of their spouses be reproduced in marble. Oursel, 'Monuments funéraires', does not confront Mâle's thesis directly but suggests that the taste of local patrons did influence changes in style and content of the funerary effigies in the fifteenth century; see esp. pp. 360 and 362. According to Mâle, *L'art religieux*, pp. 392–3, few of these funerary sculptures remain anywhere in France or Flanders, first because of the destruction carried out during the Reformation, then during the French Revolution and finally, particularly for Flanders, during the two World Wars. A church such as the Cathedral of Langres held as many as 2,000 such effigies at the beginning of the eighteenth century. See also Oursel, 'Monuments funéraires', p. 345.

himself in his very likeness, kneeling in front of an image of Our Lady, which stood at the side of his grave'.[122] In another, a husband ordered burial sculptures of himself and his wife whose resemblance to the deceased couple was to be affirmed by his executors ('de tel fachon que bon sembleur as ses executeurs').[123]

While more individualist, even more Burckhardtian, than the lineage designs of early Renaissance Florence, these northern artistic demands do not evoke the narcissism and egoism of a 'fragile' urban bourgeoisie stripped from its familial moorings as Chiffoleau, Deregnaucourt and others have argued from the post-plague French and Walloon testaments. In only two cases that I have found thus far in the Douaisien testaments antedating 1420 did a testator commissioning a burial portrait wish to be presented alone in marble: one was a parish priest; the other, a nobleman.[124] The rest came from good bourgeois families of urban Douai. They asked to be buried next to their spouses, mothers and children, commissioned burial tombs and sculpture to celebrate their conjugal affection, and had masses sung – not for their own souls alone – but for the souls of their fathers, mothers, brothers, sisters, uncles, friends ('amis et amies'), benefactors, and for all those they chose to be included in their itemised bequests dispensing their worldly wealth.

---

[122] AMD, FF 863, 1380.x.12: 'et ordonné une lame telle que boin samblera a ses executeurs . . . en telle maniere que se il avenoit que la ne peust estre gisans li dis sires Jacques, et qu'il y eust trop petit lieu mis et posés ou sarcut de sen taïon et taïe qui est scituez et assis sur le chimentiere de le dite eglise et que ychilz sarcut soit et ordonnez en boine pointure d'une personne esbochié a le samblanche du dit sire Jaque, estans a genouls devant l'image notre Dame qui la est sur un coté' (transcribed in Deregnaucourt, 'L'Autour de la mort à Douai', p. 91.)

[123] AMD, FF 867, 1399.xi.10.

[124] AMD, FF 863, 1380.x.12; and FF 869, 1402.iv.19. In another testament a widow refers to the burial tomb where the figure of her deceased husband has been sculpted above their grave; she makes no reference to her portrait; FF 867, 1399(1400).iii.29. Moreover, the trend in Douaisien marriage contracts reveals that the bourgeois and artisan classes had not lost all sense of the family as lineage; instead it gained in strength from the late fourteenth to the sixteenth centuries; see Howell, *The Marriage Exchange*; Jacob, *Les époux*, p. 240: 'Que le centre de gravité du groupe familial se soit déplacé du couple vers la parenté, c'est-à-dire dans le sen exactement inverse de la classique évolution du lignage à la communauté et au ménage, de la famille large à la famille étroite, dans laquelle tant de théories historiques et sociologiques ont vu une sorte de loi inéluctable du développement des sociétés occidentales.'

3 'Longing to be prayed for': death and commemoration in an English parish in the later Middle Ages

Clive Burgess

To fathom the connections between death and commemoration, as one acted upon the other fashioning the priorities of later medieval English Christians, it is worth developing one very obvious point as a platform for discussion.[1] Christianity, resembling other faiths, commemorates an individual whose life and teaching avowedly showed the way to deeper truth; perhaps more idiosyncratically, it has been particularly concerned to remember and, in the mass, symbolically re-enact Christ's death as an avenue to understanding and realising His teachings about life and redemption. Christians have always been concerned to contemplate and commemorate Christ's death because in so doing they address pressing questions about themselves: they believe that, just as Christ overcame death, so too they may obtain salvation by fulfilling the instructions He vouchsafed. The Church, the institution with the task of perpetuating and spreading His teachings, has mediated His message as it strives to ensure that death should have dominion over as few as possible. In short, death and commemoration are issues at the very core of Christianity. Different emphases have been applied to each, and these have changed

---

[1] This essay explores a theme that I have considered before (most obviously, perhaps, in 'The Benefactions of Mortality: the Lay Response in the Late Medieval Parish', in D. M. Smith (ed.), *Studies in Clergy and Ministry in Medieval England* (Borthwick Studies in History, 1, 1991)), but I hope that the present offering takes the material in a new and worthwhile direction. My debt to the first chapters of Eamon Duffy, *The Stripping of the Altars: Traditional Religion in England 1400–1580* (New Haven and London, 1992) is plain. Less apparent is the fact that I only realised how the theme that the editors were pressing me to write on, death and commemoration before the Reformation, might dovetail with the liturgy when I was teaching courses on Late Medieval Christianity and Culture at University College London in the autumn and spring terms of 1997–8; I doubt whether my long-suffering students knew the favour they did me, but I offer all of them my thanks.

44

radically with time and circumstance. The result has been a variety of traditions. In later medieval England, before the sweeping changes of the sixteenth century, preparations for death and the importance assigned to personal commemoration assumed a noteworthy prominence, not only as far as the teaching of the institutional Church was concerned, but also in the very striking responses of the faithful. The form and implications of these responses are the principal concern of this chapter but, by way of background, attention will be paid both to contemporary teaching on death and commemoration, and, more immediately, to the customs and conduct of local church life to appreciate quite how instruction sat with context.

As it strove to involve a population for the most part unlettered and which lived by husbandry, the institutional Church in the Middle Ages evolved a distinctive and complex liturgy.[2] The events of Christ's life and the mysteries of the faith were represented and re-enacted through services and ceremonies: as time passed through seasons and years, the Church observed a well-defined and endlessly repeated cycle of rites, and at each the celebration of the mass was invariably of central significance. The two most prominent sequences of feasts in the Church calendar were particularly associated with the life and the Passion of Christ: Advent, Christmas, the Epiphany and Candlemas were concerned essentially with the incarnation, with the mystery that God became Man; but of deeper significance, Easter asserted Christ's triumph over sin and death, and its date in turn determined the feasts of Ascension and Pentecost, of seasons like Lent, and celebrations like Corpus Christi. In addition to the feasts concerned particularly with the Saviour were many others celebrating those close to Him, like His mother, the Blessed Virgin, Her mother, St Anne, St John the Baptist and, of course, the Apostles. To these feasts were added those of eminent saints and martyrs, like Sts Stephen, Catherine and Margaret; and there were others of more general significance like those of St Michael and All Angels and the feasts of All Saints and All Souls, and this is before we come to the myriad feasts observed for saints often of more local or personal significance.[3] Many of the most

---

[2] Duffy, *Stripping of the Altars*, chap. 1 and bibliography provides a particularly useful starting point on the subject of the liturgy. See also R. Hutton, *The Rise and Fall of Merry England: the Ritual Year, 1400–1700* (Oxford, 1994), chaps. 1–3, and D. Cressy, *Bonfires and Bells. National Memory and the Protestant Calendar in Elizabethan and Stuart England* (Berkeley and Los Angeles, 1989), chaps. 1 and 2.

[3] Despite attempts by the elite of the Church to alter attitudes to sanctity, it is clear that the cult of saints enjoyed sustained and intense popularity in the later Middle Ages: see A. Vauchez, *Sainthood in the later Middle Ages*, tr. J. Birrell (Cambridge, 1997).

important feasts occurred, whether by accident or design, at significant times of the year.[4] Easter, celebrating the triumph of life over death, is in spring at the beginning of the agricultural year; Christmas and the feast of St John the Baptist immediately follow the solstices; Lammas, Michaelmas and All Saints occur at significant stages of the harvest; and so on. The truths and teachings embodied in the feasts inevitably became deeply embedded into the consciousness of believers, and the figures celebrated and commemorated were invoked in petition at critical times of the year and in particular predicaments, or thanked more generally as helpmeets. Religion, and the unfolding of the Christian message, became part of life's pattern, symbolically and in reality, repeated year after year after year. Late medieval Christians in countryside and towns – themselves centres acutely dependent on rural food production, whose populations originated for the most part from nearby counties – lived and worked in a tissue of time, memory and meaning, articulated primarily by the seasons but powerfully reinforced and elaborated by the Church.

For the great majority, the teaching and ministry of Christianity emanated from parish churches. As a building, replete with fixtures, fittings and decorations, a parish church reinforced many of the truths expressed in the faith and its liturgy. Ceremonial was enacted in spaces provided in and defined by the building – with, for instance, masses being celebrated at the holiest places, the high or side altars, and processions exploiting internal aisles and exterior features for suitable routes on certain feast days. Observances were, as a matter of course, sited in appropriate places with, for instance, vigils at the Easter sepulchre, fraternity masses in a chapel dedicated to the patron saint, and drinkings and May celebrations in the churchyard. Decoration reinforced the message. Any parishioner sitting or standing in the nave and looking towards the high altar in the chancel could be left in no doubt as to the core of the faith and the fate of his or her soul when time should end, as it would. The rood, surmounting the screen separating nave from chancel, comprised a carved figure of Christ crucified, flanked by the Virgin Mary and St John, an echo in visual form of the truth celebrated in the mass – celebrated with most circumstance at the high altar in the chancel beyond. This representation of the Passion had broader ramifications of reinforced meaning for it would, in all probability, have been set

---

[4] Cressy, *Bonfires and Bells*, chaps. 1 and 2 is particularly good on the 'rhythms' of the year, and succinctly describes how the Church had accommodated itself within earlier festivals of significance.

in a fuller visual context intended to remind the onlooker of the Judgement when the individual's response to Christ's sacrifice would be decided: roods were frequently set within a Doom painted on the surrounding chancel arch, with St Michael weighing souls under God's gaze, whilst the saved on one side ascended to the celestial city and the damned on the other were tossed or dragged into Hell's mouth. Reminding every onlooker of the essentials of the faith, this arrangement of visual stimuli acted also as a mainspring to prompt actions, be they good works, almsdeeds or service for others and in the interests of the parish. No one could be in any doubt of what was at stake and of the importance of one's actions in the here and now for the eventual outcome in the hereafter.

Thus an *aide-mémoire* became a prick of conscience, an effect further reinforced by decorations and fittings visible in the rest of the building. On side walls, in the aisles, on panels at the base of the screen and elsewhere, and in the windows were respectively murals, paintings or stained glass depicting scenes from the life of Christ, of the Virgin or of a saint, or stories from the Bible, or portraits of saints with symbols. Surfaces reinforced by image what was celebrated and commemorated in the lessons and liturgy, a feature further mirrored by carved images of Christ and the Virgin and the saints in the shrines, screen and aisles of the church. In short, the setting in which the liturgy was enacted mirrored and counterpointed the rites themselves, providing a continuous presence, and prompting prolonged veneration and contemplation of predecessors and truths perforce celebrated at set times.

The effects were cumulative: chiming in with time and experience, a regular round of observances established the tenets of the faith; moreover, the physical setting in which this was enacted became a visual mnemonic, further reinforcing dogma. But it is, in addition, to be remembered that sounds, that is of the words comprising the rites and of the music, chants and even polyphony to which services and observances were set, further compounded the mnemonic effect – and sound can carry where sightlines fail.[5] Words and phrases used at special times set indelibly in the mind; similarly chants, tunes and song might reinforce the grasp of the pious and the not so pious. If in our culture the medium may be deemed to be the message,[6] then it is worth pondering how, in a very much less

---

[5] Duffy, *Stripping of the Altars*, chap. 2 explores the power of images and words, and also the effects of the Church's programme of catechesis.

[6] Most notably, of course, Marshall McLuhan, in the title of the first chapter in his book, *Understanding Media* (London, 1964).

cluttered environment, the potency of the ceremonial, visual and aural media together comprising the experience of parish Christianity would have penetrated and shaped the consciousness and experience of late medieval Christians; and this was, of course, but a pale reflection of what was on offer in cathedrals, abbeys, hospitals and collegiate churches. The experience was nothing if not memorable; it was, of course, meant to be so.

The principles of the faith, the round of ceremonial, and the decorative, verbal and aural environments were of a piece, facilitating worship and commemorating and celebrating the saints, 'the very special dead'. Religion made past things present by constant and vivid re-enactment: life was articulated, truths taught, intercessors invoked, the past celebrated and some semblance of control over the future proffered in the process. But as the past exercised a strong influence shaping the religious experience of Christians in the century and more preceding the Reformation, so too did it elicit a distinctive and co-ordinate response as men and women, with the teachings of Christ and the Church in mind, sought to procure their salvation. It is a striking – although, on reflection, hardly surprising – aspect of late medieval pious practice that contemporaries, prompted particularly by the imperatives of the Sacrament of Penance, interwove their response within the existing liturgy, within the structures and practices deemed appropriate by and for precursors in the Church Triumphant. Members of the Church Militant and the Church Suffering, that is on earth and in Purgatory, contrived to be remembered, and even celebrated, in parallel with the liturgy and the church year by succeeding generations, usually in their own parish, but sometimes in other arenas, such as colleges, or in civic life, or by companies and confraternities. To restrict the discussion for the time being to the parish, this had implications of profound importance both for individuals and for communal religion as most experienced it in the century or more before the Reformation. It is to a closer examination of this response, considering what prompted it and what forms it took, that I now turn.

I work from the premise that, at a fairly basic level, the motive which explains why men and women were profoundly affected by and continued to respond to the teachings of the Church in the late medieval period was the hope of salvation (and, one might add, fear of the alternative). It is, therefore, important to consider quite what the Church demanded as it sought to fulfil its duties to mankind as the mediator of Christ's teachings. In addition to the essentials of belief and attendance, the Church required that individuals should receive and participate in the sacraments: the rites of passage – baptism, confirmation, matrimony, extreme unction – on the one hand, and the central rites of Christian worship – Mass and Penance – on the other. If, as suggested earlier, the celebration of mass invariably formed the focal point of corporate Christian worship, the operation of penance was of utmost importance for individuals, addressing as it did the barrier of sin excluding Man from God's providence. In contradistinction to emphases introduced as a result of sixteenth-century change, penance before the Reformation demanded a more public and ostentatious response. The most important aspect of penance, dealing with the guilt consequent on sin, was confession, and every Christian of either sex had an obligation to confess at least once annually.[7] Properly shriven and penitent, the Christian might rest assured that he or she could not be damned. But among the most auspicious of the doctrinal developments emanating from the Schools, particularly Paris in the twelfth and early thirteenth centuries, was a feasible means of dealing with the penalties inexorably attached to sins. Although strictly subordinate, paying the penalty to purge the stain of sin was necessary to complete the process and gain admission to Heaven. The point was that, as a result of changes in emphasis implicit in the new dispensation, while one might certainly make a start by good works in this life, the process could be completed (and might, indeed, be wholly satisfied) in Purgatory. Provision to expedite the progress of the soul through Purgatory rendered the spiritual imperatives of the late Middle Ages distinctive, and, as indicated above, contemporaries' responses dovetailed neatly with the characteristics of liturgical practice. Purgatory emphasised the need for good works, both for their intrinsic merit and because those who benefited were obliged to intercede for benefactors; it extolled intercession, from saints certainly, but very definitely from those still living and the dead in Purgatory. And whereas the honest poor might rest assured that, because of intrinsic virtue, their main duty was to pray for benefactors, written, preached and visual admonition left the wealthy in no doubt that they were sorely in need of intercession, and that it was their duty and in

---

[7] T. N. Tentler, *Sin and Confession on the Eve of the Reformation* (Princeton, 1977) is invaluable on the application of the sacrament of penance and of developing obligations; attention is also drawn to the useful discussion in early chapters of W. D. Myers, *'Poor, Sinning Folk', Confession and Conscience in Counter-Reformation Germany* (Ithaca, 1996). For discussion of the doctrine of Purgatory and its implications, see Duffy, *Stripping of the Altars*, chap. 10, and my 'A Fond Thing Vainly Invented': an Essay on Purgatory and Pious Motive in Later Medieval England', in S. J. Wright (ed.), *Parish, Church and People. Local Studies in Lay Religion, 1350–1750* (London, 1988), pp. 56–84.

their interest to stimulate it.[8] One of the most striking attributes of the late medieval Church was, indeed, the success it had in prompting generosity: the wealthier classes gave fulsomely both for their own spiritual benefit and the practical benefit of others. Above all else, the wealthy – be they the aristocracy, gentry or, to be discussed here, the bourgeoisie – sought commemoration. Stimulating others to intercede for them, the wealthy spent a very great deal and made themselves hardly less of a presence in death than they had been in life.[9] The contrivances to which they resorted coloured many aspects of parish life and repay close examination.

In the following, examples will be drawn from one urban parish, All Saints' in Bristol, for two reasons. First, it is important to emphasise that the practices which contemporaries fostered and funded had a cumulative effect which may best be appreciated by dwelling on provisions in a single locality. The second reason for concentrating on All Saints', Bristol, is that it has an unusually detailed archive: other late medieval parishes may have more extensive accounts or more wills but few, if any, have so broad a range of surviving material – indeed, most English parishes have no surviving muniments for the later medieval period. All Saints' has a reasonable number of surviving wills, some twenty or thirty in all.[10] More unusually, the parish has an extensive run of pre-Reformation churchwardens' accounts and two reasonably detailed inventories of equipment. Quite extraordinarily it has, in a volume known as the Church Book, a list of parish ordinances and the names of parish benefactors – 'Good Doers by whom livelode, tenements and other goods have been given to the church of All Saints'. It itemises who had given what for their own and the parish's benefit, as well as a list of pairs of churchwardens mentioning what each had achieved for their own and the common benefit during their term of

---

[8] B. L. Manning, *The People's Faith in the Time of Wyclif* (2nd edn, Hassocks, 1975), chap. 10 is still useful; for a more recent overview, M. Rubin, *Charity and Community in Medieval Cambridge* (Cambridge, 1987), and, as a local study, P. H. Cullum and P. J. P. Goldberg, 'Charitable Provision in Late Medieval York: "to the Praise of God and the Use of the Poor"', *Northern History* 23 (1993), pp. 24–39.

[9] I explore this theme more fully in 'The Benefactions of Mortality'; for broader treatment of the theme, see S. Cohn, *The Cult of Remembrance and the Black Death: Six Renaissance Cities in Central Italy* (Baltimore, 1992).

[10] Given that the mid-sixteenth-century Chantry Certificate reveals that All Saints' had a population of just less than 200 houseling members, the number of wills surviving for the fifteenth and early sixteenth centuries only serves to remind us that, excellent as the All Saints' archive is, a very great deal has been lost.

office.[11] The parish has the muniments and accounts generated by the perpetual chantry founded by the Halleways in the parish church in the 1450s, and – almost unbelievably – a very considerable cache of property deeds and of miscellanea pertaining to the life of the parish in the century or more before the Reformation. Much has been lost, inevitably depressing our impressions; but we are, relatively, very well informed as to the priorities and behaviour of the men and women in this particular parish. This is ample reason to survey their activities to discover how the dead and those about to die contrived to be commemorated and thus benefit from intercession. It also proves possible to gain some impression of how the dead perpetuated their identities, weaving benefactions and requirements into the fabric of parish practice, juxtaposing their own presence with those who still lived within a small community. Such contrivance was, of course, placed within a regime already efficiently operating to commemorate precursors, saints and significant events. The formal liturgy combined with penitential imperatives to spawn a fuller roster of both saints and sinners, as the wealthier members of the parish in particular sought to engage surviving and succeeding parishioners in a structured response of collective memory and intercession. Their personal benefit thus went hand in hand with the profit of the parish and relief of the generality as bequests provided for services, building and equipment from which all gained. Beneficiaries in life were thus bound to remember benefactors in death, and the All Saints' archive reveals both strategies and results with clarity.

There are, however, two further preliminaries – one specifically pertaining to All Saints', the other of more general application – which deserve consideration. First, as commented earlier, the decoration of the church left the faithful in no doubt as to their fate, and it is of interest to note that parishioners often took it upon themselves to remind those who came after just what was in store. That All Saints' had a rood, for instance, is clear from Alice Chestre's commission and provision of an ornately carved new rood loft, replete with many carved images 'of which three are principal – a Trinity in the middle, a Christopher in the north, and a Michael in the south side'.[12] John Haddon, vintner of All Saints', had moreover 'let make the story of the doom in the cross aisle'; that is, a parishioner paid, if not for a painting of the Day of Judgement, then

---

[11] The All Saints' Church Book has been published in full, see *The Pre-Reformation Records of All Saints', Bristol. Part 1: The All Saints' Church Book*, ed. Clive Burgess (Bristol Record Society Publications, 46, 1995) (hereafter cited as *ASCB*].

[12] *Ibid.*, pp. 16–17.

some representation on this theme proving his own mindfulness and reminding others of the last things.[13] Further, William Wytteney 'let ordain and let make at his own cost a memorial that every man should remember his own death, that is to say the Dance of Pauls, the which cost £18. God have mercy on his soul.'[14] What this was is best explained by reference to John Stow's *Survey of London*: 'There was also one great cloister on the north side of this church [St Paul's Cathedral] invironing a plot of ground, of old time called the Pardon Churchyard . . . About this cloister was artificially and richly painted the Dance of *Machabray*, or dance of death, commonly called the Dance of Pauls.'[15] Wytteney's donation cannot be accurately dated but it was probably made in the mid-fifteenth century, and was a *danse macabre*, a painting of the Dance of Death. The All Saints' churchwardens' accounts reveal that this was put up and taken down again twice annually, at St James's tide in late July and at All Saints' at the beginning of November.[16] It must have been painted either on boards, or on canvas to form a banner. It was expensive and, presumably, large or long; it would have commanded attention, reminding the living of every degree 'to remember their own death'. Parishioners were themselves prepared to admonish others, commissioning depictions which heightened an awareness of death, judgement, Purgatory and, as a result, the requisite responses which all were obliged to make and on which all depended.

Second, as a result of synodal legislation in the thirteenth century, the laity had been assigned the duty of maintaining the fabric of their parish churches, save that of the chancel for which the incumbent was liable; from a slightly later date, congregations had been made responsible for

---

[13] *Ibid.*, p. 13   [14] *Ibid.*, p. 14.

[15] J. Stow, *A Survey of London*, ed. C. L. Kingsford (2 vols., Oxford, 1908), I, p. 327. John or Jenkyn Carpenter, town clerk of London, is said to have paid for the painting in the north cloister of St Paul's 'with great expenses'; Stow also tells us (I, p. 109) that it was 'painted upon a board . . . a monument of death, leading all estates with speeches of death, and answer of every estate'. The verses were translated from French into English by Lydgate.

[16] The feast of St James was a time of heightened significance in Bristol, the main English port for pilgrims travelling to the shrine at Compostella; moreover, given that the feast was in high summer, the details of the painting may have been at their most clearly visible at this time. At an altogether darker time of the year, All Saints' Day was the parish's patronal feast and was immediately followed by All Souls', a feast of particular relevance for considerations of mortality. It is perhaps worth noting that both seasons were in the so-called 'secular half' of the year, confirming once again that much of spiritual and liturgical significance might occur between Corpus Christi and Advent. The identification of a 'ritualistic' and a 'secular' half of the liturgical year is made by C. Phythian-Adams, 'Ceremony and the Citizen', in P. Clark (ed.), *The Early Modern Town* (London, 1976), pp. 106–28.

maintaining the vessels and vestments necessary for the seemly conduct of rites and worship.[17] So, at roughly the same time as the penitential system was rejigged, practical obligations were imposed on the laity to provide for buildings and equipment, that is for the basic wherewithal for parish worship. In practice the two often combined: to fulfil or start to satisfy their penitential obligations, parishioners might repair or embellish church fabric, or donate vessels and vestments, and, parish pride apart, this was done because donors wished to be remembered and prayed for by contemporaries and successors. The more that any individual gave, the less the parish as a whole would have to contribute, so donors were justified to expect some return of gratitude. But benefactors also contrived to ensure that, were they forgotten, then their benefactions should be forfeit. So they had to be remembered officially by the parish, and provision made to ensure that they were formally prayed for. The management of endowments, fabric and equipment, and the preservation of benefactors' memories, all became vital duties. The office of church-warden evolved whereby prominent individuals undertook to discharge these responsibilities on behalf of the wider parish community.[18] Parish management was a good work, profiting the soul and deserving com-memoration – a theme to be examined in more detail below.

When investigating the response elicited by the prevailing penitential regime in a community like All Saints', a start may be made by examining the formal provision on which parishioners might rely. Early in the fifteenth century, in 1405, Robert Crosman, in addition to making various benefactions to All Saints', promised the vicar 3s 4d if he should put Crosman's name, his wife's name, and the names of their respective parents on the *tabula memoria*, and rehearse them every Sunday.[19] At the end of the century such practice was still current. In 1492, Thomas Baker gave the vicar, John Thomas, 20s so that 'every Sunday he shall specially exhort parishioners to pray for my soul'.[20] In the same year, Clement Wilteshire, Mayor of Bristol who died while in office, bequeathed John Thomas a robe of scarlet 'to pray for my soul and my first wife's soul, and

---

[17] *Councils and Synods*, ed. F. M. Powicke and C. R. Cheney (2 vols., Oxford, 1964), I, pp. 128, 367; II, pp. 1002ff., 1122–3, 1385–8; see also C. Drew, *Early Parochial Organisation in England: the Origin and Office of the Churchwarden* (York, 1954), pp. 8–9 and notes.

[18] For the origins of the office of churchwarden, see Drew, *Early Parochial Organisation*, *passim*; and a more recent study, B. Kümin, *The Shaping of a Community: the Rise and Reformation of the English Parish, c. 1400–1560* (Aldershot, 1996), chap. 2.

[19] The Great Orphan Book (in Bristol Record Office), fols. 96v–7.

[20] Great Orphan Book, fols. 245v–7; also Prerogative Court of Canterbury Registers (here-after PCC), 23 Dogget fols. 181–2v.

for the souls of parents, brothers, sisters, kin and friends on every Sunday among the other dead of the parish of All Saints' according to the usage there'.[21] Clearly a bede-roll, a list of benefactors, which the celebrant read out at high mass, was long established in All Saints', and if not explicitly commissioned all that frequently, might evidently comprise part of the spiritual armoury of the very rich no less than those of more moderate means.[22]

There was also an annual commemoration of benefactors in All Saints', known as the General Mind, which took the form of a corporate anniversary paid for from parish funds.[23] The celebration which, apart from anything else, was an important social event in the parish calendar, was held on the Thursday and Friday after Ash Wednesday – different parishes had different days, but in All Saints', notably, it coincided with a high-water mark of the penitential season.[24] Moreover, in All Saints' the General Mind was preceded by a more than usually detailed recitation of Good Doers and their good deeds on the Sunday before Ash Wednesday, a recital presumably based on the benefaction lists in the All Saints' Church Book.[25] A statement concerning the practice on this particular Sunday heads this material and offers a particularly revealing appraisal as to the effects of benefaction and memory in death as the two combined to operate in a fifteenth-century parish. It bears quotation at length.[26] The preamble reads thus: 'The names of good doers and wellwillers by whom livelode, tenements and other goods have been given unto the church of All Saints' in Bristol, unto the honour and worship of Almighty God and [the] increasing of divine service, to be showed and declared unto the parishioners on the Sunday before Ash Wednesday and at high Mass and yearly to be continued.' Practice is then expounded:

---

21 Great Orphan Book, fols. 244v–5v.
22 See also Duffy, *Stripping of the Altars*, pp. 327–37; the bede-roll, ironically, was so common a means of commemorating the dead that many testators may not have explicitly commissioned inclusion of their name, relying instead on their executors' discretion.
23 Payments for the General Mind comprise a prominent part, year after year, of the All Saints' churchwardens' accounts. The costs of the Mind gradually increased even despite a parish ordinance that, should its expense exceed 13s 4d, the senior warden should have to pay the difference from his own pocket, *ASCB*, p. 3.
24 In St John's, Bristol, the General Mind was on the Tuesday and Wednesday of Whitsun week; in St Nicholas's, the vigil and feast of St Martin; in St Stephen's, the eighth and ninth days after Easter.
25 The benefaction lists are to be found in *ASCB*, pp. 4–30; effectively there are three or four versions of the same list, each succeeding list compressing old material and adding new items.
26 The following quotations together comprise the statement concerning practice on the Sunday before the General Mind; it is to be found in *ASCB*, p. 4.

Where it has been of a laudable custom of long continuance used, that on this day the names of good doers and wellwillers by whom livelode – tenements, buildings, jewels, books, chalices, vestments and with divers other ornaments and goods, as follows – has been given unto the church unto the honour and worship of almighty God and increasing of divine service, to be rehearsed and shown yearly unto you by name, both man and woman, and what benefits they did for themselves and for their friends and for others by their lifetimes, and what they left for them to be done after their days.

The purpose is plain: 'That they shall not be forgotten but had in remembrance and be prayed for of all the parish and all of them that be to come, and also [that they should be] for an example to you that be now living that you may likewise do for yourself and for your friends while they be in this world.' And this was done so that the living remembered their benefactors: 'That after the transitory life you may be had in the number of good doers rehearsed by name and in the special prayers of Christian people in time coming'; and with, finally, a more transcendent purpose, 'that by the infinite mercy of almighty God, by the intercession of Our Blessed Lady and of all the blessed saints of heaven, in whose honour and worship this church is dedicated, you may come to the everlasting bliss and joy that our blessed Lord has redeemed you unto'. Explanation and exhortation are thus woven together to extol the benefits accruing from commemoration and intercession: it was to expedite salvation, and individuals and the community had their respective parts to play.

It is clear, on the one hand, that the authorities in All Saints', be they clerical, lay, or both together, promoted 'good doing' as an activity of the utmost importance, and on the other, that parishioners responded, either because of a sense of sin, or of need, or simply for fear of missing out. Richard Ake, for instance, gave an antiphoner worth £10 for the use of subsequent vicars 'in order to be prayed for among the benefactors of the parish'.[27] Thomas Abyndon, innkeeper, at his decease in the late fifteenth century gave the church 40s so that he should be remembered 'as a good doer'.[28] John Jenkyns, alias Steynour, another innkeeper, and his wife, Agnes, 'longing to be prayed for', gave a standing nut, that is a cup.[29] His instructions are unusual: Jenkyns prevailed upon the current vicar, John

---

[27] *ASCB*, pp. 13, 27. The date when Ake made the donation is uncertain, but it may very well have been before the beginning of the fifteenth century; it is instructive that his gift was being commemorated over a century later.

[28] *ASCB*, pp. 21–2.

[29] *Ibid.*, pp. 22, 30.

Thomas, 'that he should so order in this book, the register of good doers, that this nut should never be alienated or sold, but should remain in the treasure coffer, to the behoof [advantage] and pleasure of the parishioners in the day of the General Mind of good doers'. The cup, significantly, was to be reserved for use on the day of the General Mind to prompt specific, efficacious prayer.

Possibly the most illuminating single example of generous benefaction to guarantee commemoration in death, and one which I have mentioned in passing above and described more fully elsewhere, concerns the activity of a widow, Alice Chestre, who died in 1485, who sought both her own benefit and that of her spouse, Henry, who had predeceased her in 1470.[30] Neither of their wills suggests conspicuous wealth or noteworthy piety; the benefaction list, however, reveals just how generous Alice was, presumably with her dead husband's estate, in the years succeeding his death but preceding her own. One can only guess how many others, now all too easily dismissed because their wills are unremarkable, were in fact similarly generous. The All Saints' Church Book records her benefactions at length; here I mention only those entries accompanied by description of motive. It is recorded that Alice, 'to the worship of almighty God and his church and to have both their souls [i.e. her own soul and Henry's] prayed for specially among all good doers, has at her own cost had carved a new front to the altar in the south aisle of the church, called the rood altar, with five principal images, St Anne, St Mary Magdalen, St Giles, St Erasmus and St Anthony'.[31] In addition to stimulating parishioners' special prayers, it would also appear to have been Alice's intention to invoke the intercession of powerful mediators.[32] In addition she commissioned a hearse cloth:

> Also the said Alice, considering that there was no hearse cloth in the church of any reputation in value, saving only a hearse cloth that Thomas Halleway ordained for his own anniversary, for the love and honour she had unto almighty God and to all Christian souls, and for the ease and succour of all this parish unto whom she owed her good will and love in her day as it

---

[30] I refer to the Chestres in more detail in my '"By Quick and by Dead": Wills and Pious Provision in Late Medieval Bristol', *English Historical Review* 102 (1987), pp. 841ff; Henry Chestre's will is PCC, 1 Wattys fol. 4v; Alice Chestre's is PCC, 14 Logge, fols. 103v–4.

[31] *ASCB*, p. 16.

[32] The choice of Sts Anne and Mary Magdalene needs no comment; the others, Sts Giles, Erasmus and Anthony, were all included in the collective cult (particularly popular in the Rhineland) known as the Fourteen Holy Helpers, see D. H. Farmer, *The Oxford Dictionary of Saints* (Oxford, 1978).

appears in this church as it is afore expressed and rehearsed, she has given an hearse cloth of black worstead with letters of gold of H & C and A & C and a scripture in gold *Orate pro animabus Henricus Chestre et Alicie uxoris eius.*[33]

The exhortation is blatant, her motive plain. But she is said to have done this, in part at least, 'for the ease and succour of all this parish unto who she owed her good will and love in her day'. Cynicism is easy, but she probably was devoted to the parish; her provision, while to her and her late husband's specific benefit, was no doubt also prompted by genuine good will. The motives and emotions which found expression in such generosity were complex, and one might easily reinforce and temper the other.

The All Saints' Church Book refers to Alice's death as follows: 'On the day of O Sapientia, that is to say the 16th day of December in the year of Our Lord God 1485,[34] the soul of this blessed woman departed out of this world, on the which soul almighty God of His infinite grace take mercy, and reward her for her good deeds.'[35] It adds: 'We that are now and that are to come are bound to pray for her.' The response, if obligatory, may also have been heartfelt: Alice had done a very great deal for the parish. Any who were similarly wealthy might consider Alice's activities and the fulsome reaction she elicited from surviving parishioners, and conclude that 'altruism' might, in fact, be money well spent. The benefaction lists served *pour encourager les autres.*

Having touched, briefly, on the response orchestrated through the parish, it is worth considering individual initiatives. These, too, might well be expressed through institutional arrangements, the most common being chantries and anniversaries. The chantry was an arrangement providing for the daily celebration of masses, either in perpetuity, in which case a property endowment invariably provided the necessary income, or for a number of years, in which case the service was usually 'found' by a legatee of the individual who was to benefit from the celebration. Chantries, which undoubtedly commemorated the dead, were good works, and their founders 'good doers'. Apart from anything else, each funded a priest who, after he had celebrated mass for the founder, was to help out in the parish, with a specific obligation to assist in and bolster the celebration of the liturgy, at no cost at all to the parish. So in All Saints', for instance, John and Katherine Leynell 'ordained at

---

[33] *ASCB*, p. 17.

[34] It is worth making the point, to illustrate the way in which liturgical observance had permeated the common conception of time, that it was common form to date by reference to church feasts and saints' days.

[35] *ASCB*, p. 17

their own proper cost to find a priest to sing in this church for ten years to the worship of almighty God and the augmenting of divine service, every year 9 marks, £59 6s 8d [*sic*]'.[36] The parish, significantly, costed the service from which it benefited but which was, in point of fact, found from the Laynells' estate: the sum was treated as a gift.

The anniversary, as suggested earlier, was a re-enactment of the funeral liturgy, with exequies on the eve and a requiem on the morrow, complete with bell-ringing and the distribution of doles to the poor, intended to stimulate intercession.[37] Integral to these proceedings was the presence of the parish hearse, draped with a pall and set at either end with lighted tapers, as if the body of the deceased was once again present. Anniversaries were, as the name implies, usually performed annually, although deceased parishioners might have two or three celebrated on prescribed dates during the year. It should be noted, though, that by the later fifteenth century perpetual anniversaries were almost always part of a benefaction: the annual service was, quite simply, the visible aspect of generous property devise. In All Saints', where sufficient documentation survives to reveal what precisely was going on, parishioners such as the Chestres, the Bakers and the Fylours devised property to produce a steady income, and a proportion of this sufficed for the anniversary. Agnes Fylour, for instance, made provision for an anniversary for her husband and herself at the cost of 10s annually.[38] This was found from the revenues from a tenement in the High Street which she devised to All Saints', the rents from which yielded an overall annual income of £3 6s 8d. The parish was obliged to maintain the property but it is nevertheless plain that it, or, more strictly, succeeding generations of Agnes's co-parishioners, were the real beneficiaries. Obliged to remember Agnes and her husband, the parish provided a fitting commemoration by celebrating the anniversary with full ceremony.[39] Although, by the later fifteenth century, property devise to the parish commonly had some such reciprocal obligation attached, earlier arrangements were not quite so ambitious. In 1261, for instance, Alice Hailes devised the Green Lattice to the

---

[36] *Ibid.*

[37] For more detailed discussion of the anniversary, see my 'A Service for the Dead. The Form and Function of the Anniversary in Late Medieval Bristol', *The Transactions of the Bristol and Gloucestershire Archaeological Society* 105 (1987), pp. 183–211.

[38] Agnes Fylour's will is in The Great Orphan Book, fols. 186–6v; her anniversary is also mentioned in *ASCB*, pp. 7, 25, where it is said to have cost 12s per annum, but the extra 2s was a payment to the churchwardens.

[39] The All Saints' churchwardens' accounts reveal that the anniversary was indeed faithfully kept, coming under the direct responsibility of the parish apparently in 1485–6.

church. This was an inn on the High Street which, by the fifteenth century, yielded some £5 annually, invariably the churchwardens' single most important source of rental income.[40] It would be misleading to claim that she was lionised by the parish in the fifteenth century and, although she had specified that a light be kept and a mass of the Blessed Virgin be celebrated for her, it is impossible to tell from surviving accounts whether these were observed. Nevertheless she made the devise 'for my soul and the soul of William Hailes, my man, and for the souls of all our ancestors and successors, in order that our souls shall specially be held in memory of the church' and, in fairness to the parish, the benefaction lists in the All Saints' Church Book assign her gift priority, commemorating her generosity and commending her soul.[41] Called a 'special benefactrix', her memory was very much alive in the parish well over 200 years after her death.

In addition to institutional services and endowments, it is important to note that individuals made further benefactions. They frequently bequeathed sums of money, as mentioned earlier with the example, for instance, of Thomas Abyndon. Others gave vestments, vessels and books, shown not only by Alice Chestre but also by another wealthy widow from All Saints' in the late fifteenth century. Not only did Maud Baker give a sumptuous suit of white damask vestments embroidered with flowers of gold and shells of silver enamelled with the Grocers' arms, said in all to be worth £27, she also gave a suit of blue damask vestments 'with five wounds in the cross', and a vestment of cloth of gold. In addition she gave a chalice 'well gilded', worth £6 13s, cruets of silver, a 'goodly censer' of silver, and two latten candlesticks to stand on St Thomas's altar. She also gave a mass book 'in prent work'.[42] Many also added to the fittings in the church but, confining ourselves for the time being to the bequests made by Alice Chestre and Maud Baker, it is worth pointing out that in addition to commissioning an elaborate rood loft, Alice commissioned a new front to the rood altar, paid for a tabernacle to go over the image of Jesus and, as well as gilding Our Lady's altar, she also set up a tabernacle around this altar. Maud Baker contributed towards gilding the rood loft; she provided hangings for the high altar 'of satin of Bruges with flowers and a crucifix of gold there set out on the same', with two frontals of black velvet with crowned 'M's and 'Jhc's; she gave a 'Table of the Transfiguration of Our Lord Jesus Christ to move and excite people unto

---

[40] As perusal of the churchwardens' accounts easily verifies.
[41] *ASCB*, pp. 5, 25.
[42] Maud Baker's benefactions are listed in *ASCB*, pp. 20–1, Chestre's on pp. 15–16.

devotion'; she paid for painting two stories on two pillars in the lower part of the church 'one story over the font of the baptising of Our Lord Jesus Christ' and on the other pillar 'a figure otherwise an image of St Christopher'. These widows were wealthy and notably generous, but many another parishioner made donations, or equipped or strove to embellish the church in order that their deeds should outlast them and to guarantee commemoration, as a glance at the All Saints' Church Book confirms. It is worth reiterating, too, that without the benefaction list in the Church Book – whose existence proves that each achieved his or her ambition – we would all too often know nothing of their actions; their wills, if they survive, are frequently silent on the matter.[43] So, to an unquantifiable but appreciable degree, All Saints' derived its fittings, decoration and equipment from its parishioners either near or at their death and to perpetuate their memories. It becomes easier to imagine how All Saints', as with virtually any late medieval parish church, did indeed come to resemble a highly ornate and articulated *aide-mémoire* celebrating the Passion of Christ and the redemption of mankind, and facilitated the elaborate celebration of the liturgy and portrayed stories of Christ, the Holy Family and many of the saints. Much of the wherewithal for this was provided by the commemorative benefaction of parishioners, in just the same way as many of the clergy were funded and a good proportion of the parish income was provided, effectively, as a result of benefaction. The dead 'increased Divine Service'; the living were to manage and maintain and, of course, to pray and intercede.

Before reaching any conclusions, one or two points deserve fuller exploration. It is, for instance, important to stress that the clergy were deeply involved in the practices described, not just as teachers and facilitators, but also as practitioners. Indeed, the All Saints' Church Book has sections devoted solely to clerical benefactors, and it is plain that during the mid- and later-fifteenth century, the period for which the Book is at its most informative, every incumbent gave, some very generously, as did many another priest associated in one way or another with the parish.[44] Maurice Hardwick, incumbent from 1455 until 1471, may be singled out as the most lavish. The following represents only some of his benefactions: he gave silver to be made into clasps for the parish's best suit of vestments; he helped the parish purchase an organ; he helped to repair the church roof; he commissioned a wooden statue of

---

[43] The implication clearly being that testators had either made provision in life or left it to their executors' discretion.

[44] *ASCB*, pp. 7–12, 25–7.

St Ursula 'to excite people to devotion'; he gave altar cloths, one decorated with a crucifix, one with the Coronation of Our Lady, and another pair said to be of St Ursula; he gave a pair of red vestments; he gilded the image of All Hallows' in gold and gilded the crucifix with the sun; he also 'let set out the tabernacle at the high altar at principal feasts unto the more laud and worship of almighty God'.[45] He seems to have had a particular concern to enrich the parish liturgy. The same intention may be detected in provisions he made in April 1471, at or near to the time of his death. He gave a cloth of red velvet embroidered with flowers of gold, each of which had the text *Hymnus omnibus sanctis* in the foot, and with two letters of gold, M and H, his initials, embroidered prominently on the cloth; he specified that the cloth should hang behind the head of the image of All Hallows' at every principal feast. He gave a frontal of cloth of gold to hang over All Hallows' head at every principal feast; he gave four stained cloths of red and yellow with wreaths and the arms of the Passion in the middle, with the scripture *Dulcis est illo amor meus*, the which cloths were to be hung around the choir at principal feasts; he also gave the vellum necessary to add three quires to the antiphonal used by the vicar, and paid for the necessary chapters, collects and benisons for the year to be added, 'where there was never chapter, collect or benisons before'. In addition to embellishing the parish's liturgy, he also sought commemoration as an integral part of this liturgy: to this end, in a device indistinguishable from Alice Chestre's, he had his initials embroidered on an eye-catching cloth on show at principal feasts.

Clergy and lay are hardly to be distinguished in such matters; but in others, clergy, acting in a manner difficult for the laity to emulate, induced others to generosity and were celebrated for their actions. Hardwick, for instance, 'procured, moved and stirred Agnes Fylour to give the said house in which she dwelt in the High Street on the south side of the Green Lattice', providing the parish with an income and Agnes and her late husband with an anniversary. When Agnes's son, who lived in London, incidentally, attempted to thwart his mother's wishes, Hardwick and the churchwardens resisted him. Finally, it was Maurice Hardwick who, in addition to providing a chest in which to keep the parish muniments, 'where before they lay abroad likely to be embezzled and mischiefed', instigated the procedures to safeguard, preserve and formalise parish memory, initiating the benefaction list itself. 'He laboured to compile and make this book for to be a memorial and a remembrance for ever for the curates and the churchwardens that shall be for the time, that

---

[45] *Ibid.*, pp. 9–11.

every man to put yearly his account for one evidence of the livelode, and for to put in the names of the good doers and the names of the wardens of the church and what good they did in their days that they must yearly be prayed for.' Hardwick was far from being the only clergyman to enrich the liturgy,[46] but it is to be noted that, more unusually, Hardwick strove to preserve and improve what might be termed the practical and spiritual memory of the parish; apart from anything else, he benefited by weaving memorials to himself into the parish liturgy, but, by moving to provide and compile the Church Book, helped others to do likewise and achieve their aims more effectively.

Hardwick's stated reasons for compiling the All Saints' Church Book force us to consider quite what the churchwardens were doing and why they were persuaded to do it. The Book was 'to be a memorial and remembrance for ever for curates and churchwardens' so that the actions and achievements of each might be recorded 'that they must yearly be prayed for'. Churchwardens, it may be recalled, were the laymen who managed the congregation's responsibilities, maintaining the fabric of the parish church and the equipment for seemly worship. They generally served in pairs for a year or two at a time and, we are told in the surviving All Saints' Ordinances, were 'chosen by the most voice of the parish'.[47] In practice churchwardens played a vital role managing many aspects of parish life, sustaining and even increasing its effectiveness as a sacramental and intercessory battery for the benefit of all parishioners. Their role was essential, not least in that it was a prerequisite, if the wealthy were to be induced to generosity, that those who were preparing for death should feel confident that whatever they bequeathed or devised would be kept safely and used as intended. While much was done in consultation with the incumbent, the role of the churchwardens was both onerous and of critical importance. Considering what was involved, it is only right that the faithful discharge of the task should have been considered a good work and, as such, worthy of commemoration, so much so that much of the All Saints' Church Book is in fact a celebration of churchwardens' achievements. Not only does the volume contain a list of summaries describing what each pair who served in the early and mid-fifteenth century had achieved, providing a 'memorial and remembrance' thereby, but the accounts contained in the Book (which were a very much tidied version of whatever might originally have been submitted for audit) were

---

[46] William Warens, one of the Halleways' chantry priests, was perhaps the most notable, giving books of pricksong and a breviary to the parish, *ibid.*, p. 11.

[47] *Ibid.*, p. 3. Quite what proportion of the parish was permitted a 'voice' is debatable.

probably intended to be a detailed testimony reminding posterity of quite how much each pair of wardens had done.[48] This was to stimulate commemoration, certainly; it was, in all probability, also intended to urge others to volunteer for the task to ensure that they, too, would be remembered as benefactors whose contribution was no less important than those able to give vessels, vestments and fittings.[49] It must be emphasised, then, that the urge for commemoration and desire for inter-cession served not only to enrich the parish but also to procure faithful management, safeguarding benefaction and ensuring, presumably with the help of the clergy, who were themselves deeply involved in the indissoluble nexus of altruism and self-interest, that the liturgy was fully and properly celebrated. Once in operation, the system was clearly self-generating and self-serving: the prerequisites which might prompt generosity were themselves furthered by the promise of effective com-memoration. The durability over long periods of the practices outlined, with celebrations being maintained, endowments kept and bequests preserved, surely suggests that the system *was* both effectively regulated and efficiently discharged. Late medieval parishioners, to judge from unswerving practice, might confidently depend upon their wardens for competence and on the clergy and parish as a whole for effective and seemly commemoration.

As we approach some conclusions it is, first, to be borne in mind that, even for a parish like All Saints', Bristol, where the survival rate of material has been unusually good, a great deal has been lost, and our impressions of late medieval practice are inevitably impoverished. Even if the glass is dark, we may still conclude that in the face of death and as preparation for the eschatological processes as taught and conceived before the Reformation, parishioners behaved in a way which, if remark-able, was nevertheless congruent with and determined by other practices prominent in parish life. Existing in, and having doubtless been shaped by, a potent and highly structured devotional environment, which pervaded both the sacred and the secular, which commemorated death as a means of procuring life, and which celebrated the lives and deaths of many larger-than-life precursors, men and women were persuaded to act in ways which emulated the liturgy and improved it. They may have been the 'less special dead', but they still contrived to be remembered. They

---

[48] An argument developed at more length in the introduction to *ASCB*, pp. xxxviii–xli.

[49] Regardless of the wealth of an individual, generosity in terms of immovable or movable property may have been difficult were there heirs who had claim to the estate; labour as churchwarden was, to that extent, a more flexible but equally vital 'currency' which deserved commemoration no less than the donation of goods.

provided extra revenues and equipment. They paid for ever more elaborate fittings in the church, glorifying the mysteries of faith and celebrating
'the very special dead' in ever more fulsome ways. They supported super-
numerary clergy who further added to the liturgy, acting when necessary
as teachers and extra ministers in the parish, providing more sumptuous
celebration by serving as extra celebrants, deacons and subdeacons, and
also facilitating sophisticated musical and choral performance when
appropriate. The laity wove themselves into the liturgy. Their images,
too, might appear in the church, in glass, in brasses, and as effigies and
etchings on tombs. Their names, or initials, were emblazoned in hangings, embroidered on cloths, embossed or engraved on vessels, paving
slabs or stones, or carved in wood. As the saints had special days and
celebrations, so too might the parish dead. In addition to their funerals,
they had anniversaries, and had their names inscribed in books or on
'tables' and ensured that these were regularly read out. Corporately, in
addition to All Souls' Day, they had the General Mind. Cumulatively, it
may (or may not) have been a faint imitation but, reflecting the parish
liturgy, the dead contrived to perpetuate their presence and demanded
and elicited a response as they further glorified God and His saints. In
sum, the giving that this involved, and the services and ceremonies that
were implicit, changed parish regimes very profoundly, and particularly
stimulated the efforts of the living, be they clergy, churchwardens or
simply the parishioners obliged to pray.[50] But it is to be emphasised that
benefactors who sought commemoration were not somehow swimming
against the stream and acting in an eccentric fashion; their activity added
to the stream as they sought immersion in it. In regimes which were in
any case repositories of sacred memory, it made perfect sense that
individuals should seek to capitalise on this by dovetailing themselves
into the repertory. Telescoping time and obfuscating the division between
life and death, those who deserved memory as exempla and those who
sought commemoration as suppliants made an indelible mark both on
contemporaries' attitudes to life and death, and on parish regimes as
centres of instruction and of intercession which might offer a semblance
of influence over events and eventualities. In sweeping away the saints,
the Reformers had also to sweep away the more humble dead, subverting
– whether successfully or not – the human urge to be remembered: parish

---

[50] An argument developed at more length in my 'Shaping the Parish: St Mary at Hill,
London, in the Fifteenth Century, in J. Blair and B. Golding (eds.), *The Cloister and the
World: Essays in Medieval History in Honour of Barbara Harvey* (Oxford, 1996),
pp. 246–86.

regimes were emasculated as a result. Death lost its positive role: it was no longer a key to be turned, or a drama to be played and replayed in the midst of a growing array of props and paraphernalia.

4 Spirits seeking bodies: death, possession and communal memory in the Middle Ages

Nancy Caciola

What of those shades of the dead who lacked a proper place? In the following pages I discuss the displaced dead who wandered, restlessly, through the imaginations of late medieval urban communities. Their memories – and, according to the texts I shall discuss, their ghosts – lingered on amidst the community of the living; searching out, and sometimes finding, a physical place in which to lodge. These spirits seeking bodies haunted the late medieval landscape, and the rather spectral traces they left in medieval texts – hagiographies, miracle compilations, exorcists' manuals – provide the primary evidence for my investigation.

To place the dead permanently, in the period from the fourteenth through to the sixteenth centuries, was a complex process. Once the spirit left the body it was displaced from its accustomed habitation, and the location of its continued existence was a topic of some dispute. Theologians held that the spirits of the dead were placed immediately according to their merits, entering into one realm of a tripartite afterlife, but this was not a consensus viewpoint. The bourgeois inhabitants of some towns entertained alternative possibilities about the status of dead spirits. Many believed that certain shades of the dead might remain displaced for some time, particularly the ghosts of those who had died a 'bad death' that was sudden or violent.[1] Such spirits might wander the

---

[1] On 'good' and 'bad' deaths, see Maurice Bloch and Jonathan Parry (eds.), *Death and the Regeneration of Life* (Cambridge, 1982). I discuss this theme in a slightly different context in 'Wraiths, Revenants and Ritual in Medieval Culture', *Past and Present* 152 (1996), pp. 3–45. On ghosts in the Middle Ages, see Jean-Claude Schmitt, *Les revenants: les vivants et les morts dans la société médiévale* (Paris, 1994), now available in English translation by Teresa Fagan, *Ghosts in the Middle Ages: the Living and the Dead in Medieval Society* (Chicago and London, 1998); Claude Lecouteux, *Fantômes et revenants au moyen*

earth as maleficent spirits seeking bodies. In short, the dead might mourn their own death, their desolate existence in exile from the sensory experiences of embodiment. Hence they might seek another human body, a new place in which to dwell, through the spiritual possession of the living.

In this chapter I seek to mine the layers of cultural interpretation that are sedimented in tales about spirit possession, drawing from sources of the fifteenth and sixteenth centuries, with a geographic range stretching from Berne to Rome. I shall focus upon two distinct interpretations of these events, interrogating in particular the nature of possessing spirits. Official Church doctrine held that possessing spirits were demons or fallen angels, ancient forces of evil seeking the downfall of the human race. The dead, by contrast, had passed beyond the realm of the living, and were placed in a new afterlife of torment, purgation or blessedness; they did not seek new bodies. However, within local communities in the area I have identified, possession was thought to be the work of disembodied human ghosts seeking to regain a human body. I shall designate these different interpretations as 'demonic possession' and 'ghostly possession' respectively.

Thus, on one level, this is a paper about differing attitudes towards the dead, towards spirits and towards the human body. At a somewhat grander level, I shall also argue that these two differing interpretations of possessing spirits correspond to two fundamentally different attitudes towards the supernatural and natural worlds. On the one hand, theologians had for centuries elaborated a cosmic, transcendent, and moralistic view of the supernatural, a view dominated by powers and principalities conceived as fundamentally Other to the human realm. More characteristic of local communities, on the other hand, was an intimate, immanent and amoral view of the supernatural, one in which the building blocks of the supernatural were apt to be conceived as elements of the natural world conjoined in an unexpected or marvellous manner. I shall argue, further, that within this more intimate world view, the dead occupied a central place. The supernatural order imagined by the local communities I will discuss was dominated by dead saints and wandering ghosts, rather than by demons and angels. Thus this is also a chapter about competing religious and social epistemologies.

âge (Paris, 1986); Ronald Finucane, *Appearances of the Dead: a Cultural History of Ghosts* (New York, 1984); Nikolaus Kyll, *Tod, Grab, Begräbnisplatz, Totenfeier* (Bonn, 1972); Jean Gobi, *Dialogue avec un fantôme*, French tr. by Marie-Anne Polo de Beaulieu (Paris, 1994).

Even as these two systems of thought competed with one another, however, they overlapped. Historians of 'popular culture' must be mindful of the essential artifice of this category: the popular only exists in so far as it becomes the object of an historical analysis. The terms 'popular' and 'elite' are modern constructions that are not native to the medieval data: indeed, the dichotomy erects false boundaries between cultural idioms that intermingle freely in the sources and artefacts of the past.[2] Yet in sounding this cautionary note, I do not mean to suggest that the duality of popular and elite cultures lacks all utility, merely to note that the spectrum of culture is more complex and shaded than the dichotomy of popular and elite allows. Individuals and communities often adhered simultaneously to beliefs that we find logically inconsistent with one another. Such multiplicity is an expression of the complexity both of medieval cultures and of the intellectual and physical communities that produced them.

The evidence I shall discuss exemplifies this complex interweaving of different cultures. I begin with a close reading of a paragraph from Johannes Nider's *Formicarius*, describing the formation of a local possession cult in the city of Berne that centred on the returning spirits of the local dead. The minute observation of this constellation of beliefs within a circumscribed time and place permits an analytic precision that is necessary to the project of placing the unruly dead. This initial microstudy, in turn, will provide a sort of template that may then be compared with, and tested against, references to spirits seeking bodies from other sources. Thus from Berne, I move to a series of ghostly possession episodes across the Alps in fifteenth- and sixteenth-century Italy. Here, a close reading illuminates both divergences from and similarities with the Bernese example. In the end, these fragments of information, while often cryptic on their own, can be layered together to produce a provisional description of local popular beliefs about dead spirits and their relationships with the living. The effect is similar to a mosaic or pointillist painting, which allows the viewer a clear image or impression when viewed in its entirety, even though each smudge or tile is opaque when viewed alone.

---

[2] See Karen Louise Jolly, *Popular Religion in Late Saxon England* (Chapel Hill, 1996); Jean-Claude Schmitt, *Religione Folklore e Società nell'Occidente Medievale* (Bari, 1988), pp. 1–27; Caciola, 'Wraiths, Revenants and Ritual', pp. 3–6, especially n. 6 for further citations.

Spirits seeking bodies: the genesis of a spiritist cult

What follows is a description of how one could gain a reputation as a medium for spirits of the dead in early fifteenth-century Berne:

> There was a fraticello in the city of Berne . . . who got up at night in his house, and using stones and wood, he pretended that some spirit was present. Thus, to the admiration of many each night in that place he asserted (and many believed him) that either some divine revelation must be forthcoming, or a ghost [*anima*] was abroad, or an evil spirit. Not infrequently, he changed his voice and, in wailing accents like the ghost of some dead man who had been well known in the city, he gave responses to those who asked him questions, saying that he was the ghost of a certain recently deceased person, both those known to him and strangers, whose name he would give. He persuaded them that he would perform a pilgrimage to particular saints' shrines on [the souls'] behalf . . . and while journeying to these saints' shrines for the above mentioned souls, he acquired . . . not a little money.[3]

Johannes Nider incorporated this tale into his *Formicarius* without further explanation, doubtless assuming that his readers would perceive why the man was a fraud. Indeed, from Nider's particular cultural perspective – that of a learned Dominican Inquisitor writing between 1435 and 1437 – there were excellent reasons to dismiss the fraticello's assertion. The latter's claim that he could be voluntarily possessed by spirits of the dead contravened basic dogmas of medieval theology. According to Church[4] doctrine, the possessing spirits that sometimes invaded human bodies were fallen angels, rebellious creatures who had been transmuted into demons through a primordial sin of pride. The human dead, though possibly condemned to share an infernal abode with demons, emphatically did *not* share an essential nature with demons. Ontologically speaking, demons and the dead had absolutely nothing to do with one another. I cannot examine this entire tradition of thought here, but a brief examination of these ideas at their origin may prove instructive. In *The City of God*, Augustine – the first and most important Catholic theologian to forge a mutually exclusive demonology and necrology – addressed the issue directly:

> Apuleius says that the souls of men are demons and that, on ceasing to be men, they become *lares*, if they have deserved this reward for their good

³ Johannes Nider, *Formicarius sive Myrmecia Bonorum* (Duaci, 1602), pp. 181–2.
⁴ See Gary Macy, 'Was there a "the Church" in the Middle Ages?', in R. Swanson (ed.), *Unity and Diversity in the Church* (Oxford, 1996), pp. 107–16.

conduct, and *lemures* or *larvae* if they have been bad . . . What an abysmal pit of profligacy is opened up before men's feet by those who hold this belief, as anyone can see if he gives the matter even the slightest attention![5]

Demonic spirits and human spirits were different orders of beings. Furthermore, the corollary to this principle was equally true for Nider and his peers: living human beings could not possibly be possessed by shades of the restless dead. This tradition, again, stretches back to Augustine, who explicitly wrote against certain contemporary Christians who believed in ghostly possession.[6] Augustine instead emphasised the cosmic and eschatological dimensions of the battle between God and the Devil that is waged in human bodies through demonic possession. Demons 'influence [people] in extraordinary and invisible ways, using the subtlety of their bodies to penetrate the bodies of men without their feeling it'.[7] However, 'that power [i.e. of demons to possess a given individual] neither conquers nor enthralls any man unless he joins it by some act of sin'.[8] In short, possession can only be accomplished through an initiating act of human collusion. All this was axiomatic for Nider in the fifteenth century, a kind of cultural 'common sense'[9] that held an authoritative pedigree of tradition. Indeed, Nider undoubtedly included the tale of the soul-possessed *fraticello* in his collection of anecdotes precisely so that it might serve as a negative illustration of a 'superstitious error' in need of correction.

For a modern historian, however, Nider's story is instructive on levels that extend beyond the cautionary lessons anticipated by its author. In describing the responses of a community to a reputed medium in its midst, the story offers a valuable index of popular beliefs about spirits, possession and the dead, as well as providing social-historical evidence about constructions of individual identity and communal memory.

---

[5] Augustine, *The City of God*, tr. D. Wiesen (Cambridge, MA, 1968), pp. 188–91.

[6] See the fourth-century Zeno of Verona, who believed in ghostly, not demonic, possession. 'For the wandering unclean human spirits of both sexes enter into the corporal dwelling-places of living spirits . . . But when they . . . [are exorcised, each] will confess its sex, it will confess the time and place when it entered, it will confess its proper name, and its death. Or else it will reveal who it is by clear signs . . . we are especially concerned about those who died through some violence [*vi*] . . . You say, "Demons feign these things" . . . But why would they take feigned names, when their confessions are true in all other ways?' *De Resurrectione*, in *Patrologia Latina*, ed. J.P Migne (Paris, 1844–64), XI, pp. 373–6 (hereafter cited as *PL*). Augustine's rejection of this proposition was to become standard.

[7] Augustine, *De Divinatione Demonum*, in *PL*, p. 586.

[8] Augustine, *City of God*, pp. 348–9. See also pp. 343–7.

[9] In the sense used by Clifford Geertz, 'Common Sense as a Cultural System', *The Antioch Review* 33 (1975), pp. 5–26.

Although any recovery of local beliefs and practices is necessarily both partial and provisional, a close reading of the 'cultural facts' of the story[10] yields rather a different conception of possessing spirits from that advanced by theologians. What was considered possible within the realm of spirit possession for this community, and what kinds of evidence were accepted as probative indicators of possession? How was the nature and identity of the spirit gradually constructed and endowed with meaning?

Nider reports three inferences or chains of association made by the community in Berne that gathered around the fraticello. These determinations on the part of the community become increasingly precise in their assessment of the unseen. First they decided that there was some sort of spirit present; then its identity was debated; and finally, several specific spirits were named and interviewed. This incremental process of constructing meaning – of attaching both a recognisable identity and a communal significance to the spirit – reflects the gradual coalescence of the group from an amorphous collection of curious neighbours, to a spiritist cult centred upon a charismatic medium and his regular bouts of possession by spirits known to the community. By placing the dead, the community also places itself, a point to which I shall return.

The circumstances that initially drew attention to the fraticello occurred at night – the traditional time for spirits to walk abroad – and in his home. We can infer (from Nider's enigmatic notation that the fraticello was 'using stones and wood' as part of his pretending) that the most notable element was some sort of noise, possibly of a rattling or clapping sort.[11] From these few indications – night-time noise in the house of a semi-religious figure – it seemed credible to observers that an unseen spirit was in their midst. As gossip spread through the small world of a fifteenth-century town, the fraticello apparently became the centre of a nightly gathering of curious neighbours, who gathered to experience the visits of the purported spirit first hand. The subsequent development of the anecdote informs us of the range of identities that the Bernese thought might legitimately be attached to this unknown spirit that

---

[10] I am here utilising a notion elaborated in greater depth in 'Wraiths, Revenants and Ritual', pp. 10–11. Briefly defined, by 'cultural facts' I mean 'the most minimal description of what actions are reported to have occurred, and were held as true by the community that circulated the report'.

[11] On noise-making, see Nicole Belmont, 'Fonction de la dérision et symblisme du bruit dans le charivari', in Jacques Le Goff and Jean-Claude Schmitt (eds.), Le charivari (Paris, 1981), pp. 16–21.

suddenly wandered among the living. According to Nider, it was the fraticello who first suggested that there were three possibilities: either it was a good spirit who would be responsible for a divine revelation; or it was a human spirit, or ghost; or perhaps an evil spirit, or demon. The word that I have translated as 'ghost' throughout the paragraph is *anima*, or human soul. Thus, significantly, the population of supernatural spirits is here divided into three parallel groups, with human ghosts regarded as similar in nature and capabilities to spirits of angelic origin. This inclusiveness contrasts sharply with the theological position, which as we have seen assigned distinct essences and capabilities to human souls on the one hand, and angels or demons on the other.

In the final part of Nider's description, the terms of encounter with the spirit suddenly change. Rather than the vague nocturnal disruptions that were described earlier, we learn that the fraticello apparently became more intimate with the spirit over time. He 'not infrequently' spoke in the voice of a ghost, that is, with a wailing inflection. Furthermore, the voices that proceeded from the fraticello's body sounded familiar to the crowd, often like that of a 'dead man who had been well known in the city'. Now it becomes clear that the fraticello was regarded as a medium for the dead, and that his body was believed to be possessed by various ghosts that spoke through his mouth. Moreover, these spirits were interactive: they answered the questions of bystanders and, most importantly, explicitly identified themselves by name. There was no longer any question of divine revelations or evil spirits: the possessing entities were prominent, recently deceased Bernese. Their names were recognised, though the crowd was particularly impressed that the fraticello himself had not known all of them personally.

Nider's anecdote perhaps constitutes our most detailed medieval description of the genesis of a minor spiritist cult. An initial period of commotion, during which news of the spirit spread and locals began to frequent the home of the fraticello at night, was followed by a period of transition, in which alternative theories about the nature and identity of the spirit were proposed and debated. Finally, the group seems to have coalesced into a group of 'regulars' who structured their meetings around a series of séances. These were conducted by the fraticello, who allowed spirits of the well-known local dead to take over his body and answer questions through his mouth. Thus the fraticello ultimately learned how to become 'voluntarily possessed', that is, to control the spirits and his possession trances. Anthropological studies of spirit possession have noted that this phenomenon of domesticating or taming spirits often accompanies the public institutionalisation of a possession cult.[12] In many cultures, individuals who were at first considered to be involuntarily possessed through the guile or violence of the spirit, later establish a reputation as voluntary mediums as they mature and learn to control the spirits that frequent their lives. A somewhat similar pattern seems to be elaborated in Nider's tale, as the fraticello gradually learns to subdue the spirits and mediate their interrelationships with the living. His ultimate goal, however, is to lay the unruly spirits that haunt him to rest. His project of going on pilgrimage aims at placing the restless dead by visiting the shrines of the holy dead. The detail about the man's continued funding while on pilgrimage suggests, further, that belief in the possibility of becoming a medium for the dead was not confined within the city walls of Berne.

The interpretive choices made by this community correlate with a particular set of attitudes towards the supernatural world. It is significant that at the outset of the tale, the identity of the spirit is a cipher, an indeterminate sign, the meaning of which is only gradually worked out by the group. While the existence of angelic and demonic spirits was acknowledged by the Bernese, they focused their attention upon the spirits of the dead as the most likely supernatural beings to be wandering amongst them. Yet the excluded alternatives for the spirit's identity are equally as interesting as the preferred solution, for they aptly demonstrate the fluid and syncretistic nature of medieval belief systems. The categories of the elite culture (angels and demons) are recognised, even though it is ultimately a third category (wandering ghosts) that dominates the interpretive scheme of the group. Similarly, the cult of the saints – the heroic dead – was an important part of this community's religious field, for it is through pilgrimage to saints' shrines that the fraticello thinks to lay his spirits to rest. Thus the polarity of the 'bad' or restless dead, and the 'good' or saintly dead, represent the two most powerful sources of supernatural power in the unseen world constructed by the fifteenth-century Bernese. As we shall see, this mentality was not unique.

Masks, disguises and contested identities

The group at Berne represents an excellent example of what microhistorians have termed a 'normal exception'.[13] A given set of behaviours or beliefs may be exceptional when judged by the norms of the dominant

---

12 Ioan Lewis, *Ecstatic Religion* (New York, 1971).
13 Edward Muir and Guido Ruggiero (eds.), *Microhistory and the Lost Peoples of Europe* (Baltimore, 1991), p. xiv.

culture, here represented by the Dominican Johannes Nider, yet normal in so far as they reflect the cultural mentalities and field of possibilities maintained by a non-elite sector of society that did not produce many written narratives. The fact that the *fraticello* was not an isolated individual, but the charismatic centre of a group, testifies to the fact that a claim to incarnate the spirits of the dead was not considered exceptional by the Bernese, but within the range of the normal and the possible. Moreover, the Bernese case is not as isolated as it might at first appear. A body of evidence with significant parallels may be found in a group of roughly contemporary texts from across the Alps, in fifteenth- and sixteenth-century Italy.

I would like to begin this phase of my exploration with three short quotations that all testify generally to the belief that the spirits of the dead could possess the bodies of the living. The first was written in about 1420 by an anonymous Dominican bishop about the thirteenth-century recluse Verdiana of Castelfiorentino:

> Her power of expelling from human bodies the worst demons – which the common folk ignorantly consider to be souls divided from their bodies – could be proved by as many witnesses as there were and are men in that province.[14]

Giovanni Matteoti, the fifteenth-century hagiographer of his contemporary, Francesca Romana, makes note of the same belief, while again contesting the identity of the possessing spirits:

> Demons . . . sometimes invade the bodies of living men and women, and then they lie and say that they are the spirits of the dead, whom they often even name, in order to defame the souls of those dead people.[15]

The third quotation derives from a sixteenth-century exorcists' manual written by a Franciscan friar by the name of Buonaventura Farinerio, and published in Venice in 1567:

> When demons enter human bodies, they almost always appear to the person first in the form of a man who died an evil death, or sometimes they show themselves as one of the person's relatives.[16]

These three comments all assume spirit possession to be the work of demons masquerading as the dead in order to lead astray the faithful. Yet

---

[14] *Vita Viridianae Virgine*, in *Acta Sanctorum*, ed. Société des Bollandistes (3rd edn, Paris, 1863–87), IV (1 February), p. 265 (hereafter cited as *AASS*).

[15] *Vita Francescae Romanae*, *AASS*, VIII (9 March), p. 175.

[16] Buonaventura Farinerio, *Exorcismo Mirabile da Disfare Ogni Sorte de Malefici et da Cacciare i Demoni* (Venice, 1567), fol. 360v.

despite the contestation of identity embedded in these texts, the authors' arguments against the possibility of ghostly possession are themselves a way of preserving the contours of popular belief. Beneath these learned interpretations, a more intimate view of the universe, one populated by spirits of human, rather than of cosmic origin, may be discerned. In general, the Italian references tell us more about the spirits than does Nider, who concentrates his attention on the putatively fraudulent medium. Several observations are immediately striking. First, spirit possession was widely seen by the 'common folk' to be the work of 'souls divided from their bodies'. That is, possessing spirits are disembodied souls seeking to regain the privileges of a human body through possession. The second quotation amplifies this description, giving an additional fragment of information: as in Nider's spiritist cult, these possessing souls usually revealed their human identities. Naming was thus a central component of what might be called the ritual drama of a possession episode, as performatively enacted by a community.[17] We may assume, further, that the names given by the spirits were usually known to the witnesses and participants in this drama, for Giovanni Matteoti notes that revealing a human name is a means of 'defaming' the memory of the individual concerned. This strategy would be meaningless if the name were not familiar to the crowd. The question of defamation is linked to a final observation: the moral status of the deceased. The last quotation specifies two groups from among the dead that were deemed most likely to become spirits seeking bodies: those who 'died an evil death', or else relatives of the possessed victim. Presumably the 'defamation' of the deceased is connected with the expectation that possessing ghosts are shades who died an evil death.

The question of 'bad' or 'evil' death had been a conceptual category of some significance throughout the Middle Ages. The moral significance of one's life was thought to be complemented by the specific kind of death one met: whether it was peaceful and expected, or sudden and violent. Thus the precise manner of one's death, as much as the moral quality of one's life, had bearing upon one's fate in the afterlife. In the thirteenth

---

[17] I am here drawing upon the literature on performance theories of ritual. See Lawrence Sullivan, 'Sound and Senses: Toward a Hermeneutics of Performance', *History of Religions* 26 (1) (1986), pp. 1–33; Catherine Bell, *Ritual Theory, Ritual Practice* (New York, 1992); Roy Rappaport, *Ecology, Meaning, and Religion* (Berkeley, 1979), pp. 173–222; Edward Schieffelin, 'Performance and the Cultural Construction of Reality', *American Ethnologist* (1985), pp. 707–24; Jonathan Z. Smith, *To Take Place: Toward Theory in Ritual* (Chicago, 1987); Ronald L. Grimes, *Readings in Ritual Studies* (Upper Saddle River, 1996).

century, for example, the Cistercian monk Caesarius of Heisterbach had enumerated four kinds of mortality in his *Dialogue on Miracles*: the death of those who live well and die peacefully; of those who live sinfully but die well; of those who live well but die badly; and finally, of those who both live and die badly.[18] Caesarius follows this lesson with an illustrative discussion of each kind of death and the fates of the souls concerned. Those who die badly, through violence or guile, are shown as unquiet souls, wandering the earth either as maleficent spirits, or as corporeal revenants.[19] A similar conception seems to have been at work in the late medieval Italian belief in the depredations of dead spirits seeking bodies. For example, this is likely to have been what Alessandra Strozzi had in mind when, in a 1459 letter to her son Filippo on the occasion of his brother's death, she mused that 'whoever dies suddenly or is murdered . . . loses both body and soul'.[20] The body is lost through physical death; the soul, through a bad death. To be torn too suddenly from life leads to restless wanderings, a death without place.

These general observations about the contours of popular belief may be supplemented by specific anecdotes about ghostly possession, in which we see the belief 'in action'. Indeed, the comments made by learned authors about 'demons who lie and say that they are spirits of the dead' correspond quite closely to some specific case-histories of spirit possession recorded in miracle accounts. At times, possession stories are merely evocative of the belief in possession by the spirits of the dead, without being precise. For example, the apparent spirit possession of a little boy described in the *Vita* of Columba of Rieti occurs after he 'found a dead cat on the public street. And when, with childish curiosity, he lifted up the head by the ears, and uncovering the eyes, looked into them, he was struck numb . . . and made mindless and mute.'[21] This tale seems to preserve, in vestigial form, a connection between possession and death, although it is non-specific and the dead being is an animal. Similarly, the *Life* of Zita of Lucca recounts two cases of possession in which the spirits, when interrogated, reveal apparently human names. One identifies himself as Pintello de Controne, presumably a person known locally. In the other case, a woman is simultaneously possessed by two spirits, who give their names as Napoleone

---

[18] Caesarius of Heisterbach, *Dialogus Miraculorum*, ed. Joseph Strange (Cologne, 1851), II, p. 266.

[19] Caciola, 'Wraiths, Revenants and Ritual'.

[20] Gene Brucker (ed.), *The Society of Renaissance Florence: a Documentary Study* (New York, 1971), p. 48.

[21] *Vita B. Columbanae Reatinae*, AASS, XVIII (20 May), p. 190.

and Solidario.[22] All three names seem more likely to be designations of local dead people than of infernal spirits. In both cases, the victims are freed through the intervention of Zita.

A more detailed set of examples may be drawn from the *Miracles of John Gualbert*, a fifteenth-century text from Florence that includes several fascinating cases. Gualbert died in 1073, but the miracle collection was compiled some 400 years later, making this text precisely contemporary to the other testimonies presented thus far. The author was a Florentine monk of Gualbert's Vallambrosan order, Jerome de Raggiolo, who undoubtedly recorded this series of miracles with an eye to Gualbert's possible canonisation.[23] By the time Raggiolo wrote in the late fifteenth century, Gualbert's relics – particularly his arm – enjoyed a reputation for outstanding exorcistic virtue. The possessed were brought to his shrine in large numbers, and it is their testimony, that of their family members, and that of the monks performing the exorcisms with the help of Gualbert's relics, that is abstracted in Raggiolo's text. Some tales give quite a bit of circumstantial background to the process of the possession, including information about the identity of the spirit, what the victim was doing just prior to the possession, and how the spirit gained power over the individual. In several cases, the spirit either explicitly identifies itself as a ghost – though as we might expect, Raggiolo contests this – or else the circumstances of the possession and exorcism clearly imply that the spirit was understood to be a ghost by the victim and onlookers. In one instance, even Jerome de Raggiolo jokes about the belief, when he tells of a fool possessed by a 'ridiculous demon' whose primary amusement is to sing psalms and hymns in such hilarious parody, that he moves even sombre religious men to irrepressible laughter. So intent was this spirit upon its liturgical songs, 'that you would think', remarks Jerome, 'it was the soul of some priest!'[24]

The first truly detailed example of possession by a ghost in this text conforms closely to the pattern suggested above by elite authors: possession by the displaced spirit of one of the 'evil dead':

> While . . . a cadaver was hanging tied to the scaffold [*cruce*] with a chain, this man, who had been driven insane by love, by chance took the road next to the scaffold. As is human nature, he raised his eyes to the frightful corpse

---

[22] *Vita S. Zitae Virgine Lucae, AASS*, xii (27 April), pars. 85, 66.

[23] The text has been discussed by Pierre Sigal, 'La possession démoniaque dans la région de Florence au XVe siècle d'après les miracles de Saint Jean Gualbert', in *Histoire et société: mélanges offerts à Georges Duby* (3 vols., Aix-en-Provence, 1992), iii, pp. 101–12.

[24] *Miraculi S. Joannis Gualberti Abbatis, AASS*, xxix (12 July), p. 388.

. . . [and] from above, as he himself was accustomed to tell it, he heard a hissing sound . . . The demon entered into him while he was in this state of fear, and began to dominate him and to use him as a dwelling-place.[25]

In this extraordinary fragment of testimony, it is nearly possible to hear this lovelorn fifteenth-century youth recount his own story, 'as he himself was accustomed to tell it'.[26] The hiss that comes from above apparently was understood by the victim as the sound made by the spirit of the executed criminal as it left the dead body hanging on the scaffold and slipped into his own body. Immediately afterwards he was possessed. The character of the possessing spirit conforms to the pattern observed by the exorcist Buonaventura Farinerio, for criminal execution is, of course, the very worst kind of death, indicating an evil life leading to a violent end. Furthermore, the tale indicates that the status of the victim also was seen as a contributing factor in his possession: the combination of long-term lovesickness and recent terror apparently rendered this individual especially vulnerable to spiritual invasion. This is a theme that will recur.

In two other tales from the same text, Jerome de Raggiolo discusses possessing spirits who explicitly claim to be ghosts, and aggressively contests the identity of the spirit:

> Another woman came to us . . . and the demon that had invaded her, as many are accustomed to do, confessed that it was the soul of a certain Ligurian named Beltramo. It must be noted that this is an impudent lie that must be restrained by the authority of Holy Mother Church, so that the average common man might perceive that such a thing is hardly possible, and thus be instructed in true religion . . . First of all, it is proved by the authority of the Prophet who says, 'the spirit goes and does not return' (Ps. 77:39). Nothing tells us where it goes: either it flies through the air purging itself; or it dwells in an earthly place that is deserted and uncultivated, or else not deserted; or it seeks a place unknown to us, which we call Purgatory. But that it should go back into a human body again we consider, and declare, to be a blasphemy [*nefas*]. Besides, of no people has it been read, that two souls of the same condition and nature, and experiencing various things together, [might] occupy a place in one body.[27]

Several aspects of this incident are worthy of comment. First, there is Raggiolo's comment that 'many [spirits] are accustomed' to identify themselves as shades of the dead, testifying to how common the belief

---

[25] *Ibid.*, p. 391.
[26] See Carlo Ginzburg, *Clues, Myths, and the Historical Method*, tr. John and Anne Tedeschi (Baltimore, 1989), pp. 156–64; Muir and Ruggiero, *Microhistory*, pp. vii–xxviii.
[27] *Miraculi Joannis Gualberti*, p. 416.

was in fifteenth-century Italy. Moreover, the text later notes that this Beltramo had died violently – ambushed and then slaughtered in a forest by local criminals for the sake of his money. Thus the link between the unquiet dead and the violently killed is again reinforced. Third, there is the intriguing series of arguments against the belief, including both biblical authority as well as a physiological argument that two human souls cannot share the experiences of one body. Jerome de Raggiolo, like other churchmen of his day, accepts the possibility that spirits might linger on earth,[28] but not within human bodies. We know from the subsequent anecdote, however, that arguments against ghostly possession were largely unsuccessful. In this tale, the exorcism of another individual possessed by a spirit claiming to be one of the displaced dead leads to a spontaneous public debate on the nature of possessing spirits. The priest contests the spirit's identity to no avail:

> The demon who had invaded her asserted that it was the soul of a certain man [named] Mazzanto, who was murdered with a dagger by a certain scoundrel over a game of dice. Everyone who was present pressed forward to affirm that this was true. However the priest argued with them, bringing forth . . . many opinions of men outstanding in virtue and learning, through which he demonstrated that when the souls of men first leave their bodies they go to the place they have merited: that is, they find a sweet place; or they find a harsh land for purging or else for eternal torment. They do not find another body to enter. As for those others [i.e. possessing spirits], they are evil spirits . . . [But] he hardly could convince them that this was true.[29]

The belief that possessing spirits were the evil dead seems to have been too deeply rooted in the community to be uprooted by the mere theological disquisitions of a priest. In this particular example, the crowd was particularly impressed by the specificity of the spirit's knowledge. The account of the precise circumstances of Mazzanto's bad death provoked a stirring response among the bystanders, who pressed forward excitedly to hear and corroborate the story. In such a case, community memory had priority over the priest's abstract theological argument about the afterlife and the different kinds of supernatural spirits. The unseen world reflected the seen world: the supernatural was populated by the 'natural' spirits of the local dead.

In addition to tales involving the 'bad dead', one case in the *Miracles of John Gualbert* involves the other category of possessing ghosts identified in the exorcists' manual above: relatives. Spirit possession was not any less to be feared for being the work of a known, but deceased, member of the

---

[28] See Gobi, *Dialogue avec un fantôme*.   [29] *Miraculi Joannis Gualberti*, p. 417.

community. In this instance, a girl is possessed after encountering 'an old woman lying on her bed, holding her right hand between her cheek and the pillow'.[30] The girl does not recognise the old lady, but the description certainly is vivid, giving a sense of the rhythms of real speech. When the spirit is later conjured, it tells the priest it will leave, 'if you make sure to have Gregorian Masses with the offerings for the dead celebrated on my behalf'. Thus far, this anecdote is rather similar to two others in Raggiolo's text, in which possessing spirits refuse to leave the bodies they have taken unless masses for the dead are sung for specific, recently dead individuals – that is, presumably, on their own behalf.[31] In this particular case, however, not only is the ghost named and prayed for, it ultimately is identified as the girl's great-grandmother. The primary witness whose testimony is preserved was the girl's father; he noted that the spirit was that of 'the recently deceased mother of my father'.[32] The old lady thus returned to the comfort of her family by first haunting, then possessing, her descendant.

Another case of ancestor-possession – though this time unsuccessful – may be found in the hagiography of Bernardino of Siena. This text, roughly contemporary with Jerome de Raggiolo's, explains in some detail how possession by the dead was believed to occur, although it simultaneously argues that possession is in reality the work of demons:

> It happened not far from the town that a certain mountain man [*montanus*] came to the term of his life. Three days after he was buried, the voice of an unclean spirit was heard outside the house simulating the spirit of the dead man . . . The rebellious and envious spirits . . . succeed more easily in [their goals] if they can slip into the minds of careless people through any weakness.[33]

As in the case of the lovesick victim discussed above, a state of depression – mourning – is apt to make one particularly vulnerable to spirit possession. Longing for the presence of the lost loved one may allow a possessing spirit to 'slip into the minds of careless people through any weakness'. The period directly after burial seems to be targeted in particular in this passage, noting that the attempted possession takes place within three days of the funeral; similarly, we are told that the great-grandmother who possessed her descendant in the Gualbert miracles had died quite recently.

---

[30] *Ibid.*, p. 440.   [31] *Ibid.*, p. 421.

[32] *Ibid.*, p. 441. Sigal, 'Possession démoniaque', p. 106, identifies the spirit as the girl's grandmother, but this is a misreading.

[33] *Analecta S. Berneardino Senensis, AASS*, xvii (20 May), p. 140.

There thus seems to be a relatively short interval in which shades of the dead were believed to cling to life, seeking a new living body to possess after an interval of haunting. As in Berne and elsewhere, it is always the recent local dead who seek new bodies from among the living in their community. These are the displaced shades who long for a new habitation: the communities that gather to interrogate them attempt to construe their identity and understand their motivations by asking about their names; where they were from; the times and manners of their deaths; and their families. These were thought to be key points in establishing the nature of the spirit, its place within the community while alive, and the best way to place it to rest by placing it within its new community: that of the dead. Yet at the same time, the high level of public interest in these events testifies to a broad social interest in temporary communion with the dead. Jerome de Raggiolo communicates an intense sense of excitement when he describes local responses to ghostly possession: in one case, 'everyone . . . pressed forward to affirm that [the manner of the spirit's death] was true'; in another, we hear from the victim of possession, 'as he himself was accustomed to tell it' – indicating that this was a tale much in demand. The opportunity to interview the dead, while it did not obviate the desire to heal the possessed victim, was greeted with great excitement. It is easy to see how, in these circumstances, cases such as those described in the Italian sources might become transmogrified into the situation described by Nider, in which an individual first claims to be haunted, then possessed, and finally acts as a voluntary medium for a local group that forms its own local spirit cult.

Social constructions of the supernatural

'The supernatural', writes Peter Brown, 'becomes the depository of the objectified values of the group.'[34] This chapter has elaborated two different conceptualisations of the supernatural world. On the one hand is the model of the universe advanced by ecclesiastical authors. These men identified possessing spirits with fallen angels, and argued that dead spirits cross over into a new realm, a tripartite afterlife of reward and punishment that is disconnected from our present existence. On the other hand, it is clear that within certain local communities shades of the

---

[34] Peter Brown, *Society and the Holy in Late Antiquity* (Berkeley, 1982), p. 318. Brown is working within a Durkheimian tradition: see Emile Durkheim, *The Elementary Forms of the Religious Life* (London, 1915).

bad dead, or of relatives, were believed to linger among the living, and occasionally to seize the opportunity to regain a body through possession. We have seen two variants of this latter belief: in Berne, the case of a fraticello who acted as a voluntary medium for such spirits; and in Italy, where cases of ghostly possession were seen as involuntary and violent. The Bernese anecdote focuses more upon the living medium and his community; the Italian evidence reveals more about the status of the dead. In both cases, however, visits to saints' shrines were seen as a solution to the depredations of spirits seeking bodies.

Can we, according to Brown's dictum, extrapolate social values from these different constructions of the supernatural world? In the remaining pages of this chapter, I would like to explore the social-historical dimensions of these differing mental constructs. For the process of collectively constructing the spirit's nature and meaning is a fundamentally social act, deeply expressive of community priorities and interests. Theologians utilized possession exempla as a means to explore questions of individual soteriology and universal eschatology, while local communities regarded the same events as opportunities ritually to reconstruct community boundaries and definitions, to place themselves amid the memories of local history and of their ancestors.

While I cannot do justice to the complexities of medieval theology here, a few observations can help to foreground contrasts between the elite and the popular conceptions of possessing spirits. A religion both transcendent and soteriological, medieval Catholicism developed an anthropology that was based upon a perception of congruence between the microcosm of an individual and the macrocosm of the universe. And in turn, the cosmos imagined by medieval theologians may be described as the material backdrop – almost a material analogue – to a vast eschatological conflict between God and the Devil, the Ancient Enemy of the human race. Microcosmic choices towards sin or righteousness reflect a macrocosmic, ancient tension that pervades the whole of creation and history. After death, a soul's assignment to Hell, or to Purgatory and/or Heaven, positions it eternally on the side of evil or of good. One leaves behind the body to exist among the righteous or the sinful, the blessed or the fallen, angels or demons, for all eternity. Dead spirits do not seek new bodies; they already are placed within a new spiritual realm, from whence there is no return. As one medieval encyclopaedist phrased it, 'after death there is no means of gaining merit . . . Afterwards, there is no possibility of returning to the body or to the world.'[35] This gap between worlds

---

[35] Vincent of Beauvais, *Speculum Morale* (Duaci, 1624; repr. Graz, 1964), pp. 710–11.

could only be crossed by the living when they joined the dead; never by the dead seeking to rejoin the living.

Within this system, the spirit possession of a material human body by a fallen angel inevitably was bound up with moral questions of sin and retribution. As Augustine noted, demons have no power over the individual unless she first sins, a doctrine that was more or less upheld throughout medieval discussions of spirit possession. Indeed, some sources seem to suggest that sin actually alters the physical constitution of the body and permits easier entrance to the demonic spirit.[36] Demons thus play a retributive role within the universal scheme of divine providence, and possession signals a negative soteriological state: only fallen Christians attract fallen angels. Moreover, since demonic spirits and human spirits are different orders of creation, possession is violent and painful: a hybrid, wrenching violation of immense power brought to bear upon fragile flesh. At this moment, the human body not only reflects but actually incarnates the tensions of the macrocosm. A possessed individual is not herself, but Other: her voice, actions and consciousness are all those of the demon whose personality is dominant. Finally, as a reflection of this unique state of alterity, possession also places the victim in a socially liminal position.[37] The demoniac is beyond the bounds of human society because she no longer retains an independent identity: she is in thrall to the demon in her body. In short, one's individual spiritual state, soteriological status and the broader social order are all tightly interwoven within this rationalist system, in which human events and choices reflect broader cosmic and moral conflicts.

By contrast, in turning to the supernatural world constructed by local communities, we see a universe that is far more intimate in its structure, if less systematic in its meanings. The building blocks of the supernatural often are shown as natural in themselves: it is their unwonted combination that produces a miraculous effect. Indeed, in many communities it was the human dead that dominated the local supernatural, rather than beings of an entirely different essence, such as angels and demons. For example, although the community in Berne acknowledged the possibility that the spirit in their midst might be an angel or a demon, it is a series of ghosts that are eventually identified as the agents in the possession of the

---

[36] Some of these issues are explored in an article currently being written, 'Mystics, Demoniacs, and the Physiology of Possession in Medieval Europe'.

[37] Although Barbara Newman has emphasised that demoniacs might exercise leadership roles and gain prestige through possession, 'Possessed by the Spirit: Devout Women, Demoniacs, and the Apostolic Life in the Thirteenth Century', *Speculum* 73 (July 1998), pp. 733–70.

fraticello. This is a more 'humanistic' view of the unseen world, one in which the activities of transcendent beings are remote and ineffable, while the memories, experiences and local common sense of the community form a vivid cultural basis for constructing the supernatural. Furthermore, the cure for possession – visiting a saint – involves the invocation of yet another category of the human dead: those heroic dead whose sufferings merited them a participation in the reserves of divine supernatural power. In viewing the human body as a possible repository for displaced human souls, these communities constructed for themselves a supernatural that was more knowable because smaller in scale.

The procedure of identifying the possessing spirit – of gradually attaching meaning and familiarity to the invading entity – is an act of collective memory. In the creative process of constructing meaning, we see local knowledge, memories and idioms interwoven to express the evolving self-definitions of the group as well as its collective anxieties. Rather than the automatic placement according to merits that theologians endorsed, these local communities felt that certain souls among the dead needed to be placed in a more active way. The defining boundaries of the entire community – including both living and dead – were at stake. With good deaths, community boundaries were effortlessly fractured and immediately reconstituted as the dead left the community of the living and entered into their new 'age class'.[38] These shades were believed to accept their new place. In cases of bad death, however, the process of placing the dead was more complex and gradual. Death became a process, not an event. Not only did these dead have to make their initial entry among the dead too suddenly, while still desperately attached to life; but those left behind likely experienced a heady mixture of ambivalence, titillation and vague guilt in recalling the violent ends of murder victims or executed criminals. Collective memories of such deaths would linger as a mental apparition that could become vividly present. A similar, though less sinister, process could be said to occur in the case of relatives. In these cases, significantly, it is always the family that makes the identification of the possessing ghost, not the broader community as a whole. The recent deaths of family members haunted the imaginations of survivors, as the bad dead haunted the thoughts of a town more generally, providing a group of 'usual suspects' in the event that someone were possessed. Such local memory was considered probative and irrefutable by the group, as demonstrated by the sceptical reactions Jerome de Raggiolo attributed to a local crowd when a priest attempted to dispute with them about the

---

[38] Patrick Geary, *Living with the Dead in the Middle Ages* (Ithaca, 1994), p. 36.

nature of a possessing spirit. When the hapless ecclesiastic explained the theology of spirits and bodies, demons and the dead, the local folk remained unimpressed. After all, the possessing ghost had given his name, Mazzanto, and had specified in minute detail the known and remembered circumstances of his bad death. Experience was firmly credited over authority.

Furthermore, within these local communities the moral valences of possession were the inverse of theological belief. Victims might be rendered vulnerable through mourning or other forms of depression, but were not understood as sinful. Evil is displaced from the living, and projected instead onto the ghost who takes possession. By specifying that possessing spirits are the shades of those who died a bad death, sin and violence are linked to the dead spirit, not the living victim. In consequence, the social aspects of the possession drama tend to be conceived in rather a different way from theologians' representations. When viewed theologically, possession engenders an absolute alterity: the demoniac is seen as incarnating an ancient and cosmic supernatural being dedicated to nothing less than the downfall of the human race. She is socially, morally and mentally dis-integrated for the duration of her possession. As viewed through the lens of this popular culture, however, possession may become a temporary means to social integration beyond the threshold of death. A former member of the community seeks to possess one of the living both to re-experience embodiment and to reconnect with the community of the living. The living, moreover, evidently felt some sympathy for such spirits: taken too soon from the body, such spirits had not yet come to terms with the fact of their own death. They thus desperately attempt to regain life by obtaining another body, wrested from among the living. Although the possession was seen as disruptive for the possessed individual, the motives of the possessing spirit were perfectly understandable. The conversations and interviews conducted with such possessing ghosts – a theme that is particularly marked in the Bernese example, but that is also seen in episodes such as the ghost Mazzanto – signal the reconstitution of a community that temporarily includes the dead individual once again. This social aspect of possession thus both mediates group memories and restores past circles of community. In the case of the bad dead, finally laying such a ghost to rest also exorcises collective anxiety and guilt about the individual's violent end. Once fully placed among the dead, the collective memory of the individual's violent end can be allowed to fall into obscurity.

Ultimately, the entire scenario of possession and exorcism lays the errant spirits of the dead to rest in the imagination of the community.

Whether relatives or sinners, possessing ghosts must complete the process of death by abandoning the new body they have taken. The community or family places itself under the protection of a local saint, or good shade, and thus lays to rest the unquiet shade that has tried to force its way back among the living. It is a reconstitutive ritual that redefines the community at its centre – the living – and at its peripheries – the dead. Ultimately, such episodes place the living even as they place the dead, repositioning both within new social groupings as the population of a given town constantly passes away and renews itself.

5 Malevolent ghosts and ministering angels: apparitions and pastoral care in the Swiss Reformation

Bruce Gordon

During a crossbow competition in Basle in 1541 Hans Knüttel, a well-known archer, collapsed and died.[1] Panic swept through the crowd as the people quickly identified the cause of this unexpected death: the plague had returned. The autumn of 1541 was a season of death in Basle as the city was scourged by an affliction which made no distinctions of status or learning; the hebraist Sebastian Münster wrote to Konrad Pellikan in Zurich to report that he had ceased all scholarly endeavours to remain with his family behind closed doors in the presentiment of death.[2] Münster would survive another ten years before plague would carry him off, but many of his learned colleagues were not so fortunate.[3] Simon Grynaeus, the pre-eminent Graecist, and one of the most learned men of the age, was a victim of the 1541

I wish to acknowledge Rainer Henrich of the Bullinger Briefwechsel Edition in Zurich and Christine Linton in St Andrews for their considerable assistance in the preparation of this paper. An earlier version of this paper was given to the Denys Hay Seminar at the University of Edinburgh and I profited greatly from the lively discussion on that occasion.

[1] Emmanuel Le Roy Ladurie, *The Beggar and the Professor. A Sixteenth-Century Family Saga*, tr. Arthur Goldhammer (Chicago, 1997), p. 70. On the plague in Basle, the best contemporary source remains Felix Platter, *Sieben regierende Pestilenzen 1539–1611*. A manuscript copy of this work is in the Basle Universitätsbibliothek, sig. A.X.III.5.a.

[2] *Briefe Sebastian Münster*, ed. Karl Heinz Burmeister (Ingelheim am Rhein, 1964), p. 44. The letter is simply dated 1542. Münster wrote 'invalescenteque pestilenti morbo nihil fere egi nisi quod omnes Domini vocationem expectavimus'. Despite the virulence of the plague, Münster was to complete the first edition of his *Cosmology* two years later in 1544.

[3] Münster's letter to Pellikan makes clear the extent of the grim harvest taken by the plague from the Basle intellectual elite. In addition to Grynaeus and Karlstadt, he mentioned Hieronymous Artolphus (rector of the university and professor of logic), Johannes Alfinius (faculty of arts), Acetarius (former Franciscan) and Antonius Wild (schoolmaster at St Peter's).

pestilence.[4] Among the endless stream of bodies borne up the Todengä-slein for burial by the church of St Peter was that of Andreas Bodenstein von Karlstadt, who had succumbed on Christmas Eve.[5] Karlstadt's death, however, proved as controversial as his life. Oswald Myconius, the irresolute head of the Basle church who had often been pilloried by Karlstadt, recounted to Heinrich Bullinger in a letter of 14 January 1542 the strange circumstances of the Saxon's end.[6]

> On the day before he fell ill, that is the 18th of December, Karlstadt, while he was in the pulpit preaching, observed a demon moving about the pews, though with considerable irritation he believed at that time that it was merely a man who was aping him. However, when the demon approached him he was dressed in white, when he moved away, he appeared dressed in black.[7]

Myconius further reported that when Karlstadt asked his friends about this audacious intruder, they claimed to have seen nothing.

> Then he realised that he had seen his own demon and he was deeply disturbed. He went home and found the pigs in his garden, where someone had put them, and his anxiety grew. On the following day he became ill, and six days later [24 December] he died. After his death his wife said, 'wherever we were there had always been a malevolent spirit'. Karlstadt's son Adam added, 'and in Zurich he [the spirit] often appeared as a black dog'.[8]

The story of Karlstadt's death made sensational copy, and by March 1542 the demonic tale had reached Luther, who took an especial interest in the circumstances of his arch-enemy's departure. The Basle printer, Johannes Oporinus, wrote to Joachim Camerarius in February 1542 a richly embroidered account of the events.[9] In Karlstadt's house, and around his grave, according to Oporinus, one could hear a terrible din; stones flew about, making it unwise for anyone to remain there. Further, Karlstadt's widow had asked the ministers of Basle to lead their congregations in prayer for deliverance from her afflictions. Myconius and Oporinus were not alone, other accounts were put about which embellished the tale, telling how Karlstadt's own children, as well as the other occupants of his

---

[4] On Grynaeus, see Peter G. Bietenholz, 'Simon Grynaeus', in his *Contemporaries of Erasmus* (3 vols., Toronto, 1986), II, pp. 142–6.

[5] Although Karlstadt was buried in St Peter's church, his epitaph is now lost, cf. François Maurer, *Die Kunstdenkmäler des Kantons Basel-Stadt* (8 vols., Basle, 1966), v, p. 23.

[6] The documents relating to this story are found in Hermann Barge, *Andreas Bodenstein von Karlstadt* (2 vols., Leipzig, 1905), II, pp. 509–515. The story is also discussed in Mark Edwards Jr, *Luther and the False Brethren* (Stanford, 1975), pp. 183–5.

[7] The text of Myconius's letter is partially printed in Barge, *Karlstadt*, p. 614.

[8] *Ibid.*   [9] *Ibid.*, pp. 510–11.

house, had been tormented by visitations from the revenant reformer. The possessions of the dead man were thrown into the sewer or on the fire, with the loss of many important items.

The story of Karlstadt's death is a complex narrative to which rumour and anxiety, along with a sprinkling of character assassination, all contributed. Hermann Barge, in his monumental biography of Karlstadt, may be correct in his belief that the whole account was fabricated by Myconius in a calumnious act of revenge upon a man who had treated him so disdainfully.[10] Against this, however, it must be noted that Myconius willingly prosecuted the wish of Karlstadt's widow that Luther be informed that her husband had died without a malign word against his old rival.[11] Apart from a possible provenance in the troubled relations of the Basle church, the story of Karlstadt's death has several striking elements, not least being the willingness of the international Protestant network to take it seriously. Luther and Melanchthon, among others, were persuaded that the hand of the Devil was present in Karlstadt's death. The interpretative framework of the story, as it made its way around Europe, was constituted by the categories of the 'good' and 'bad' death. The account may have had a mendacious hue, but to sixteenth-century churchmen death involved a complex web of relations between this world and the next, and the fantastic remained an integral component of those relations. Signs from beyond the grave were an important and legitimate part of establishing or discrediting the memory of the deceased. The appearance of the Devil would surprise no one, and that he would kill a prominent reformer was understood in terms of a moral tale which was to be interpreted by the living. Luther drew from this the unhappy conclusion that Karlstadt had, after all, revealed himself to be a member of the church of Satan.[12]

It may surprise us to read of visions of demons and the haunted graves of reformers, but in the lands of the Swiss Confederation, as elsewhere in Europe, demons, ghosts and the revenant were deeply secured in local cultures. Through the work of nineteenth-century folklorists we are afforded a view, even if the glass is dark, of the mental world of sixteenth-century communities in Protestant lands.[13] In the villages of the Zurich

---

[10] *Ibid.*, p. 510.

[11] Melchior Kirchhofer, *Oswald Myconius. Antistes des Baslerischen Kirche* (Zurich, 1815), p. 333. Amazingly this remains the best study of Myconius. Kirchhofer argued that Myconius, whose own wife became seriously ill during that plague year, conducted himself graciously in the period following Karlstadt's death.

[12] Edwards, *Luther and the False Brethren*, p. 185.

[13] I follow here the persuasive line taken by Ronald Hutton in his 'The English Reformation and the Evidence of Folklore', *Past and Present* 148 (1995), pp. 89–116.

Oberland, for example, there is a legend that if you peer through the keyhole of the parish church at midnight on New Year's Eve you will see gathered around the Lord's Table the images of those who will die in the coming year.[14] From Basle comes another example from the sixteenth century: a local nobleman was being held in the castle of Rötelen in the Vogtei Hochberg.[15] When he was brought out of his cell to be executed he took a small knife and slit his own throat, dying almost instantly. As the nobleman's death was a suicide, the executioner took his body to dispose of it in the Rhine – a traditional form of ritual cleansing for a community in which a suicide had taken place. The corpse was placed on a horse, and as the party approached the river a sudden lightning storm arose, throwing the hapless rider and his horse in the air. The horse was rendered blind and the injured executioner fled home, abandoning the body. The story was a warning of how Satan can both drive the desperate to suicide and thwart the community's means of purging itself from such a death.

A brief glimpse of how people interpreted ghost stories is found in a letter of Johannes Haller, chief minister of the church in Berne, to Heinrich Bullinger from the spring of 1570.[16] The matter concerned the death of a Bernese magistrate, Johannes Sager,[17] who:

> When he had dined at home and gone to lie down [was] seized violently by a misfortune, managing only to cry: 'what will happen to me?' Afterwards, he could make no sign, either by words or gestures, that anyone could understand. The next day, towards evening, he finally died in the midst of this struggle.

Soon after his death Sager began to appear to others:

> A few days later, rumours began to circulate about certain apparitions,

---

[14] Cf. William Plomer (ed.), *Kilvert's Diary 1870–79* (Harmondsworth, 1977), p. 229 for a nearly identical nineteenth-century Welsh belief. I am grateful to Peter Marshall for this reference.

[15] C. Buxtorf-Falkeisen, *Baslerische Stadt- und Landgeschichten aus dem sechszehnten Jahrhundert* (3 vols., Basle, 1863), II, p. 80.

[16] Johannes Haller to Heinrich Bullinger, 14 May 1570. Zurich Staatsarchiv E II 370, 422f. I am grateful to Rainer Henrich of the Bullinger Briefwechsel Edition for this reference.

[17] Sager or Saager was an established burgher family in Berne which had served on the city council from 1402. The Johannes of this story held a number of leading offices in the Bernese state: Landvogt of Aarberg in 1553, on the Small Council of Berne and as Venner (second in importance to the Schultheiss – executive head – with especial control over military and financial matters), and then as Bauherr in 1564. His son, Hans Rudolf (1547–97), was one of the leading Bernese politicians of the second half of the sixteenth century. *Historisches-Biographisches Lexikon der Schweiz* (7 vols., Neuchâtel, 1929), VI, p. 784.

which, passing through his fields, were troublesome at night. One man complained loudly that he had been flung into the nearest hedge and severely injured. Others spoke of lights which were seen around those places in which bricks are made.

The moral of the story, however, was to be found in one especial encounter with Sager's ghost:

> Eventually, a certain upright, known, virtuous and godly man, whilst spreading manure on his master's field, which was adjacent to Sager's, saw the ghost approaching him from a distance through the snows which were still falling onto the hedge. The man, having forgotten about [Sager's] death, believed [Sager] to be alive. When [the ghost] drew near, it launched into a speech about certain obscure matters which the man could not understand, though he claimed to have grasped one thing which was a reference to the poor: 'Arms volk, arm lüth' (O poor folk!, O poor people!). Then the terrified man remembered that [Sager] had died, and he said to the ghost 'If you had treated the poor well during your life, you would already have discovered [that].'

The effect of this remonstration upon the ghost was immediate; his face became contorted and then began to burn. From the expiring ghost came a blast of hot air which felled the man in the field, and he was confined to bed seriously ill for several days. The man was required to appear before the magistrates to defend his account, which, according to Haller, he did with vigour. The story, which seems to have been a passing sensation, had a sad ending as the man's wife, who was pregnant at the time of the encounter, gave birth to a stillborn daughter. This is how Haller ends the account, except to ask Bullinger not to say anything about it, for '[Sager's] relatives and connections are powerful [people], who are unwilling for such things to be published.'

The story offers some interesting parallels with the Karlstadt tale: in both cases the appearance of a ghost is interpreted by Protestant writers as an indication of a bad death. Familiar aspects of ghost stories are prominent: quick deaths, appearances close to home, indications of demonic activity and the terrorising of locals. Crucial to Haller's account, as it would be for the work of Ludwig Lavater to be discussed later, was the verification of the story by an honest, pious man. The fact that Haller recounted the events to Bullinger, a confirmed persecutor of ghosts, reveals something of the concerns of Protestant church leaders about entrenched beliefs about ghosts. In both stories it is clear the presence of ghosts brought social discord; their appearance stirred up contested memories about the person in the community. The association of a ghost with a person's memory was an effective way of damaging that person's posthumous standing amongst the people by bringing into doubt the nature of the person's deeds and beliefs. In the case of Sager, the good and honest workman identifies the magistrate's failure to look after the poor, and it is clearly on account of this sin that the man is being punished in the next world. The Karlstadt tale is constructed to indicate that it was his preaching, and therefore his beliefs, which led to his death at the hand of the Devil. In both cases it was not in the interests of the ruling authorities to allow these stories to spread, for ghost stories could be used as a form of indirect attack upon established powers.

Ghost stories continued to find a place in Swiss literature through the seventeenth century. An unpublished Basle chronicle tells of a young girl in the house of Franz Werras who was frequently visited. On each occasion this lurid apparition would instruct her to follow him with a shovel to the cellar, where, at the ghost's behest, she was to start digging. There she found some coins and human bones. The ghost then declared, 'You have helped me to find rest and I shall no more appear to you. Forty-five years ago an eighteen-year-old boy was cut to pieces and buried here. Since then I have had no rest.' The ghost then let out three cries and vanished, never to return. The chronicler remarked that apparitions of the night generally did not speak.[18]

Another account from the seventeenth century reveals a different perspective on ghostly apparitions, this time among educated men.[19] In 1681 there was a case of witchcraft against Esther Wüstin, who was well known for her prophecies and who claimed to have conducted a long discussion with a ghost in the cellar of a cooper concerning the location of some buried treasure. The view of doctors Megerlin and Passavant was that to speak to a ghost without uttering a blessing was not wrong, for some good could come of this intercourse, such as the freeing of homes from malevolent guests, or indeed the locating of treasure. The chronicler brought the account to a close with the laconic observation that many people have seen ghosts, but few have the heart to speak to them. The imprisonment which Wüstin had already served was seen as sufficient punishment. In both of these seventeenth-century ghost stories, where the religious content is rather oblique, there is a hint of change, a suggestion that spectral accounts had moved away from their ecclesiastical settings, becoming secular stories of less interest to the Church. The heightened interest among Protestants of the Reformation period in the relationship of apparitions to the dead began to wane markedly in the following century.

---

[18] Buxtorf-Falkeisen, *Baslerische Stadt- und Landgeschichten*, III, p. 108.
[19] *Ibid.*, p. 109.

Much of the sixteenth-century material on ghosts, however, is found in chronicles or in the works of religious writers where such stories were employed to make particular points, most especially the guile and ubiquity of the Devil or the false religion of the Catholics. A passage from Hans Ardüser's Graubünden chronicle is evidence of the latter. Ardüser took the 1581 story of the appearance of the Virgin Mary to a shepherd on a mountain near Oberhalbstein as material for a polemic against the superstitious nature of Catholicism.[20] The apparition, which he called a ghost (*ein gespennst*), took the form of the Mother of God in order to deceive the people; and this, he lamented, it achieved with alacrity, for the people poured out of villages carrying banners to the site of the visitation, building a chapel in thanksgiving. In this case a ghost story has become an expression of confessional rivalries in the Graubünden, a means of discrediting Catholic popular piety.

Indeed, most references to ghosts are extremely negative and are generally made within the context of the intestinal battles between confessions. But even in the association of ghosts with false religion and the work of the Devil we find vestiges of older traditions in the Protestant world. The Devil's attempt to prevent the body of the nobleman being thrown in the river reflects his desire to disrupt the normal process by which the bodies of those who have committed suicide are discharged from the community. The young woman in Basle to whom the ghost reveals the bones is the active agent in bringing peace to this unquiet spirit. Only through the actions of a living person can the dead find rest. The Wüstin story from Basle bespeaks the continuing belief in commerce between the living and the dead. In all tales we find the survival of the medieval connection between ghosts and locality. Ghosts remain attached to particular places, seeking to conclude unresolved business and imploring the aid of the living. In short, ghost stories remained common currency throughout the early modern period, and Protestants, as we shall see again, retained and understood structures and details which gave these spectral accounts meaning.

The Protestant treatment of ghosts existed on several levels. Theologically, following medieval writers, there could be no toleration of the revenant, as the souls of the departed are incapable of returning to this world. While Protestant writers stood shoulder to shoulder with Catholics in denying the return of the dead, the whole matter was cast in a different light by their denial of Purgatory. This rejection of a doctrine which had won wide support in the fifteenth century determined that Protestants

---

[20] *Hans Ardüser's Ratische Chronik*, ed. J. Bott (Chur, 1877), p. 69.

would have to offer an alternative interpretation of the supernatural.[21] There is no evidence that the attack on Purgatory by Protestant reformers was a popular measure; it was essentially a necessary doctrinal issue, but one which had profound consequences for religious and social practices in the lands of the Reformation. Protestants had to be able to articulate a different relationship between the living and the dead in communities which believed in apparitions and portents. Simply to deprive people of traditional sources of spiritual comfort on doctrinal grounds was evidently hopeless, and certainly not the basis for a new church order. Protestants had to find ways of attending to the basic needs of the people, of speaking in a language which would be understood in the farmhouse and of drawing upon the natural rhythms of daily life. Thus it should not surprise us that in the middle decades of the sixteenth century, when Protestantism was primarily concerned with establishing a *cura animarum*, the treatment of the supernatural became more evident in the vernacular literature. Protestant writers sought to explain the natural world to the faithful in terms consonant with the theological principles of the Reformation. This was undertaken in cognisance of the fact that the success of the Reformation hung on the ability of the new churches to deliver where the pre-Reformation Church had in so many lands failed, in the provision of pastoral care. For Protestants this meant the creation of a vocabulary for the supernatural which was at once based on scripture, but at the same time addressed the realities of daily life in the villages. This was undertaken by a shift in the language of death and the supernatural.

This shift took place through a conscious and unconscious syncretism in which Protestant writers incorporated various aspects of medieval death culture into their own theological perspective. Hence the Protestant view of death, as seen in the Swiss lands, was an amalgam of medieval and evangelical theology as well as popular belief. Clearly, the notion of revenancy could not be retained, but many aspects of the roles played by the revenant in medieval culture were of importance and therefore needed to be re-cast. Most significantly, reciprocity, communication, kinship and the transcendence of God, concepts central to the doctrine of Purgatory and the medieval spiritual world, could not simply be cast aside. In essence they were retained through a new emphasis upon angels – biblically sound beings who act as protectors, intercessors and communicators in order to assuage the anxieties of the quick.

---

[21] See Peter Marshall's chapter in this volume; also his 'Fear, Purgatory and Polemic in Reformation England', in W. G. Naphy and P. Roberts (eds.), *Fear in Early Modern Society* (Manchester, 1997).

Ghosts and angels, though long part of medieval religious culture, occupied a particular moment in the European Reformation. This was the period marked by the implementation of Protestant polities, ranging from the middle decades of the sixteenth century through to the middle of the seventeenth century. The establishment of Protestant churches required various forms of accommodation. The cultures in which the reformations took place were constructed around notions of kinship and reciprocity which would not admit change and, indeed, the reformers themselves showed little inclination to transform the world into which they had been born. The presentation of apparitions, of angels and of death itself was couched in terms intended to retain older notions of kinship and the transcendence of the divine.[22] Very real theological change in the sixteenth century must be set against degrees of continuity.

The fullest and most influential work on angels and ghosts in the sixteenth century was *Das Gespensterbuch* by Ludwig Lavater, first printed in Zurich in 1569.[23] Lavater was a Zurich minister who briefly held the post of chief minister before his death in 1582. The work was quickly translated into German and then French, Spanish and Italian. The English translation appeared in 1572 with the title, *Of ghostes and spirites walking by nyght, and of strange noyses, crackes, and sundry forewarninges.*[24] The book had wide circulation not only in Protestant but also in Catholic circles, and later French Catholic writers Noel Tallepied and Pierre Le Loyer acknowledged their debts to Lavater's work, even if they did not accept his theological positions.[25]

---

[22] Jürgen Beyer has demonstrated the importance of angels in sixteenth- and seventeenth-century Lutheran culture. See his 'A Lübeck Prophet in Local and Lutheran Context', in Bob Scribner and Trevor Johnson (eds.), *Popular Religion in Germany and Central Europe, 1400–1800* (Basingstoke, 1996), pp. 166–82.

[23] Ludwig Lavater, *Von Gespaenstern, unghüren, faeln, und anderen wunderbaren dingen, so merteils wenn die menschen sterben soellend, oder wenn sunst grosse sachennd enderungen vorhanden sind, beschaehend, kurtzer und einfaltiger bericht* (Zurich, 1569), referred to as *Das Gespensterbuch.* There has been some work done on Lavater's text, cf. Dominic Langwehr, 'Ludwig Lavaters Gespensterbuch von 1569 im Rahmen der zeitgenössischen populären Literatur von Zürich', unpublished Lizentiatsarbeit (Zurich, 1982); also his 'Gut und böse Engel contra Arme Seelen. Reformierte Dämonologie und die Folgen für die Kunst, gezeigt an Ludwig Lavaters Gespensterbuch von 1569', in U. Altendorf and P. Jetzler (eds.), *Bilderstreit. Kulturwandel in Zwinglis Reformation* (Zurich, 1984), pp. 125–34.

[24] The text has been printed in an edition by J. Dover Wilson and May Yardley (Oxford, 1929).

[25] Noel Tallepied, *Psichologie, ou Traité de l'apparition des espirits à scavoir des âmes séparees, fantosmes, prodiges et accidents merveilleux, qui précèdent quelquefois la mort des grands personnages ou signifiell changemens gemens de la chose publique* (Paris, 1588); Pierre Le Loyer, *IIII Livres des spectres ou apparitions et visions d'espirits, anges et demons se monstrons sensiblement aux hommes* (Angers, 1586).

Lavater's goal was to collate all the witnesses from biblical, patristic, medieval and contemporary sources for the existence of ghosts. From this vast wealth of material he was determined to understand why men and women see apparitions, to explain the nature of these spectres; and to advise people how to conduct themselves when confronted by a ghost. The work, as its full title reveals, was intended to treat the issue of ghosts in a pastoral context. *Das Gespensterbuch* was not simply a didactic exercise in which ghosts and angels were cast as moral agents. The underlying logic of the text was a firm conviction that ghosts appear to the living. His proof was not experiential, but secondary, based on the accounts of pious and learned Christians such as Melanchthon: 'Philip Melanchthon writes in his book *De anima* that he himself has seen some ghost, and that he knows many people of good credit, who not only claim to have seen ghosts themselves, but have talked to them at great length.'[26]

Das Gespensterbuch is a long work, which for the most part consists of anecdotal information shaped by clear-cut theological argument. Much of the material is based on older ideas of ghosts, such as, for instance, their propensity to be found in certain locations: in the wilderness (woods and mountainous areas), where battles have been fought and where executions are carried out.[27] Other sites include graveyards, monasteries, castles or any place where the 'black arts' are practised.[28] Lavater's account of the attachment of ghosts to particular locations has clear echoes of late medieval ideas of Purgatory.[29] The appearance of ghosts is also connected with tumult and change, for great events (battles, plagues, revolts) are announced by forerunners and apparitions.[30] The world is full of spirits, benevolent and malign, and the reason for this, according to Lavater, is revealed in scripture. Lavater saw in Isaiah's prophecy against Babylon evidence that God had unleashed spiritual forces in the world to punish the wicked for their apostasy.[31] Two central points arise

---

[26] Lavater, *Gespensterbuch*, fol. 36r.   [27] *Ibid.*, fol. 46r.

[28] On this point, see Jean-Claude Schmitt, *Ghosts in the Middle Ages: the Living and the Dead in Medieval Society*, tr. Teresa Lavender Fagan (Chicago, 1998), esp. pp. 171–90. Heinrich Bullinger also wrote extensively on this subject, see his *Wider der schwartzen Kunst, Aberglaubigs segnen, unwahrhafftigs Warsagen, und andere derglichen von Gott verbottne Kunst* (Frankfurt-am-Main, 1586).

[29] Jacques Le Goff, *The Birth of Purgatory*, tr. Arthur Goldhammer (Aldershot, 1984).

[30] Lavater, *Gespensterbuch*, fol. 47v.

[31] Lavater referred to the following text: 'Listen, a tumult on the mountains as of a great multitude! Listen, an uproar of kingdoms, of nations gathering together! The Lord of hosts is mustering an army for battle. They come from a distant land, from the end of the Heavens, the Lord and the weapons of his indignation, to destroy the whole earth.' Isaiah 13:4–5.

here which merit iteration: the spiritual world is ultimately controlled by God, and all spirits, regardless of disposition, exist only in relation to humans. They are not, however, constrained to the visible world, for another landscape inhabited by ghosts is dreams. Citing the biblical examples of Joseph, Peter and Paul, Lavater argued that God makes use of the dream world to communicate messages to the living. St Augustine, whose views on Purgatory wavered, was clear that the dream world belonged to God, and he was cited by Lavater as an authority.[32]

Ghosts take many forms: they can appear with the visage of a long-lost child, spouse or friend, or of an unknown person. They can seem to be either a man or a woman; some are handsome, others hideous. Some ghosts appear on foot, others ride, and they can make a variety of noises. As Karlstadt's son recounted, these spirits can also take animal form as dogs, cats, deer, and especially as wolves.[33] Lavater wrote:

> The nature and frequency of ghostly appearances is uneven, as one will understand from the examples that I have provided. They manifest themselves in numerous ways: sometimes they take the form of a person who is known to us, either still alive or long dead. Other times they take the form of an unknown person. To the men of the forest (*waldbruederen*) and monks, ghosts frequently appear in womanly guise in order to stir them to immoral acts. They also appear as animals: they take the form of four-footed animals (dog, pig, horse, goat, cat, rabbit), as flying animals, and as creeping beasts . . . such as snakes, which the pagans greatly honoured and used in acts of repentance.[34]

Lavater accepted the medieval idea that ghosts are almost always known to those who see them and that they appear in particular locations for particular reasons.

Lavater's interest in ghost stories fifty years after the outbreak of the Reformation may strike the reader as somewhat odd. The sustained attack on Purgatory by evangelical writers in the early years of the Reformation had surely, one would think, sounded the death knell for ghosts. Medieval ghost tales were based upon the idea that the dead returned from Purgatory because their lives were not yet complete.[35] They still belonged to the community of the living. There could be no

---

[32] On Augustine and ghosts, see Le Goff, *Birth of Purgatory*, pp. 79–82; Schmitt, *Ghosts in the Middle Ages*, pp. 17–27.

[33] Lavater, *Gespensterbuch*, fol. 48v.   [34] *Ibid.*, fol. 48r.

[35] This idea that ghosts are the dead returning from Purgatory was never taught definitively by the Church; it was, however, a widely held popular belief. On this point see the essay by Nancy Caciola in this volume.

place, however, in the Protestant economy of salvation for the return of the dead from the 'Third Place', as Lavater quickly acknowledged:

> That neither the souls of the faithful nor of infidels wander upon the earth when they have been severed from their bodies I shall make plain and evident to you by the following reasons. First, it is certain that those who depart die either in faith or unbelief. Concerning those who depart in right belief, their souls are kept by Christ in possession of eternal life. Those who die in unbelief straightway become partakers of eternal damnation.[36]

Lavater employed the story of the rich man and Lazarus (Luke 16:19–31) as the biblical foundation for his rejection of revenancy:

> That the souls of the faithful and unfaithful, who after their death are either in Heaven or Hell, do not return to the earth before the Day of Judgement, may be understood from the parable of the rich man clothed in purple and Lazarus, as we read in Luke. For when the rich man asked Abraham to send Lazarus to him to cool his tongue, Abraham answered, saying that there is a great gulf set so that no one can pass from here [from Abraham's Bosom] to you [Hell], nor can one pass from you to us. And when he sought him, that he might send Lazarus to his father's house to admonish his five brethren, he [Abraham] said to him: they have Moses and the prophets, let them hear them. And again if they do not hear Moses and the prophets neither will they believe, though one rose from the dead.[37]

Across the Protestant front there was a broad consensus that the dead could not return to the living. At the moment of death their fate is determined, with only two possible destinations, Heaven or Hell. This seemingly simplified geography of the afterlife, however, was not without its problems. Protestants quickly faced questions relating to the temporal sequence of their interpretation of death. If the dead are immediately in Heaven or Hell from the moment their terrestrial life ends, then what about the time between death and the Last Judgement? Some reformers were attracted to the idea of a sleep of the soul, and indeed Luther referred to elector Johann, who had died in 1530, as 'one of the holy sleepers'.[38] Calvin emphatically rejected the notion of sleep, preferring to use the language of Abraham's Bosom, a type of antechamber for the elect in which they have a foretaste of eternal bliss as they await the consummation of time.[39] Equally, the damned are able to contemplate their punishment, sensing something of the heat of the eternal fires. Although

---

[36] Lavater, *Gespensterbuch*, fols. 59v–60r.   [37] *Ibid.*, fol. 61r.

[38] Susan Karant-Nunn, *The Reformation of Ritual: an Interpretation of Early Modern Germany* (London, 1997), p. 148.

[39] Heinrich Quistrop, *Calvin's Doctrine of the Last Things* (London, 1955), p. 92.

Protestants recognised that there was probably some 'other' form of existence between this world and eternity, they would admit of no movement within these 'transitory' states. The bliss or horror of eternity was perhaps not complete, but the die was cast. In this sense the notion of reciprocity which so animated late medieval ecclesiastical life, grounded in the doctrine of Purgatory, was severed from the vine. Ghosts, therefore, as Lavater explicitly spelled out, cannot be the dead returning to this world.

A book about ghosts which denies their existence in its opening chapters would not seem to have much to hold the interest of the reader. Lavater's purpose, however, extended well beyond a simple denial of revenancy along standard Protestant lines. His principal aim was pastoral, not doctrinal. Lavater sought to explain what people saw when visited by apparitions, and how they should conduct themselves. To this end Lavater alighted upon the biblical text 1 Samuel 28, the story of the witch of Endor:[40]

> if Samuel indeed appeared, that must have happened either by the will of God or by a work of magic. But it was not God's will that Samuel should return, for he has condemned necromancy and forbids us to seek the counsel of the dead. That the Spirit of God should act contrary to this, or permit the saints to act thus, or was present with those who so acted, cannot be allowed. Or that these things were done by force or act of magic we likewise reject, for the wicked spirit has no rule or power over the souls of the faithful to bring them out of their places when he wishes if they be in the hand of God, and in the Bosom of Abraham (*Schoß Abrahe*). Neither has he any power over filthy or unclean swine, for he was driven (as we read in Matthew 8) to beg leave before he could enter into a herd of swine. How then should he have power over the souls of men?[41]

The ghost of Samuel, according to Lavater, was a demonic apparition which only confirmed the despondent Saul's loss of God's favour: the deception only served to compound the king's mendacity. In contrast, had the apparition been sent by God, it would have served a pastoral role:

> if he [the ghost] had been the true Samuel, he would have no doubt exhorted Saul to repentance, to have him seek aid from God, to have him put his whole confidence in Him or at least to have given him some comfort, or counselled him to fight against his enemies with courage, for although prophets do often beat and threaten men, so they also revive and solace them. But because this

---

[40] On medieval interpretations of this passage, see Jean-Claude Schmitt, 'Le spectre de Samuel et la sorcière d'Endor. Avatars historiques d'un recit biblique. I Rois 28', *Etudes Rurales* 105–6 (1987), pp. 37–64.

[41] Lavater, *Gespensterbuch*, fol. 68v.

Samuel said nothing other than that God was displeased with Saul, and had already forsaken him, we may believe that he was not the true Samuel but a mere counterfeit. The ancient fathers write that the true Samuel was not seen.[42]

The tension in Lavater's book is created by his acceptance of apparitions, but denial of ghosts. What men and women see and hear, Lavater explained, are angels. They are not the dead, but they can take the form of the dead in order to fool the living; for there are good and malevolent angels, though, sadly, the latter appear more frequently. This was by no means a new argument; Lavater, in setting out the Protestant view of human experiences in the world, was reprising a traditional position. He spoke in terms of a spiritual battle carried out in the natural world, with human souls as the prize. Satan can take the form of familiar visage or voice to trick a person, or to frighten him, but Satan cannot bring the dead back into this world.

Lavater's principal interest lay in instructing the Christian person in how to behave when confronted by an apparition, and this fills much of the last three chapters of his eight-chapter book. When visited by an angel, it is impossible to know whether the angel's intentions are benevolent or malign, for those in Satan's service are much cleverer than humans. Therefore, Lavater argued, one must not enter into conversation. If it appears evil, then a statement of faith should be uttered, and nothing more. If it appears to be a good angel, or if the person is not sure, remain quiet, for if the angel has a purpose from God then nothing that person says or does will have any effect. If a person is plagued by apparitions the local church should pray for him or her, thus deploying the bonds of kinship in the spiritual battle. The primary weapon of a malevolent spirit is psychological, for in moments of extreme fear a person is in grave danger of losing faith. The Church, as the community of the faithful, is the first line of protection against this affliction. Lavater's counsel is towards passivity on the part of lay people; they were to affirm their faith in the face of adversity and the supernatural. The unstated principle in the work is that although there are different forms of spirits, in the end lay people are unable to discern their character with any certainty. This must be left to those, like himself, properly trained in interpreting God's will, making the Protestant position ultimately as clerical as the Catholic.

Das Gespensterbuch is an encyclopedic treatment of Protestant belief about ghosts and angels. As a collector of ghost stories and folklore Lavater provides us with crucial insights into the beliefs of the sixteenth century. As

---

[42] *Ibid.*, fol. 70r.

a theologian he has provided a compendious treatment of Reformed Protestant beliefs about the afterlife. As a church leader he has crafted the text to enable ministers and lay people to deal pastorally with experiences of the supernatural. The book clearly belongs to the genre of instructional and didactic literature of the second generation of reformers; it is a remarkable compilation of material and theological argument. Yet at its core there remains an uncertainty. The fine lines of the Protestant denunciation of revenancy become obscured in the anecdotes collected by Lavater. He was well aware that the people remained persuaded of the reality of wandering spirits and that the dead still dwelt among the living. This might be decried by Protestant preachers as the work of the Devil, but that did nothing to diminish the force of this belief, which, as the Karlstadt case illustrates, had a hold on the reformers themselves. The renewed emphasis upon angels by Protestants was rooted in an attempt to bring this very real world of apparitions within a theologically sound context.

In Coburg at Michaelmas in 1530 Martin Luther preached:

> Dear child, curse not, otherwise the Devil is beside you and he will throw you into the water or lay some misfortune in your path. However, so that the child does not become hysterical, one should also say, but, dear child, our Lord God has also placed an angel by your side, so that when the Devil seeks to throw you in the water, or to frighten you in your sleep, he will protect and restore you.[43]

The archangel Michael, according to Revelation 12:7, led the armies of Heaven against Satan in a cosmic battle which Luther interpreted as taking place in the life of each and every Christian. The Christian life, Luther admonished his hearers, was a constant struggle between evil and good: Heaven and Hell are immediately present to each person in the form of angels and devils locked in a combat for the salvation or damnation of the soul. The language was hardly intended to be figurative: Luther adamantly believed in the presence of angels and devils arrayed against one another.

Luther's sermon captures the sense of intimacy of the angels, an idea which would spread across the Protestant world in the sixteenth century. Every man and woman, at every moment in his or her life, is surrounded by angels, for whose presence they should give thanks every day. The Devil, on the other hand, is closer than one's shirt or skirt, though this is recognised by only a few. The importance of angels and devils for Luther,

---

[43] Martin Luther, 'Sermo de anglis', *D. Martin Luthers Werke: Critische Gesamtausgabe* (55 vols., Weimar 1883–1987), XXXII, p. 120.

as for the later Reformed tradition, was that they were agents of human emotions. They stirred feelings of fear and anxiety, as well as bringing comfort and solace. There is a sense in which humans, as fallen beings, are only moved by external forces, angels and devils. Without these agents they remain impervious to damnation and salvation. Temptation is a sign that the Devil is at hand, whilst the fact that there is order in the world (villages, families, work) indicates the prevalence of benevolent angels. Citing Matthew 8:28, when Christ meets the demoniacs in the country of Gadarenes, Luther argued that every poor soul has to deal not with one devil but with a whole host at one time. This is countered by a host of angels. The devils are much cleverer and stronger than humans, and the whole order of the empire would be overthrown in less than an hour if it were not for the protective force of angels.

Luther's sermon and other writings exercised a decisive influence on the development of Protestant pastoral literature. The early Reformation remained beholden to medieval categories of good and bad deaths, of preparation for death and the reality of apparitions. Through the appropriation of angels, Protestants attempted to make sense of the experiential world, to provide spiritual solace in forms recognisable to the people. By linking angels with human emotions they could counter the fear stirred by ghosts with the assurance of God's presence in the lives of the people. This was not merely a remote God of sermons, but a God who allowed himself to be anthropomorphised in the form of angels.

A 1561 collection of sermons by Ambrosius Blarer serves as another example of this current.[44] Blarer, who lived from 1492 to 1564, was a native of southern Germany and an active proponent of reform in Württemberg and his native city of Constance, before being forced to flee to the Swiss Confederation following the imposition of the Interim in 1548.[45] He was a talented musician and liturgist and an inspiring preacher who had little interest in doctrinal exactitude, preferring to dwell on the Christian life. The sermon collection of 1561 runs to 114 leaves and was the work of Jacob Fünklin, who recorded what Blarer preached. Fünklin wrote in his preface that he had undertaken this work because so many people requested copies of Blarer's sermons, and that Blarer was unlikely to have them printed.[46]

The theme of the sermons, as the title suggests, was Christian prepara-

---

[44] *Der geistlich Schatz Christenlicher vorbereitung und gloubigs trosts wider Tod und Sterben . . . .gepredigt durch Ambrosium Blarer* (Zurich, 1566).

[45] On Blarer, see Bernd Moeller, 'Ambrosius Blarer (1492–1564)', *Theologische Realenzyklopädia*, ed. G. Müller (Berlin and New York, 1977–), vɪ, pp. 711–15.

[46] Blarer, *Der geistlich Shatz*, sig. A iii.

tion for death. In this sense, Blarer followed the traditional *ars moriendi* form commonly employed, as Susan Karant-Nunn has shown, in Lutheran devotional literature.[47] What distinguished Blarer's work from the great number of texts on dying which appeared later in the century was its relatively loose structure. Blarer was not particularly interested in prescribing necessary acts or rituals, the death-bed is not the focus of attention, and the sacraments were hardly mentioned. In this sense his work has the character of Luther's writings on the subject. Blarer intended treating the daily life of the Christian, for, as he remarked at the opening of his first sermon, every hour brings the moment of death closer. The purpose of the work was to provide a correct spiritual framework for the people's emotions.

Central to Blarer's sermons was the attempt to answer questions which people had put to him about death, the status of the dead and the next world. Would a man recognise his wife in Heaven? What if she was not there? One theme which emerged repeatedly was the fear of the people that they might lose their salvation on account of physical pain at the time of death, when the excruciating agony of a final illness causes a person to scream out blasphemies, or to rant and rave in a state of delirium. Does this mean that the Devil has won? Blarer's answer was generous. The pain and loss of rationality afflict the godly as well as the godless, but with a difference. Reason is indeed God's gift to humanity, but its departure does not indicate a withdrawal of his favour from the elect, for the moment of death is no longer considered crucial. The faithful have lived their lives according to God's word, and for this they shall receive their due reward. Pain is the Devil's pyrrhic victory, a consequence of humanity's fallen nature, but it is not the final word. Those gathered around the death-bed should reflect upon a life of faith rather than the fevered ravings of a person's last minutes.[48] The good death comes at the end of a good life, and those who still enjoy their health should give thanks to God and amend their lives whilst there is time.[49] The Protestant emphasis upon providence is thus employed to bring comfort to those experiencing the horrors of death.

Much of Blarer's discussion of death, especially in his second sermon, dwelt upon the importance of kinship in life and death. When speaking about the relationship between the dead and the living, however, the timbre of Blarer's argument is changed. Rather than asserting providence against the world of experience, he draws deeply from people's sources of

---

[47] Karant-Nunn, *Reformation of Ritual*, pp. 162–70.
[48] Blarer, *Der geistlich Schatz*, fols. 16v–17r.   [49] *Ibid.*, fols. 26r–26v.

identity to develop a more affective view of the bonds with those who have departed. Once more the starting point is fear, this time fear of loss. Blarer freely admitted that it hurt desperately when a person loses his or her beloved:

> Separation greatly hurts the natural man and this makes death abominable and hard for him. He may have a dear wife, or a wife may have a dear husband. He may have children, a brother, sister, or good friends, good neighbours with whom he has spent many fine years with many good times. This is an especial price to pay.[50]

Loss is a consequence of sin, but Blarer's consolation lay in the hope of reunion:

> Those for whom death is unbearable, because they must leave their beloved, must realise (and thereby console themselves) that he should not only think from whom he must travel when he dies, but rather to which people he will come after this life.[51]

Blarer continued that those who have lost a wife, child, brother, sister, father, mother or other should never doubt that they will see them again in the next world, and that this time they shall never have to say goodbye. The relationships which one has on earth will be made eternal in Heaven. This, as Blarer well understood, was a problematic position for Christian theology, which for the most part argues that marriage is an earthly institution. Like all good pastoral writers, however, Blarer allowed himself a considerable degree of ideological latitude and a certain elasticity of language in addressing people whose lives were nothing short of brutal. Blarer's language is redolent of the southern German culture in which he preached and lived; he spoke of friends gathering once again around their *Stammtisch* in Heaven. He used the language of the farmhouse and of the tavern as images of eternal life. Thus through these series of sermons on death and the dead we find an interlacing of providential and experiential language in response to very basic concerns of the people.

It is in this context that Blarer, like so many other writers, introduced angels ordained by God to stand ready to aid the Christian:

> to secure our way into the next life God has ordained the beloved and holy angels that they might serve our welfare by being with us at all times. They walk with us in the journey of life to the judge, and they rejoice greatly when we live a holy and godly life in this world.[52]

---

[50] *Ibid.*, fol. 35v.   [51] *Ibid.*, fol. 37r.
[52] *Ibid.*, fol. 56r–56v.

Blarer portrayed angels as protectors from the fear of death engendered by the continuing belief in Purgatory and ghosts.

Angels, therefore, became the spiritual forces working for good in a fallen world. 'Wherefore', wrote Heinrich Bullinger in the ninth sermon of the Fourth Decade, 'we shall not miss much of the mark, if we say that angels are good spirits, Heavenly substances (I mean incorruptible), created for the ministry or service of God and man'.[53] Calvin wrote in his *Harmony of the Gospels* that, 'to the angels is committed the care of the whole Church and that they succour individual members so far as their necessity and situation demands'.[54] Protestant writers of the sixteenth century essentially adopted *in toto* medieval angelology. Heinrich Bullinger, that most unspeculative of Protestant writers, loftily stated his lack of interest in the orders of the angels, citing Augustine's words that they may be true, but he could not know. Yet he then admitted that there is in scripture ample evidence for the various types of angels, and he affirmed the traditional threefold order: first, seraphim, cherubim and thrones; secondly, lordships, virtues and powers; and thirdly, principalities, archangels and angels.[55] Each of these names referred to specific functions of the angels in the offices of Heaven. Thrones, for example, are those angels which continuously worship God face to face; lordships are the means by which God carries out his rule of the cosmos; powers are God's army; cherubim are wisdom and seraphim love. Bullinger's sermon on the angels reflects the unquestioning manner in which Protestant writers adopted established teachings on angels. All were careful to distinguish that angels are spiritual essences created by God and given bodies in order that they might be visible to humans. These bodies are not like human bodies: they are incorruptible and are really only borrowed for the occasion. Angels are not the dead, they have never sinned.

Having appropriated the essential medieval doctrine of angelic bodies, Bullinger outlined why God makes use of them: 'For among other innumerable and the greatest benefits of God, whereat not without cause we are astonished, this is not to be counted the least, that he hath given us angels to be our servants.'[56] God has no need for angels. They are entirely for human benefit, for they carry out his ministry in the world. This is the central point of the frequent use of angels in Protestant vernacular

---

[53] Henry Bullinger, *The Decades: The Fourth Decade*, ed. T. Harding (Cambridge, 1851), p. 328.

[54] John Calvin, *Harmony of the Gospels*, ed. T. Torrance (3 vols., Edinburgh, 1972), ii, p. 218.

[55] Bullinger, *Decades*, p. 338.

[56] *Ibid.*, p. 339.

literature. The pivotal biblical text, cited again and again, was Hebrews 1:14: 'Are not all angels spirits of the divine service, sent to serve for the sake of those who are to inherit salvation?'

According to Protestant writers, God entrusted the angels with the safekeeping of Christ's Church. Following from their Greek name, angels are messengers of God who move swiftly on account of their weightless bodies. From scripture these writers discern a variety of activities within the angelic ministry to humanity: angels praise God and sing hymns; they bring news from the next world to this one; they set themselves against false prophets; they carry out the commands of God; they protect the faithful and they punish the wicked. Angels have no personality of their own. That they have a human form is a concession from God to the sensual nature of humanity. Their human characteristics are pure divine accommodation. As Bullinger wrote:

> For otherwise those blessed spirits can rejoice, in whom there is no human affection; which affections nevertheless are not only attributed to them, but to God himself tropically or by a figure, and as they say ἀνθρωποπαθῶς, that is, after the affection of man, to the end that our minds may better understand and more easily conceive spiritual things, as it were by parables.[57]

Angels, therefore, are a means by which God allows humans to understand his presence in the world anthropomorphically.[58] But the force of the argument goes beyond this. The angels act because they love humans; their whole existence is to care for them, to serve them. In so doing, they only carry out God's will. Therefore, by analogy, the service and love they demonstrate in the world is nothing other than God's care for humanity. Rudolf Gwalther, Bullinger's close friend and successor, in preaching on Acts 10, the story of the angel and Cornelius, gives the following explication for God's use of visible messengers:

> But not contented to have appointed all things to serve our use, he sendeth out his angels also, (as Paul teacheth) for the mynistrie of those who that be his. And such is the maner of this apparition, that it is voyde of al suspicion of craft or subtletie. For in the clear light, about the ix hour of the day, doth the angel come in unto him, in a visible fourme, (yet representing some more majestie, than is in man) and calleth Cornelius by his propre name,

---

[57] *Ibid.*, p. 340.

[58] Peter Carrell has argued that the appearance of Jesus as an angel in Revelation 1:13–16 and 14:14 was fundamentally pastoral, demonstrating Christ's closeness to the Church. This, I would argue, is essentially what the Protestant reformers were attempting to convey. Cf. Peter R. Carrell, *Jesus and the Angels. Angelology and the Christology of the Apocalypse of John* (Cambridge, 1997), p. 218.

thereby to make him the more attent to receyve the commandments of God. For God useth so plainely to deal with us, that we need suspect no guyle, such, as commonly useth to be in apparitions of devils, which are always dark and doubtfull. And yet not withstanding Cornelius his great and fervant study of religion, he is abashed, at the sight of the angell. Which thing as it may be attributed to the infirmitie of man, so is it the property of the godly, to be afraid at the presence of godly majestie.[59]

Although God is beyond all human emotions, he has enabled humans to conceive of his passions through the ministry of angels. The angels were the Protestants' understanding of God's emotions in the created order.

Having externalised human emotions in forms which the people might recognize, the Protestant writers drew again from Scripture to explain how God's protection of the faithful was immediate. This was through the language of guardian angels. The crucial text here was Matthew 18:10–11: 'Take care that you do not despise one of those little ones; for I tell you, in Heaven their angels continually see the face of my Father in Heaven.' This text is cited in virtually every Protestant sermon on angels, though interpretations awarded it varied considerably. For Luther, it was clear evidence that each Christian has his/her own guardian angel who accompanied that person to protect him or her from evil. Luther advised the faithful in his Michaelmas sermon to give thanks to God every morning for the continuing protection of their angel.

Later Protestant thought, as found in the sermons of Ambrosius Blarer and John Calvin, was less inclined to speak of individual guardian angels. Throughout his sermons Blarer referred to the protective work of die Engeln, plural. Calvin was clearly troubled by the subject, writing on Matthew 18:10:

Some take this verse as if God ascribed a particular angel to each individual; but this is weak. For Christ's words do not say that one angel is devoted to this or that person all the time; and indeed it conflicts with the whole teaching of Scripture, which bears witness that the angels camp around the godly (Ps 34.7) and that many, not just one, are appointed as guardians of each believer.[60]

Angels were clearly not the dead. Nor, according to Protestants, could they be equated with saints' cults. The intense Protestant interest in angels, however, had much to do with their understanding of death. The

---

[59] Rudolf Gwalther, In acta apostolorum per divum lucam descripta, homiliae CLXX lll (Zurich, 1567). I have only had access to the English translation, An Hundred, threescore and fiftene homelyes or sermons, uppon the Acts of the apostles (London, 1572), p. 428.

[60] Calvin, Harmony of Gospels, II, p. 218.

Protestant language of angels and ghosts of the sixteenth century was an attempt to harness popular beliefs and shape them with the biblical understanding of such things. It was an attempt to place popular belief on the moral field created by Protestant readings of the Bible. We must be careful, however, to avoid seeing this merely as a didactic programme of inculcation. There were various dynamics at work. Protestant writers wrote about apparitions and angels because they themselves believed in them. They too craved the reciprocity and mediation offered by the rituals against which they had turned their faces. There was no question of returning to these rites *per se*, but an examination of Protestant ritual and writing as it emerged through the sixteenth and seventeenth centuries reveals the extent to which many of these affective elements of medieval religion were embraced under a different guise. There is a good deal left to be said about Protestant notions of intercession in the sixteenth century. How far angels took up the intercessory roles performed by the dead remains to be examined. The period of the Reformation was a time of overlapping influences which manifested themselves in blatant inconsistencies of belief and practice. The subject of death, ghosts and angels throws some light on the extent to which sixteenth-century Protestants still occupied the houses of their fathers. The measure of religious change and continuity is not an exact science, for the old and new cohabited in the hearts and minds of all early modern people.

Ghosts were roundly denied by Protestants on the ground that it was unacceptable to conceive of the dead returning to living. This was not new: Augustine had been extremely eloquent on that point. Throughout the lands of the Swiss Reformation, however, ghosts continued to make their presence felt to both the common people and the Protestant reformers. Although the latter declared these apparitions to be demons or malign angels, the ways in which ghosts were described on the pages of Protestant tracts reveal the extent to which traditional forms and interpretations retained their hold. The matter was primarily a pastoral one. Protestants accepted that people continued to believe in ghosts, and they, as the Karlstadt tale makes evident, were credulous participants in the spiritual battle which manifested itself in apparitions. To speak to the people about death and the dead Protestants conjoined traditional beliefs with their refined theological positions in a marriage which was not without its contradictions. The importance of angels for pastoral care, in aiding the faithful to deal with the vicissitudes of existence, meant that there was a considerable degree of accommodation on the part of sincere and persuaded Protestants. They were interested in ghosts and angels because these forces were real and an integral part of each community.

Clearly medieval notions of mediation were still very present in Protestant teachings on angels. The whole point of pastoral care, as these men understood very well, was to comfort with the familiar. This would eventually change as religious and social beliefs evolved, and as Protestants and Catholics alike continued their war on popular superstition, but in the sixteenth century, once we move beyond the internecine polemic which so clearly delineated the two camps, we find many shared assumptions about some very old questions.

6 'The map of God's word': geographies of the afterlife in Tudor and early Stuart England

Peter Marshall

The idea of the survival of the human personality after death has from the earliest days been a hallmark of Christian belief. Moreover, like most other religions, Christianity came to assign the souls of the dead to locations invisible to and (usually) unreachable by the living; not merely to one undifferentiated 'place of the dead', but to a variety of places with distinct orientations both in respect to the created world, and to each other. In their reconstructions of the intellectual outlook and spatial imagination of the Middle Ages, historians have recognised that the formation of a 'geography of the afterlife' was a process not peripheral but central to contemporary religious and eschatological concerns.[1] In modern Christian thought, by contrast, life after death (in so far as it impinges at all) tends to be imagined in terms of some kind of radical transformation of consciousness, rather than an experience of spatial relocation to another place in the universe. A recent 'history of Heaven' concludes that in the late twentieth century Heaven has become 'a state of vague identity'. As for Hell, another modern survey puts it bluntly: 'Hell has become something of an embarrassment.'[2]

As this chapter will demonstrate, however, unease with the affirmation of a precise spatial location for disembodied souls is not an exclusively modern phenomenon. In the course of the seventeenth century an increasing number of English religious radicals would be prepared to reject the very notion of a localised afterlife, to assert that Heaven and

---

[1] See C. Carozzi, 'La géographie de l'au-delà et sa signification pendant le haut moyen âge', *Popoli e Paesi nella Cultura Altomedievale* (Spoleto, 1983), and most significantly, J. Le Goff, *The Birth of Purgatory*, tr. A. Goldhammer (Aldershot, 1984).

[2] C. McDannell and B. Lang, *Heaven: a History* (New Haven and London, 1990), p. 352; A. Turner, *The History of Hell* (London, 1993), p. 238.

Hell were no more than spiritual states experienced in this life.[3] At the same time more respectable intellectual sceptics would begin that process of interrogation of traditional eschatologies which D. P. Walker has styled *The Decline of Hell*, a recognisable milestone on the road to those happy hunting grounds of the historical profession, Modernity and Secularisation.[4] In tracing the origins of seventeenth-century rejections of Heaven and Hell it has been usual to cite the rapid dissemination of sceptical ideas in the turmoil of civil war, or to point to a sub-stratal tradition of sceptical and 'atheistical' speculation, a lineage of true unbelievers.[5] The emphasis here will be rather different, concerning itself in the main not with the opinions of deviants and dissidents, but with the discourses of generally 'respectable' theologians. It will be argued that over the period from the break with Rome up to roughly 1630, distinct cracks in the edifice of conventional belief about a localised afterlife can be detected spreading slowly, almost imperceptibly, from within the bastions of orthodox Christianity itself. This took place primarily because, over the course of the English Reformation, reformers of all kinds were determined to dissociate themselves irrevocably from the typologies and language of pre-Reformation 'geographies of the afterlife', in particular from the notion of a 'third place', Purgatory. In doing so they can be seen to prepare the ground and set the terms for a fundamental reappraisal of the relationship between the known physical world on the one hand, and what David Cressy has recently called the 'conceptual geography of salvation', on the other.[6]

The 'geographies' of the future life which reformers would discard with such vehemence in the sixteenth century were the product of a long collective process of imaginative construction. They drew eclectically on classical traditions, scriptural exegesis and visionary accounts of otherworldly journeys. The vision literature of the early Middle Ages popularised the

---

[3] K. Thomas, *Religion and the Decline of Magic* (Harmondsworth, 1973), pp. 202–3; C. Hill, *The World Turned Upside Down* (Harmondsworth, 1975), pp. 151–83, 185, 214, 221–2, 228, 339, 397; N. Smith, 'The Charge of Atheism and the Language of Radical Speculation 1640–1660', in M. Hunter and D. Wooton (eds.), *Atheism from the Reformation to the Enlightenment* (Oxford, 1992), pp. 136–7, 139, 158.

[4] D. P. Walker, *The Decline of Hell: Seventeenth-century Discussions of Eternal Torment* (London, 1964).

[5] P. C. Almond, *Heaven and Hell in Enlightenment England* (Cambridge, 1994), p. 43; Smith, 'Language of Radical Speculation', p. 134; Thomas, *Religion and the Decline of Magic*, pp. 145, 198–200, 202; Hill, *World Turned Upside Down*, pp. 26–7, 175.

[6] D. Cressy, *Birth, Marriage, and Death: Ritual, Religion, and the Life-cycle in Tudor and Stuart England* (Oxford, 1997), p. 396.

idea that souls would pass to various locations in the next life, and it made the association between entrances to the other world and places on this earth, such as Mount Etna, or the so-called 'St Patrick's Purgatory' in Ireland.[7] Yet as Aaron Gurevich has observed, early medieval beliefs about the afterlife lacked 'spatial integrity': 'the Other World of visions is a conglomerate of uncoordinated points'.[8] The magisterial work of Jacques Le Goff has traced a process which he terms a growing 'spatial conception' of the afterlife, and the emergence by the twelfth century of 'a new geography of the other world, which was no longer made up of tiny receptacles . . . but consisted rather of vast territories'. The crucial development came towards the end of the twelfth century with the coining of the noun 'Purgatorium' as the definitive identification of the place where the majority of souls would be confined for a lengthy period after death.[9] In fact, by the late Middle Ages, the clear consensus of theological opinion was that there were five distinct places occupying the 'space' of the next life: Heaven, Hell, Purgatory, a *Limbus Infantium* for the souls of children who had died before receiving baptism, and a *Limbus Patrum* which had housed the souls of the patriarchs who died before the incarnation, and which Christ had visited after his death on the cross in the so-called 'Harrowing of Hell'.

There were, however, latent in medieval teaching about the afterlife a number of disputed or unanswered questions. The existence and theological rationale of Purgatory had been formally defined by the Councils of Lyons in 1274 and Florence in 1439, but no such official sanction had been provided for the teaching on the Limbos. Nor had any definitive answer ever been offered to the question posed by the Cistercian Caesarius of Heisterbach in the thirteenth century: 'ubi est purgatorium?'.[10] Nonetheless, there seems to have been little objection to the idea that this was a question worth asking, and that it ought in principle to be possible

---

[7] On medieval vision literature, see T. Wright, *St Patrick's Purgatory: an Essay on the Legends of Purgatory, Hell, and Paradise, current during the Middle Ages* (London, 1844); H. R. Patch, *The Other World according to Descriptions in Medieval Literature* (New York, 1970); J. Le Goff, 'The Learned and Popular Dimensions of Journeys in the Otherworld in the Middle Ages', in S. Kaplan (ed.), *Understanding Popular Culture: Europe from the Middle Ages to the Nineteenth Century* (Berlin, 1984); A. Gurevich, *Medieval Popular Culture: Problems of Belief and Perception*, tr. J. M. Bak and P. A. Hollingsworth (Cambridge, 1988), chap. 4; E. Gardiner (ed.), *Visions of Heaven and Hell before Dante* (New York, 1989); A. Morgan, *Dante and the Medieval Other World* (Cambridge, 1986).

[8] Gurevich, *Medieval Popular Culture*, pp. 132–3.

[9] Le Goff, *Birth of Purgatory*, quotes at pp. 32, 228.

[10] R. A. Bowyer, 'The Role of the Ghost Story in Medieval Christianity', in H. R. Ellis Davidson and W. M. S. Russell (eds.), *The Folklore of Ghosts* (Cambridge, 1981), p. 183.

to 'map' the afterlife, to establish schema for the geographical relations of the constituent parts. Most firmly established was the idea of the proximity of Purgatory and Hell, resulting in what Le Goff, following Arturo Graf, has called an 'infernalisation' of Purgatory.[11] Aquinas thought it likely that 'the place of Purgatory is situated below and in proximity to Hell, so that it is the same fire which torments the damned in Hell and cleanses the just in Purgatory; although the damned being lower in merit, are to be consigned to a lower place'.[12] Among pre-Reformation English sources, *The Ordynare of Crysten Men* of 1502 stated that Paradise and Hell were at the extremes of geographical distance, that 'this present worlde is bytwene Hell & paradyse' and that Purgatory was 'one part of Hell'.[13] Still more categorical was the *Lytel Boke, that speketh of Purgatorye*, appearing on the very eve of Henry VIII's break with Rome. This laid down that Hell, *Limbus Infantium*, Purgatory and *Limbus Patrum* were situated under the earth, stacked one on top of the other in that ascending order.[14] By the early 1530s, however, pronouncements of this sort were already anathema to an undercurrent of reformist opinion, a current that was shortly to merge with the inexorable spate of official policy.

The story of the campaign against Purgatory and prayer for the dead, culminating in the Edwardian dissolution of the chantries, is becoming an increasingly familiar one in the historiography of the English Reformation.[15] Yet the scholarship to date has shown little interest in continuing Protestant attacks on Purgatory after the climacteric of 1547, and it has scarcely engaged at all with what will be the central concern of this chapter, debates about the 'geography' of the afterlife. As I hope to demonstrate, intense hostility to the Roman teaching on the next life remained a staple of anti-papal polemic throughout the period. While this polemic attacked Purgatory on a number of fronts – its association with clerical abuses, its inculcation of unchristian fear, its alleged disparagement of Christ's Passion – a persistent theme was the absurdity of the

---

[11] Le Goff, *Birth of Purgatory*, pp. 205–8, 252, 310–15.

[12] Aquinas, *Summa Theologica*, cited in M. Joseph, 'Discerning the Ghost in Hamlet', *Publications of the Modern Language Association of America* 76 (1961), p. 497.

[13] Cited in R. L. White, 'Early Print and Purgatory: the Shaping of an Henrician Ideology' (Australian National University PhD thesis, 1994), p. 53.

[14] *Here begynneth a Lytel Boke that speketh of Purgatorye* (?1531), sig. Aiiv.

[15] A. Kreider, *English Chantries: the Road to Dissolution* (Cambridge, MA, 1979); E. Duffy, *The Stripping of the Altars: Traditional Religion in England 1400–1580* (New Haven and London, 1992).

Catholic geography of the afterlife, its tendency to particularise and localise imaginary realms, to map out the confines and borders of the hereafter.

Unsurprisingly, the vision literature of the Middle Ages, with its vivid material evocation of the topography of Purgatory and Hell, its paths, bridges, rivers, valleys and angelic guides, proved an irresistible target for Protestant satire. In the Elizabethan burlesques *Tarleton's News out of Purgatory* and *Greenes Newes both from Heaven and Hell*, bemused souls undertake taxing journeys in search of the 'third place that all our great-grandmothers have talked of'.[16] Arguably of greater literary merit, but of similarly polemical intent, was John Donne's *Ignatius his Conclave* (1611). Here the writer falls into an ecstasy and with the help of a pair of miraculous spectacles, 'the same by which Gregory the Great and Beda did discern so distinctly the soules of their friends', he was able to see 'all the roomes in Hell open to my sight'.[17]

In the same work, Donne epitomised Limbo and Purgatory as 'the Suburbs of Hel', an image employed by other anti-papist writers including Pierre Viret, Anthony Wooton, Sir Edward Hoby and Thomas Beard.[18] With their contemporary resonances of sprawl, disease and disorder, the suburbs well evoked the sense of squalid materiality these writers wished to associate with the Romish teaching on Purgatory.[19] Another tack was to associate the subdivisions of the afterlife with the theme of unlawful possession. In his 1567 *Defence of the Apology of the Church of England*, Bishop John Jewel made scornful reference to 'your lists and gainful territories of Purgatory'.[20] To the Jacobean bishop, Thomas Morton, the papists' *Limbo Puerorum* was 'like a new inclosure . . . lately taken out of the common of Hell . . . our Adversaries limite the borders of Hell according to their own fancies'.[21]

To some writers what was most staggering about the Church of

---

[16] J. Belfield, 'Tarleton's News out of Purgatory (1590): a Modern-Spelling Edition, with Introduction and Commentary' (Birmingham University PhD thesis, 1978) (quote on p. 285); R. B. McKerrow (ed.), *Greenes Newes both from Heaven and Hell* (London, 1911).

[17] John Donne, *Ignatius his Conclave*, ed. T. S. Healy (Oxford, 1969), pp. 5–7.

[18] *Ibid.*, p. 9; Donne, *Essays in Divinity*, ed. E. M. Simpson (Oxford, 1952), p. 27; Pierre Viret, *The Christian Disputations*, tr. J. Brooke (London, 1579), fols. 225v–226r; Anthony Wooton, *An Answere to a Popish Pamphlet* (London, 1605), p. 49; Edward Hoby, *A Letter to Mr T. H.* (London, 1609), p. 79; Thomas Beard, *A Retractive from the Romish Religion* (London, 1616), p. 9.

[19] S. Rappaport, *Worlds within Worlds: Structures of Life in Sixteenth-century London* (Cambridge, 1989), pp. 11, 86, 213; I. Archer, *The Pursuit of Stability: Social Relations in Elizabethan London* (Cambridge, 1991), pp. 12–13, 185–6.

[20] John Jewel, *Works*, ed. J. Ayre (4 vols., Cambridge, 1845–50), IV, p. 845.

[21] Thomas Morton, *A Catholike Appeale for Protestants* (London, 1609), pp. 197, 198.

Rome's imaginary landscape of the afterlife was the certainty with which its apologists claimed to be able to place its every feature. A character in Jean Veron's 1561 dialogue, *The Huntyng of Purgatory to Death*, is made to remark that notaries are not as careful in their deeds to record the situation of lands and houses, as popish doctors are 'to measure and limite Hell, the lymbe and purgatorie'.[22] According to William Fulke, perhaps the most energetic of all Elizabethan writers against Purgatory, 'there is no man knoweth his owne house better the[n] we may know every corner of Purgatory'.[23]

Yet while on the one hand attacking the Catholics for their utter and absurd certainty about the geography and topography of the afterlife, an equally, if not more fruitful line of attack was to draw attention to the extent to which Catholic teaching was hopelessly inconsistent and contradictory on this score. The charge that papists were unable to agree 'about the place where Purgatory should be' became a leitmotif of anti-popish polemic, William Barlow noting that authorities were unresolved whether it was 'extensive as a cover over Hell, in latitude; or collaterall with Hell, severed by a partition, in longitude, or circular about Hell, in severall celles, as the spottes of an apple about the quore'.[24] As to *Limbus Patrum*, James Ussher pointed out that as it was now redundant, papists disagreed about its distinction from the limbus of children.[25] The English translation of a work by the Huguenot Pierre Du Moulin helpfully suggested that since 'the Franciscans, according to their rule, do not goe into Purgatory single, but by two and two . . . this Limbo lying in the way to Purgatory, seemeth a very convenient place to lodge him who being departed hence alone, must attend his companion'.[26]

At the beginning of the seventeenth century, no papist defence of Purgatory was more carefully pored over than the *Liber de Purgatorio* of Rome's most renowned controversialist, Robert Bellarmine. This work

---

[22] Jean Veron, *The Huntyng of Purgatory to Death* (London, 1561), fol. 159v.

[23] William Fulke, *Two Treatises written against the Papistes* (London, 1577), p. 170.

[24] William Barlow, *A Defence of the Articles of the Protestant Religion* (London, 1601), p. 138; Thomas Rogers, *The Catholic Doctrine of the Church of England*, ed. J. S. Perowne (Cambridge, 1854), p. 215; Christopher Carlile, *A Discourse concerning Two Divine Positions* (London, 1582), fols. 93r–v, 99r–100v, 160r–1v; William Fulke, *The Text of the New Testament of Iesus Christ translated out of the vulgar Latine by the Papists* (London, 1589), p. 119; Andrew Willett, *Synopsis Papismi* (London, 1592), p. 312; Henry Smith, *Sermons* (London, 1592), pp. 534–5; Richard Field, *Of the Church: Five Bookes* (London, 1606), p. 95; Joseph Hall, *The Peace of Rome* (London, 1609), p. 48; William Leigh, *The Soules Solace agaynst Sorrow* (London, 1612), p. 32.

[25] James Ussher, 'An Answer to a Challenge by a Jesuit in Ireland', in *The Whole Works of the Most Rev. James Ussher*, ed. C. R. Elrington (17 vols., Dublin, 1829–64), III, pp. 278–9.

[26] Pierre Du Moulin, *The Waters of Siloe*, tr. I. B. (Oxford, 1612), p. 35.

had given cautious approval to a tradition originating with Bede, that within Purgatory there was a place free of punishment, for souls not yet ready to receive the beatific vision, a place described as a fresh and pleasant meadow.[27] This had Protestant polemicists falling over themselves to argue that Bellarmine had unilaterally invented a fifth place in Hell.[28] James I himself joined in mocking Bellarmine on this score, and was able to combine his two great passions, theology and hunting, by asking Bellarmine to tell him 'if that faire greene Meadow that is in Purgatorie, have a brooke running thorow it; that in case I come there, I may have hawking upon it'.[29]

It should by now be clear that a central component of the Protestant strategy for demolishing Purgatory, *Limbus Patrum* and *Limbus Infantium* was to epitomise them in terms of their spurious geographical locations and spatial relationships to each other, to demonstrate the unreality of these places through an ironic evocation of their very concreteness. But the ramifications of this *modus operandi* could be felt beyond the specific doctrinal dispute with the Catholics over the existence of Purgatory and Limbo. The problem of the appropriateness of envisaging the condition of the soul after death in terms of its spatial location lay quite clearly near the heart of two internecine conflicts which beset English Protestantism. The first of these was the sixteenth-century debate over the destination of the soul immediately after death, the so-called 'sleep of the soul'.[30] The second was the long-running 'Descensus Controversy', the debate over how Protestants should understand the article in the Apostles' Creed that Christ 'descended into Hell', a phrase which in its very construction clearly raised questions about the location of Hell.[31]

The idea that the souls of the faithful did not proceed immediately to the beatific vision, but 'slept' until the end of the world, was associated in the early sixteenth century with the teaching of Martin Luther. It appealed to a number of early English reformers, William Tyndale and John Frith

---

[27] R. Bellarmine, 'Liber de Purgatorio', in his *De Controversiis Christianae Fidei* (5 vols., Ingolstadt, 1601), II, p. 793.

[28] Randall Hutchins, 'Of Specters', tr. and ed. V. B. Heltzel and C. Murley, *Huntingdon Library Quarterly* 11 (1947–8), p. 423; Andrew Willett, *Testrastylon Papisimi* (London, 1599), p. 180; Morton, *Catholike Appeale*, pp. 198–9, 429; Du Moulin, *Waters of Siloe*, p. 35.

[29] James I, *An Apologie for the Oath of Allegiance* (London, 1609), p. 43.

[30] The best survey of this controversy is N. T. Burns, *Christian Mortalism from Tyndale to Milton* (Cambridge, MA, 1972), chap. 3.

[31] D. D. Wallace, 'Puritan and Anglican: the Interpretation of Christ's Descent into Hell in Elizabethan Theology', *Archiv für Reformationsgeschichte* 69 (1978).

among them, because it seemed to restore soteriological meaning to a final judgement which could otherwise appear as a kind of eschatological rubber-stamping.[32] By the mid-Tudor period, however, the idea was coming to be decisively rejected by the Protestant establishment, partly because it had acquired an association with Anabaptism, but also because it seemed to revive in Reformed theology the notion of a third place in the next life, distinct from Heaven and Hell. John Hooper spoke for an emerging English Protestant orthodoxy on this question when he repudiated 'the fond opinion of the sleepers, which affirm that the spirits of the saints are not yet in Heaven, but do sleep in a certain place unknown to us'.[33] In fact, early proponents of soul-sleeping ideas had shown a clear determination not to get caught up in questions about where exactly the souls of the dead would reside. According to Tyndale, this was 'a secret laid up in the treasury of God', and Frith remarked that 'God would that we should be ignorant where they be.'[34] The most eminent continental opponent of the soul-sleepers, John Calvin, expressed himself in almost identical terms by noting that 'many torment themselves greatly with discussing what place they occupy . . . It is foolish and rash to enquire into hidden things.'[35]

Rhetorical diffidence of this sort was characteristic of mature Protestant discussion of the destinations of the dead, but it found itself tested in the tilt-yards of polemical debate. Protestant taunts about the inability of the Catholics to pinpoint or agree about the location of Purgatory invited an obvious riposte. A man 'may have both the example and the like doubt of Hell itself' observed the exiled William Allen in 1565.[36] The same conclusion was reached in the course of the Jacobean debate between Sir Edward Hoby and the Jesuit John Floyd. Noting the disparate locations in which medieval authorities had placed Purgatory, Hoby observed '*Quod ubique est, nullibi est*, it is in so many places, that indeed it is in no place.'[37] Floyd in turn accused Hoby of incipient atheism: 'Doe not

---

[32] Burns, *Christian Mortalism*, p. 101.
[33] John Hooper, *Later Writings*, ed. C. Nevinson (Cambridge, 1852), p. 63. See also Henry Bullinger, *The Decades: the Fourth Decade*, ed. T. Harding (Cambridge, 1851), pp. 389–90; Thomas Becon, *Prayers and Other Pieces*, ed. J. Ayre (Cambridge, 1844), p. 182; Veron, *Huntyng of Purgatory*, fol. 1r.
[34] William Tyndale, *Expositions and Notes*, ed. H. Walter (Cambridge, 1849), p. 185; John Frith, *Work*, ed. N. T. Wright (Oxford, 1978), p. 192.
[35] John Calvin, *The Institutes of the Christian Religion*, tr. H. Beveridge (2 vols. in 1, repr. Grand Rapids, MI, 1989), II, p. 267.
[36] William Allen, *A Defence and Declaration of the Catholike Churchies Doctrine touching Purgatory* (Antwerp, 1565), fol. 117r.
[37] Hoby, *Letter to Mr T. H.*, p. 79.

learned christians likewise dissent about the situation of Hell? . . . Will any true Christian argue in your forme? Hell is in so many places, that it is indeed noe where?'[38] Hoby's response was to ground himself upon a founding principle of the Reformation: 'As for Hell, though Learned men exactly know not the site thereof, yet doth the word of God plainly teach that there is a Hell . . . so that we are tied to a necessitie of beleefe . . . But as for Purgatorie, it is neyther averred nor described in the Mappe of Gods word.'[39]

That the existence of Hell could be established definitively from the 'map of God's word', the scriptures, was a position accepted by all mainstream reformers, but further than this the cartographic analogy was hopelessly misleading. Dispersed through a series of more or less gnomic Old and New Testament texts, the scriptural teaching on Hell was cryptic and encoded, and required for its deciphering the negotiation of a whole series of historical and philological problems.[40] As the Elizabethan and Jacobean controversies over the meaning of Christ's descent into Hell were to show, appealing to scripture to pin down the likely location of Hell proved hugely divisive. Protagonists on what we might loosely call the 'Puritan' side of these debates, those who preferred a spiritual interpretation of the credal article, tended to stress the variety of figurative uses of 'Hell' in scripture, and usually argued that the Hebrew word 'sheol' was better translated as 'the grave' or 'death' rather than Hell, and was more properly applicable to bodies than to souls.[41] Some controversialists made much of the passage in Ephesians 2:2 which implied the Devil's abode was in the air; thus to have visited Hell in the literal sense, Christ would have had to have *ascended.*[42] Hugh Broughton (a learned, if somewhat eccentric hebraist) went as far as to say 'they are much deceaved who thinke Hell to be in this world, lowe in the earth'.[43] None of the main participants in the Descensus Controversy ever sought explicitly to

---

[38] John Floyd, *Purgatories Triumph over Hell* (St Omer, 1613), p. 125. See also Theophilus Higgons, *The First Motive* (Douai, 1609), p. 155.

[39] [Edward Hoby], *A Curry-combe for a Coxe-combe* (London, 1615), p. 205.

[40] For a broad outline of the issues, see Turner, *History of Hell*; R. Hughes, *Heaven and Hell in Western Art* (London, 1968), chap. 4. The relevant scriptural texts are usefully collated by J. Delumeau, *Sin and Fear: the Emergence of a Western Guilt Culture*, tr. E. Nicholson (New York, 1990), pp. 374–5.

[41] Viret, *Christian Disputations*, fol. 290r; Carlile, *Discourse concerning Two Divine Positions*, fol. 137v; Henry Jacob, *A Treatise of the Sufferings and Victory of Christ* (Middleburg, 1598), pp. 122–3; Du Moulin, *Waters of Siloe*, p. 32

[42] Carlile, *Discourse concerning Two Divine Positions*, fols. 105v–107r; Jacob, *Sufferings and Victory of Christ*, p. 146; Andrew Willett, *Loidoromastix* (Cambridge, 1607), pp. 25–6.

[43] Hugh Broughton, *Declaration of Generall Corruption of Religion . . . wrought by D. Bilson* (Middleburg, 1603), unpaginated.

deny that there was a place, commonly called Hell, which God had reserved for the souls of the damned. Yet clearly inscripted within the theological positions adopted by even 'moderate Puritans', like William Whitaker, William Perkins or Andrew Willett, was a palpable unease with the conception of the afterlife as a series, or even a pair of concatenated localities, allowing, however exceptionally, of travel between the constituent parts: 'Christ's locall descension was but to the grave.'[44]

On the other side of the debate, 'conformist' spokesmen like Thomas Bilson, Adam Hill, Richard Parkes and John Higgins vigorously upheld a more literalist interpretation of the descent, and at times were prepared to assert that Hell was situated under the earth.[45] Yet common to virtually all the participants in these controversies was a growing coyness about where precisely Hell might be, a pragmatic consensus that since scripture did not pronounce definitively on the question, to enquire of it too closely was presumptuous and dangerous.[46] As Archbishop Ussher piously admonished, 'it is not to be inquired in what place it is situated, but by what means rather it may be avoided'.[47] Even conformists such as Adam Hill and John Higgins who were prepared to make the case against their Puritan opponents that Hell was beneath us felt that no more precise enquiry was warranted.[48] Preaching in 1626 on the text 'in my father's house are many mansions', John Donne complained of the 'wantonness' of the fathers and the 'wildness' of the schoolmen in their attempts to explicate this passage. He poured particular scorn on an author who 'afraid of admitting too great a hollowness in the Earth, lest then the Earth might not be said to be solid, pronounces that Hell cannot possibly be above three thousand miles in compasse'.[49] The following year the Norwich minister Samuel Gardiner similarly castigated those

---

[44] William Whitaker, *A Disputation on Holy Scripture*, tr. and ed. W. Fitzgerald (Cambridge, 1849), p. 538; William Perkins, *A Golden Chaine* (Cambridge, 1660), pp. 372–3; Andrew Willett, *Limbo-mastix* (London, 1604), p. 55 (quote).

[45] Thomas Bilson, *The Survey of Christs Sufferings* (London, 1604), p. 619; Adam Hill, *The Defence of the Article: Christ descended into Hell* (London, 1592), p. 10; Richard Parkes, *The Second Booke containing a Reioynder to a Reply* (London, 1607), p. 4; John Higgins, *An Answer to Master William Perkins* (Oxford, 1602), pp. 21–2.

[46] Veron, *Huntyng of Purgatory*, fols. 155r–v; Carlisle, *Discourse concerning Two Divine Positions*, fol. 105v; Viret, *Christian Disputations*, fol. 28v; Jacob, *Sufferings and Victory of Christ*, p. 153; Willett, *Synopsis Papismi*, pp. 607–8; Perkins, *Golden Chaine*, p. 373; Donne, *Essays in Divinity*, p. 36.

[47] Ussher, 'Answer to a Challenge', p. 378.

[48] Hill, *Defence of the Article*, p. 62; Higgins, *Answer to Perkins*, pp. 19–20.

[49] John Donne, *Sermons*, ed. E. M. Simpson and G. R. Potter (10 vols., Berkeley and Los Angeles, 1953–62), VII, p. 137. The allusion is to Sebastian Münster, *Cosmographiae Universalis* (Basle, 1550), pp. 11–12.

who took it upon themselves to define the situation of Hell 'in a hollow cave, or center of the earth, and so punctually doe describe unto us the space thereof, as if with a reed or metwand in their hand they had taken the iust measure of it'.[50]

By the later sixteenth century English Catholic writers as well as Protestants seemed increasingly reluctant to pronounce definitively on the precise dimensions or location of Hell. In 1529 Thomas More was quite certain that Hell 'nothynge ellys sygnyfyeth unto us . . . but ye habytacyons of sowlys byneth or under vs in ye low placys under ye ground'.[51] Half a century later Robert Persons, while accepting that the consensus of the fathers was that Hell was under the earth, admitted that it was uncertain 'whether it be under ground or no'.[52] Such caution also increasingly characterised Catholic discussions of the location of Purgatory. William Allen pronounced that 'it is better to be in doubt of these secretts, then to stande in contentious reasoning of thinges uncertaine'.[53] In the early seventeenth century, the Catholic controversialist, Anthony Champney, was prepared to commit himself no further than to state that 'after this life there is a purgatorie, or place where the soules of the faythfull . . . are detained untill they be wholly purged', while Sylvester Norris displayed a similarly minimalist attitude in 1622 by insisting 'we stand not upon the name, but uphold the thing, that is, a certaine penall estate, or cleansing . . . after this life'.[54] By the early part of the seventeenth century, right across the confessional spectrum, learned discussions of the whereabouts of Hell, and in the case of Catholics, Purgatory, seem to reflect a new sensibility, characteristically tempered by a kind of 'reverential agnosticism', a reticence about precise locations and (in contrast to the Middle Ages) a reluctance to define or situate the afterlife in geographical relation to the physical world.

This more guarded approach was equally evident in treatments of 'Abraham's Bosom'. By the end of the Middle Ages, the dominant trend of Catholic theology was to identify this place (mentioned in Luke 16) with the *Limbus Patrum* harrowed by Christ, thus locating it within the

---

[50] Samuel Gardiner, *The Devotions of the Dying Man* (London, 1627), p. 332.

[51] Thomas More, *The Supplication of Souls*, ed. F. Manley *et al.*, Yale edn of the *Complete Works of St Thomas More* (New Haven and London, 1990), VII, p. 186.

[52] Robert Persons, *The Christian Directory* (St Omer, 1607), pp. 229–30.

[53] Allen, *Defence and Declaration*, fol. 117r.

[54] Anthony Champney, *A Manual of Controversies* (Paris, 1614), pp. 76–7; Sylvester Norris, *An Antidote or Treatise of Thirty Controversies* (St Omer, 1622), p. 299. Norris thought it most likely, however, that Purgatory was under the earth: *ibid.*, p. 302.

macrocosm of the subterranean infernal world.[55] The reformers rejected this, but had difficulty knowing what to make of this unquestionably scriptural destination for dead souls.They refuted vehemently the suggestion that Abraham's Bosom could be any part of Hell (the rich man in Hell was noted to have 'lift up his eyes' and seen Lazarus 'afar off'), but often they recognised that patristic writers had distinguished it from Heaven, seeing it as a kind of atrium of Paradise where the faithful did not yet enjoy that full blessedness which would be theirs at the final judgement.[56] Some Protestant authorities retained something of this outlook, Veron writing that Abraham's Bosom was a paradise, 'but yet not so perfect as it was afterwards'.[57] Nonetheless, a desire to avoid needless speculation on the question was frequently expressed.[58] Without committing themselves to any precise cosmological location, however, the clear trend among Protestant writers was simply to affirm Abraham's Bosom as a synonym for Heaven. William Fulke averred, for example, that 'Abraham's bosome was a place of comfort. And other place of comfort then Heaven or Paradise, which is all one . . . I finde none in Scripture.'[59] In a devotional context, the identification of Abraham's Bosom with Heaven seems to have become almost entirely unexceptional. An early Jacobean funeral sermon by Robert Pricke stated it as certain that the souls of the faithful immediately 'meete with the Lord Iesus in Paradise: are gathered in the bosom of *Abraham*'.[60] A few years earlier, Nathaniel Gilby had told the dying earl of Huntingdon that 'angels attended to cary his soule to the bosome of Abraham'.[61] The death-bed declaration of faith which Philip Stubbes placed in the mouth of his teenage bride in 1591 included the comforting certainty that the blessed would recognise each other in the life to come, as 'the riche man lying in Hell, knewe *Abraham* and

---

[55] Le Goff, *Birth of Purgatory*, pp. 157–8; P. Binski, *Medieval Death: Ritual and Representation* (London, 1996), p. 210; Allen, *Defence and Declaration*, fol. 275v; Richard Bristowe, *A Reply to Fulke* (Louvain, 1580), p. 154.

[56] Binski, *Medieval Death*, p. 183, Ussher, 'Answer to a Challenge', p. 291; Hoby, *Currycombe for a Coxe-combe*, p. 153; Beard, *Retractive from the Romish Religion*, pp. 414–15.

[57] Veron, *Huntyng of Purgatory*, fol. 314v.

[58] Henry Bullinger, *The Decades: the First and Second Decades*, ed. T. Harding (Cambridge, 1849), p. 139; Bilson, *Survey of Christs Sufferings*, p. 541.

[59] William Fulke, *A Reioynder to Bristows Replie* (London, 1581), p. 149. See also William Fulke, *A Defence of the Sincere and True Translations of the Holy Scripture*, ed. C. H. Hartshorne (Cambridge, 1843), p. 285.

[60] Robert Pricke, *A Verie Godlie and Learned Sermon* (London, 1608), sig. Eir.

[61] M. C. Cross, 'The Third Earl of Huntingdon's Death-bed: a Calvinist Example of the *Ars Moriendi*', *Northern History* 21 (1985), p. 102.

Lazarus in Heaven'.[62] The pastoral appeal of this elision of Abraham's Bosom and Heaven might also be adduced from the knowing solecism of Shakespeare's *Henry V,* where Hostess Quickly says of the dead Falstaff, 'sure he's not in Hell, he's in Arthur's bosom, if ever man went to Arthur's bosom'.[63] To most Protestant Englishmen and women, the significance of Abraham's Bosom probably lay in its familiarity and accessibility as a pledge of salvation and redemption, not in concern over its theological nuances, or its positioning within a hierarchy of Heavens. One early Stuart writer roundly attacked those who argued about the location of Abraham's Bosom as 'rather producing scruples then instruction', adding that 'what ever they say, I take [it] to have been in Heaven, in which (we know) there are many stations, however they perplexe themselves in marshalling our lodging there'.[64]

In some ways equally perplexing, however, was the case of that other Lazarus of the gospels, the brother of Martha and Mary, whom Christ raised to life after he had lain four days in the tomb.[65] In the Middle Ages, the case of Lazarus provided the inspiration for lurid evocations of the horrors that lay beyond the grave,[66] but in the Reformation period it could be made to serve a more overtly polemical purpose. Where had the soul of Lazarus resided while his body lay in the grave? It was inconceivable that Christ would have summoned back a soul from Hell, and to have wrenched it from the enjoyment of eternal bliss in Heaven would seem an act of injustice. As William Allen put it, 'it is sure and most certaine, that it had sum place of abyding after the separation from the fleshe', the implication being, of course, that this place could logically only be Purgatory.[67] This was an objection that Protestant writers were obliged to take seriously. Calvinists such as the Englishman Andrew Willett, the Frenchman Pierre Du Moulin and the Scotsman William Guild could all agree that there was no compelling reason for thinking Lazarus was not in Heaven. As Guild put it, 'private good must ever give

---

62 Philip Stubbes, 'A Christal Glasse for Christian Women', in *The Anatomie of Abuses,* ed. F. J. Furnival (London, 1877), p. 204.

63 *Henry V* ii.iii.9–19. For other references to Abraham's Bosom used in this sense in Shakespeare, see *Richard III,* iv.iii.38; *Richard II,* iv.i.94–5.

64 David Person, *Varieties: or a Surveigh of Rare and Excellent Matters* (London, 1635), p. 183.

65 John 11:1–44.

66 Wright, *Patrick's Purgatory,* p. 167; Duffy, *Stripping of the Altars,* pp. 81–2, 340–1, pl. 127–8; C. Daniell, *Death and Burial in Medieval England, 1066–1550* (London, 1997), pp. 10–11, 82; G. England and A. W. Pollard (eds.), *The Towneley Plays,* Early English Text Society, 71 (1987), pp. 387–93.

67 Allen, *Defence and Declaration,* fol. 277r; Bellarmine, 'Liber de Purgatorio', p. 798.

place to the manifestation of Gods glorie'.[68] Yet Guild covered himself by assigning the question to 'the secret thinges [that] belong onely to God.'[69] This was the line taken earlier by Hugh Latimer, in the parallel case of the temporary location of the soul of Jairus's daughter: 'my own answer is this: I cannot tell, but where it pleased God it should be, there it was . . . other answer nobody gets at me, because the scripture telleth me not where she was'.[70] In his controversy with William Allen, Fulke reflected similar exasperation with 'foolish and unlearned questions . . . gendering strife rather than edificatio[n] . . . you shall never prove the common case of the departed in Christ by these fewe peculiar cases. For when so ever and how so ever it pleased God, that their soules remained, it was determined of God that they should be restored to their bodies.'[71] The question, however, retained the capacity to perplex: the renowned Elizabethan preacher, Henry Smith, included it in a list of 'questions gathered out of his own confession . . . which are yet unanswered'.[72] Some years later, reflecting on his own 'catalogue of doubts', Sir Thomas Browne expressed a determination to believe 'that *Lazarus* was raised from the dead, yet not demand where in the interim his soule awaited'.[73]

Thus far, this chapter has been describing developments that seem essentially endogenous, arising from the exigencies of theological debates between Catholics and Protestants, and among Protestants themselves, as they evolved over the century following the break with Rome. However, this may be to ignore the question of whether these changes in the discourse about the geography of the afterlife could have been linked to broader intellectual changes in this period, changes relating to improved physical knowledge of the earth, and of its place in the cosmos. According to Le Goff, the genesis of Purgatory was intimately connected with the growing knowledge of the world in the high Middle Ages. The increasing concern with the spatiality of the other world mirrored developments in terrestrial cartography, the attempt to 'introduce realism into topographical representation' on maps which had previously been 'little more

---

68 Willett, *Synopsis Papismi*, p. 307; Du Moulin, *Waters of Siloe*, p. 307; William Guild, *Ignis Fatuus or the Elf-fire of Purgatorie* (London, 1625), p. 41.
69 Guild, *Ignis Fatuus*, p. 41.
70 Hugh Latimer, *Sermons*, ed. G. E. Corrie (Cambridge, 1844), p. 550.
71 Fulke, *Two Treatises*, p. 442.
72 *The Sermons of Mr Henry Smith* (2 vols., London, 1866), ii, p. 420.
73 Thomas Browne, 'Religio Medici', in *Major Works*, ed. C. A. Patrides (Harmondsworth, 1977), pp. 87–8.

than an assemblage of topographical ideograms'.[74] If this is so, then it is at least arguable that the much greater advances in astronomical and geographical knowledge made in the sixteenth century stimulated an antithetical reaction. Any comprehensive discussion of the dual impact of the voyages of discovery and the Copernican revolution on early modern religious thought is, of course, way beyond the scope of this chapter. Yet it is fascinating to note the ways in which the imagery of cosmography, and the employment of cartographic and cosmological motifs, seeped into discussions of eschatology in late sixteenth- and early seventeenth-century England. Astronomical tropes are central to the humour of Donne's *Ignatius his Conclave*, which hinges upon the Jesuits' founder making good use of Galileo's telescope, and agreeing with Satan to found a new colony of Hell on the moon.[75] In more sombre and elegiac mode, Donne's 1627 memorial sermon for Lady Danvers artfully deploys the language of terrestial discovery as a mere simulacrum for man's understanding of the 'new Heavens and new earth' spoken of in St Peter's second epistle:

> in these discoveries . . . our *Maps* will bee unperfect. But as it is said of old *Cosmographers*, that when they had said all that they knew of a *Countrey* . . . they said that the rest . . . were possesst with *Giants*, or *Witches*, or *Spirits*, or *Wilde beasts* . . . yet wee must say at last, that it is a *Countrey* inhabited with *Angells*, and *Arch-angells*.

Donne concludes: 'Where it is *locally*, wee enquire not . . . Of these new Heavens, and this new earth we must say at last, that wee can say nothing.'[76] Here the signifiers of cartography are juxtaposed with the metaphorical promises of scripture to suggest that the former can do no more than evoke the complete impermeability of the latter. Other Protestant writers were less subtle. In 1561 Jean Veron had scoffed that he did not doubt that popish doctors 'could verye well make and compasse a Mappe or c[h]arte of those lowe and infernall regions'.[77] To Thomas Morton, Purgatory and the Limbos of fathers and of children were places 'without the horizons of mans wit'.[78] Hoby sneered that without Homer, Plato and Virgil 'you would never have knowne how to have set your compasse, for the discoverie of this new found world. And yet, if a man should ask the best navigator of you all, in what degree, & how many leagues *Purgatorie* is from the *Infernall Cape*, I think he would be put to

---

[74] Le Goff, *Birth of Purgatory*, pp. 229–30.   [75] Donne, *Ignatius his Conclave*, pp. 79–81.
[76] Donne, *Sermons*, VIII, pp. 81–2.   [77] Veron, *Huntyng of Purgatory*, fol. 161r.
[78] Morton, *Catholike Appeale*, pp. 197–8.

his trumps.'[79] Similar motifs emerged in the exchanges of the Descensus Controversy. In 1607 Richard Parkes was stung by Andrew Willett's charge that he seemed to be encouraging belief in *Limbus Patrum*, and retorted that 'it should seeme you know in what clymate of your *Necrocosmus* it is *sited*: for how else can you judge of the aspect?' He went on to attack another Puritan opponent, Henry Jacob, as 'one of the skilfullest Cosmographers of this our age, in the description of New-found lands'.[80] What we are witnessing here seems a kind of epistemological dissociation, a growing perception that the categories appropriate to the pursuit of knowledge about this world were inadmissible in theological discourse about the world to come. It is revealing that Archbishop Ussher ascribed the eschatological fallacies of classical and early Christian writers to their imperfect knowledge of the shape of the world, specifically their belief that the horizon cut the world in half, and that the antipodes were an uninhabited, invisible kingdom of the dead.[81] The Scottish writer, David Person, mounted a comprehensive attack in 1635 on those who regarded the metaphysical world as a proper object for experimental investigation. Among his targets were 'curious *Ouranographers*' who applied meteorological criteria to determine the part of Heaven into which Enoch and Elijah were assumed. He also condemned '*Topographers*' who wondered whether Hell could be 'in the centre of this Terrestiall globe' and whether volcanoes might be 'the vents and chimneys of Hell'. Person castigated such enquiries as the product of frivolous and divisive curiosity, and warned that 'God disappointeth the expectations of the most curious'. Interestingly, however, he commended the 'practical curiosity' of Christopher Columbus.[82]

While most Protestant writers displayed a growing reluctance to speculate on the locations of Heaven and Hell, an interesting counterpoint was the concern they increasingly displayed with the location of the earthly paradise described in the book of Genesis. As Jean Delumeau has recently shown, the early modern period witnessed a flood of conjecture on this issue, the question providing much of the impetus for the growing provision of maps in Protestant bibles.[83] But the geographical issues here had more to do with biblical history than eschatology. In early modern Europe, both Catholic and Protestant authorities tended to reject the

---

[79] Hoby, *Letter to Mr T. H.*, p. 79.   [80] Parkes, *The Second Booke*, p. 4.
[81] Ussher, 'Answer to a Challenge', pp. 373–7.
[82] Person, *Varieties*, pp. 183–5, 188, 194, 199.
[83] J. Delumeau, *History of Paradise: the Garden of Eden in Myth and Tradition*, tr. M. O'Connell (New York, 1995), esp. chap. 7. See also C. Delano-Smith and E. M. Ingram, *Maps in Bibles 1500–1600: an Illustrated Catalogue* (Geneva, 1991), pp. xvi, xxv–xxvi.

medieval idea that after the Fall the Garden of Eden had been miraculously relocated to the Heavens. Despite some enthusiastic interest in possible New World locations, the most common conclusion was that reached by the Englishman John Salkeld in 1617: the earthly paradise had been destroyed by the flood and no longer existed.[84] With the expansion and mapping of the known world, the idea that Hell and Paradise could be situated in this world, under exotic volcanoes or on distant islands, was looking increasingly anachronistic, surviving only as self-consciously literary and philosophical conceits: More's *Utopia*, Bacon's *New Atlantis* or Harrington's *Oceana*.[85]

If in this period what we might call 'real space' was displacing 'eschatological space', this may be linked to a growing readiness in some quarters to assert that the quiddity of Heaven and Hell lay not in their locations, but in their psychological and existential meanings for the individual Christian. Such views are most readily associated with the 'ranter' tracts of the 1650s, and have been linked with a continental tradition of mystical religious writings.[86] Yet language which stressed the immanence of Heaven and Hell was by no means the sole prerogative of a radical fringe. Once again, the Descensus Controversy was a factor here, as 'Puritan' writers sought to reconcile their acceptance of the creed with their desire to exclude a grossly material conception of Christ's presence in Hell. Andrew Willett insisted that 'that the place of Hell causeth not the torment, but the wrath and curse of God: for even out of hel God may make a man to feele the torments of Hell'.[87] Henry Jacob likewise insisted that '*Hell* as we take it, (that is the sense of Gods wrath) is even in this life, found sometyme.'[88] The topos was not an exclusively Puritan one. The 'avant-garde conformist', William Barlow, allowed diverse interpretations of 'Hell' which were not 'exorbitant from the Scriptures tacke'. These included the 'miserablest state which may befall a man'.[89] To John Donne, 'the Hell of hels, the torment of torments, was the everlasting

[84] Delumeau, *History of Paradise*, pp. 149, 152–7; John Salkeld, *A Treatise of Paradise and the Principall Contents thereof* (London, 1617), p. 39.

[85] Gurevich describes the idea of an island location for Hell and Paradise as 'rooted in the consciousness of the inhabitants of the European North' in the Middle Ages: *Medieval Popular Culture*, p. 131. On island utopias, see J. C. Davis, *Utopia and the Ideal Society: a Study of English Utopian Writing 1516–1700* (Cambridge, 1981).

[86] Almond, *Heaven and Hell*, pp. 46–7.   [87] Willett, *Synopsis Papismi*, p. 609.

[88] Jacob, *Sufferings and Victory of Christ*, p. 79.

[89] Barlow, *Defence of the Articles*, p. 172. The classification of Barlow is Anthony Milton's: *Catholic and Reformed: the Roman and Protestant Churches in English Protestant Thought, 1600–1640* (Cambridge, 1995), p. 23.

absence of God'.[90] In 1631 the Catholic Richard Smith was able to claim (with some exaggeration) that 'Protestants expressly say, that Hell is not place, no corporall place, no prison; that it is nothing but a wicked conscience.'[91]

In fact, the passages Smith provided in support of this charge were not as heterodox as they might appear. The notion that devils always carried their Hell around with them was a conventional one, sanctioned in the fifteenth century by that founding charter of witch-hunting and daemonology, the *Malleus Maleficarum*.[92] Its most famous exposition is to be found in Marlowe's *Dr Faustus*, in Mephistopheles' declaration that 'Hell hath no limits, nor is circumscrib'd / In one self place, but where we are is Hell, / And where Hell is, there must we ever be.' Yet Mephistopheles also provides a more traditional affirmation of Hell's location 'within the bowels of these elements'.[93]

To assert so volubly, however, that Hell could be a condition in this life, that it had resonant symbolic meanings which could claim parity with, or even be prioritised over its transcendent (and locational) reality, was to invite speculation that it was no more than a condition in this life, that it had no existence beyond a symbolic or metaphorical one. As early as 1550 the Edwardian divine Roger Hutchinson had complained of 'Libertines' who taught that 'there is neither place of rest ne pain after this life; that Hell is nothing but a tormenting and desperate conscience'.[94] Such accusations of 'atheism' are of course notoriously problematic, and can, and should be read as the constructions and projections of contemporary persuasive discourses, rather than as objective socio-religious commentary. Yet by the early seventeenth century there clearly were some in intellectual circles who were coming to regard any emphasis on the localised and spatial aspects of the afterlife as a vulgar misconception pertaining to the multitude. Thomas Browne thought that teaching the torments of a subterranean Hell 'makes a noyse, and drums in popular eares', adding that 'though wee place Hell under earth, the Devills walke and purlue is about it; men speake too popularly who place it in those

---

[90] Donne, *Sermons*, v, p. 226.
[91] Richard Smith, *A Conference of the Catholike and Protestante Doctrine* (Douai, 1631), p. 510. See also John Radford, *A Directorie teaching the Way to Truth* (England, secret press, 1605), pp. 459–60.
[92] Cited in R. H. West, *The Invisible World: a Study of Pneumatology in Elizabethan Drama* (repr. New York, 1969), p. 82. See Bilson, *Survey of Christs Sufferings*, p. 633; Browne, 'Religio Medici', p. 125; C.A. Patrides, 'Renaissance and Modern Views of Hell', *Harvard Theological Review* 57 (1964), pp. 228–9.
[93] *Doctor Faustus* II.i.122–6.   [94] Burns, *Christian Mortalism*, p. 59.

flaming mountaines, which to grosser apprehensions represent Hell'. To Browne, its true significance was that 'I feele sometimes a Hell within my selfe.'[95] In the mid-seventeenth century it became characteristic of the so-called 'Cambridge Platonists' to believe Hell to be, in John Smith's phrase, *'rather a Nature* than *a Place'*.[96] Most orthodox opinion would have balked at this phraseology, but something of this outlook had been presaged decades earlier in the writings of a considerable number of Elizabethan and Jacobean theologians, and perhaps also in those expressions of utter agnosticism about the conditions of the future life which in the later Elizabethan and early Stuart periods become a distinct literary topos. One thinks immediately of Hamlet's 'dread of something after death / The undiscovered country from whose bourn / No traveller returns', and also of Claudio's *cri de coeur* in *Measure for Measure*: 'to die, and go we know not where'.[97] Francis Bacon suggested that 'men fear death, as children fear to go in the dark'.[98] Thomas Browne later made a similar point, yet more graphically: 'a Dialogue between two Infants in the womb concerning the state of the world, might handsomely illustrate our ignorance of the next'.[99] In such rarefied intellectual circles at least, attitudes towards the afterlife seemed to be becoming, literally and metaphorically, dislocated.

If the argument of this chapter itself has a location, it might be seen as occupying the chronological and conceptual space between two influential books, Jacques Le Goff's *Birth of Purgatory*, and D. P. Walker's *Decline of Hell*. Le Goff chronicles how the Christian afterlife achieved a kind of spatial integrity in the high Middle Ages with the formalisation of beliefs about Purgatory. Walker shows how over the course of the seventeenth century received ideas about Hell and the eternity of infernal punishment came increasingly to be questioned. He notes that 'the Protestant rejection of Purgatory must be of great importance in attempts to discover why the doctrine of Hell began to be questioned when it did', but it is striking that he makes no real effort to follow up this insight.[100] Other modern cultural studies of death in post-Reformation England make only passing mention of the 'absence', 'abandonment' or 'loss' of Purgatory, almost as if the doctrine had been rather carelessly

---

[95] Browne, 'Religio Medici', p. 125.
[96] C. A. Patrides, *Milton and the Christian Tradition* (Oxford, 1966), pp. 280, 176.
[97] *Hamlet* III.i.80–82; *Measure for Measure* III.i.118–27.
[98] Francis Bacon, *Essays* (London, 1965), p. 6.
[99] Browne, 'Hydriotaphia or Urne-Buriall', in Patrides, *Works*, pp. 302–3.
[100] Walker, *Decline of Hell*, p. 59.

mislaid.[101] It has been a concern here to demonstrate that attacks on Catholic teaching on Purgatory and the afterlife remained a commitment of Protestant theologians throughout the Tudor and early Stuart periods. This hostile attention often focused on the supposed locations of Purgatory and Limbo, and in the process it facilitated, even if it did not primarily intend, a process of 'despatialising' the afterlife, of abstracting or even internalising it, of moving decisively away from a concern with its geographical configuration and its vicinity to the physical world. There is, of course, a danger of overstating the case here: the concept of a localised Hell was to have an extremely long shelf-life after 1600, implicitly underpinning many Hellfire sermons over the decades and centuries to come. The Enlightenment itself was not an automatic solvent: in 1714 Tobias Swinden was to argue that the sun must be the site of Hell, on the 'rational' grounds that the centre of the earth was too small to contain the enormous number of damned souls, and fire could not operate there without air. Three years later William Whiston trumped the proposition by asserting that the scientific and scriptural evidence proved Hell to be contained within a comet.[102] In the 1860s an American clergyman, W. R. Alger, compiled a massive *Critical History of the Doctrine of a Future Life*, with the avowed intention of showing that 'the doctrine of a locall Hell . . . is plainly proved by historic evidence to be a part of the mythology of the world, a natural product of the poetic imagination of ignorant and superstitious men'. Yet as Alger was compelled to admit, 'most people still think [Hell] is the interior of the earth'.[103] The diagnosis here, though, would seem to be a clear case of cultural lag. In England at least, the intellectual underpinnings of a literalist belief in a subterranean Hell and a cosmologically localised Heaven were already under strain two and a half centuries earlier.

In a memorandum of 1536 the humanist Thomas Starkey warned of the effects of the radical preaching he saw going on around him: 'with the despising of Purgatory, [the people] began little to regard Hell, Heaven, or any other felicity hereafter to be had in another life'.[104] This was clearly an exaggerated fear, but in a certain sense it might have been

---

[101] N. L. Beaty, *The Craft of Dying: a Study in the Literary Tradition of the Ars Moriendi in England* (New Haven and London, 1970), p. 154; C. Gittings, *Death, Burial and the Individual in Early Modern England* (London, 1984), p. 155; N. Llewellyn, *The Art of Death: Visual Culture in the English Death Ritual c. 1500–c. 1800* (London, 1991), p. 79.

[102] Walker, *Decline of Hell*, pp. 39–40, 100–1; Almond, *Heaven and Hell*, pp. 125–30.

[103] W. R. Alger, *The Destiny of the Soul: a Critical History of the Doctrine of a Future Life* (10th edn, New York, 1878), pp. 698–9.

[104] Cited by Kreider, *English Chantries*, p. 115.

allowed to stand as the epigraph to this chapter. The campaign against Purgatory, *Limbus Patrum* and *Limbus Infantium* brought with it not merely a 'down-sizing' of the afterlife, the painless substitution of a binary for a tertiary model of the Other World. Rather, it both effected and reflected the beginnings of a fundamental reconceptualisation, a tectonic shift in accepted and permissible modes of representation. The repudiations that this involved may have been more acceptable in so far as they were seen to correspond with contemporary developments in exploration, cartography and cosmology. Before the Reformation, to elucidate the geography of the afterlife was the legitimate business of theologians, devotional writers and homilists. To attempt to do the same in post-Reformation England, however, was characteristically to engage not with a physical, but with a metaphysical question, and increasingly perhaps, a metaphorical one.

7 Contesting sacred space: burial disputes in sixteenth-century France

Penny Roberts

The confessional tensions that arose in sixteenth-century France made the burial of the dead, specifically the Huguenot dead, a hotly contested issue. Whilst Huguenots strove to prevent their co-religionists from being 'polluted' by what they considered to be the idolatrous practices surrounding Catholic rituals, in turn Catholics obstructed Huguenot burials in established cemeteries which they regarded as 'pollution' of consecrated ground.[1] The resulting clash of sensibilities between the faiths was to be articulated through disputes concerning not only the place of burial but also the manner of death. In addition to theological differences such disputes encompassed concepts of community and the necessity for exclusion of those of another faith. By focusing on the issue of confessional burial it is possible to explore the changing social as well as religious dynamic of French communities split by the Reformation.

The perils of a body finding rest in a confessionally divided community are clearly illustrated by the following account. In 1558, Claude Portesain, a poor Huguenot goldsmith, was imprisoned in the town of Troyes for showing irreverence towards the Catholic Church and specifically its clergy. In prison, we are told, he stood firm in his faith, refusing to go to mass, and as a result was beaten so badly by the Catholic inmates that he died. This is where we pick up the story as reported by the Huguenot author, Nicolas Pithou:

---

[1] This language of pollution has informed our understanding of the violence of the French religious wars since the 1973 article in *Past and Present* by Natalie Zemon Davis, 'The Rites of Violence', reproduced as chap. 6 in her *Society and Culture in Early Modern France* (Stanford and London, 1975), pp. 152–87. However, not all Huguenots abandoned the popular belief in the power of consecrated ground, as studies of rural Calvinism have shown. See, for instance, Raymond A. Mentzer, 'The Persistence of "Superstition and Idolatry" among Rural French Calvinists', *Church History* 65 (1996), pp. 220–33.

There was no question of burying him in the accustomed place for one of his status, rather the cruel and pitiless gaoler hastily had a ditch dug outside the prisons, in a place where all the refuse of the quarter was dumped, and threw the corpse into it, with so little earth covering it that its feet stuck out. Enemies [of the faith], acting with all possible cruelty, expressed their wrath towards the deceased by stabbing and slashing at the poor corpse's legs with knives. This pitiful spectacle continued for some time, until the archer, Michel Charles [friend and neighbour of the deceased], and others of the faith, alerted to this inhumanity, removed the body one clear night, and carried it to the Notre-Dame cemetery. Fearing that if they made a new grave it would be discovered by means of the disturbed earth which would look freshly turned over, having found a recently made grave they put the corpse inside on top of another which had been buried a few days before. But since they did not have time to dig as deep as necessary, because they were so frightened of being surprised, the body was not buried as deep as it should. So that some time later, dogs scratching on the grave uncovered its legs. On realising this, the Catholics retrieved the corpse from the cemetery and buried it in a place where everyone was accustomed to urinate and defecate.[2]

The story of a Huguenot corpse being subject to abuse, disinterment and unsavoury burial could be replicated several times from contemporary sources. A similar fate befell a young soldier in Chartres, for example, who refused to confess to a priest before his execution and was brutally attacked by the crowd who later dug up his corpse three times, and also Pierre Petot, a mason of Beaune in Burgundy, whose body was dragged through the streets by vinegrowers' wives and buried secretly in a field, both in 1562.[3] Such examples raise a number of issues regarding relations between the faiths at this time. Not least, they reflect an extreme contempt and hatred for the deceased whose body is physically expelled from the community by its removal from sacred ground, much as the Huguenots were believed to have effectively separated themselves off from the community of the living by their rejection of Catholic devotional practices and thus forfeited their right to rejoin that community in death. Catholics were most offended by the Huguenot rejection of the existence of Purgatory (one of the most direct links between the living

---

[2] Bibliothèque Nationale, Paris (hereafter BN), MS Dupuy 698, fols. 107–8r (my translation).

[3] *Histoire ecclésiastique des églises réformées au Royaume de France*, ed. G. Baum, E. Cunitz and E. Reuss (3 vols., Paris, 1883–9), I, pp. 841, 865. For further examples from Rouen and Paris, see Philip Benedict, *Rouen during the Wars of Religion* (Cambridge, 1981), p. 64, and Barbara B. Diefendorf, *Beneath the Cross: Catholics and Huguenots in Sixteenth-Century Paris* (Oxford, 1991), pp. 62, 73.

and the dead, with the prayers and donations of the former easing the progress of the latter), and their criticism of the pomp and ritual of Catholic funeral practices, which was reflected in the sobriety and simplicity of their own rites. As a result, Huguenot corpses were treated with a disrespect completely at odds with conventional attitudes towards the dead, a point that has been long established in studies of religious violence in France at this time.[4]

Before we can begin to analyse such areas of contention, however, we need to consider existing burial practices and attitudes to death among the Catholic majority, and to what extent and in what ways the Huguenot stance challenged or offended these customs. The French historiography of death in the early modern period is extremely rich in detailing the beliefs and attitudes of early modern Europeans to their own and to others' deaths.[5] The relationship between the living and the dead, we are told, was a close one, allowing for fewer inhibitions about being in the presence of the dead than the modern-day sanitisation of death. According to Catholic belief, death – an important rite of passage in any religious culture – resulted in the passing of the soul into Heaven (rarely), Limbo (for the unbaptised few), Purgatory (most often) or Hell (only for the most ungodly) according to an individual's behaviour on earth. Here they would stay (with some movement between these locations, in part through the intercession of the prayers of the living) in anticipation of the Last Judgement when they would be reunited with their bodies. In this context, Alain Croix notes that cemeteries were viewed as dormitories of the dead, awaiting the final wake-up call, with their sometimes grand gateways indicative of the important transition souls had made.[6] Furthermore, it was popularly believed that the soul stayed in the vicinity of the body for the first month after death, though this was a view at odds with Catholic orthodoxy. Thus, although it is argued that with the development of the doctrine of Purgatory the resurrection acquired secondary importance for Catholics, both they and Protestants remained wedded to the concept.[7] However, whilst it is claimed by some authors that Luther

---

4 See, in particular, Davis, 'The Rites of Violence', and Denis Crouzet, *Les guerriers de Dieu: la violence au temps des troubles de religion, vers 1525–vers 1610* (2 vols., Paris, 1990).

5 Philippe Ariès, *Essais sur l'histoire de la mort en Occident du moyen âge à nos jours* (Paris, 1975), and *L'homme devant la mort* (Paris, 1977); Pierre Chaunu, *La mort à Paris: XVIe, XVIIe et XVIIIe siècles* (Paris, 1978); Alain Croix, *La Bretagne aux 16e et 17e siècles: la vie, la mort, la foi* (2 vols., Paris, 1981); Michel Vovelle, *La mort et l'Occident de 1300 à nos jours* (Paris, 1983).

6 Croix, *La Bretagne aux 16e et 17e siècles*, II, p. 1095.

7 Chaunu, *La mort à Paris*, pp. 258–9.

initially supported the idea of the 'sleep of the dead' (though with the body and soul remaining united in anticipation of a communal day of judgement), Calvin maintained that the soul of the faithful was united with God immediately after death – a more traditional and, some have argued, individualistic approach, freeing the soul from the captivity of the body.[8] It was the Calvinist view that was to prevail among the Huguenots.

It is usually argued that the Reformation drove a wedge between the living and the dead – a *rupture brusque*, as Vovelle has called it – in particular with its rejection of Purgatory and the efficacy of intercessory prayers.[9] Although Protestants held that the fate of the dead could no longer be affected by the actions of the living, there was no sense in which they were indifferent to the process of death itself. Salvation remained the central issue for both faiths, and the Protestant emphasis on the immediacy of the beatific vision for the saved arguably made the need for a 'good death' even more crucial in their eyes as a sign of divine grace. This was particularly important for the first-generation Huguenots who considered the good death (often through martyrdom) of their co-religionists to be a confirmation of their own confessional choice. Thus, Huguenots were enjoined to embrace death in the reassurance of their election; any signs of doubt or fear were to be suppressed. In practice, however, it was recognised that this was an onerous burden for any but the most stalwart to tackle on their own. Protestants rejected the intercessory role of the priest in administering the last rites (confession, communion and extreme unction), as well as the lights, crucifix and other Catholic paraphernalia of the death-bed, but consolation was still to be provided to the dying by a minister, family and friends. In recognition of this need, manuals of instruction, Huguenot equivalents of the fifteenth-century *Ars moriendi*, were published, offering advice both to the dying and to those attending them.[10]

It is clear, at least in the early decades of the Reformation, that where the Huguenots were a persecuted minority the death-bed struggle would be particularly fraught. Not only did it involve the dying wrestling with doubts that assailed them regarding their own worthiness, but also the need to prevent Catholic attempts to administer the last rites. A particularly vivid account of such a struggle is once more provided by the memoir of Nicolas Pithou, regarding the fate of a Huguenot tanner,

---

[8] *Ibid.*, pp. 249–51, and Vovelle, *La mort et l'Occident*, pp. 205–10.

[9] Vovelle, *La mort et l'Occident*, p. 209. See also Clare Gittings, 'Urban Funerals in Late Medieval and Reformation England', in Steven Bassett (ed.), *Death in Towns: Urban Responses to the Dying and the Dead, 100–1600* (Leicester, 1992), esp. pp. 173, 181.

[10] For examples of these, see Chaunu, *La mort à Paris*, pp. 252–3.

Pierre Boissonnot, in January 1559. Boissonnot was caught between the pressure exerted by his wife and brother to confess to a priest (so as to prevent the forfeiture of the family inheritance) and that of his Huguenot friends and his own conscience. After the parish priest had visited him, Boissonnot spoke with his fellow Huguenot, Chantefoin, who 'seeing him so terrified and troubled in his conscience, cited some passages from the Scriptures to reassure him'.[11] But Boissonnot insisted that he would be damned for having denied Jesus 'before men' as a result of the visit. Nevertheless, on his friend's advice, he remained resilient in the face of his relatives' attempts to make him receive the Host, which he promptly spat out. Chantefoin was delighted and declared to him, 'that he had fought valiantly and had shown himself to be a true champion of Jesus Christ, exhorting him to persevere and to always have recourse to God'. Yet, Boissonnot was still in despair. 'Seeing which Chantefoin told him that he must play another tune, and rejecting all these reveries that the devil had aroused in his mind, put all his confidence in God, relying on the death and passion of our Lord Jesus Christ.' Soon after it became clear that Boissonnot was near to death and the priest was sent for in order to give him the last rites:

> Now he found the invalid in a pitiful state, for he had already, in everyone's judgement, completely lost his sight, hearing and speech. In short it was as if he was already dying, it only remaining for the priest to anoint him. The invalid allowed him from the beginning to do all that he wished, without moving or making a sound. But when it came to taking off his stockings in order to grease his feet, he jumped up with a start; leaning on his elbows and casting his gaze here and there seeing so many candles lit in the room, and the priest dressed in his surplice, a stole at his neck . . . 'Don't you want', said he speaking to the priest, 'to be paid for your grease and your oil? Villain, if I was up and had my strength, I would throw you downstairs. Go, and clear out fast.' This amazed all those present . . . And when everyone had left the room, Chantefoin, coming near to the bed asked the sick man what he wished to say and whether he wished to put his total confidence in our Lord Jesus Christ. 'Yes indeed' (he replied), 'I have spoken to Him, He has forgiven all my trespasses, and has told me that before midnight, I will be with Him in his eternal kingdom.'

The moral of the tale is clear. Despite the efforts of the priest and Boissonnot's wife, more concerned with her future security than her

---

[11] BN, MS Dupuy 698, fols. 109–13. For a fuller version of my translation of this passage, see William G. Naphy (ed.), *Documents on the Continental Reformation* (London, 1996), pp. 73–6.

husband's salvation, the tanner dies a good Calvinist death with the assistance of his co-religionists. Nevertheless, despite Boissonnot's defiant stance, his widow was still keen to avoid opprobrium towards herself and her children by appeasing the parish priest. As a result of her pleadings, Boissonnot's body was buried in the parish church, much to the consternation of some local Catholics. Nor were such concerns with safeguarding an inheritance by outward conformity uncommon, especially amongst the Huguenot nobility.[12]

Amid the turmoil of confessional strife, it is not surprising that Reformed ministers were often able only clandestinely to provide consolation for the dying. With the advent of the Wars of Religion, and in particular the edicts of pacification which sought to end them, ministers were excluded from conducting worship and thus from residing in many towns, although they were in certain circumstances permitted to attend the sick. A not uncommon clash between the Cardinal of Lorraine and the Chancellor Michel de l'Hôpital in 1566 regarding this provision (and in response to an appeal from the Catholics of Dijon) underlines the differences of opinion that could coexist at the highest decision-making levels, in this case the royal council.[13] The Cardinal opposed King Charles IX's decision to grant ministers access, arguing that this would not only be the source of renewed trouble but that it would encourage clandestine worship in places where it was not otherwise permitted, and that the dying should seek consolation from local Catholic clergy instead. The Chancellor retorted that this would be to condemn the Huguenots to die like beasts by depriving them of the Word when they were most in need and, rather than preventing further trouble, would foment it. Whilst this dispute has much to tell us about the personal animosity of these men (as well as their differing views as to whether Huguenots would find consolation from a priest acceptable), it also reveals two quite opposing strategies towards the same end, that of preventing a return to the troubles.

Since Huguenots were keen to avoid priestly intercession at the hour of death, claiming a 'sudden' death was a convenient means by which failure to summon a priest could be explained.[14] However, although in theory the living had no further role to play except in securing a decent burial for the deceased (as in the case of Claude Portesain), severing ties

---

[12] For example, see Raymond A. Mentzer, *Blood and Belief: Family Survival and Confessional Identity among the Provincial Huguenot Nobility* (West Lafayette, IN, 1994), pp. 180–1.

[13] BN, MS Dupuy 322, fols. 146–7r.

[14] Mentzer, *Blood and Belief*, p. 180.

in the form of intercessory prayers did not weaken the Huguenots' concern to ensure that the corpses of their friends and loved ones were treated with dignity and respect. Nevertheless, their preference for a simple funeral and burial offended their Catholic neighbours. The Huguenot rejection of the Catholic rituals of the laying out of the corpse, the offices of the dead, and the elaborate funeral procession and burial service, caused offence not just on religious grounds but could be interpreted as a snub to the community, a rejection of the gestures of 'collective piety' which brought the community together at the death of one of its number.[15] For if, as Finucane argues, the manner of disposing of the dead 'reflects social or cultural norms and ideals', then the Huguenot negation of these norms goes some way to explaining the hostility which their actions generated.[16] This hostility manifested itself primarily over two issues: the use of Catholic cemeteries and the conduct of funerals.

The normal pattern was for individuals or their families to have as much pomp at a funeral as they could afford, including several priests and members of the poor in the cortège, which was to be accompanied by torches and the ringing of bells. The request for a simple funeral had been interpreted as an act of extreme piety and self-abnegation before it became associated with Huguenot practice. Humanists, too, encouraged sobriety on such occasions, as was exemplified at the funeral of Guillaume Budé in 1540, lending such practices a certain respectability. However, as early as the 1530s, requests for simple funeral rites came to be viewed with suspicion and the orthodoxy of the deceased (and their next of kin) brought into question. These issues were brought into sharp focus by a case that was to become infamous in Protestant Europe, that of the so-called 'spirit of Orléans' of 1534. The wife of the city's *prevost* had explicitly rejected the customary practices, of which Johann Weyer gives us a useful description:

> In France, when a person passes away, funeral criers hired for the purpose go around through the more crowded parts of the city and sound their cymbals, calling together the multitude. Then they proclaim the name and titles of the deceased; urging the people to pray to God for him, they announce the time and place of the burial. When the funeral procession is conducted,

---

[15] John Bossy, *Christianity in the West, 1400–1700* (Oxford, 1985), p. 32.

[16] R. C. Finucane, 'Sacred Corpse, Profane Carrion: Social Ideals and Death Rituals in the Later Middle Ages', in Joachim Whaley (ed.), *Mirrors of Mortality: Studies in the Social History of Death* (London, 1981), p. 41.

mendicant monks are usually employed, and many lights are carried before.[17]

According to Weyer, the disgruntled Franciscans, in whose church the woman was buried, constructed a rather elaborate ruse to make it appear that her soul was not at peace. In supposed consultation with her restless spirit they established that her anguish was due to her Lutheran heresy; as a solution they suggested exhuming the body and performing an exorcism. However, the imposture was discovered.[18] The stipulation of a simple funeral became such a contentious issue that even those whose orthodoxy was not previously in doubt could fall victim. In 1558, the body of a Catholic mercer of Tours who requested a quiet burial was pulled out of its coffin, abused and thrown out of the cemetery. A similar fate awaited those who criticised any aspect of Catholic devotions.[19] As a result, the burial of those whose confessional allegiance was in any way suspect became an issue fought out in Catholic cemeteries.

Underlining the thin demarcation between the living and the dead, cemeteries were often open spaces, in towns one of the few public places where people could meet together and the setting for a number of communal activities: dances, markets, games, fights, agitation and gatherings of all kinds. Even Huguenots in some notable instances made use of them for public prayers and sermons; sometimes unofficially, or quite legally, as in Chastellerault in Poitou, where the royal commissioners sent to enforce the edict of pacification of 1563 established a site for worship in a disused cemetery in the *faubourgs*.[20] In some cases, part of a cemetery might be given over to cultivation or pasture; indeed, a common problem was straying animals, with instances of pigs and dogs digging up bones in a cemetery at Nantes in 1581 (demonstrating that this was not only the

---

[17] G. Mora *et al.* (eds.), *Witches, Devils and Doctors in the Renaissance. Johann Weyer, De praestigiis daemonum* (Binghamton NY, 1991), pp. 439–41. There are various versions of the story in French texts, e.g. *Histoire ecclésiastique*, I, pp. 30–3.

[18] In other circumstances exorcism was to prove a powerful weapon of the Counter Reformation in France. See D. P. Walker, *Unclean Spirits: Possession and Exorcism in France and England in the Late Sixteenth and Early Seventeenth Centuries* (London, 1981), pp. 4, 19–33 (and pp. 15, 33–42, on fraud in such cases); Denis Crouzet, 'A Woman and the Devil: Possession and Exorcism in Sixteenth-Century France', in Michael Wolfe (ed.), *Changing Identities in Early Modern France* (Durham, NC and London, 1997), pp. 191–215.

[19] *Histoire ecclésiastique*, I, pp. 175–6, 905, 969.

[20] BN, MS français, 15878, fol. 96; see also *Mémoires de Claude Haton contenant le récit des événements accomplis de 1553 à 1582, principalement dans la Champagne et la Brie*, ed. Félix Bourquelot (2 vols., Paris, 1857), I, p. 148.

fate of individuals like Claude Portesain).[21] The need to keep animals out was one argument advanced for the enclosure, and even locking, of cemeteries, which was an increasingly common occurrence by the seventeenth century and also reflected a greater reverence for such sites. As the years passed, burial space was increasingly at a premium; few grave-markers were used and bones were often dug up and mixed up in the process of making new graves. The increasingly accepted solution to this problem was to place the bones in ossuaries or charnel-houses, most extensively in Brittany, and, notably, in Paris at the Cimetière des Innocents.[22]

The precise location of where someone was buried reflected their status when alive and was thus of great significance. There was both a geography and a social hierarchy of sacred burial space. The most prestigious site was usually in the church (or local convent) with the most sought-after spots nearest the altar. These were filled by members of the clergy and the upper echelons of local society. This was decided not just in terms of local standing, but ensured by the prohibitive cost of such sites to the majority. It is not surprising that the burial of a notorious 'heretic' like Pierre Boissonnot in his parish church should have caused such a stir, nor that his widow saw this as the best way of trying to establish a reputation for piety. Certain groups were segregated or excluded altogether from burial in consecrated ground. Stillborn and unbaptised infants, beggars, plague victims and lepers, for example, could be allocated their own plots or even a separate cemetery. In theory, suicides, excommunicates and heretics were to be refused burial in sanctified ground altogether, but this was not always upheld in practice.[23]

As tensions between the faiths grew in sixteenth-century France, so did Catholic objections to Huguenot burials in their cemeteries. It was argued that in rejecting the administration of Catholic sacraments, including extreme unction, the Huguenots had forfeited their right to burial in sacred ground. Huguenots, for their part, wished to be buried

---

[21] Croix, *La Bretagne aux 16e et 17e siècles*, II, pp. 1095–7. Cf. Christopher Daniell, *Death and Burial in Medieval England, 1066–1550* (London and New York, 1997), pp. 111, 123.

[22] Edward Muir, *Ritual in Early Modern Europe* (Cambridge, 1997), p. 50. Elizabeth Musgrave, 'Memento Mori: the Function and Meaning of Breton Ossuaries 1450–1750', in P. C. Jupp and G. Howarth (eds.), *The Changing Face of Death: Historical Accounts of Death and Disposal* (London, 1997), pp. 64–7.

[23] Croix, *La Bretagne aux 16e et 17e siècles*, II, pp. 1001–5; Daniell, *Death and Burial in Medieval England*, p. 35.

with their ancestors in the customary way, although as time wore on they sought permission to establish their own cemeteries near to their sites of worship. Whilst by the early 1560s (with the arrival of suitably trained ministers) Huguenots were performing their own baptisms and marriages, the demand to have their own cemeteries came more gradually, with the obligation of provision embodied in an edict of 1570, which that of Nantes in 1598 reinforced. This may suggest that the Huguenots did not themselves find the issue of burial problematic, but that it was more likely prompted as a result of Catholic antagonism. Indeed, where Huguenots were in the majority, the established cemetery continued to be used much as before, 'retaining its purpose as a sacred place'.[24] Furthermore, whilst Huguenots had little objection to the interment of their co-religionists in Catholic cemeteries (provided it was not accompanied by Catholic rites), Catholics were distinctly less happy about accepting Protestant burial practices. Cases brought before the Chambre de l'Edit de Castres in the late 1590s demonstrate these differences in attitude. In the case of a Catholic woman buried in Protestant soil according to Protestant custom, the court granted that the body be exhumed and reburied according to the Catholic rite; whereas the Protestant minority of Saint-Pargoire sought permission to use the communal Catholic cemetery whilst awaiting provision of a site of their own.[25] In addition, both faiths were to be accused of desecrating the graves of the other, as was reported in the case of the Huguenots of Le Mans during their takeover of the city in 1562, and by Catholics against the graves of the Huguenots of Autun at La Barre, who complained that they were also being obstructed from burying their dead at the site.[26]

By erecting an 'us and them' attitude with regard to the regulation of burials, the advent of the Reformation also changed perceptions of the definition of sacred space. By excluding Protestant burial, the previously communal churchyard, the repository of a collective ancestry, became symbolic of the confessional rift within society. Huguenots, too, came to accept their separation from the community in

---

[24] Vovelle, *La mort et l'Occident*, p. 232, although he traces a change in the cemetery's magical status; Chaunu, *La mort à Paris*, p. 260, suggests that its sacrality was even stronger than before.

[25] Raymond A. Mentzer, 'L'édit de Nantes et la chambre de justice du Languedoc', in Michel Grandjean and Bernard Roussel (eds.), *Coexister dans l'intolérance: l'édit de Nantes* (Paris and Geneva, 1998), p. 335. I am grateful to Professor Mentzer for sending me an extract from this essay.

[26] On Le Mans, Archives Départementales de (herafter AD) la Sarthe, Archives Communales du Mans, 985; on Autun, BN, MS français 4048, fols. 66–7.

death, whilst the establishment of their own cemeteries may in turn have reinforced the sense of solidarity within their own communal group. Although it is tempting to view the Huguenots as victims in such circumstances, a defiant stance often preceded or challenged their exclusion from parish cemeteries. In Bordeaux, just prior to the outbreak of the first civil war in the spring of 1562, there seems to have been a groundswell of popular support among Reformers (or possibly a deliberately orchestrated campaign) to defy regulations on the conduct of funerals and to procure a cemetery of their own. Whilst the bishop and clergy resisted this development, the local military commander, the seigneur de Burie (usually no friend of the Huguenots), supported their case before the *parlement* on 27 February.[27] Burie's main concern was that, because the Huguenots were refused burial in church or cemetery both inside and outside the town, the embalmed corpses of their dead were lying in their houses which was contrary to humanity.[28] He thus supported their request for the restitution of their burial rights. There was already a certain nervousness among the clergy in Bordeaux because of the unrest which had accompanied a funeral at the church of Saint Rémy early in the previous November; this is reflected in a case before the archbishop's court in February 1562.[29] A surgeon, Jehan de Poulhon, and his wife had been reported by their parish priest for objecting to the presence of Catholic clergy at the burial of their son. Three times the surgeon's wife maintained this stance and insulted the parish priest and ecclesiastical officials when they paid her a visit to discuss arrangements for the funeral. Her husband, who had originally approached the parish priest so as to gain access to the church, was always said to be absent on these occasions. This may have been a ploy to distance him from blame; certainly his failure to appear when summoned before the court suggests that he supported his wife's stance. Such displays of overt anticlericalism did not actually lead to direct accusations of *Huguenoterie* in this instance, but the correspondence with the timing of the campaign to secure a site for Reformed burial in Bordeaux cannot have been coincidental. It appears once again that, whilst the Huguenots were happy to continue using parish cemeteries and even churches

---

27 BN, MS français 3186, fol. 10r.
28 See Chaunu, *La mort à Paris*, p. 260, for Huguenot rejection of embalming under normal circumstances.
29 BN, MS français 3186, fols. 174–5r. On the earlier incident see MS français 3159, fol. 31r.

for burial, tensions with local Catholics regarding this issue were increasing.[30]

The provisions and enforcement of the edicts of pacification which punctuated the wars detail the authorities' attempts to deal with such tensions through the regulation of Reformed burial. Prior to the wars burial, 'according to the new religion' or 'in the Genevan fashion', was rarely if ever tolerated, and seems to have been rigorously pursued by the courts. A variety of cases survive from the jurisdiction of Dijon and Lyons, and especially that of the *parlement* of Bordeaux.[31] Here a decree of the court dated 23 February 1562, prohibiting Huguenot burial in towns or consecrated ground, was reiterated in royal letters of 26 March 1562 and 19 March 1563, as well as by the governor Monluc, on 20 April 1563, and subsequently in regional towns such as Bazas, Libourne and Marmande.[32] The Catholic inhabitants of Bazas reported that on 19 April, a widow, assisted by her fellow Huguenots, had her daughter buried 'in the Genevan way' in the cemetery of Saint-Jean, contrary to the recent edict which had allowed services to be conducted in the suburbs of the nearby town of La Réole. At Libourne the Huguenots remonstrated against Monluc's ordinance which they believed ought to have been modified in accordance with the most recent edict. At any rate, the frequent repetition of the decree in the *parlement's* jurisdiction suggests that contraventions were a frequent occurrence. The defiant stance of the reformers in Libourne also points to a tightening of royal regulation of burial provision. A detailed account of a Huguenot funeral and burial conducted by members of the church at Montauban reveals just what such services 'in the Genevan style' involved:

> all those of the Reformed religion in broad daylight two-by-two behind the corpse, covered with a white cloth and a green cover over it, carried by six artisans, to the great amazement of all the townspeople, who followed this new spectacle as far as the St Michel cemetery; where, having buried the body, the minister Le Masson took up a prominent position and preached a

---

[30] *Histoire ecclésiastique*, I, p. 871, regarding a riot which ensued at Saint-Rémy on 1 November 1561 as a result of Huguenots requesting the keys to the cemetery so that they could bury a child. It is suggested here that previously the Huguenots had buried their dead in this cemetery without obstruction.

[31] E.g. Archives Municipales de (hereafter AM) Dijon, B 200, fol. 169r (17 Mar. 1564); B 201, fol. 91r (26 Jan. 1565); B 203, fol. 63v (13 Aug. 1566); AM Lyon, GG 77, no. 9 (25 Oct. 1566); AM Bordeaux, GG 983a (14 Apr. 1561).

[32] AD la Gironde: 1B 243, nos. 386–8 (26 Mar. 1562); 1B 257, nos. 163, 214 (Apr. 1563, Bazas); 1B 258, no. 87 (Libourne, 11 May 1563); 1B 260, no. 158, and 1B 265, fol. 67 (both Marmande, 14 July 1563).

sermon about burial and resurrection, which he concluded with ordinary prayers and singing of the commandments.[33]

Just prior to the outbreak of war, this was the first public display by members of the Montauban church, and it would seem that on this occasion it was more edifying than provocative. Later on, in more tense circumstances, however, the Catholic citizenry might well have interpreted it as an act of defiance which would have provoked unrest, something that the authorities were keen to avoid.

The edicts of pacification formalised previous royal policy with regard to the conduct of Reformed funerals and the securing of final resting-places for their dead. By the royal edict of interpretation (of the earlier March edict) dated 14 December 1563, detailed restrictions were imposed on the burial of Huguenots.[34] A site was to be acquired outside the town in which they lived; the funeral party was to be restricted to twenty-five to thirty people; and the interment was to take place in the hours of darkness between dusk and dawn (as much for the safety of the participants as to prevent offence to local Catholics). Whilst this was to be the general rule, Paris was singled out, as so often in the edicts: here burials were to take place in the deceased's parish cemetery; the death was to be reported by a member of the household or family to the *chevalier du guet* (head of the nightwatch) who was responsible for organising a gravedigger and as many of his sergeants as he thought appropriate to accompany the body and to ensure that there was no scandal; and the burial was to take place at night with no funeral party in attendance. These stipulations were extended to other major towns, such as at Toulouse, Lyons and in Provence (where the proviso was made that local Huguenots could find a separate site if they preferred).[35] The *chevalier du guet* became notorious for exploiting his position and charging Huguenots exorbitant fees for carrying out his duties, as was the case in Lyons, since they had no choice but to employ him.[36] The more general provision for burials could also be modified, especially with regard to the numbers allowed to attend: limited to fifteen in Autun, ten to twelve in Languedoc, and only eight in Mâcon.[37] In the

---

33 *Histoire ecclésiastique*, I, p. 913.

34 BN, Imprimés, F 46825, Actes royaux, nos. 25–9.

35 Bibliothèque Municipale de (hereafter BM) Toulouse, T 21 (5), 'Lettres de declaration et interpretation de l'édit' (Br Fa D 604); AM Lyon, GG 77, no. 20; AD Bouches-du-Rhône (annexe), B 3329 (Parlement de Provence), fol. 51.

36 AM Lyon, GG 78, no. 34. See also François Garrisson, *Essai sur les Commissions d'Application de l'Édit de Nantes: première partie – règne de Henri IV* (Paris, 1964), pp. 241–2.

37 BN, MS français 4634, fol. 129 (Autun); 4048, fol. 173 (Mâcon); C. Devic and

area around Bordeaux in 1565, a sergeant was ordered to carry a white stick before the cortège in order to prevent trouble.[38] In October 1563 (two months before the edict of interpretation clarified the position), the governor of Burgundy, Gaspard de Saulx-Tavannes, remonstrated with the royal commissioner, Jean de Monceaulx, for allowing burials and baptisms at the town of Autun contrary to the March edict. In particular, he commented on the frequent need for such services because of the daily round of births and deaths, and that burials would inevitably be accompanied by sermons and assemblies in the Reformed tradition, even though royal permission had not been specifically granted for Reformed worship in the town.[39] Here again we see a differing interpretation of the provisions of an edict, this time between agents of the crown both entrusted with its enforcement, with one applying the rules more restrictively than the other.

It is clear from other evidence that such stipulations were not always applied so strictly. In Grenoble in the summer of 1564, the municipal council suggested a site near or belonging to the Jacobins outside the town, but as it did not belong to the municipality they pointed out that there could be some delay in obtaining permission.[40] So in the meantime, they advised the Huguenots to carry on burying their dead as before, and said that they would ask the chapter of Notre Dame and the clergy of Saint Laurent if they might make use of their cemeteries for this purpose. In other places too, Catholic cemeteries continued to be used, notably in Poitou (where the faiths were not separated in death until the early seventeenth century), but it is significant that these were areas in which the Reformed Church was then strong.[41] In most places, the use of Catholic cemeteries for Huguenot burials was fiercely opposed and continued to be so into the seventeenth century (although most exhumations were done under official supervision, in contrast to the rough treatment of Claude Portesain).[42] Even in Dauphiné, the practice of burying Huguenots in Catholic cemeteries was prohibited in December

---

J. Vaissète, *Histoire générale de Languedoc, avec les notes et les pièces justificatives* . . . (16 vols., Toulouse, 1874–95), XII (1889), cols. 704–6.

[38] BN, MS français 15881, fol. 294r. The carrying of a white stick before a corpse indicated death from plague, making an interesting analogy between the diseased and the 'heretical', both seen as sources of 'infection' of the community.

[39] BN, MS français 4634, fol. 129 (20 Oct. 1563).

[40] AM Grenoble, BB 19, fols. 62 (25 June) and 74v (7 July).

[41] Garrisson, *Essai sur les Commissions d'Application de l'Edit de Nantes*, pp. 241–2.

[42] For examples of early seventeenth-century objections to Huguenot burials in Catholic cemeteries, see AD la Charente, G 398 (at Charmant, June 1600) and G 491 (at Touzac, 28 Aug. 1601). On exhumations, see Croix, *La Bretagne aux 16e et 17e siècles*, I, p. 94.

1566 following the reassertion of Catholic dominance in Grenoble.[43] Even when it was allowed, as we have seen, this was usually on a temporary basis until the Huguenots acquired a site of their own. Nevertheless, the obstruction of such provision for their own sites was often a deliberate policy of the local authorities. In Dijon, for example, whilst the Huguenots sought and won royal support for the acquisition of a plot for a cemetery in the city *faubourgs* in 1564, the municipal authorities and the provincial governor continued to drag their feet until the official stipulation of the edict of 1570 obliged them to make such provision.[44] Yet even in Dijon, mercy could be extended in an individual case, as when they granted the request of a Huguenot merchant whose son had drowned to bury him at night 'however he wished'.[45] However, in 1571, the Huguenots of Angoulême complained to the crown that the local authorities had not yet honoured the provisions of the previous year's edict.[46] An edict of 1576 stipulated that the site granted for burial should be *le plus commode* (the most suitable); a frequent complaint of the Huguenots was that the sites granted were inaccessible or otherwise unacceptable (a common problem faced, too, in the case of sites for worship).[47] Even after satisfactory sites were established, the antagonism did not necessarily end there. Aside from sporadic attacks on those going to and fro, it rumbled on in some towns into the seventeenth century, as in Mâcon in 1647, when the municipal authorities were criticised by the *parlement* for allowing a convent to encroach on a Huguenot cemetery that had been long established.[48] Likewise, the Huguenots of Nantes appealed in 1665 for the restoration of two of the three sites assigned to them for burial purposes in 1601 and which had since been taken out of their control.[49]

In some towns, such as Lyons, places of burial were to take centre-stage in disputes between the faiths. Following the edict of Amboise of 1563, the Huguenots of Lyons successfully appealed to the *maréchal* de Vieilleville (who was responsible for enforcing the edict in the Lyonnais)

---

[43] AD la Drôme, B 996 (Justice Mage de Valence), fol. 259.

[44] AM Dijon, B 200, fols. 184v–5r (12 Apr. 1564); B 202, fols. 129v, 136v (Jan. 1566); B 207, fol. 208v (22 May 1571). In Brittany, many of the municipal authorities were able to hold out until the commissioners sent to enforce the 1598 Edict of Nantes obliged them to provide a site, and in the case of Nantes much longer: see Croix, *La Bretagne aux 16e et 17e siècles*, II, pp. 1002–3.

[45] AM Dijon, B 200, fol. 169r (17 Mar. 1564).   [46] AM Angoulême, AA 5, fol. 62r.

[47] F. A. Isambert, *Recueil générale des anciennes lois françaises, depuis l'an 420, jusqu'à la Révolution de 1789*, (29 vols., Paris, 1822–33), XIV, P. 283.

[48] AD Saône et Loire, Archives Communales de Mâcon, GG 124, nos. 8–12.

[49] AM Nantes, GG 650 (1665–1788).

to grant a site known as the Terreaux where they could hold services and bury their dead.[50] This, they argued, had been agreed to by the municipal authorities, the nuns of Saint-Pierre (whose garden it bordered and who set strict limits on what they could construct) and by His Majesty when he had passed through on his tour of the realm in 1564. Moreover, it had been nothing but a ditch when they had acquired it, which they had filled in and enclosed with high walls at a cost of at least 8,000 *livres*. In 1571 they complained to the governor Mandelot that the authorities were obstructing access. This was countered by the Catholic inhabitants' remonstrances of 1572, that the site had been usurped from the community who had thereby lost its rent and the place where they had previously slaughtered their animals.[51] The Huguenots responded in turn that the designation of Terreaux should be confirmed, since they had been permitted the site by an edict and so much had already been invested in it. They also pointed out that the royal officials ought to be doing something about the fact that there was nowhere else in the region where the authorities had yet conceded a place of burial. In 1600 the commissioners for the enforcement of the Edict of Nantes in Lyons granted part of a garden adjoining a hospital cloister by the Rhône for burials, to which the Huguenots could make a gateway from the street and build a separating wall. Yet in 1604 they were still requesting burials at Terreaux and complaining of the inconvenience and danger of the designated site because of the abuse which they suffered as they went to and fro.[52] The final insult came in June 1606, when the site was granted by the authorities to the Jesuits for the building of a college and a church.[53]

Faced with the obligation of providing a burial site, the authorities not surprisingly preferred the Huguenots to purchase one outside the town at their own expense, thereby also avoiding further inconvenience to civic order. It is clear that funerals and burials were seen as a potential source of unrest, both as a result of Huguenots gathering together as well as the Catholic reaction to their presence. In Mâcon, on 8 November 1563, the Huguenots themselves requested an external site because of the trouble they had encountered in the town when burying their dead.[54] They suggested five locations that would suit them in the suburbs, from which governor Tavannes (more amenable than in other instances) chose Saint-Estienne in consultation with the municipal authorities. Although

[50] AM Lyon, GG 77, no. 20; GG 84.
[51] AM Lyon, GG 78, nos. 21, 34; BM Lyon, MS Coste 426.
[52] AM Lyon, GG 86, nos. 2, 4, 5.   [53] BM Lyon, MS Coste 434.
[54] BN, MS français 4048, fol. 171r.

the Reformed churches of Lyons and Autun attempted to maintain burials near to their place of worship, the pattern was to sever the links between the site of worship and that of burial where 'the prayers of the living and the remains of the dead coexisted'.[55] Yet, as we have seen, this disintegration of the coexistent community of the living and the dead came about for practical rather than doctrinal reasons. 'New' Huguenot cemeteries might be located at some distance, perhaps near to the largest community in a region. For example, at the turn of the century, the Huguenots of Rennes in Brittany were prepared to carry their dead to Vitré (more than twenty miles to the east) where a new cemetery had been established for the Huguenot dead.[56] Evidently, Huguenots were keen to establish stable places of burial; hanging onto a cemetery once established was crucial for obvious reasons. They were much less mobile than, for instance, sites for Reformed services (though the relocation of these could be just as hotly contested) and, as we have seen, they were sometimes linked to each other, making the reallocation of sites for worship with each successive edict of pacification a source of anxiety.[57]

In practical terms, there were a number of factors which decided the fate of Huguenot corpses: the attitude of the presiding authorities, and even single officials (usually high-ranking, such as royal governors); the degree to which the relatively generous provision of successive edicts of pacification could be upheld (largely dependent on these same authorities and their interpretation of this provision); and the ability of the Huguenots to retain or maintain a site once it was established. Aside from demonstrations of confessional hostility, the debate which accompanied this regulation also focused on the common human decency to be extended to the treatment of the dying and the dead, of either faith. Much was inevitably dependent on the relative strength of the faiths in a given locality, as well as the degree of protection of their rights they could expect from the local governor (less so the royal commissioners sent to enforce the edicts whose fleeting presence could only be temporarily effective). The issue of confessional burial was a complex one, and the variety of local strategies implemented to deal with it attests to the fact that no simple or generally

---

[55] Musgrave, 'Memento Mori', p. 70. The breaking of the association between church and cemetery is also evident in other contexts, e.g. in Germany, see Vovelle, *La mort et l'Occident*, p. 232, and in more depth, S. Karant-Nunn, *The Reformation of Ritual: an Interpretation of Early Modern Germany* (London and New York, 1997), esp. p. 178.

[56] Croix, *La Bretagne aux 16e et 17e siècles*, II, p. 1002, n. 414.

[57] On disputes regarding sites for Reformed services, see Penny Roberts, 'The Most Crucial Battle of the Wars of Religion? The Conflict over Sites for Reformed Worship in Sixteenth-Century France', *Archiv für Reformationsgeschichte* 89 (1998).

applicable solution could be found. Opinion was divided; royal declarations on the subject were accepted but often reinterpreted to suit the local situation; whilst Huguenot concerns became focused on establishing and defending their ownership of a particular site. Whether successful or not, the Huguenot campaign to establish their burial rights altered the sacred topography of France, redefining both the association between the living and the dead, as well as what constituted suitable sites for burial. In this way, the ambiguous and contested place of the Huguenot dead can be seen to have formed part of the strategies of confessional separation and exclusion which were to characterise the Wars of Religion. Burial disputes thus represent a crucial barometer of relations, and tensions, between the faiths within French communities during an intense period of civil and religious strife.

8 'Defyle not Christ's kirk with your carrion': burial and the development of burial aisles in post-Reformation Scotland

Andrew Spicer

In 1609 the courtier and diplomat Sir James Melville died at his estate at Halhill, Fife.[1] He was laid to rest at Collessie, in a small, gabled rectangular mausoleum. This building, at the edge of the churchyard, looks out across the countryside and the following inscription is proclaimed to passers-by on the road below:

> Ye loadin pilgrims passing langs this way,
> Paus on your fall, and your offences past
> Hou your frail flesh, first formit of the day
> In dust mon be dissolvit at the last
> Repent amend on Christ the burden cast
> Of your sad sinnes who can your savls refresh
> Syne raise from grave to gloir your grislie flesh
>
> Defyle not Christ's kirk with your carrion
> A solemn sait for God's service prepar'd
> For praier; preaching and communion
> Your byrial should be in the kirk yard
> On your uprysing set your great regard
> When savll and body joynes with joy to ring
> In Heaven for ay with Christ over head and king.[2]

Although now roofless, decayed and the epitaph badly eroded, Melville's mausoleum still provides an intriguing indication of the change in attitudes towards death and burial in post-Reformation Scotland.

---

[1] On his career, see *The Memoirs of Sir James Melville of Halhill*, ed. G. Donaldson (London, 1969).

[2] Recorded in *The New Statistical Account of Scotland* (15 vols., Edinburgh, 1845), IX, p. 27. The mausoleum is pictured in H. Colvin, *Architecture and the After-life* (Yale, 1991), pp. 301, 303 and recorded in J. Gifford, *The Buildings of Scotland: Fife* (London, 1988), p. 130.

At the Reformation the Kirk reacted against the traditional ceremonies and customs associated with death and burial. The rejection of Purgatory, the efficacy of good works and also prayers for the dead, together with the adoption of the doctrine of predestination, all served to undermine the lengthy round of services and masses for the dead associated with burial in the pre-Reformation Church. Such elaborate rituals were rejected as superstitious and superfluous; the doctrine of predestination taught that the consequences of death and the achievement of salvation could not be altered through human actions. The Kirk therefore made provision for a simple service of burial contrasting markedly with the external observances of Catholicism. The body was to be taken to its place of burial without singing and readings, then to be interred soberly without any kind of ceremony. While readings, singing and sermons might all serve to admonish the living and encourage them to prepare for death, some worried that they might be seen as being beneficial to the deceased and hence were to be avoided.[3]

In its desire for simplicity and its strictures concerning burial, the Kirk was little different from other Reformed Churches. However, the Kirk also rejected the practice of kirk-burial, the interment of corpses within the church building itself. Here the Kirk differed significantly from the position adopted in the Netherlands where the churches virtually became graveyards.[4] Kirk-burial was rejected in Scotland for a number of reasons. It was opposed for purely practical reasons; it disturbed the fabric of the building with the floor being broken up for burial.[5] Such burials were also considered to be insanitary; the Kirk ordered that they should take place somewhere 'lying in the most free aire' and at a depth of six feet. Furthermore the *First Book of Discipline*[6] considered kirk-burial to be unseemly in a building which was assigned for preaching and the administration of the sacraments, a view which is endorsed by Melville's epitaph.[7] Not only were such burials unseemly but they could also be seen to foster superstition and the continuation of

---

3 *The First Book of Discipline*, ed. J. K. Cameron (Edinburgh, 1972), pp. 199–200; A. Spicer, '"Rest of their Bones": Fear of Death and Reformed Burial Practices', in W. G. Naphy and P. Roberts (eds.), *Fear in Early Modern Society* (Manchester, 1997), pp. 167–9.

4 Spicer, '"Rest of their Bones"', pp. 167–83.

5 *Visitation of the Diocese of Dunblane and Other Churches, 1586–1589*, ed. J. Kirk, Scottish Record Society, new series, 11 (1984), pp. 3, 14, 30.

6 *First Book of Discipline*, p. 201; *The Booke of the Universall Kirk of Scotland*, ed. T. Thomson (Edinburgh, 1839–45), p. 43. See also Spicer, '"Rest of their Bones"', pp. 170–1.

7 *First Book of Discipline*, p. 201.

pre-Reformation beliefs. This was discussed at great length by the minister of Lanark, William Birnie, in his tract, *The Blame of Kirk-buriall tending to perswade cemeteriall civilitie* which was published in Edinburgh in 1606.[8] The minister argued that burial in a house of prayer might encourage belief in the efficacy of prayers for the dead. Such an opinion, he argued, was furthered by kneeling on graves or being able to see the graves of the deceased while praying. Birnie claimed that such burials were but the thin end of the wedge and were just one step away from encouraging a priest to say masses for the dead.[9]

However, the Kirk's attempt to discourage such burials could raise strong emotions. Sir William Hamilton of Sanquhar, an elder of the church and a major figure in Ayrshire, died in August 1572 bequeathing his 'saule to god & my bones to ye ere'.[10] His son, John Hamilton, broke into the church at Mauchlin, while the kirk session was meeting nearby, with a crowd of 200 people. They threw aside the table boards which had been used that morning for the Lord's Supper and buried Sir William. The bishop of Glasgow was charged by the General Synod to discipline those involved.[11] In 1607 Adam Menzies of Enoche appealed to the Privy Council concerning the dispute over the burial and disinterments of his son at the church of Durisdeer. The burial in the church was seen to be 'his undoubtit rycht and continuall possessioun of his saide antecessoris' and in a place used for 'the bureying of the deid bodyis thairin of the house of Enoche in all aigeis bigane'.[12] These two examples reflect some of the difficulties that the Kirk faced in its opposition to kirk-burial and the risk that it faced of alienating men of local standing. However, the cases also reveal two other areas which were seen to be threatened: the tradition of being buried with one's ancestors and the legal rights of burial possessed by some lairds.

There was a long-standing tradition of being buried with one's forebears; in fact, the coffin-routes to clan burial grounds were an important part of the communications network of the Highlands.[13] Burial amongst one's ancestors served to demonstrate the permanence

---

[8] W. Birnie, *The Blame of Kirk-buriall tending to perswade cemeteriall civilitie*, ed. W. B. D. D. Turnball (London, 1833). The volume is unpaginated.

[9] Birnie, *Blame of Kirk-buriall*, chaps. 11, 17, 19.

[10] Scottish Record Office (SRO), cc8/8/73; G. Hamilton *A History of the House of Hamilton* (Edinburgh, 1933), pp. 777–8; M. H. B. Sanderson, *Ayrshire and the Reformation: People and Change, 1490–1600* (East Linton, 1997), pp. 9, 14, 105, 138.

[11] *Booke of the Universall Kirk*, pp. 272–3, 294.

[12] *The Register of the Privy Council of Scotland*, ed. J. Hill Burton *et al.* (36 vols., Edinburgh, 1877–1933),vii, p. 315.

[13] J. Dawson, 'The Origin of the "Road to the Isles": Trade, Communications and Campbell

and stability of a family and it was a tradition which remained strong even after the Reformation.[14] Considerable effort was taken to ensure that the deceased's body was recovered and was buried amongst his family. The body of Lord Hugh Fraser of Lovat who had died at Tolly, Mar, in January 1577 was conveyed to Beauly Priory for burial. Five hundred men from the Fraser clan accompanied by '24 gentlemen heads of families as officers to manage them with good conduct in the rode' were sent to collect the body and were joined by representatives of other clans *en route*. As the 'wether [was] beyond expectation serene and fair', the journey from Tolly took eight days.[15] However, conveying the deceased to the traditional family plot could prove to be a major undertaking: the case of the first earl of Buccleuch is perhaps an extreme example. The earl died in London in November 1633 while returning from the Netherlands; 'being sent home by sea, [the ship] was by Storme of Wether drivin over to Norway, where ye said Corps remened 5 monethes and at last was brought home in John Simpsons Ship in Kirkcaldy and landed at Leith, who thereafter ye said Corps had remened twinty days in ye Kirk was transported to his house of Brandsholme and remened there till ye 11 day of June 1634 where he was from that to ye Kirk of Hawick'.[16] One further interesting example is George Sinclair, fourth earl of Caithness, who died in 1582; his will stipulated that his body was to be buried in Edinburgh and his heart was to be encased in lead and buried next to his wife in the burial 'aisle' of the church at Wick. His body was interred in Rosslyn Chapel which had been founded in *c.* 1446 by his great grandfather, William Sinclair, earl of Orkney and Caithness.[17] Such practices were condemned by Birnie who criticised 'the superstitious opinion of the perogatiue of some sepulchrall places, for their hallowed moulds, . . . [and] these farland conuoyences of the dead to their homed tombes, defrauding the weary corps of the desired rest'.[18]

The prohibition of kirk-burial also challenged the legal rights and

Power in Early Modern Scotland', in R. Mason and N. Macdougall (eds.), *People and Power in Scotland. Essays in Honour of T. C. Smout* (Edinburgh, 1992), p. 83.

[14] The desire of Huguenots to be buried amongst their ancestors caused particular problems in France in this period. Spicer, ' "Rest of their Bones" ', p. 177. See also Penny Roberts's chapter in this volume.

[15] James Fraser, *Chronicles of the Frasers. The Wardlaw Manuscript*, ed. W. Mackay, Scottish History Society, 47 (1905), pp. 174–5.

[16] Court of the Lord Lyon, D1 34 Funeralls, pp. 68–9; J. Balfour Paul, *The Scots Peerage* (9 vols., Edinburgh, 1904–14), II, pp. 233–4.

[17] SRO, cc8/8/12; Balfour Paul, *Scots Peerage*, II, pp. 332–40; R. Fawcett, *Scottish Architecture from the Accession of the Stewarts to the Reformation, 1371–1560* (Edinburgh, 1994), p. 171.

[18] Birnie, *Blame of Kirk-buriall*, chap. 8.

prerogatives of some lairds over their local church. Landowners or heritors were usually patrons responsible for the financial concerns of the parish and church building, excluding the chancel. Patronage was acknowledged as being a heritable property-right which was normally conveyed with a barony or lands to which it was attached. Furthermore, there was a marked increase in the number of patrons after the 1587 Act of Annexation, as the crown dispersed episcopal and monastic estates with the rights of patronage to the annexed churches.[19] It had become commonplace for patrons to be buried inside the church and this right was jealously guarded, as can be seen in the case of Adam Menzies of Enoche. Although the dispute centred on the issue of kirk-burial, it seems to have been motivated by Sir William Douglas of Drumlanrig's challenge to the Menzies's legal right of burial.[20] However, this privilege was also attacked by Birnie.[21]

In seeming to threaten the rights and traditions of the landed elites, the Kirk's attempt to prohibit burial inside churches inevitably resulted in opposition and disputes.[22] In his broad survey of the architectural responses to death, Professor Howard Colvin has examined the construction of the burial 'aisle' (an annex or lateral projection from the main body of the church) in Scotland which served to satisfy the demands of the Kirk but also the wishes of the landowners with regard to burial. To an extent it could be argued that an accommodation was reached on the issue of kirk-burial.[23] However, the establishment of such 'aisles', although important, represents only a part of the picture of how certain families adapted to the changes of the Reformation with regard to burial without compromising their traditions and rights.

Before the Reformation, monastic churches were popular places of burial for the élite. They often occupied sites of ancient sanctity, possessed relics making them centres of pilgrimage, and had communities which could pray for the soul of the departed. Iona had been the ancient burial place of the Scottish kings but was then replaced by Dunfermline Abbey which possessed the relics of St Margaret. While later monarchs selected other places of burial, all of the Scottish kings – with the exception of

---

[19] J. Kirk, 'The Survival of Ecclesiastical Patronage after the Reformation', in his *Patterns of Reform: Continuity and Change in the Reformation Kirk* (Edinburgh, 1989), pp. 421, 424–5. On the maintenance of the church fabric, see *The Books of Assumption of the Thirds of Benefices. Scottish Ecclesiastical Rentals at the Reformation*, ed. J. Kirk, British Academy: Records of Social and Economic History, new series, 21 (1995), p. xlii.

[20] *Register of the Privy Council of Scotland*, vii, pp. 315–17, 337–8.

[21] Birnie, *Blame of Kirk-buriall*, chap. 19.

[22] Spicer, ' "Rest of their Bones" ', pp. 170–4.

[23] Colvin, *Architecture and the After-life*, pp. 296–306.

Plate 8.1   *Beauly Priory, Inverness-shire. The East End. [Crown Copyright: Reproduced Courtesy of Historic Scotland]*

James IV – were buried in monastic houses.[24] However, monastic churches were not the exclusive preserve of royalty: in England some communities actively sought burials in their precincts.[25]

Beauly Priory near Inverness was closely associated with the Frasers of Lovat who were the successors of John Byset who had founded the Valliscaulian house in *c.* 1230. In the early fifteenth century, Hugh Fraser of Lovat complained to the pope about the ruinous condition of the house and began a rebuilding programme which included the Chapel of the Holy Cross.[26] By the sixteenth century the Priory had become the favoured burial place for the Frasers of Lovat; for example, Hugh Fraser of Lovat and his son were buried there after being killed in a clan fight in 1544.[27] (See Plate 8.1.)

---

[24] M. Dilworth, *Scottish Monastic Houses in the Late Middle Ages* (Edinburgh, 1995), p. 58.

[25] C. Daniell, *Death and Burial in Medieval England, 1066–1550* (London, 1997), pp. 91–2.

[26] Dilworth, *Scottish Monastic Houses*, p. 7; Fawcett, *Scottish Architecture from the Accession of the Stewarts*, pp. 88–9; D. MacGibbon and T. Ross, *The Ecclesiastical Architecture of Scotland* (3 vols., Edinburgh, 1896), II, pp. 245–51; J. Gifford, *The Buildings of Scotland: Highlands and Islands* (London, 1992), pp. 149–53.

[27] The tomb was apparently identifiable in the eighteenth century: E. C. Batten, *The Charters*

At the Reformation, although Catholicism was proscribed, the monastic houses in Scotland did not disappear overnight but gradually withered away.[28] At Beauly, Hugh, fifth Lord Fraser of Lovat had acquired the barony and lands of Beauly from Walter, Abbot of Kinross in *feu ferme* in November 1571; this grant of the Priory's lands and buildings was subsequently confirmed by the crown.[29] Although the Priory church had really lost its religious role with the Reformation, it continued as a burial place for the family. In 1576 Hugh Fraser of Lovat was buried there at Candlemas before the high altar in a funeral noted for its 'solemnity and magnificence'. His sister-in-law and brother were buried at Beauly in 1611 and 1612 respectively.[30] Such burials continued at Beauly until 1633 when Simon Fraser was buried there, but the family then constructed a mausoleum about five miles away at Kirkhill due to the ruinous condition of the Priory.[31] However, the church was not abandoned and continued to be used for burial by other branches of the Fraser family. The family's continued use of their traditional burial place after the Reformation is intriguing. The Priory had lost its *raison d'être*, and the community of monks had withered away, but burials continued to take place around the high altar and even today there are several seventeenth-century table-top tombs at the east end of the church. Whether the continued use of this building was merely the result of tradition or of a residual belief in the sanctity of the site is a moot point.

However, some families chose to reject their traditional monastic burial places after the Reformation. John Erskine, earl of Mar wrote his will in August 1568 at Stirling and ordered that he was to be buried in the choir of the church at Alloa. He went on 'I ordaine ane honourable sepulchre to be maid and ye relicts of my forbears which are in the abbey of Cambuskynneth to be transportit ther.'[32] The Erskine family did already have links with Alloa; Alexander, third Lord Erskine, had founded a chaplainry in the church in 1497.[33] The reason for the move to Alloa is

---

of the Priory of Beauly (Edinburgh, 1877), pp. 223, 225. In 1287 Sir Simon Fraser of Lovat was buried before the high altar; Hugh Fraser was said to have been buried at Beauly in 1440. Gifford, *Highlands and Islands*, p. 149; Batten, *Charters of the Priory of Beauly*, p. 97.

[28] Dilworth, *Scottish Monastic Houses*, pp. 78–80.

[29] Gifford, *Highlands and Islands*, p. 150; Balfour Paul, *Scots Peerage*, v, pp. 528–30.

[30] Fraser, *Chronicles of the Frasers*, pp. 175, 241; Batten, *Charters of the Priory of Beauly*, pp. 279–80.

[31] Fraser, *Chronicles of the Frasers*, pp. 219, 242, 249, 266. On the new mausoleum at Kirkhill, see below, pp. 163–4.

[32] SRO, GD 124/3/9, CC8/8/3.

[33] *The New Statistical Account of Scotland*, VIII, Clackmannan – Alloa, p. 37.

unclear although it is close to the family seat of the Erskines. Subsequent earls of Mar were buried at Alloa and by 1652 the third earl could describe the church as 'the burryall [place] of our Ancestores'.[34] In the eighteenth century the exiled Jacobite earl of Mar designed an elaborate pew and burial place for his family, which looked more like a stage set, to be built at Alloa. The pew was to be reached by a double flight of stairs and the vault was to be surmounted by an ornamented black marble obelisk.[35]

Perhaps even more interesting than the monasteries is the fate of the collegiate churches and chantries after the Reformation. Collegiate churches in Scotland were essentially late medieval foundations, and were established principally to pray for the souls of the founders and also often served as family burial places. About fifty such colleges were founded, mainly in the Lowlands of Scotland. These buildings took a variety of forms: some were attached to existing churches in the church-yards of the founder's parish church; others were completely new build-ings. With the Reformation and the rejection of the efficacy of prayers for the dead, these institutions became redundant. However, as many as thirty of these foundations survived the Reformation, becoming parish churches, family burial places and university chapels.[36] An examination of several of these collegiate churches provides a useful indication of the attitude of the landed elites towards burial and the extent to which the role of these institutions had changed in the post-Reformation period.

In *c.* 1425 Thomas, first Lord Somerville built a chapel at Carnwath, Lanarkshire, adjacent to the parish church.[37] This became a collegiate chapel with a foundation for a provost and six prebendaries to pray for the souls of the founder and his family. The chapel became the burial place for the Lords Somerville and still contains the altar-tomb of Hugh, Lord Somerville and his wife, who died in 1549.[38] The fifth Lord Somerville, who died in 1569, was the last member of the family to be buried at Carnwath.[39] By the end of the sixteenth century the Somervilles seem to have adopted the choir of the church at Cambusnethan as their burial place. The abandonment of the chapel probably owed more to the family's alienation of the barony of Carnwath, and presumably with it the

---

[34] SRO, GD 124/3/52; D. MacGibbon and T. Ross, *The Castellated and Domestic Architecture of Scotland* (5 vols., Edinburgh, 1887–92), I, pp. 155–6.

[35] Colvin, *Architecture and the After-life*, pp. 341–3.

[36] Fawcett, *Scottish Architecture from the Accession of the Stewarts*, pp. 142–4.

[37] *Ibid.*, p. 30.

[38] MacGibbon and Ross, *Ecclesiastical Architecture of Scotland*, III, pp. 349–50.

[39] Balfour Paul, *Scots Peerage*, VIII, p. 21.

Plate 8.2   *Maybole Collegiate Church, Ayrshire. Part of the seventeenth-century extension. [Crown Copyright: Reproduced Courtesy of Historic Scotland]*

rights to the former collegiate chapel, than any concern about the Kirk's attitudes towards burial. The chapel continued as a burial place during the seventeenth century for the Lockharts who assumed the barony.[40] Carnwath therefore provides a good example of how such collegiate chapels continued to serve as the resting place for a local family even after the Reformation had proscribed masses for the dead.

Maybole in Ayrshire was one of the earliest and simplest collegiate chapels established in Scotland. In 1371, John Kennedy of Dunure founded the chapel at Maybole and by 1382 had received permission

---

[40]   Balfour Paul, *Scots Peerage*, VIII, pp. 24, 25, 26. On the adoption of choirs as burial places in the post-Reformation Church, see below, pp. 160–1.

from the bishop of Glasgow to establish a college of priests, by which time the construction of the buildings was complete. The college of three priests and a clerk was to pray in perpetuity for the salvation of the souls of the founder and his family.[41] The college continued to function for a time after the Reformation as mass was publicly celebrated there in 1563.[42] The church had served as a burial place for the Kennedy family and this role continued after the Reformation. In 1578 Sir Hugh Kennedy of Girvanmains requested in his will that his body be 'buryit in ye college kirk of mayboill at ye south end of ye hie alter' and eight years later, Dame Margaret Kennedy asked to be buried 'in ye college kirk of Maybole besid my umqle sone Erle of cassills'.[43]

Not only did the collegiate church at Maybole continue to be used by the Kennedy family for burial after the Reformation, it was repaired, developed and extended in the seventeenth century for further burials (see Plate 8.2). An agreement was drawn up in 1632 by the provost of Maybole, Ralph Weir of Brennane, on the advice of the earl of Cassillis, the patron of the college, for the repair of the building because 'of the ruinous estate & decay of the said College' which 'was apoyntit for the burial place of the said Earle his Lordships predecessors & certaine others of his Lordships friends'. The earl and branches of the Kennedy family were to contribute to the repair of the college in return for which they were each to receive burial rights and access to the building. The interior of the repaired church was to be divided up amongst various branches of the Kennedy family as burial plots or rooms; the earl and his heirs were assigned an area the whole width of the church and fifteen feet in length from the east end of the church. The next fifteen feet of the Kirk was to be split between the families of Hew Kennedy of Girvanmains and Thomas Kennedy of Ardmillane and so on, dividing it into seven plots in total.[44] The seventeenth-century entrance to the church surmounted by the Kennedy coat of arms presumably dates from this period.[45] The college therefore continued to function long after the Reformation as the burial place of the Kennedys and continued to have a provost and prebendaries, although their religious role had disappeared.[46]

Collegiate churches such as Maybole were so small as to be little more than chantry chapels. At Straiton in Ayrshire, seven miles from Maybole,

---

[41] Fawcett, *Scottish Architecture from the Accession of the Stewarts*, pp. 24–5, 142, 145.
[42] I. Cowan and D. E. Easson, *Medieval Religious Houses. Scotland* (London, 1976), p. 224.
[43] SRO, cc8/8/6, cc8/8/29.
[44] SRO, GD 25/9/2/7.
[45] MacGibbon and Ross, *Ecclesiastical Architecture of Scotland*, III, pp. 341–3.
[46] SRO, GD 25/9/2/7.

the south transept was adapted as a chantry chapel in 1475 by John Kennedy of Blairquhan. Today a holy water stoup survives, as do the piscina, credence table and aumbry as well as a pedestal for a statue. The tomb of John Kennedy who died in 1501, complete with crest and traces of the original colouring, survives beneath the Gothic window. At the Reformation this transept was sealed off from the main church and served until the nineteenth century as the burial place of the lairds of Blairquhan. The transept is the only remaining part of the thirteenth-century church, the main body of the church being rebuilt in the eighteenth century.[47]

As these three examples demonstrate, certain religious establishments which became redundant through the Reformation, especially those specifically charged with providing prayers for the souls of the founder and his family, continued to have a role. Families which had established these foundations continued to use them as places of burial in spite of the changed circumstances. In a sense this might have been their wish to continue the tradition of a family burial site or it might relate to a deeper superstition or belief in the sanctity of such buildings. Whatever the reasons for such practices, it was difficult for the Kirk to challenge them in what were redundant religious buildings, because to do so would be to recognise a sanctity or significance which it had already refuted.

With the Reformation the interiors of parish churches were adapted for the new demands of Reformed worship. The emphasis was directed away from the regular celebration and spectacle of the mass towards the preaching of the Word of God. The pulpit became the focal point in services, replacing the altar; whereas the altar had been placed at the east end of the church behind a rood screen, distant from the congregation, the pulpit was placed in a central position where the minister and congregation could clearly see and hear each other. In a number of churches the pulpit was placed in the centre of the longest wall, and with the construction of galleries and the introduction of seating, the congregation came to be ranged around it. Clearly, the form of adaptation varied from church to church; for example, St Giles's in Edinburgh was divided into several churches each with galleries for the congregation.[48]

Although the Reformed Church aspired to administer the Lord's

---

[47] MacGibbon and Ross, *Ecclesiastical Architecture of Scotland*, III, pp. 396–7; G. Hay, *The Architecture of Scottish Post-Reformation Churches, 1560–1840* (Oxford, 1957), p. 250. Other information about the aisle comes from unpublished material at Straiton.

[48] Spicer, 'Architecture and the Reformation', in A. Pettegree (ed.), *The Reformation World* (Routledge, forthcoming); Hay, *Architecture of Scottish Post-Reformation Churches*, pp. 21–8; D. Howard, *Scottish Architecture from the Reformation to the Restoration, 1560–1660* (Edinburgh, 1995), pp. 172–7.

Supper weekly, this was clearly impractical and as a result it was held infrequently. The reformers emphasised that this was a congregational and corporate event and the church was required to set up special tables for the administration of the sacrament. Initially in larger churches, the chancels were used for the administration of the Lord's Supper; this happened at Crail, Culross and Perth where the chancels became communion 'aisles'. However, in most churches the small size of the chancel meant that this was not feasible and long tables were erected along the length of the building enabling the communicants to sit down together for the Lord's Supper.[49]

These liturgical changes meant that the chancel had become, in many cases, redundant. As a result, in some churches the chancel was sealed off from the main body of the church to be used by the local laird as a burial 'aisle'. As has already been seen, the Erskine earls of Mar had taken over the choir at Alloa and the Somervilles the choir of Cambusnethan for their burial places. At Old St Peter's church in Thurso, Caithness, the Sinclairs of Forss took over the chancel and a separate communion 'aisle' was built. The Wemyss family took over the chancel of the early sixteenth-century church at East Wemyss, Fife; the Aytouns of Inchdairnie took over the chancel at Kinglassie.[50] However, it was not only redundant chancels which were adapted as burial vaults. At Haddington, the former sacristy of the church was adapted in the early seventeenth century by the first earl of Lauderdale into a burial 'aisle'. The Lauderdale monument on the north wall commemorates, in effigy, the earl's father (John Maitland, Lord Thirlestane, Chancellor of Scotland who died in 1595) and mother, as well as the earl himself and his wife.[51] The vault beneath became the burial place for at least seventeen members of the Maitland family from the seventeenth to the nineteenth century.[52] The adaptation of the chancel or part of the existing building as a burial vault by the local laird might be seen as being a matter of convenience; but for some, it could also reflect the survival of the tradition of burying the elite in what was perceived to be the holiest part of the church building, where the mass had been celebrated.[53]

[49] Hay, *Architecture of Scottish Post-Reformation Churches*, pp. 25–6, 179–81; Howard, *Scottish Architecture from the Reformation*, p. 172.

[50] Gifford, *Highlands and Islands*, pp. 35, 130; Gifford, *Fife*, pp. 203, 273.

[51] C. McWilliam, *The Buildings of Scotland: Lothian (except Edinburgh)* (London, 1978), pp. 232, 235; Howard, *Scottish Architecture from the Reformation*, p. 206.

[52] D. H. Caldwell, 'A Group of Post-Medieval Noble Burials at Haddington', *Transactions of the East Lothian Antiquarian and Field Naturalists' Society* 15 (1976), pp. 25–37.

[53] For the popularity of this location in medieval England, see Daniell, *Death and Burial in Medieval England*, pp. 97–9.

The conversion of redundant chancels into burial 'aisles' also meant that a part of the church which had previously been the responsibility of the parish priest was now maintained by the laird. At Borthwick the kirk session complained to the Presbytery of Dalkeith about the ruinous condition of the parish church in 1606, the choir and vestry being in a particularly parlous condition. The walls and roof were giving way and the woodwork was decaying. The representatives from the Presbytery examined the structure and met the parishioners, who were opposed to raising the money for repairs from amongst themselves. They concluded that 'the best meane for reparing of the said kirk and vphalding of the same Revestrie Tobe the dispositioun of the same Revestrie to sum gentleman of the said parochin for ane buriall. The samyn serving for na vther vse'. With the consent of the Presbytery, Sir James Dundas of Arniston agreed to pay 250 marks for the vestry which was 'to be ane buriall for him and his posteritie'. The arrangement was ratified in an Act of Parliament which also stipulated that 'the said Sir James furneist the Charges and expenss in repairing of the said kirk'.[54] In his will, he requested that he be buried at Borthwick and he was interred 'in a little isle of his oune in that kirk' on 7 October 1628.[55] The purchase of the vestry is indicative of the dynastic ambitions of Sir James Dundas, whose father had bought him the estate of Arniston in 1571, and who later served as Governor of Berwick to James VI.[56] His father, George Dundas, of Dundas had been interred in the 'buriall place perteyning to ye hous of Dundas within ye kirk . . . of South quensferie' where a fragment of his tomb survives.[57]

Not only were parts of the church adapted for burial but new burial vaults were constructed on the sites of former chancels or at the east end of churches. At Terregles near Dumfries, a 'quire' or burial chamber was built at the end of the east end of the church during the 1580s. As a semi-octagonal apse and at the east end, it continues the medieval tradition but it does not seem to have had any liturgical significance.[58] Although Sir

---

[54] T. Thomas and C. Innes (eds.), *The Acts of Parliament of Scotland* (Edinburgh, 1814–75), IV, p. 499; G. W. T. Omond, *The Arniston Memoirs. Three Centuries of a Scottish House 1571–1838* (Edinburgh, 1887), pp. 6–7.

[55] Court of the Lord Lyon, D1–34 Funeralls, pp. 47–8; Omond, *Arniston Memoirs*, pp. 12–13.

[56] M. D. Young (ed.), *The Parliaments of Scotland: Burgh and Shire Commissioners* (2 vols., Edinburgh, 1992–3), I, pp. 214–15, 216.

[57] SRO, cc8/8/34; McWilliam, *Lothian*, p. 432; *Parliaments of Scotland*, I, p. 216.

[58] The date of the structure is unclear and is given variously as 1583, 1585 and 1588, and seems to be based upon the date inscribed on the cornice: Fawcett, *Scottish Architecture from the Accession of the Stewarts*, p. 227; J. Gifford, *The Buildings of Scotland: Dumfries*

John Maxwell of Terregles, fourth Lord Herries was a strong supporter of Mary, Queen of Scots, he was also a staunch Protestant. However, his son the fifth Lord Herries had converted to Catholicism and attended mass in 1584. As the fourth Lord Herries seems to have been responsible for the structure, it is unlikely that it was intended as a liturgical chancel although it may have been a remodelling of an earlier structure but for use as a burial 'aisle'.[59] The fourth Lord Herries was interred in the 'quire' in 1583 and his wife requested to be buried beside him. The 'aisle' also contains the tombs of two of their sons, Sir Robert Maxwell of Spottes and Edward Maxwell of Lamington, and their wives.[60]

Terregles is not, however, an isolated example of a burial vault being built at the east end of a church. At Oldhamstocks, Lothian, the minister Thomas Hepburn seems to have built a burial 'aisle' (although it is not referred to in his will) at the east end of the church. There is a heraldic panel with the arms of the minister and his wife Margaret Sinclair and dated 1581.[61] A red sandstone 'aisle' was built in 1616 by George Munro of Milntown at the east end of the church of Kilmuir Easter, Cromarty. Munro was also a minister and played a prominent role in the establishment of the Reformed Church in Ross and Cromarty. The family does however seem to have had long-standing links with the church as Munro's father and grandfather were buried there.[62] Other examples of this type of burial vault survive at Drumelzier, Peebleshire (an 'aisle' was erected for James Tweedie in 1617) and Bowden, Roxburghshire (a laird's loft was constructed over a burial vault at the east end of the church in

---

and Galloway (London, 1996), p. 538; MacGibbon and Ross, *Ecclesiastical Architecture of Scotland*, III, pp. 614–15; Royal Commission on Ancient and Historical Monuments of Scotland (RCAHMS), *Ancient and Historical Monuments – Stewartry of Kirkcudbright* (Edinburgh, 1914), pp. 253–5; W. Fraser, *The Book of Carlaverock. Memoirs of the Maxwells, Earls of Nithsdale, Lords Maxwell and Herries* (2 vols., Edinburgh, 1873), I, plate facing p. 569.

59 Fawcett, *Scottish Architecture from the Accession of the Stewarts*, p. 227; Gifford, *Dumfries and Galloway*, p. 539; K. Brown, 'The Making of a *Politique*: the Counter Reformation and the Regional Politics of John, Eighth Lord Maxwell', *The Scottish Historical Review* 66 (1987), pp. 152–3, 158.

60 SRO cc8/8/12, cc8/8/32; Fraser, *Book of Carlaverock*, pp. 568–9; Balfour Paul, *Scots Peerage*, IV, p. 411.

61 SRO, cc8/8/15; McWilliam, *Lothian*, p. 371; MacGibbon and Ross, *Ecclesiastical Architecture of Scotland*, III, pp. 594–6; RCAHMS, *Inventory of Monuments and Constructions in the County of East Lothian* (Edinburgh, 1924), p. 74; *Fasti Ecclesiae Scoticanae. The Succession of Ministers in the Church of Scotland from the Reformation*, ed. H. Scott *et al.* (Edinburgh, 1915), pp. 412–13. Another heraldic panel refers to a later minister also called Thomas Hepburn who served the parish from 1642 onwards.

62 Gifford, *Highlands and Islands*, p. 430; J. A. Inglis, *The Monros of Auchinbowie and Cognate Families* (Edinburgh, 1911), pp. 2–6.

Plate 8.3   *Lovat Mausoleum, Kirkhill, Inverness-shire. [Crown Copyright:
Royal Commission on the Ancient and Historical Monuments of Scotland]*

1644 for Robert Ker, first earl of Roxburghe).[63] In fact at Oldhamstocks
and Bowden these additions have subsequently been converted into
chancels.[64]

The decision to build at the east end of the church was also a
reflection of how responsibility for the choir had passed from the parish
priest or the appropriating institution to the local laird. The dispersal of
church lands through temporal lordships, particularly after the 1587 Act
of Annexation, conveyed with it the rights to the east end of the church.
As a result, the local laird had a legal right to adapt existing chancels or to
build at that end of the church.[65] However, there could also be practical
reasons for the decision to build at the east end, as can be seen at Kirkhill.
The Frasers of Lovat decided to build a mausoleum at the east end of the
existing church at Kirkhill when they arranged to move their burial place

[63] RCAHMS, *Peebleshire. An Inventory of the Ancient Monuments* (2 vols., Edinburgh, 1967),
     II, pp. 195–6; RCAHMS, *An Inventory of the Ancient and Historical Monuments of
     Roxburghshire* (2 vols., Edinburgh, 1956), I, pp. 66–7.
[64] McWilliam, *Lothian*, p. 372; RCAHMS, *Roxburghshire*, p. 66.
[65] See above, note 19; Hay, *Architecture of Scottish Post-Reformation Churches*, p. 20; Fawcett,
     Scottish Architecture from the Accession of the Stewarts, p. 217.

from Beauly. According to the Wardlaw manuscript, 'their first design was to have erected the chapell at the wester end of the church, but the hight of the rock impeded that, so that they chused the litle bottom at the easter end of the church, which of old was the buriall place of the Mackayes in Clune, who now had removed to Kintail'.[66] The location of the mausoleum in fact meant that the east window of the church, which had been given in the mid-fourteenth century by the widow of the third Lord Fraser of Lovat, was blocked.[67] (See Plate 8.3.)

Burial 'aisles' were not solely added at the east end of churches; lateral 'aisles' were constructed projecting from the church wherever it was convenient to build. These burial 'aisles' really should be seen in context and against the background of late medieval chapel construction. During the fifteenth century there was a gradual development of lateral chapels built onto a church by a particular family, which could serve as a burial place and often had endowments for the foundation of a chantry. Such chapels were a reflection of familial piety as well as the status and aspirations of the family concerned.[68] After the Reformation, the local lairds continued to build burial places for their families which were divided from the church interior by a wall, and so satisfied the Kirk's prohibition of burial within the church.

At Kinfauns, Perthshire, a gabled rectangle, almost square, was constructed to the south of the medieval church. The heraldic panel over the entrance is dated 1598 and although much eroded it probably bore the arms of John Chatteris of Kinfauns, who built the 'aisle'. The interior of the chamber is supported by elegant rib-vaulting, decorated with the arms of the Chisholm and Chatteris families.[69] There are two mural tablets on the east and west walls, each divided into three sections by pilasters. One tablet commemorates John Chatteris and his wife Janet Chisholm and their son George Chatteris, and displays their heraldic devices.[70] The mural tablet on the east wall has an elaborate coat of arms and initials; there is no inscription. It can be conjectured that these might be the arms of Helen Chisholm, the wife of Henry Lindsay alias Chatteris, thirteenth earl of Crawford, who died *c.* 1598.[71] The burial 'aisle' seems unfinished

---

[66] Fraser, *Chronicles of the Frasers*, p. 266.

[67] Gifford, *Highlands and Islands*, p. 210.

[68] Fawcett, *Scottish Architecture from the Accession of the Stewarts*, pp. 227–30.

[69] Hay, *Architecture of Scottish Post-Reformation Churches*, pp. 29–30, plate 6a.

[70] Inscriptions at Kinfauns; Hay, *Architecture of Scottish Post-Reformation Churches*, pp. 29–30.

[71] Henry Lindsay had been adopted by John Chatteris of Kinfauns and had taken the name and arms of Chatteris which was confirmed by Act of Parliament in 1587. In the arms, H

Plate 8.4   *The Skelmorelie Aisle, Largs, Ayrshire. A view of the laird's loft over the burial vault. [Crown Copyright: Reproduced Courtesy of Historic Scotland]*

with empty sections of the mural tablets and with blank cartouches. Although Sir John Lindsay, the thirteenth earl's eldest son, was buried at Kinfauns in 1615, the estate had already been sold by the earl of Crawford in 1612.[72]

At Ballantrae on the Ayrshire coast, a new church was constructed by a branch of the Kennedy family, the laird of Bargany, at the end of the sixteenth century. The parish church of Innertig was 'altogidder ruinous and decayed' and so Thomas Kennedy, who was an ardent reformer, provided land for the church and a glebe in a more populated area of the parish. The church was erected in the burgh of Ballantrae, close by the castle of Ardstinchar, 'for heiring of the worde and vse of ye sacramentis'.[73] Nothing remains now of this church apart from an 'aisle' which was erected to Gilbert Kennedy, sixteenth baron of Bargany between 1602 and 1605. Kennedy had been murdered by his distant cousin, the fifth earl of Cassillis, in local feuding during an ambush near Maybole. His widow, Jean Stewart, died shortly after her husband.[74] Their bodies were then carried in procession from Ayr to Ballantrae for burial in 1605, accompanied by the Lords Semple, Loudoun, Abercorn and Montgomerie.[75] A monument with the recumbent effigies of the laird and his wife was erected in the 'aisle'.[76]

Both of these burial 'aisles', through their use of heraldry and fashionable monuments, served to emphasise the importance of the families interred there.[77] However, the status of the laird could be furthered by the building of lofts or pews over the burial vault. The laird was able to attend services unobserved, having his own private access to the loft through an external staircase. Although the burial 'aisles' at Kinfauns and Ballantrae may have opened onto the main body of the church at ground

---

and L impaled with a C could refer to the Earl and 'H C' to his wife, Helen Chisholm. The arms displayed show the Crawford arms with an escutcheon bearing the Chatteris arms, impaled with those of Chisholm. Balfour Paul, *Scots Peerage*, III, p. 32; *The Complete Peerage of England, Scotland, Ireland, Great Britain and the United Kingdom*, ed. V. Gibbs *et al.* (12 vols., London, 1910–40), III, p. 517.

[72] Balfour Paul, *Scots Peerage*, III, pp. 32–3.

[73] *Acts of Parliament of Scotland*, IV, p. 555; *The Parliaments of Scotland*, I, pp. 386–7.

[74] Balfour Paul, *The Scots Peerage*, II, p. 476, VI, p. 516.

[75] *Ayr Burgh Accounts, 1534–1624*, ed. G. S. Pryde, Scottish History Society, third series, 28 (1937), p. 228.

[76] Hay, *Architecture of Scottish Post-Reformation Churches*, p. 208.

[77] The monuments erected were clearly an important display of the status of the individual. On this subject see Howard, *Scottish Architecture from the Reformation*, pp. 203–7; G. Donaldson, 'The Dunbar Monument in its Historical Setting', in *Dunbar Parish Church* (East Lothian Antiquarian and Field Naturalists' Society, 1987), pp. 1–16; D. Howard, 'The Kinnoull Aisle and Monument', *Architectural History* 39 (1996), pp. 36–53.

level, providing some private accommodation for services, they are not as impressive as those 'aisles' which were specifically constructed for this dual purpose. In fact the building of burial vaults with lairds' lofts above, directly opposite the pulpit to the south of the nave, converted existing rectangular buildings into the T-shape so characteristic of Scottish post-Reformation church architecture. Elaborate screens built across the front of these lofts provided another opportunity to display heraldic devices and further emphasise the family's status; a typical example is the screen built for the Forbes family loft at Pitsligo in 1634.[78]

One of the earliest post-Reformation burial 'aisles' which seems to have originally had a laird's loft was built at Banff by Sir George Ogilvy of Dunlugus, who had been provost of the town. The 'aisle' projects from the south of the nave and was erected in 1580 to commemorate Ogilvy's parents, Sir Walter Ogilvy of Dunlugus and his wife Alison Hume who had died in 1558 and 1557 respectively. They are commemorated in an arched altar tomb within the vault, although this is now sadly vandalised.[79]

The medieval form of the 'aisle' built at Banff is in complete contrast to the 'aisles' built by Alexander Seton, first earl of Dunfermline at Dalgety Bay in Fife and that built by Sir Robert Montgomerie of Skelmorelie at Largs, Ayrshire. Both of these buildings reflect a more sophisticated form of architecture and the influence of the court. Alexander Seton was James VI's Lord Chancellor and was part of the influential group of courtier builders of the early seventeenth century. He was the patron of the Master of the King's Works, William Schaw, and carried out building works at Fyvie Castle, Aberdeenshire and Pinkie House, Midlothian.[80] In his will, Seton requested that he be buried at 'my littell ile biggit be my selff at ye kirk of my hous at Dagatie'.[81] The 'aisle' was erected c. 1610 at the west end of the church and completely dominates the building, taking the form of a small tower house. The burial vault is on the ground floor but above is

[78] Hay, *Architecture of Scottish Post-Reformation Churches*, pp. 191, 193, plate 33; Howard, *Scottish Architecture from the Reformation*, pp. 200–1.

[79] C. D. Abercromby, *The Ogilvies of Banff* (Aberdeen, 1939); *The Parliaments of Scotland*, II, pp. 549–50; Hay, *Architecture of Scottish Post-Reformation Churches*, pp. 30, 205; inscriptions in the Ogilvy vault.

[80] Howard, *Scottish Architecture from the Reformation*, pp. 30, 50, 64, 83, 87, 103, 106, 213, 218; M. Bath, 'Alexander Seton's Painted Gallery', in L. Gent (ed.), *Albion's Classicism: the Visual Arts in Britain, 1550–1650* (New Haven, CT, 1995), pp. 79–108. On Seton's career, see M. Lee Jr, 'King James's Popish Chancellor', in I. B. Cowan and D. Shaw (eds.), *The Renaissance and Reformation in Scotland. Essays in honour of Gordon Donaldson* (Edinburgh, 1983), pp. 170–82.

[81] SRO, c/c/53.

the laird's loft, which opens onto the church, complete with a retiring room with a fireplace. The walls of these rooms are stone-panelled with frames for heraldic panels.[82] The whole structure was intended to impress and the chancellor's extravagant funeral served to emphasise this.[83]

Another example of early seventeenth-century court architecture is the 'aisle' which was added to the medieval church of Largs in *c*. 1636 by Sir Robert Montgomerie of Skelmorelie in memory of his wife Dame Margaret Douglas. The 'aisle' is noted both for its painted ceiling and also for the laird's loft, which was built over the burial vault. The painted ceiling includes texts from the Genevan Bible, signs of the zodiac, the coats of arms of the tribes of Israel as well as a depiction of the four seasons. 'Summer' includes a primitive view of the church with the burial 'aisle' attached. The laird's loft itself is built of local stone which is then elaborately decorated with strapwork. The loft now vacantly looks out on a wall as the remainder of the church was demolished in 1802 leaving it as a somewhat redundant burial place.[84] (See Plate 8.4.)

The burial of the landed elites therefore caused several problems for the Kirk in the post-Reformation period. As has been seen, in some cases families did not change their burial practices and continued to use buildings which in the eyes of the Church had ceased to be religious buildings at the Reformation. However, in other places the desire to continue family traditions and exercise their rights of burial, or in other cases to emphasise the standing of a particular family, ran contrary to the Kirk's desire to prohibit burials inside churches. As a result a *modus vivendi* was reached with the construction of burial 'aisles'. In some cases redundant chancels were sealed off or new aisles were built, adjoining the church, for burial. However, while these aisles were technically separate from the church itself, they were part of the same building. Furthermore, where a laird's loft was constructed over the burial vault, opening onto the main body of the church, the separation between the dead and the living was particularly tenuous.

The design and construction of these 'aisles' served to emphasise the status and importance of the families that used them. Elaborate tombs were now concealed from view, no longer a public statement on display

---

[82] Gifford, *Fife*, pp. 170–1; A. MacKechnie, 'Design Approaches in Early Post-Reformation Scots Houses', in I. Gow and A. Rowan (eds.), *Scottish Country Houses* (Edinburgh, 1995), p. 21.

[83] Court of the Lord Lyon, D1 34 Funeralls, pp. 28–31.

[84] A. MacKechnie, 'Evidence of a post-1603 Court Architecture in Scotland?', *Architectural History* 31 (1988), p. 115; HMSO Guide, Skelmorelie Aisle; Howard, *Scottish Architecture from the Reformation*, p. 203.

to the whole congregation but private family monuments. So burial aisles such as those built at Dalgety Bay and Largs in the latest architectural style leave the observer in no doubt about the status or pretensions of the builder. While some landowners such as Sir James Melville were prepared to build separate mausoleums away from the church itself, for many the continued demands of tradition, status and ancient rights remained strong. The emergence of the burial 'aisle' is, therefore, a reflection of these continued demands and their influence on the development of church architecture in post-Reformation Scotland.

9 Whose body? A study of attitudes towards the dead body in early modern Paris

Vanessa Harding

Early modern cities present the historian of death with a rich field of study: the combination of large numbers of people struggling for economic well-being and social identity and status, with high normal and even higher epidemic death rates, and severe limitations on the availability and possible uses of space, meant that the disposal of the dead was bound to be a major concern. The interests of the living competed with those of the dead, but could never wholly override them: all must have been conscious of a future personal interest in the treatment of the dead, as well as perhaps an emotional involvement with some of the recent dead.

This chapter examines attitudes towards the dead body, as exemplified by arrangements for funerals and burials, in Paris between around 1550 and 1670.[1] It seeks to establish, not so much what people said should happen to the bodies of the dead, but what happened in practice – the care, or lack of it, which the living accorded to the corpses of their contemporaries and predecessors – and to use this to further our understanding of the mentality of early modern urban dwellers. It is part of a wider enquiry, to explore the attitudes of the living to the dead in Paris and London, and to consider the ways in which this can illuminate the nature of these two metropolitan societies, in the sixteenth and seven-

---

[1] It is based on archival research in Paris, principally the eighteenth-century antiquaries' extracts (Bibliothèque Nationale (hereafter BN), MSS Français 32838, 32588, 32589) from some of the now-lost burial registers of early modern Paris, and other parish material in the Archives Nationales (hereafter AN). Two invaluable studies are Pierre Chaunu, *La mort à Paris: XVIe, XVIIe et XVIIIe siècles* (Paris, 1978) which draws, among other things, on a large number of thèses de maîtrise which analyse wills, pious provision and testamentary discourse; and Jacqueline Thibaut-Payen *Les morts, l'église, et l'état dans le ressort du Parlement de Paris aux XVIIe et XVIIIe siècles* (Paris, 1977). See also J. Hillairet, *Les deux cent cimetières du vieux Paris* (Paris, 1958).

170

teenth centuries.[2] Looking at the treatment of the corpse can also take discussion of the body, and the ways in which it is apprehended and understood, a stage further than the predominant focus on the living; dead bodies were as variably constructed, as liable to objectification (even commodification), as exposed to contest and competition over meaning as living ones. This particular study highlights the issues of control and ownership, among the complexity of reactions to the materiality of bodies, and offers an insight into power relations in a wider social and spatial environment.

One important theme, however, that I have not attempted to bring into the discussion is the spiritual dimension of death, burial and commemoration. The presumption of an afterlife and a continuing immaterial entity called the soul is obviously fundamental to the practices discussed, and deserves much fuller treatment than could be given here. The salvatory needs of the soul dictated many of the rituals enacted over the body, and belief in the resurrection of the body as an aspect of immortality added a significant complication to thinking about the appropriate treatment of mortal remains. It is possible, nevertheless, to consider the dead body as, primarily, belonging to this world, and its treatment as a reflection of priorities and concerns to do with life rather than the afterlife.

Identity and personalisation

The moment of death and the irresistible progress of time present a new range of problems for society in relation to the body. For how long does the dead human body retain the meanings and values it held in life, once it no longer has an incumbent but is perceived by outsiders only? If the body is composed or constituted socially as well as physically, is there a close synchrony between the dissolution of the person and physical decomposition? I will argue that, while there are some themes that run consistently through the attitudes of the living to the bodies of the dead, there is an important distinction between attitudes to the corpse that can be identified with a person, and attitudes to the 'depersonalised' corpse.

---

2 This will take the form of a monograph, *The Living and the Dead in Early Modern London and Paris*. See also V. Harding, '"And One More may be Laid There": the Location of Burials in Early Modern London', *London Journal* 14 (1989), pp. 112–29; V. Harding, 'Burial on the Margin: Distance and Discrimination in the Early Modern City', in M. Cox (ed.) *Grave Concerns: Death and Burial in England, 1700–1850* (Council for British Archaeology Research report 113, York, 1998), pp. 54–64.

What was a permissible way to treat one category might not be at all acceptable for the other.

The ways in which people treated the bodies of their close relatives, friends or neighbours reflected a strong sense of both the individuality and the social persona of the deceased, and this identification muted or delayed other feelings about the corpse – superstition, fear, anxiety. A body without those individualising and personalising associations, however, was viewed more starkly as a source of danger – moral or environmental – or at least trouble and expense. At the same time, every body is viewed from a number of different standpoints: almost every corpse is a personalised body for someone, and every dead body presents some danger and has to be safely disposed of. It is the balance between the two that is crucial: the extent to which relatives, friends or colleagues can impose their own perception of a particular corpse on a wider circle of society is in itself a measure of social power. Those who in life had the smallest or least influential social circle, and especially those who through poverty or sickness had lost control over their own destinies and even over their living bodies, becoming dependent on charity or hospital care, were also those whose bodies after death were most likely to be treated pragmatically and impersonally. This was in practice a very large category: in Paris, especially after the creation of the Hôpital-Général in 1656, deaths in institutions made up a very significant proportion of the total. In 1670, the first year of the Bills of Mortality, 21,461 people died in the whole of Paris; over 5,000 of these died in hospitals, including over 4,000 in Hôtel Dieu.[3]

The length of time over which the personalised view is sustained is also important. Even the most highly individualised corpse is subject to the irreversible processes of physical decay which will make its presence unacceptable to the living before long. Post-mortem decay literally dissolves the integrity of the physical body, merging the deceased with 'the earth from whence he came'; consciousness of decay, of the physical changes that the corpse undergoes that take it further and further from the recognisable human individual, also undermines the sense of personalisation. Social or rather financial power can resist this, deferring the consciousness of decay, and therefore the loss of personal identification, for the longest possible period. Embalming can postpone decay itself; much more common and important is the establishment of a secure

---

[3] BN, Printed books, Reserve, L k/7 6745: printed bills of mortality from 1670. Cf. L. Bernard, *The Emerging City. Paris in the Age of Louis XIV* (Durham, NC, 1970), pp. 132–55.

burial site, in which the corpse will be protected against intrusion and exhumation which would inevitably draw attention to its physical metamorphosis. Marking the burial site, erecting epitaphs naming or even visually representing the dead, and reciting their qualities, can also support the illusion that the grave contains the body of a person, not a dissolving corpse. The endowment of memorial services and explicit occasions for recollection, directed as they are towards spiritual ends, may seem to lead attention away from the body, but in many cases such services were said over the grave-site, and thus recalled again the physical existence of the deceased. Lead coffins, which themselves survive indefinitely, but which conceal or disguise the decay of the body they contain, also preserved a physical focus for prayer and commemoration.

Few of such rituals of protection and preservation were available to the more modest Parisians and the poor, though they did not lose their identity immediately. Their deaths would have been recorded in the original parish registers; the chaplain at Hôtel Dieu was charged with noting the names and *pays* of the sick in his book, and also with writing them on a piece of paper which he was to attach to their arms 'that they may be known at death and also in life'.[4] The poor could do little, however, to protect the bodies of their fellows once consigned to the ground, especially when burial took place in mass graves (*fosses communes*), as seems to have been common in sixteenth- and seventeenth-century Paris: the individual was rapidly and wholly assimilated into the category of 'the dead'. Those whose family and friends were buried in this way must have been aware that in a very few years – well within the memory of the living – the surviving skeletal remains would be dug up and stored, without any sense of the personal.[5] On the other hand, this process, that separated and extinguished the individual so rapidly, also transmuted the body from a cadaver to a relic, and recovered some spiritual meaning for the physical remains.

Another complex aspect of the personalisation/ loss of personalisation of the corpse is the attitude of the living person towards his or her own future physical state. Nobody ever sees his or her own corpse: even at the point of death, the living subject is not directly faced with the reality of post-mortem physical changes, familiar as he or she may be with the discourse of decay. However conscientiously an individual might observe the exhortation to contemplate mortality and physical corruption,

---

[4] L. Brièle, *Inventaire-sommaire des Archives Hospitalières anterieures a 1790. Hôtel Dieu* (4 vols., Paris, 1882–9), ii, p. 107.
[5] See Hillairet, *Les 200 cimetières*, pp. 12–13.

however vivid his or her imaginative projection, essentially there remained a distinction between the body he or she understood himself or herself to inhabit, and the idea of the body – the corpse or cadaver – that was the object of contemplation. Consequently, while the requests or prescriptions of the dying for the treatment of their own bodies after death quite obviously demonstrate the 'personalisation' of the corpse, there is a real difference in viewpoint from the responses of the survivors to the real corpse. The nuisance-value or environmental hazard of one's own corpse was rarely envisaged. It is clear that many believed that their body would retain some sensibility after death, and their provisions reflect this. The request for burial in a particular or familiar place, near to friends or family, presupposes some idea of post-mortem communion or contact. Even those who explicitly acknowledged the inevitability of decay made some defence against it, such as Nicolas Lambert, *conseiller du roi* and *secretaire de ses finances*, who recognised in his holograph will of 1646 that his body would soon be reduced to corruption and ashes according to nature, but nevertheless asked that it be treated with honour and modesty according to his condition, because it had been the domicile of his soul and the recipient of holy communion.[6]

Clearly, responses to the dead body varied in other ways too. Social categorisations of the living informed attitudes to the dead, perhaps particularly when the categorisation was itself involved with the cause of death, as with heretics and excommunicates, criminals (especially traitors) and suicides. As persons who were outside normal society, their bodies were liable to be treated in ways that emphasised their exclusion from the normal. In some cases the corpse had to bear the full brunt of society's disapproval of its owner's actions in life; ritual degradation of the body, dismemberment, distribution were a way of taking revenge.[7]

Heretics (Protestants) in Paris suffered all kinds of humiliations and penalties after death as well as before. Isolated incidents in the 1560s, when some burials according to reformed rites in Catholic churchyards, including the Innocents, were dug up and cast out, indicated that this would be an arena of conflict. Even after Protestant funeral rights and burial locations were in theory secured, they were subject both to official restriction and to popular attack. Further attempts to share traditional burial grounds with Catholics were resisted, and finally forbidden.

---

[6] Will printed in Chaunu, *La mort à Paris*, p. 516.
[7] Hillairet, *Les 200 cimetières*, pp. 282–4; cf. J. Merrick, 'Patterns and Prosecutions of Suicide in 18th-century Paris', *Historical Reflections / Réflexions Historiques* 16 (1) (1989), pp. 24–5, 29.

Protestants were confined to using cemeteries on the outskirts of the city, formerly used for plague victims, victims of fifteenth-century massacres, and the dead of Hôtel Dieu. Vexatious prosecution and rigorous application of the burial laws made life more and more difficult, until, with the revocation of the Edict of Nantes in 1685, even these grounds were closed. The bodies of those who died outside the Church were thereafter subject to exemplary punishment, including being dragged through the mud.[8]

Others who were in some way not full members of society might also be treated differently: the most obvious, and difficult case, is that of children, especially chrisoms, neonates and stillborns. Were these really human, did they deserve the full rites and respect accorded to adults or those of years of discretion? How far could 'personalisation' of the corpse operate in these cases, when the living being had barely developed any individuality, though it might inherit a social persona from its parents?[9]

Those who had already 'died to the world' by entering an enclosed religious community formed another distinct group in or on the edge of society, but in this case it was a privileged group: their obsequies would be fully observed and attended, their careful burial guaranteed. In any case, these bodies did not impinge upon public sensibility, because they were kept out of public view. As an ideal of safe and sacred burial they may have influenced the burial choices of the laity: convent burial apparently became a more popular choice in the course of the seventeenth century, with the revival of the religious orders in the Catholic Reformation.[10]

The bodies of those who died of an infectious disease (principally plague in this period) constitute another special case, given anxieties about the role of the corpse in the dissemination of disease. The firm direction of affairs in Paris meant that orders relating to plague burials were strictly enforced, with bodies being buried quickly and not in churches.[11] The rigour of the law could be modified, however, by other considerations: one young man of good family, Pierre Séguier, who died of the plague in 1591, was buried – on that account – in the churchyard,

---

[8] Hillairet, *Les 200 cimetières*, pp. 264–72; Thibaut-Payen, *Les morts, l'église, et l'état*, pp. 94–185. See also the chapter by Penny Roberts in this volume.

[9] See Philippe Ariès, *Centuries of Childhood. A Social History of Family Life*, tr. Robert Baldrick (New York, 1965), pp. 38–40. See the contribution by Will Coster in this volume.

[10] Chaunu, *La mort à Paris*, p. 321; Hillairet, *Les 200 cimetières*, pp. 143–264.

[11] Hillairet, *Les 200 cimetières*, p. 284.

but a few months later permission was given for his exhumation and reburial in the church near his ancestors' chapel.[12]

The impact of gender on burial practices is hard to discern, or at least to expose. Men and women of the same family and status appear to have merited equal treatment. Chaunu found no 'sexual dimorphism' in sixteenth-century burial choices.[13] Not enough is recorded of the burials of children to see whether there was discrimination at this level. Clearly, gender was a defining aspect of some status groups – principally the clergy – which obtained privileged burial for themselves, and at the opposite end of the scale there were widows and prostitutes, notably poor and/or socially reprehended groups. The convents of men appear to have attracted a greater number and variety of elite burials than the convents of women,[14] but the men's houses were on the whole larger, wealthier and more prestigious than the women's, as well as more numerous, so the difference is probably not directly significant. It could even be argued that in this respect, as in others, mortality tends actually to erase gender, at least in the medium term.

If the distinction between the personalised corpse and the depersonalised one is fundamental to the response of the living to the dead, and the category matters too, there is still a range of common emotions. These include feelings of actual tenderness, reverence, superstitious awe, horror or revulsion, and fear of contamination, often in combination. Such emotions might be felt by one individual at different times towards different corpses; or they might be experienced in relation to a single corpse by the different people who confronted it. In order to explore the interplay of responses to the dead body, this chapter follows the corpse chronologically from death-bed to interment and beyond. The length of time the corpse remained among the living, the rituals enacted over it, the respect paid to it, and the precautions taken to protect it after it was left in the grave or tomb are all important elements in the argument.

Death to burial

Pre-modern burials were normally swift, with a small number being very protracted. The speed with which bodies were buried in Paris seems at least to have matched urban norms in early modern England, where perhaps 65 to 70 per cent had been buried by the second day after

---

[12] BN, MS Fr 32589, 15 Sept. 1591.   [13] Chaunu, *La mort à Paris*, pp. 320–1.
[14] See Hillairet, *Les 200 cimetières*, pp. 143–232.

death.[15] Given the selective nature of the surviving burial records, totally reliable statistics for Paris are not available, but examination of a sample of 600 cases from the parish of Saint-André-des-Arts between 1550 and 1670 offers some plausible figures. Of these, largely bourgeois or *noblesse de robe*, 24 per cent were buried on the day of death, 50 per cent on the day after, and 16.5 per cent on the third day, so that just over 90 per cent had been buried by the end of the third day after death. Funerals of the poor are not represented in this sample: these would probably bring down the death–burial interval still further. There would be little reason for delay: no elaborate arrangments to be made, a common grave already open, not to mention the cramped living conditions of the poor and the unlikelihood of preservative measures.[16]

Long-distance convoys were largely confined to the highest groups in society – burial outside Paris was usually on the deceased's family estate – so in that sense a long death–burial interval is a mark of class. The expense of a large convoy over several days must have been considerable, and in such cases embalming was probably essential. The convoy of Maître Jean de l'Aultry, *conseiller ordinaire du Roy* and vicomte of Levignan and Bèze, left Paris four days after his death, but it must have taken several more days to reach Bèze near Dijon.[17] The body of Dame Gasparde de la Chastre remained in the chapel of her husband's family at Saint-André-des-Arts for seventeen days before it was taken away for burial at Villebon.[18]

While the body was treated formally, even ritually, it was not shunned. In the interval between death and burial, bodies were kept in private houses, handled, watched and prayed over, and their presence was accepted with apparent equanimity. The way in which the corpse was treated in the interval between death and burial tends however to emphasise the dichotomy between personalised and depersonalised bodies. The bodies of the middling and upper classes were treated carefully and with respect; those of the poor received more casual treatment.

The corpses of the better-off normally remained in the place of death until removed for service and/or interment. The registers of Saint-André-des-Arts often note the place of death ('mort en son hotel', 'mort en l'hotel de Thou', 'mort chez son frère Claude, logé en la rue Pavée') and

---

[15] S. Porter, 'Death and Burial in a London Parish: St Mary Woolnoth, 1653–99', *London Journal* 8 (1982), pp. 76–80.

[16] BN, MS Fr 32589 (eighteenth-century extracts from the burial registers of the parish of Saint-André-des-Arts). This is the source of the data in this and the following paragraph.

[17] *Ibid.*, entry for 5 Mar. 1645.   [18] *Ibid.*, entry for 4 July 1616.

this would be logical if this is where the convoy started from.[19] The bodies of persons who died in the street, whether accidentally or violently, could not have stayed there, of course, but the baron de Thiers, attacked by enemies on his way home after supper, died in the house of an unrelated person and his body remained there for five days, before being removed to the family chapel in the parish church. It is also possible that the convoy of Messire Jacques le Coigneux, *conseiller au Parlement*, started from the house of the linendraper on the pont Saint-Michel where he had died suddenly the previous night.[20] The vicar of the dean of Paris, who claimed funeral rights over the bodies of clerics in his domain, recorded the house, and often the room, in which death took place, and clearly expected to collect the body from that place. On a couple of occasions the body was waiting for him and his associates in the courtyard of the house, but on others he may well have entered the chamber.[21] Instructions to the parish gravedigger (repeated in a number of parish vestry books in the later seventeenth century) make it clear that he was expected to deliver the pall, the bier and if necessary trestles to the house where the dead person was, and bring them back with the body; an eighteenth-century gravedigger complained of having to go up to the fifth or sixth floors of some houses to collect bodies. The fact that these would have been the bodies of poorer persons – and for charity funerals the gravedigger got very little, if anything – added to his grievance.[22] On the other hand, the *emballeurs* (those deputed to shroud the dead) of Hôtel Dieu were also paid to seek and remove bodies from private houses and take them to Hôtel Dieu, presumably for shrouding and a charity burial.[23]

If French practice was similar to English, the corpse would be washed, dressed at least in a shift,[24] wrapped in a shroud, placed in a coffin or bier, and covered with a pall, ready for the watch or vigil. Since death–burial intervals were normally so short, this can rarely have lasted the three days suggested by Chaunu.[25] Parish records give some confirmation of the rituals around the corpse. Parishes could supply both the pall to cover the body, and the *argenterie*, the silver cross and branches for the

---

[19] *Ibid., passim.*   [20] *Ibid.*, entries for 8 Apr. 1565 and 18 Jan. 1623.

[21] AN, L510, microfilm no. 27.

[22] AN, LL805, p. 255; BN, MS Fr 21609, fol. 37; AN, L663 (unnumbered eighteenth-century papers concerning charity burials at Saint-Jean-en-Grève).

[23] Brièle, *Inventaire-sommaire*, II, p. 103.

[24] Though Chaunu, *La mort à Paris*, p. 350, says that the poor remained naked under the shroud.

[25] *Ibid.*, p. 350.

candles, for the vigil: it was the gravedigger who delivered them to the house of the deceased, after negotiation with the family and the parish clergy. Most parishes had a range of palls and silverware, available at graduated prices to suit all pockets (and to demonstrate the deceased's wealth and status).[26] At the other end of the scale, many parishes had a charity pall, which they supplied free.[27]

The rituals of the vigil had a dual function: to make the dead body safe while it remained among the living, and to begin the process of helping to save the soul. The safety of the body can be interpreted in several ways: the ritual of sprinkling it with holy water, after death and also again at the start of the funeral convoy, suggests that it was the safety of the observers that was at issue, as perhaps do the prayers said around it, but the constant presence of watchers also helped to save the body itself from outside intervention. Such intervention might have simple robbery of the corpse in mind, or theft of the body itself. The bodies of the dead of Hôtel Dieu were exposed to both dangers, even from those entrusted to look after them. They had already sacrificed some control of their bodies and possessions to the hospital, which took the clothes of those who died there, and either sold or reused them; the smaller hospital of Saint-Louis derived 120 *livres* from the sale of rings and other *gentillesse* of persons dying there in 1636.[28] In the 1650s Hôtel Dieu contracted with a wigmaker for the sale of the hair cut from the heads of the sick, but they did refuse a request, made in 1658, from the king's surgeon, to extract the teeth of the dead, even though he said it was for the public good.[29] Although anatomising of corpses was not widely practised in this period, surgeons were already beginning to look on the hospital as a useful source of bodies, legitimately or illegitimately obtained. In 1626 certain *emballeurs* were sacked for selling a corpse to a surgeon. They had shrouded the corpse and put it in the cart to be taken to the cemetery of la Trinité, but by arrangement they stopped just outside the hospital gate and handed over the body.[30] The gravedigger at la Trinité was accused in 1659 of despoiling corpses of their shrouds and even their shirts, and of selling the bodies to the surgeons.[31]

The masters of Hôtel Dieu, which saw itself as primarily a religious

[26] For example, at Saint-Jean-en-Grève: AN, LL805, pp. 253–5; BN, MS Fr 21609, fol. 37.

[27] For example, at Saint-André-des-Arts: AN, LL687, fol. 183v.

[28] Brièle, *Inventaire-sommaire*, II, pp. 103, 116, 226; L. Brièle, *Collection des documents pour servir à l'histoire des hôpitaux de Paris* (4 vols., Paris, 1881–7), I, p. 7.

[29] Brièle, *Inventaire-sommaire*, II, pp. 110, 115.   [30] *Ibid.*, p. 107.

[31] Brièle, *Collection*, I, p, 138.

establishment, resisted the idea of scientific or experimental anatomy, and in 1655 ruled that no body, male or female, of any age or cause of death, be given to the surgeons for anatomy/dissection, such being contrary to Christian charity and humanity. However, they would permit surgeons of the house to open bodies if that would help them to establish the cause of death or relieve other sick or poor. The opening must be done in the manner in which the bodies of private persons were opened, and with great restraint and circumspection; afterwards, the body was to be shrouded and buried as usual.[32] This firm statement of principle was not sustained in practice. Twice in the following year house surgeons were reprimanded for conducting autopsies without permission; in 1659 they were ordered to return the body of a child they had removed for autopsy. But by 1665 the masters authorised the house surgeons to open the bodies of those who died of the stone, for information, and allowed a Danish surgeon to have three or four heads for dissection, to furnish illustrations for a book. In 1667 they agreed – perhaps reluctantly – to Colbert's request that members of his proposed academy of surgeons could open the bodies of Hôtel Dieu dead, but by 1681, the religious of the hospital complained that the surgeons were not treating the bodies properly: they did not reconstruct them for burial, but made skeletons of them and thus denied them Christian burial, which according to the canons of the Church should only be denied to the executed and excommunicates.[33]

The convoy and funeral

The body had a central part to play in the funeral: its presence was essential to a sequence of rituals, from the convoy to the funeral service or services and the interment. It could also be the focus of demarcation disputes, when different groups might claim possession of the body as a symbol of their financial or jurisdictional rights.

If the vigil was the more private part of the funeral ceremony, the convoy brought the body into the light of day and the public space of street and church. Beginning usually from the place of death, the convoy accompanied the body to church for the funeral service, and if necessary on to the place of burial. The vicar of the dean of Paris described the procedure for the convoy in 1568 of Messire Nicole le Maistre, a canon of Notre Dame, *conseiller en Parlement* and president of the College of

[32]   Brièle, *Inventaire-sommaire*, II, pp. 111–12.
[33]   *Ibid.*, pp. 113, 114, 115, 120, 122; Brièle, *Collection*, I, p. 218.

Prémontré. The vicar arrived with some of the priests of the cathedral at the man's house, to find the body laid ready in the courtyard and vigils being said. He sprinkled the body with holy water and, after the vigils were over, vested himself in rochet, surplice, stole, etc., in the presence of the vicar of Saint-Cosme, the parish in which the man died. He then took up the body and with *de profundis* and the orisons *inclina* and *fidelium*, to which his own accompanying priests gave the responses, proceeded with torches and other lights and a cross carried before him to the church of the Cordeliers where the deceased had chosen burial. Several ecclesiastical dignitaries, two presidents of *Parlement* and other canons of Notre Dame accompanied the procession; two *conseillers en Parlement* carried corners of the pall.[34] The procedure was no doubt similar when the convoy was made up of parish priests, with family, friends and colleagues participating; it was common too to have a dozen poor people and/or some of the *enfants bleus*, the children from the city's orphan hospital. The *jurés-crieurs des corps et du vin*, one of Paris's privileged guilds, organised some convoys, announcing the funeral or sending out printed invitations, bringing together mourners, attendants and the poor men or women.[35] In most cases it appears that the body was carried by bearers on foot, but some convoys *en carosse* are noted, including some with lead coffins, and it seems unlikely that a lead coffin could have been carried any distance on foot.[36]

The early modern period in Paris probably saw a more widespread use of coffins, both for interment but also for the convoy alone. Hôtel Dieu bought two *coffres ou bières* to carry bodies to the cemetery of the Innocents in 1517, and at Saint-Jean-en-Grève the parish had a *bière couverte* used for charity convoys.[37] For the middling and upper sorts, coffined interment was probably the norm. Such burials paid a premium, because they occupied the ground much longer: it was agreed that at the central city cemetery of the Innocents, burials of *corps nudz et sans coffre ou bière* would cost 5 *sous tournois* (of which 2 *sous* went to the grave-digger), while a *fosse à coffre* cost 35 *sous*, of which 5 *sous* went to the gravedigger.[38] Both wooden and lead coffins were used by the later seventeenth century: the latter, which lasted almost indefinitely, were used for burials in private chapels and vaults, but several churches either

---

[34] AN, L510, microfilm no. 27.
[35] Chaunu, *La mort à Paris*, pp. 351–61; BN, MS Fr 21609, fols. 106–14 .
[36] E.g. at Saint-André-des-Arts: AN, LL687, fol. 183v.
[37] Brièle, *Inventaire-sommaire*, II, p. 184; AN, L663.   [38] AN, L571/2.

banned them for burial in the generality of the church, or charged double for allowing their use.[39]

Most convoys must have passed in an orderly fashion, without incident, but difficulties were possible. Parish priests were generally regarded as having the right to bury their parishioners, and receive the dues therefor, but exceptions were possible, and these could lead to trouble. The issue was generally the sharing of fees and rewards, but in practice disputes focused on possession of the body. Religious houses usually succeeded in claiming the bodies of their domestics, even when they lived outside the precinct, and the parish priest got nothing. Other individuals could choose burial in a church other than their parish church; parish priests were supposed to convoy the body to the chosen place of burial and hand it over, certifying that the individual had died in communion with the Church, for which they would share the lights of the convoy with the house of burial. However, the loss of the actual burial meant a loss of revenue to the priest and parish; it seems that they resented this encroachment on their privilege and sometimes the handing-over was done with a very bad grace. Thibaut-Payen cites some such cases in seventeenth-century Paris, when bodies were merely dumped at convent gates, and the parish reclaimed its pall or mortuary cloth, leaving the coffin bare; there was an actual affray in the street between the priest of St Paul and the Jesuits in 1655, before *Parlement* settled that bodies must be conveyed into the nave of the burial church before being handed over.[40]

The dean of Paris's vicar kept his register of convoys because he was entitled to keep the torches and lights from the procession as a reward; usually he agreed amicably with other claimants, waiving strict protocol (such as his right to take the torches at the entry to the church) in the interests of a seemly funeral, but more than once he resorted to litigation after the event to enforce his rights. In 1569 he went to collect the body of a chaplain of Notre Dame who had died in the presbytery of the parish of St Geneviève les Ardents, but the parish priest refused to hand it over. The vicar asserted the dean's rights, but the priest refused again, and began to sing the *de profundis*; so the vicar left, to pursue his claim by litigation – successfully. A similar case later the same year, against the curé of Ste Madeleine en la Cité, was also successfully prosecuted.[41]

Charity convoys were furnished by the parishes, which sometimes

---

[39] AN, LL686, part 2, fol. 64v; AN, LL805, pp. 253–5.
[40] Thibaut-Payen, *Les morts, l'église, et l'état*, pp. 20–2, 40–66.
[41] AN, L510, microfilm no. 27.

used a special pall, and the gravedigger was required to deliver and collect the bier, trestles, etc. as for other funerals.[42] The Hôtel Dieu evidence suggests that those who died in the hospital were taken fairly unceremoniously, shrouded but not coffined, on a bier, cart or chariot, to one of the hospital's burial grounds (the Innocents, la Trinité or, by the late seventeenth century, Clamart).[43] Often more than one body at a time was taken; in times of great mortality the carts must either have been heavily laden or have gone several times a day. However, it was not quite without ceremony: the cart was accompanied by an ecclesiastic carrying a cross, and by two lit torches in summer, or two large lanterns (*fallotz*) in winter.[44] These may suggest that the carts only went at night, or in the early morning, but this is not confirmed by regulation until 1681, when the gatekeeper of the porte Saint-Victor was given 4 *livres* a year for getting up to open the gate to let the cart for Clamart through at 4 a.m.[45]

Not all those who died in hospital lost all control over their funerals. Hospitalisation of the sick was much more common in Paris than in England, as indicated above, and patients might come from reasonably prosperous families. Hôtel Dieu clearly anticipated that some of its dead would be claimed for private burial, and in 1618 it was accepted that the families of those who died at the hospital of Saint-Louis who wished to bury them separately and with a convoy could do so for a sum of not less than 3 *livres*, including payments to the master, chaplains, gravedigger, *emballeurs* and torchbearers.[46]

The funeral service or services were said over the body itself, in the church, on its bier or hearse and again surrounded by candles and covered in a pall. Chaunu states, based on the sixteenth-century literature of the *arts de mourir*, that prayer for a body physically present was believed to be more valuable than prayer in its absence and, according to one of his seventeenth-century will samples, 95 out of 105 persons ordering obsequies wished them to be done in the presence of the corpse, so that it could participate for a last time in the mass.[47] The full gamut of funeral services, with high and low masses and all the psalms and prayers, was a long drawn-out process, however, and may well have begun before the body reached the church.

An obvious way in which the deceased person could control the whole context within which his or her corpse would be obsequied was through

---

[42] See AN, L663.
[43] Brièle, *Inventaire-sommaire*, II, pp. 107, 110, 113, 115, 118; Hillairet, *Les 200 cimetières*, pp. 23–38, 245–9.
[44] Brièle, *Inventaire-sommaire*, II, p. 110.   [45] Brièle, *Collection*, I, p. 220.
[46] *Ibid.*, p. 55.   [47] Chaunu, *La mort à Paris*, pp. 348, 359–60.

the choice of burial location. This choice, for Paris, has been quite extensively discussed by Chaunu and his students.[48] A large proportion of their sampled willmakers in the sixteenth and seventeenth centuries took the opportunity of specifying the location; even those who did not, but left it to their executors, may well have made their choice clear before death. The choices made seem to reflect a strong sense of the humanity of the corpse: while particularly sacred locations were certainly favoured, family and traditional associations were even stronger. Of a sample, 82 per cent made some choice of location; over half of these made a very precise choice, and nearly half of these asked to be buried near some member of the family or *lignage*. About 37 per cent of the sample, in all, wished to find themselves in death in the society of a dear one; a much smaller number chose 'devotionally'.[49] This suggests that the willmakers were not only thinking of their own corpses as preserving something of their own personality and feelings, but that they also had a strong sense that the bodies of their deceased relatives – in some cases long dead – retained a personal identity. The language is often affective: Etienne Tonnellier, curé of Saint-Eustache – a religious – wished to be buried in the vault where his late uncle and cousin lay 'so that death shall not separate those whom affection (*amitié*) united in life'.[50]

After the funeral

From the moment of interment, or rather from the decision as to where interment was to take place, the experiences and expectations of the better-off and the more modest diverged markedly. Some testators had secured a permanent resting-place in a chapel or vault, with their body being protected from obvious decay by its lead coffin, from spiritual danger by the sacred location and the repetition of prayers and celebrations over it, from human interference again by the sacred location and by the legal agreements with the church; it might even be secured against human oblivion by being marked with an epitaph or declamatory monument, which again called attention to the body's presence with the words 'Cy git . . .' (here lies).[51] Others, however, had no resources either to leave by will or to spend on a funeral. Although private marked graves in

---

[48] *Ibid.*, chaps. 11–14. For London, see Harding, ' "And One More may be Laid There" ', pp. 112–29; V. Harding, 'Burial Choice and Burial Location in Later Medieval London', in S. R. Bassett (ed.), *Death in Towns: Urban Responses to the Dying and the Dead, 100–1600* (Leicester, 1992), pp. 119–35.

[49] Chaunu, *La mort à Paris*, pp. 325–6.   [50] *Ibid.*, p. 508.

[51] See AN, LL434/B (Epitaphier of the cemetery of the Innocents).

churchyards continued to exist, the practice of opening large pits for the burial of many corpses was well established by the early sixteenth century, and probably much earlier.

The pressure of numbers must have forced Parisians into a kind of brutal pragmatism about burial for the masses from an early date: if the city had 3–400,000 inhabitants in the later Middle Ages (or even only 200,000), it might have needed to bury 8–15,000 bodies a year, and epidemics would multiply the numbers. It would not have been possible to bury all these in individual graves, and resort to mass interment must have been inevitable. By the sixteenth century we have explicit evidence. In 1512 the gravedigger at la Trinité made a pit containing 136.5 *toises* or fathoms; in 1549 his successor dug another great pit. One of 885 *toises* was dug in 1570, and in 1587 the gravedigger was paid 2 *écus sol* for digging several large fosses down to the water-table, each able to hold 700 or 800 bodies. The thousands buried there in the 1620s could only have been accommodated in mass graves.[52] The secondary literature gives no date for the earliest use of mass graves at the Innocents, but it too appears to have been established practice by the sixteenth century, and certainly forms part of the popular perception of that location.[53]

A final, and somewhat paradoxical, insight into the personalisation/ depersonalisation of the corpse is given by one practice that had a variety of meanings, according to context: exhumation. This could reflect either an unusually successful retention of the corpse's identity, or its opposite, complete loss of that identity.

The records of Saint-André-des-Arts offer several examples of the former: a child that was buried and exhumed ten days after death to be restored to its seniors in another church; a young plague victim, hastily interred in his parish churchyard but exhumed six months later to be reburied with his family inside the church; the case of Dame Gasparde de la Chastre's body, transported eighteen days after her death to Villebon, and buried there, but exhumed and brought back to Paris the following year, to be buried beside her husband who had just died.[54] These cases certainly assert the continuing human identity of the corpse, months after death; but they also assert it in the context of a greater, family, identity, in which, arguably, the individual is subsumed. Is this the ultimate in the

---

[52] Brièle, *Inventaire-sommaire*, ii, pp. 182, 193, 200, 219–23; Brièle, *Collection* (1887), iv, p. 32.

[53] Hillairet, *Les 200 cimetières*, pp. 23–38.

[54] BN, MS Fr. 32589, entries for 29 May 1561, 15 Sept. 1591, 4 July 1616, 8 May 1617.

personalisation of the corpse; or is it the ultimate manipulation of someone else's corpse to make a point?

Exhumation could also mean the loss of identity, with the body exposed to assault or dismemberment. The exhumation of Protestant corpses is a case in point,[55] but more mundane motives might also operate: in 1673 the prévot de Paris condemned persons who broke into the cemetery of Clamart to steal the teeth and hair of the dead.[56] Exhumation was however a normal part of the management of cemeteries, and in that context it offered a complex meaning. Part of the point of the mass graves was that, because they were filled up within a few weeks or months, and contained only shrouded not coffined bodies, which may have been layered with lime, the bodies decayed fairly evenly, and it was possible to open them up after a number of years (between nine and fourteen, according to eighteenth-century calculations).[57] The skulls and large bones were cleaned and stored in a charnel, the residue cleared, and the pit re-used for a new phase of burials.[58] No personal identity could survive this process, but it was essentially a respectful one, and it transformed the body from a dangerous decaying corpse into a safe, even sacred, physical form. The bones of the Christian dead offered a moral lesson, a reminder of mortality, and also conferred some sanctity on the place where they were stored. Despite the continual recycling of burials, the cemetery of the Innocents had an important place in the mythology of Parisian identity, and there was considerable opposition to its closure in the later eighteenth century.[59]

The experience of the dead, if one can so put it, in early modern Paris, ranged from long-term physical preservation and maintenance of identity to rapid dissolution and personal oblivion. The great majority lost any control over their bodies soon after death (and sometimes before), and some indeed were very inadequately protected against external interference. Their bodies were treated pragmatically, as material objects that posed a particular set of problems – moral as well as environmental, perhaps, but overwhelmingly practical. However, it is arguable that the price of individualisation was to remain earth-bound; if assimilation into

---

[55] Thibaut-Payen, *Les morts, l'église, et l'état*, pp. 159–71.

[56] Brièle, *Inventaire-sommaire*, II, p. 23.   [57] BN, MS Joly de Fleury 1207.

[58] It was essentially the contents of parish charnels and pits, as well as those of the Innocents, which were transferred to the Catacombs before and especially after the Revolution: Hillairet, *Les 200 cimetières*, pp. 300–8.

[59] M. Foisil, 'Les attitudes devant la mort au XVIIIe siècle: sépultures et suppressions de sépultures dans le cimetière Parisien des SS-Innocents', *Revue Historique* 510 (1974), pp. 303–30.

a greater whole, representative of Paris as a timeless community, can compensate for the loss of a personal identity, then the dead buried at the Innocents had actually achieved translation to a higher sphere of being, a kind of apotheosis, that perhaps paralleled the idea of the absorption of the soul into a Christian heaven.

10 Women, memory and will-making in Elizabethan England

J. S. W. Helt

Despite the recent expansion of historical interest in the interrelated subjects of death, dying and disposal, our understanding of remembrance of the dead in early modern England remains curiously unbalanced. We know a great deal about the important role of commemoration in the popular religion of pre-Reformation England, and about the medieval intercessory foundations where priests and monks remembered the dead on behalf of families, as ritual performances of memory that 'affirmed corporate identity, transcending the boundary between living and dead, and issued a direct challenge to the negation of the human endeavour by the finality of the grave'.[1] But our understanding of remembrance in post-Reformation mortuary culture is comparatively less complete. The impact of the Reformation on the emotional and psychological processes of grief and mourning has drawn the attention of researchers, and especially the efforts of Protestants to create a structure of death and bereavement adequate to deal with the

---

Portions of this chapter were presented during the Third International Conference on Death, Dying and Disposal at Cardiff University and I would like to thank the participants for their insightful comments and criticisms.

[1] V. Bainbridge, 'The Medieval Way of Death: Commemoration and the Afterlife in Pre-Reformation Cambridgeshire', in M.Wilks (ed.) *Prophecy and Eschatology*, Studies in Church History Subsidia, 10 (Oxford, 1994), pp. 183–204; C. Daniell, *Death and Burial in Medieval England, 1066–1550* (London and New York, 1997); P. Geary, *Phantoms of Remembrance: Memory and Oblivion at the End of the First Millennium* (Princeton, NJ, 1994); E. Duffy, *The Stripping of the Altars: Traditional Religion in England 1400–1580* (New Haven and London, 1992), especially pp. 299–376; C. Burgess, '"A Fond Thing Vainly Invented": an Essay on Purgatory and Pious Motive in Late Medieval England', in S. J. Wright (ed.), *Parish, Church and People: Local Studies in Lay Religion, 1350–1750* (London, 1988), pp. 56–85 and '"For the Increase of Divine Service": Chantries in the Parish in Late Medieval Bristol', *Journal of Ecclesiastical History* 36 (1985), pp. 48–65; A. Kreider, *English Chantries: the Road to Dissolution* (Cambridge, MA, 1979).

disruptive effects of death.[2] The funerary preferences of the gentry and their memorial concerns about social authority and deference have received considerable scholarly attention, as has the symbolic role played by funerary rites in local disputes over religion.[3] Within the context of the English Renaissance, the semiotics of memory have recently earned insightful analysis as well, revealing the mnemonic devices linked to mortal memory by early modern writers and artists.[4] All of these studies demonstrate the importance of mortuary customs as a means to understand the cultural history of early modern England, yet few have illuminated the particular role of women in memory, as rememberers and as remembered, in the mortuary customs of post-Reformation England.[5]

This essay seeks to add to the existing discourse on remembrance and to help uncover the place of the dead within the parish communities of Elizabethan England by focusing attention on the ways that women mobilised the symbolic content of their wills in preparation for death. It argues that women's wills performed a custodial role as sources of post-mortem memory, designating the remembered and the rememberers, and that women's gifts of material property and wealth to family, friends and neighbours served as gendered markers which sustained and maintained a sense of spiritual and material affinity between the dead and the living community. This analysis follows on studies of English funerary customs by Clare Gittings and David Cressy, as well as the ground-breaking work

---

[2] K. Thomas, *Religion and the Decline of Magic* (Harmondsworth, 1973), pp. 722–3; M. Rifkin, 'Burial, Funeral, and Mourning Customs in England, 1558–1662' (Bryn Mawr College PhD thesis, 1977).

[3] D. Cressy, *Birth, Marriage, and Death: Ritual, Religion, and the Life-cycle in Tudor and Stuart England* (Oxford, 1997) and 'Death and the Social Order: the Funerary Preferences of Elizabethan Gentlemen', *Continuity and Change* 5 (1989), pp. 99–119; D. Beaver, ' "Sown in Dishonor, Raised in Glory": Death, Ritual, and Social Organisation in Northern Gloucestershire, 1590–1690', *Social History* 17 (1992), pp. 389–419; C. Gittings, 'Urban Funerals in Late Medieval and Reformation England', in S. R. Bassett (ed.), *Death in Towns: Urban Responses to the Dying and the Dead, 100–1600* (Leicester, 1992), pp. 170–83 and *Death, Burial and the Individual in Early Modern England* (London, 1984); L. Stone, *The Family, Sex and Marriage in England, 1500–1800* (London, 1977).

[4] W. Engel, *Mapping Mortality: the Persistence of Memory* (Amherst, MA, 1995); N. Llewellyn, *The Art of Death: Visual Culture in the English Death Ritual, c. 1500–c. 1800* (London, 1991).

[5] M. Prior, 'Wives and Wills, 1558–1700', in J. Chartres and D. Hay (eds.), *English Rural Society, 1500–1800* (Cambridge, 1990), pp. 210–25; C. Cross, 'Northern Women in the Early Modern Period: the Female Testators of Hull and Leeds, 1520–1650', *Yorkshire Archaeological Journal* 59 (1987), pp. 83–94; N. Evans, 'Inheritance, Women, Religion, and Education in Early Modern Society as Revealed by Wills', in P. Riden (ed.), *Probate Records and the Local Community* (London, 1985), pp. 53–70.

on western mortuary traditions by Philippe Ariès, and is modelled on anthropological studies of death rituals in modern societies. Anthropologists and sociologists have long emphasised the complex patterns within cultures that secure them from fragmentation and allow for constructive social interchanges. Death, because of its finality, leaves cultures vulnerable to disintegration as individuals are alienated by the loss of family members and friends, and as social groups suffer the loss of integral members. Responses to this disruption, both in the moments before physical death and in the liminal, or intermediate, period following death, serve to confirm and close the position of the living individual in the community and to repair the bonds of society broken by the loss of a life. Of the various ritual responses to death and the liminality of the deceased person, the ritual act of gift-giving is understood by anthropologists as a means by which societies mark the status of the deceased person and signal his or her active presence in the community after the death of the body. Formed by the dying in the moments before death and enacted by designated rememberers in the intermediary period following that death, ritual gift-giving serves to moderate the 'disintegrating impulses' produced by death by signalling the continuity of the relationship between the deceased and the living. The expressions imbedded in this relationship, however, reflect not a universal experience of death and liminality but one which is shaped by the ordering principles within a particular society. Thus, there are many mortuary cultures and the place of the dead within each of these is defined by the distinctive qualities of the deceased, including the individual's gender. To ignore these subtleties is to mask the complexity of particular social configurations, and, in an effort to help improve our understanding of the place of the dead in early modern England, this essay seeks to illuminate the gendered nature of women's wills as custodial structures for remembrance of the dead.[6]

---

[6] M. Bloch and J. Parry (eds.), *Death and the Regeneration of Life* (Cambridge, 1982); J. Goody, *Death, Property, and the Ancestors: a Study of the Mortuary Customs of the Lodagaa of West Africa* (Stanford, CA, 1962); R. Hertz, 'A Contribution to the Study of the Collective Representation of Death', in *Death and the Right Hand*, tr. R. Needham and C. Needham (New York, 1960); A. van Gennep, *The Rites of Passage*, tr. M. Vicedom and S. Kimball (Chicago, 1960); M. Mauss, *The Gift*, tr. I. Cunnison (London, 1954). For a summary analysis of the recent anthropological work which provides the basis of viewing gift-giving in the will as a reciprocal and commemorative exchange restoring the social fabric, see P. Metcalf and R. Huntington, *Celebrations of Death: the Anthropology of the Mortuary Ritual* (2nd edn, Cambridge, 1993), pp. 10–14, 36–7, 113–28; P. Ariès, *The Hour of Our Death*, tr. H. Weaver (London, 1981); Gittings, *Death, Burial, and the Individual*; Cressy, *Birth, Marriage, and Death*, pp. 379–473, esp. p. 443, and 'Funerary Preferences of Elizabethan Gentlemen,' esp. pp. 113–16.

The study is based on an analysis of 1,276 women's wills probated in the three Archdeaconry Courts which held jurisdiction over Elizabethan Essex, edited by the former county archivist F. G. Emmison. This number represents all of the available women's wills from the collection, and constitutes roughly one-sixth of the total wills probated in these courts during the period under consideration. This series of volumes of Elizabethan wills was chosen because sixteenth-century Essex was a relatively prosperous and literate county where, it is estimated, about 20 per cent of the population probated wills. The collection was selected also because it provides accurate abstracts of all original and registered Essex wills for the period and it is readily available for reference. While no printed will is above suspicion, when checked against the original wills and probate registers available in the Essex Record Office no reason was found to believe that the wills were not accurately rendered. Although the selection of these sources ensures that the conclusions drawn here are local in nature, this essay also seeks to open up larger questions concerning the place of the dead in early modern England.[7]

The contents of these documents must, of course, be used carefully and with an awareness of the influence of scribal opinion and the forces of coercion or compulsion which were brought to bear on the dying woman by the family members and friends pressing around the deathbed in the last moments of the will-maker's life. After a lengthy debate, it is now widely thought that most sixteenth-century wills included highly conventional statements, most especially in the religious preamble, and that many of their seeming individual expressions were dictated by the scribe rather than to him by the testator.[8] But their formulaic nature does not entirely undermine their usefulness as evidence because even conventional expressions were shaped by social customs and priorities, including those attendant upon the gender of the will-maker. Moreover, even if the

---

[7] *Wills of the County of Essex (England)*, ed. F. G. Emmison, vol. I: *1599–1565* (Washington DC, 1982); vol. II: *1565–1571* (Boston, 1983); vol. III: *1571–1577* (Boston, 1986); *Essex Wills, the Archdeaconry Courts*, ed. F. G. Emmison, vols. IV–VII: *1577–1603* (Chelmsford, Essex, 1987–1990). Hereinafter, wills from this collection are cited as *Essex Wills* and briefly by volume/will number. Spelling and punctuation are modernised throughout. An additional note on terminology is appropriate here. Formally, 'will' refers to that part of the instrument that deals with immoveable property, and 'testament' concerns that part of the document distributing money and moveable goods. In this essay, these terms are used loosely and synonymously to refer to the entire instrument.

[8] C. Marsh, 'In the Name of God? Willmaking and Faith in Early Modern England', in G. H. Martin and P. Spufford (eds.), *The Records of the Nation* (Woodbridge, 1990), pp. 215–49; C. Burgess, 'Late Medieval Wills and Pious Convention: Testamentary Evidence Reconsidered', in M. A. Hicks (ed.), *Profit, Piety and the Professions in Later Medieval England* (Gloucester, 1990), pp. 14–33.

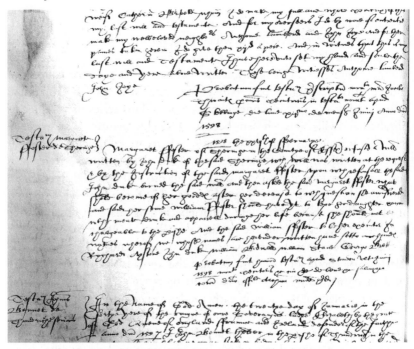

Plate 10.1   *Registered (nuncupative) will of Margaret Foster, 1598.*
[Reproduced courtesy of the Essex Record Office]

form of the will was initially supplied by the scribe, testators exercised the right to approve or reject the will's contents, and especially the right to determine their bequests of property and personal belongings. While unusual in its depiction of the process of will-making, Margaret Foster's nuncupative will demonstrated the decisive influence that one woman had concerning the final content of her testament. Her will was, according to the testimony of six witnesses, drawn up 'at her request and instruction'. Dissatisfied with this document, however, she rejected it and 'upon which refusal [John Duke] burned the will and asked her what should become of her goods'. She answered briefly and pronounced her wishes to all those in attendance and the words she actually spoke (or as far as the witnesses remembered) later were entered into the probate register as her verbal will leaving her worldly belongings for the benefit of her daughter so that 'she should not be chargeable to the parish'.[9] (See

---

[9] *Essex Wills*, VII/855. After the Statute of Wills of 1540 (32 Henry VIII cap. 1), inheritable lands could not be transferred by a verbal will. Nuncupative wills were restricted only to the disposition of goods and chattels and thus were more often used by the poor. Estimates

Plate 10.1.) Influenced by custom and by the people surrounding the death-bed, testamentary bequests of women's worldly belongings nonetheless identified the cultural priorities of the testator and her community, and through their mobilisation of the symbolism of giving within the parish community revealed the role of gender in the making of remembrance.

Before the arrival of the Protestant Reformation in England, remembrance was shaped in the moments before death by a fear of Purgatory and an awareness of the pains that awaited there.[10] Since the souls in Purgatory were those of redeemed Christians, they deserved to be remembered by the living because the dead depended on the community of the living to relieve them of their sufferings. Moreover, the living owed their departed family members and friends a responsibility based in blood kinship, affection or Christian duty to 'do like friends' and remember the dead.[11] In providing their sometimes elaborate and lavish gifts for the masses, prayers and almsdeeds needed to relieve the suffering of their departed soul, testators expressed these bonds of obligation between the living and the dead and revealed the ties that bound families and communities together across the chasm of death. As a reminder to the living of their obligation to remember the dead, one popular pre-Reformation devotional text reported that the souls in Purgatory cried out to the living to fulfil their responsibility to provide for intercession, saying 'have pity, have mercy, have mercy on me; at least you my sons and daughters, nieces and nephews, cousin and cousins, and you others unto whom I have left my goods'.[12]

This reciprocal relationship between the living and the dead was, of course, destroyed by the Protestant rejection of Purgatory as 'a fond thing, vainly invented and grounded upon no warranty of Scripture' and the abolition of the intercessory rites of the medieval 'cult of the dead' as 'blasphemous fables and dangerous deceits' that were 'injurious to the precious redemption of our saviour Christ'.[13] In Elizabethan England,

---

based on wills receiving probate underestimate the total number of verbal wills declared in early modern England since the incentive for the poorer and middling sorts to evade the courts was high because of the expense of probate.

[10] On Reformation-era depictions of the fear of Purgatory, see P. Marshall, 'Fear, Purgatory and Polemic in Reformation England', in W. Naphy and P. Roberts (eds.), *Fear in Early Modern Society* (Manchester, 1997), pp. 150–66. G. R. Keiser, 'The Progress of Purgatory: Visions of the Afterlife in Later Medieval English Literature', *Analecta Cartusiana* 117 (1986), pp. 72–100 provides a vivid survey of pre-Reformation images of Purgatory.

[11] Duffy, *Stripping of the Altars*, 338–57; M. D. Sullivan, 'Two Fruitful Sermons of John Fisher' (University of Notre Dame PhD thesis, 1961), pp. 19–22.

[12] *Ordinary of Christian Men* (London, 1505) sig. L1 ii (v).

[13] W. H. Frere and W. M. Kennedy (eds.), *Visitation Articles and Injunctions of the Period of*

remembrance by one's family and friends was no longer necessary to ensure a soul's safe passage through the 'third place' because, according to Reformed doctrine, once the soul departed the body it was bound either for Heaven or for Hell and there was nothing that the living could do to influence its condition. Prompted both by changing attitudes and by the limits of official religion, traditional bequests for commemorative masses and the once-common requests for prayers for departed souls disappeared from the content of wills after 1558.[14] Combined with the Protestant mandate that all post-mortem ritual activities were 'rather comforts to the living than helps to the dead'[15] testamentary gift-giving and funerary rituals seemingly became secularised indicators of social position in the highly status-conscious society of late sixteenth-century England.[16] The conclusion thus may be drawn that 'early modern funerals were more for the living than for the dead' and that despite some persisting aspects of traditional funerary display, the dead were forcibly alienated from the community of the living during the Reformation and gradually forgotten because the dead no longer depended on the living for commemorative ritual or intercessory prayer.[17]

Although stripped of their traditional role of providing a prompt for remembering souls suffering in Purgatory, the material gifts contained in Elizabethan wills demonstrated the continuing importance of testamentary gift-giving for commemorating corporate identity in post-Reformation England. Within their gifts, women expressed the value of their estates not simply as collections of economic commodities to distinguish their place in the local social status hierarchy, but as

---

the Reformation (3 vols., London, 1910), III, p. 186; C. Hardwick, *A History of the Articles of Religion* (London, 1895), p. 123; J. Lamb, *An Historical Account of the Thirty-Nine Articles* (Cambridge, 1829), pp. 13–19.

[14] For the disappearance of these traditional bequests from wills of other English counties, see G. J. Mayhew, 'The Progress of the Reformation in East Sussex, 1530–1559: the Evidence from Wills' and R. Whiting, '"For the Health of My Soul": Prayers for the Dead in the Tudor South-West', *Southern History* 5 (1983), pp. 38–67 and 68–94; L. Attreed, 'Preparation for Death in Sixteenth-Century Northern England', *Sixteenth Century Journal* 13 (1982), pp. 35–66.

[15] John Ayre (ed.), *The Sermons of Edwyn Sandys* (Cambridge, 1841), p. 12.

[16] Cressy, 'Funerary Preferences of Elizabethan Gentlemen', p. 108, and *Birth, Marriage, and Death*, p. 443; R. Houlbrooke, 'Death, Church and Family in England between the Late Fifteenth and Early Eighteenth Centuries', in R. Houlbrooke (ed.), *Death, Ritual and Bereavement* (London, 1989), pp. 1–42, and Gittings, 'Urban Funerals', p. 178 all clearly express this transformation of the celebrations of death from the religious to the private and secular.

[17] Gittings, *Death, Burial and the Individual*, p. 164; Cressy, *Birth, Marriage, and Death*, p. 396, and 'Funerary Preferences of Elizabethan Gentlemen', pp. 99–100; Duffy, *Stripping of the Altars*, p. 475.

collections of spiritualised goods entrusted to the public document of the will as a custodian of memory and as a means to convey this memory.[18] Through the will's active stewardship of the property that served as a symbol of divine benediction in life, and through its distribution of this property in bequests 'to the glory of God', women testators attached their memory to acts of communal generosity.[19] The reciprocal act of giving and receiving designated rememberers within the community of the living and celebrated the spiritual and material cohesiveness of the relationship between the remembered and her family, social networks and parish community. It is from these spiritually charged bequests of material property and wealth to family members, friends and neighbours that the distinctive quality of the constructions of memory found in women's wills emerges clearly.

As legal documents containing instructions for the transfer of land and property, all sixteenth-century wills were distinguished by the laws governing inheritance. Reflecting the differing position of men and women in property law in early modern England, the gender distribution of the Essex wills was markedly bipolar: married testators were overwhelmingly male, while widowed and single will-writers were predominantly female. Of the 1276 women's wills in this collection, only ten were plainly identified as belonging to married women, and their testaments showed that these wives did not administer the entire marital estate but were performing their duties concerning legacies of lands and goods from previous marriages.[20] In distributing the family estate, widowed women likewise acted according to law and local custom, following the detailed formulations necessitated by procedure and sometimes openly acknowledging their fulfilment of the conditions set out in a deceased spouse's

---

[18] Wills were public documents in that typically they were made in the presence of friends and family attending the death-bed, and the very nature of this public announcement is made clear by the extensive lists of witnesses appended to each probated will. Additionally, wills were public documents in that the original text was transcribed at the Archdeaconry Court by a probate clerk and, perhaps, reviewed by the bishop of London on occasion as part of visitation proceedings. This process ensured that the will's contents were displayed to the community.

[19] Duffy, *Stripping of the Altars*, pp. 504–5; Beaver, 'Death, Ritual, and Social Organisation', pp. 395–8; C. Litzenberger, *The English Reformation and the Laity: Gloucestershire, 1540–1580* (Cambridge, 1997), pp. 122–3. On the influence of Christian humanists in the development of sixteenth-century notions of stewardship, see M. Todd, *Christian Humanism and the Puritan Social Order* (Cambridge, 1987), pp. 133–8.

[20] *Essex Wills*, II/357, II/610, II/823, III/350, III/570, III/573, III/1048, V/1160, VII/645, VII/761. This proportion is not atypical. See Beaver, 'Death, Ritual, and Social Organisation', p. 394.

will in doing so.[21] In performing the legacies of their dead husbands, and for single women those of deceased parents or grandparents,[22] these women served as passive markers indicating the filiation of family property. But in addition to their passive role in remembering as individuals by whom land and property were transmitted, women performed an active role in remembering through their own bequests of personal belongings and money to family, friends and neighbours.[23] These gifts were characterised by a profound devotion to detail and only rarely did women will-makers provide for general distributions of their personal property by their executors. In these cases, the nearness of death may have forced testators to express their last wishes briefly, as it likely did for Agnes Wede who pronounced to the women attending her at the death-bed, 'I give to Robert Coppin all that I have, he to take all and to pay all', and for Elizabeth Sterves whose will, witnessed only by two women of Barking, announced simply, 'I make John Cornelius, brewer of London of All Saint's parish near to the Tower of London, my executor.'[24]

Although they were made on the threshold of death, women's wills typically expressed careful consideration, as certain goods were set aside as remembrances for named individuals or particular groups of people. When Christiane Abell prepared her will, she began the distribution of her worldly belongings with the bed on which she then rested. Moving on, the cushions and blankets that supported and covered her, then the various things scattered around her dwelling were distributed, with careful attention being paid to the kitchen utensils.[25] Joan Ellis began in reverse order, but achieved the same end as her will documented each piece of moveable goods to be given away.[26] Even more informative about the disposition of her goods than either of these two women,

---

[21] Prior, 'Wives and Wills', pp. 201–25; B. A. Holderness, 'Widows in Pre-Industrial Society: an Essay upon their Economic Function', in R. Smith (ed.), *Land, Kinship, and Life-Cycle* (Cambridge, 1984), pp. 423–44; C. Howell, 'Peasant Inheritance Customs in the Midlands, 1280–1700' and M. Spufford, 'Peasant Inheritance Customs and Land Distribution in Cambridgeshire from the Sixteenth to the Eighteenth Century', in J. Goody, J. Thirsk and E. P. Thompson (eds.), *Family and Inheritance: Rural Society in Western Europe, 1200–1800* (Cambridge, 1976), especially pp. 151–2 and 166–7. *Essex Wills*, i/133, i/161, 1338, i/589, ii/327, ii/360, ii/707, iv/283, iv/351, iv/813, vi/781, vi/1004, vii/473.

[22] *Ibid.*, ii/457, v/414, vi/187, vi/571.

[23] Geary, *Phantoms of Remembrance*, p. 63. The following discussion of material bequests relies heavily upon M. Howell, 'Fixing Movables: Gifts by Testament in Late Medieval Douai', *Past and Present* 150 (1996), pp. 3–45.

[24] *Essex Wills*, iv/588, ii/233.

[25] *Ibid.*, iv/740.

[26] *Ibid.*, vii/99.

Eleanor Baker did not stint in her detailed descriptions of her personal property; her list of clothing to be given away 'if God work His way with me' differentiated her things by colour and by quality, naming some by fabric and others by their worn, 'work-a-day' condition.[27] As a detailed inventory of the belongings of a wealthy mid-Elizabethan widow in the textile-producing county of Essex, Margaret Over's will was unsurpassed and it is clear that the testator and her scribe methodically accounted for all of her worldly belongings and provided for their appropriate distribution.[28] At the other end of the social spectrum, women like Mercy Asplande and Joan Mills, whose inventory exhibited a value of only 38s, expressed similar care with their own less extensive personal estates.[29] Even more destitute was Elizabeth London, whose probate clause states simply 'pauper', but she too included detailed bequests for the distribution of meagre belongings and clothing.[30] Although poor, and sometimes on the verge of destitution, these women had something to bequeath to family, friends and community as remembrances – parental portions, personal belongings or savings from being in service – and so they too left wills containing their detailed instructions for the distribution of these worldly belongings.

While about 13 per cent of these testators were young single women in service or women for whom death struck unexpectedly early in life,[31] the same inheritance law which regulated women's role in making bequests of familial land and property helped to guarantee that the typical woman will-maker was aged – usually widows such as Joan Lytman and Margaret Hallyday who left bequests to their 'children's children' or Agnes Hills of High Ongar who left a pewter platter to her great-granddaughter, or even spinsters like Jane Knyf and Agnes Raphen who had outlived most of their families – and thus it also helped to ensure that she would have many people to remember in her gift-giving and who would remember her after she died.[32] In determining who was to receive their gifts of personal belongings, these women will-makers

---

[27] *Ibid.*, I/47.
[28] *Ibid.*, III/325.
[29] *Ibid.*, V/615, V/1135.
[30] *Ibid.*, I/449.
[31] See especially *Essex Wills*, I/33, II/279, II/357, II/610, II/823, III/142, III/350, III/570, III/573, III/584, III/1048, IV/588, IV/615, V/57, V/227, V/745, V/1006, V/1160, VI/1120, VII/645, VII/761.
[32] *Ibid.*, III/53, V/183, VII/122, I/10, V/838. See also I/108, I/203, I/250, I/370, I/504, I/560, I/749, II/146, II/310, II/734, III/276, III/577, III/652, III/657, III/706, III/756, III/849, III/912, III/993, IV/343, IV/697, IV/740, IV/965, V/287, V/414, V/755, V/870, V/962, V/1057, VI/538, VI/914.

were confronted by a bewildering array of decisions. They selected the recipients of their goods from networks of kin and community based on social custom and their own priorities, giving money and goods in unequal measure to sons and daughters, to stepchildren, godchildren, and to friends and neighbours. They rewarded service, punished disloyalty, fulfilled obligations, repaid debts and celebrated the emotional ties that bound them to their communities both in life and beyond the moment of death.

Women's wills most often identified members of the nuclear family or, in lieu of them, members of an extended circle of kin to be the recipients of remembrances. Certainly, Anne Patten's nuncupative will was unusual in that all her goods were to be distributed exclusively among a small circle of her friends and that 'neither her father nor any of her brothers or sisters-in-law should have any part or pennyworth thereof, rather than they should she would have it burnt'.[33] But Patten was not alone in looking to others for remembrance, and, expressing a similar sentiment, Agnes Smyth's verbal will denied her children any part in her legacy by giving all of her belongings as a reward to the daughter of Henry Creswell who stood by her in her dying days.[34] By contrast, Agnes Beston gave all of her belongings to her son but when she was prompted to 'give her daughter somewhat for a remembrance, if it were but one of her gowns' she answered 'every time [that] she would not'.[35] More commonly, though, women behaved generously to their own and perpetuated a sense of familial cohesiveness in their material gift-giving. Dividing her goods equally between her son and four daughters, Margaret Amott's will methodically distributed the contents of each room in her dwelling between these children.[36] Agnes Wright, a widow of Rochford, made her daughter Joan the primary beneficiary of her gifts, while Agnes Brett, a single woman, bequeathed all her goods to her uncle, in consideration of which he was to 'bestow part of them on her brothers and sisters.'[37] Natural children usually were preferred to stepchildren and Joan Chamberlen specifically noted that the residue of her goods were to be distributed 'amongst my natural children, part and part alike' but Margaret Pytman gave to her husband's son 'over and above the portion that the law does give him . . . for love and goodwill'.[38] Extended kin,

---

[33] *Ibid.*, vii/137. See also iv/54.
[34] *Ibid.*, iv/54.
[35] *Ibid.*, v/1093.
[36] *Ibid.*, vi/166.
[37] *Ibid.*, vi/162, vi/526.
[38] *Ibid.*, iv/455.

including nieces and nephews as well as the children of cousins, inherited as well[39] and, occasionally, this extended kin group was supplemented by godchildren, who were in a few cases preferred to blood relatives.[40] For both Thomasine Heyman and Katherine Coolle, the boundaries of this flexible kin-group also included the man 'with whom I have contracted in marriage'.[41]

From the thousands of named individuals and personal gifts detailed in these wills, a trend emerges revealing the particular and vital bond that linked women together as rememberers and suggests that for these Elizabethan women remembering was a collective activity performed by the gendered social groups with which they had identified in life. While men's wills were concerned chiefly with the lineal descent of property to wives and children, women's gift-giving typically encompassed a gendered social network of family, friends and neighbours within the parish community in which local women and girls were the preferred recipients of itemised bequests. Mary Cucocke, a single woman of Rivenhall, left detailed gifts to named female beneficiaries, but left her male heirs only a monetary legacy from the sale of a cow.[42] Agnes Wilsonne likewise named her female heirs and detailed the goods to be distributed to them, but her only male heir, her brother, received a bequest simply for 'the rest of my goods'.[43] While such gifts commemorated the closer connection between the testator and her female heirs, other wills placed even greater emphasis on women as rememberers; notably neither Maud Powlter nor Alice Dasune included any men or boys in their gift-giving, and women alone were to receive their goods and lands.[44] Likewise, the named recipients of Elizabeth London's gifts were women from six distinct local families, while Katherine Ravens of Ardleigh concentrated her giving on women and included among her beneficiaries three women of different families in addition to her sister.[45]

Widows, the group to which many of these testators belonged in the closing days of their lives, were commonly found among the women

---

[39] *Ibid.*, vi/219.
[40] See especially *Essex Wills*, i/6, i/53, i/77 (goddaughters only), i/780, iii/1023 (preferred over natural children), iv/258, v/9 (poor relations only), v/183, v/362 (unmarried godchildren only). Cressy, *Birth, Marriage, and Death*, pp. 149–60 considers the bond of godparentage to belong 'to that circle of latent or dormant resources that could be made effective in times of need'.
[41] *Essex Wills*, v/958, vi/209.
[42] *Ibid.*, iv/324.
[43] *Ibid.*, vi/493.
[44] *Ibid.*, i/77, ii/310. See also iv/88, iv/615, vi/33, vi/389.
[45] *Ibid.*, i/449, iii/553.

receiving testamentary gifts in these wills, thus reinforcing the notion that remembrance was considered a collective activity carried on by the social group to which a person had belonged in life. The will of the widow Margaret Payne listed more than a dozen women who were to receive gifts of money and of personal articles, and a majority of these were clearly identified as widows.[46] Joan Ames gave the bulk of her worldly things to four other widowed neighbours, providing for each an article of her clothing and 12d, while in her will the widow Margery Bailie provided gifts of her clothing for three of her counterparts in South Ockendon.[47] Such gifts conveyed a sense of communal identity and reciprocal remembering among women and widows, but these markers were also distributed in ways designed to embed the memory of the testator's place in the local social hierarchy. Certainly, the widowed friend who received a rich velvet saddlecloth as a part of Anne Locksmith's testamentary gifts was being prompted to remember her benefactor, but not with the same sense of deference as the six poor widows invited to receive mourning garments at the burial of this wealthy widow.[48] In most cases, though, the gifts that women set aside for poor women and needy widows were not so elaborate, and usually involved simple donations of old clothing or household articles. Six poor women each received articles of old clothing under the directions of Margaret Mason's will, while that of Margaret Wyer set aside one of her old petticoats and a lockram kerchief for one neighbour and an 'old lockram rail' for another aged widow.[49] Maude Crushe's donation of a gift of her bed-sheets to several poor women and a poor widow of Billericay 'that has a lame boy' and Joan Bartlet's donation of her 'very worn sheets' to three needy women of her parish were also typical of the sort of aid supplied by women's wills to other needy women.[50]

As an action well founded in the authority of custom, stimulated by Protestant doctrine and encouraged by Christian humanists, this symbolic act of giving to the community's poor and needy was at the heart of women's actions reaffirming the spiritual and material bond between living and dead. Despite a lengthy debate over the scale and motives

[46] *Ibid.*, II/754.
[47] *Ibid.*, III/56, IV/184.
[48] *Ibid.*, VII/139.
[49] *Ibid.*, V/146, II/29.
[50] *Ibid.*, III/496, III/762. J. Bennett, 'Conviviality and Charity in Medieval and Early Modern England', *Past and Present* 134 (1992), pp. 19–41; F. Heal, *Hospitality in Early Modern England* (Oxford, 1990); S. Brigden, 'Religion and Social Obligation in Early Sixteenth Century London', *Past and Present* 103 (1984), pp. 67–112.

behind charitable giving in Elizabethan England, too little attention has been drawn to the subject of the gender distribution within this group of philanthropists. In Essex, where just over one-third of all Elizabethan wills included some donation to charity, giving was disproportionately led by women, whose wills accounted for only one-sixth of the total testaments but who provided for nearly one-third of all charitable bequests. During the early years of Elizabeth's reign, more than 40 per cent of women's wills contained a gift to the poor and needy in the local community, and at its lowest level during the closing years of the sixteenth century, the proportion of women's charitable giving never dipped below 20 per cent. Such gift-giving on the death-bed, of course, plainly constituted a continuation of one's life's work and Agnes Lawrence's will provided for a distribution of alms to the poor of St James, Colchester only 'if so be I shall not happen to distribute the same with my own hands in my time of sickness before my death'.[51] As an expression of the giver's life, these death-bed donations also were a continuation of the testator's place in the local social hierarchy and 'a final and dramatic demonstration of the ability to distribute alms', and thus an example of the ways in which the local elite represented the vertical bonds of deference and authority that characterised sixteenth-century life.[52] But as final acts of remembering done within the social networks of parish communities between known givers and known recipients, and done even by poor women, servants and maidens to the benefit of their equals,[53] gift-giving to the poor and needy also stressed the horizontal interdependencies binding women together within parish society.

The named and the nameless 'poor and needy' who most commonly benefited from testamentary gift-giving were not only those on the margins of local society; because the 'poor' was a flexible category, defined by the need and willingness to accept aid, the recipients of charity included not only 'sturdy beggars' and idlers but also those members of the parish community who were suffering poverty as a temporary condition.[54] These 'poor' neighbours certainly included numerous girls, mothers and ageing widows, some of whom were the recipients of specific gifts from a benefactor, but others of whom found relief among the

---

[51] *Essex Wills*, vii/641.
[52] Cressy, 'Funerary Preferences of Elizabethan Gentlemen', p. 108.
[53] *Essex Wills*, i/449 ii/351, iii/127, iii/276, iv/965, vi/8, vi/914
[54] Bennett, 'Conviviality and Charity', p. 20; C. Dyer, *Standards of Living in the Later Middle Ages* (Cambridge, 1989), p. 234; P. Slack, *Poverty and Policy in Tudor and Stuart England* (London, 1988), p. 7; M. McIntosh, 'Local Responses to the Poor in Late Medieval and Tudor England', *Continuity and Change* 3 (1988), pp. 209–45.

general recipients of alms-doles at the testator's funeral or through a distribution 'to the poor and most needy'[55] usually conducted by the will's executor but also occasionally by the local 'collectors for the poor'.[56] The foreknowledge that their giving helped the needy women of their communities may have inspired women will-makers to provide for such gifts more frequently than their male counterparts because, as women, the security of their own position in the local socio-economic system was threatened by the disadvantages of their age (either aged or young) and marital status (either widowed or single).

Women's wills manifested many aspects of charity, as the term was understood at the time, and also revealed that in Elizabethan England distributions to charitable causes were marked by a gender distinction: men's wills more often gave to the poor-box or for general distributions at the discretion of the executors[57] while women's wills more often gave for specific needs.[58] In a period in which increasing numbers of their friends and neighbours were falling into poverty as the local textile-based economy suffered,[59] women seemingly drew some inspiration for their giving from Christ's injunctions in Matthew 25:35–40. Based on this passage, traditional religion had taught that money should be given to 'repair hospitals, help sick people, mend bad roads, build up bridges that had been broken down, help maidens to marry or make them nuns, find food for prisoners and poor people, put scholars to school or some other craft, help religious orders, and ameliorate rents or taxes.'[60] Likewise, the Elizabethan text of the *Reformatio Legum Ecclesiasticarum*, published by John Day for the martyrologist John Foxe in 1571, included a prompt to testamentary charity in a section entitled 'Concerning Wills':

> Moreover, these are numbered among pious causes: when something is brought to the relief of prisoners, to the refreshment of the poor, to the maintenance of orphans, widows, and afflicted persons of any kind,

---

[55] For examples of this common formulation see *Essex Wills*, 1/338, 1/718, v1/420. Such distributions were also made through the office of the local collector of the poor-rate. See *ibid.*, 1/250, 11/812, v/537.

[56] *Ibid.*, 11/660, 111/367, v11/541; Bennett, 'Conviviality and Charity', p. 40; Gittings, *Death, Burial and the Individual*, pp. 152, 161–4.

[57] Cressy, 'Funerary Preferences of Elizabethan Gentlemen', pp. 104–5, 108.

[58] Women's donations to the poor men's box, also referred to as the 'Lord's Box', were notably rare. See *Essex Wills*, 1/338, 11/87, 11/812, 11/874, 111/205, 111/267, 111/522, 1v/4, v/477, v/537.

[59] J. Pilgrim, 'The Cloth Industry of Essex and Suffolk, 1558–1640' (University of London MA thesis, 1939).

[60] From *Vision of Piers Plowman*, based on W. K. Jordan's rendering in his *Philanthropy in England, 1480–1660* (New York, 1958), p. 112.

particularly and especially when something is designated by will for the marriage of poor girls, to cover the nakedness of needy students living in the academies, for the repair of public roads.[61]

Sustained by the authority of custom and by Protestantism, these works were encouraged at the death-bed by the attending cleric who was to remind the dying that 'they ought at this time be much more ready to help the poor and needy, knowing that to relieve the poor is a true worshipping of God' and who was to 'call upon, exhort, and move [his] neighbours to confer and give, as well as they may spare'.[62] In gendered terms, however, these works also may have appealed to women will-makers for the ways that they designated the remembered and the rememberers through acts that celebrated the spiritual and material cohesiveness of their community within which, at any given time, some were the givers of charitable gifts and others were the beneficiaries of them.[63]

While some women's wills included the more general instruction for the executor to distribute gifts 'in deeds of charity to the pleasure of God',[64] Elizabethan women testators typically supplied specific directions concerning the application of their legacies to particular charitable causes. Their spirited gift-giving to widows and to other needy women and girls has been previously noted, but the content of these donations merits further consideration. In a region famous for its textile production, it is not surprising that Essex wills contained numerous gifts of cloth or clothing to the poor; but in this giving, gifts from women to women predominated. In preparing her will, Alice Whood designated several named poor of Laindon to receive charitable gifts, with the married men receiving either food or money and their wives receiving an old petticoat, two lockram kerchiefs, a coat and a canvas apron among them.[65] Supplying more than one-half of all recorded testamentary gifts to the needy for raiment, women's wills provided not just mourning garments for ritual display at the funeral, but also the daily wear needed by the

---

[61] James Spalding (ed.), *The Reformation of the Ecclesiastical Laws of England* (Kirksville, MO, 1992), pp. 288–9.

[62] Frere and Kennedy, *Visitation Articles and Injunctions*, III, p. 14.

[63] For a discussion of a similar point of view within the context of 'help-ales' see Bennett, 'Conviviality and Charity', pp. 38–40 and her reply to Maria Moisà in *Past and Present* 154 (1997), pp. 235–42. See also F. G. Emmison, 'The Care of the Poor in Elizabethan Essex', *Essex Review* 62 (1953), pp. 7–28.

[64] *Essex Wills*, I/510, I/718, II/623, III/411, III/912, V/4.

[65] *Ibid.*, III/367.

living community.[66] Bequests of 'my common wearing gear' or 'lockram kerchiefs' or of 'two old coats' were welcome gifts for needy women, as was Margaret Water's gift of several pieces of clothing to a blind girl of Coggeshall, and these served as daily remembrances of the widows and the young single women who gave them.[67]

Although women's wills also frequently included bequests for the more vicarious acts of repairing almshouses and local churches, and for the building or maintenance of neighbourhood roads and bridges,[68] the qualities of women's testamentary gift-giving were demonstrated with particular clarity in their charitable provisions to feed the hungry and give drink to the thirsty. Women's wills pursued this charitable act with zeal, and nearly one-third of all recorded testamentary gifts for food or drink in Elizabethan Essex were made by women will-makers. These gifts of food were usually expressed in the form of a funeral feast and, although these could sometimes be sumptuous affairs, they more typically were simple buffets of bread, cheese and beer for the enjoyment of the funeral party, friends and poor neighbours attending the funeral.[69] The purpose of the feast was not simply to differentiate the local community and to reinforce the elevated social standing of the donor, as the widow Margaret Nevard's will revealed by the way that it narrowed the symbolic distance between donor and recipient by ordering that her most valuable livestock, including the 'fattest hogs' and 'fattest sheep', be killed for the enjoyment of all those at her feast, and as Joan Brown's will indicated in its inclusive invitation for all of her 'friends and neighbours' to enjoy her hospitality at the funeral alongside the local poor.[70] In addition to these funeral feasts, women distributed direct gifts of rye, wheat or barley to their needy neighbours.[71] This form of charitable gift and its expression of commensality, or the sharing of food, between the donor and the recipient may have appealed to women testators for whom the preparation and serving of food had been a central part of their life's work. Likewise, women will-makers might have been drawn to gifts of food and drink by the way that these gifts reinforced corporate identity by directing aid to the local poor

---

[66] See especially *ibid.*, I/712, II/29, III/325, III/368, III/514, III/762, III/947, IV/872, VII/590.

[67] *Ibid.*, I/712, V/146, V/967, VII/884.

[68] *Ibid.*, III/509, IV/503; I/375, I/885, II/623, IV/726, IV/966, V/62; I/718, II/611, II/623, III/590 III/912, IV/821, VI/1014.

[69] *Ibid.*, III/484, IV/400. Not all bequests for such conviviality were restricted to the day of the burial itself, but sometimes took place at the month's mind or anniversary date of the burial, or at a designated holy day: I/72, I/301.

[70] *Ibid.*, I/675, I/806, IV/303.

[71] *Ibid.*, IV/614, IV/664, VII/412, VII/440.

and especially to needy women. These acts of commensality and the conviviality which they encouraged between the living celebrants and their recently deceased hostess affirmed the interdependence of humanity and symbolically enacted the role of the dead individual in the living community.[72]

The preceding discussion has shown that testamentary gift-giving played a central part in the efforts of dying women to define their post-mortem identity and to secure their place within the living communities of Elizabethan England. In seeking to construct this identity, women will-makers mobilised the material and spiritual value of all their worldly belongings and designated their family members, friends and neighbours as rememberers who, in accepting gifts from the dead, commemorated their relationships with the deceased. This act of memory, formed through the custodial document of the will, served to reinforce the social hierarchy but also to sustain the horizontal interdependencies that marked both the place of the living and the dead in local structures of family, social network and community. The arguments proposed here are not meant to question the value of discussions of the ritual performances of burial and funeral rites, or to undermine the importance of studies of other forms of remembering in literature or in art. Rather, the goal has been to emphasise that wills provide insight into the role of women in memory that cannot be obtained from other sources, and to encourage closer scrutiny of the evidence available from women's wills in exploring the social and cultural characteristics embedded in the mortuary culture of early modern England.

---

[72] Bloch and Parry, *Death and the Regeneration of Life*, p. 28; van Gennep, *Rites of Passage*, pp. 164–5.

11 Death, prophecy and judgement in Transylvania

Graeme Murdock

Transylvania appears destined to be forever associated with death in western imagination. Although neither the brutal deeds of Vlad the impaler, Walachian warrior prince of the fifteenth century, nor the cruel crimes of the late sixteenth-century mass murderess, Erzsébet Báthori, actually took place on Transylvania's soil, and investigations of vampirism in the mid-eighteenth century extended from Serbia to Poland, the reputation of the principality as a land of blood seems fixed, thanks mostly to the projections of Gothic horror literature.[1] During the early seventeenth century Transylvanian princes, their relatives and leading nobles of the principality died as a result of murderous human actions, and by the apparent intervention of divine and diabolic powers. Whilst this hardly reduces the rather exotic nature of the history of death in Transylvania, the interpretation which was placed upon the deaths of members of the Transylvanian ruling elite during the seventeenth century, which I shall examine here, falls nevertheless within a pattern of political and religious significance which was attributed to death across the continent, and within the role sometimes given to the dead in the calculations of Protestant elites during the early modern period.

The Transylvanian principality emerged as a semi-autonomous state under loose Ottoman suzerainty during the second half of the sixteenth century. Ottoman invasion of the northern Balkans had divided the medieval Hungarian kingdom into three parts, with southern Hungary under Ottoman control, western and northern counties of Royal Hungary

---

[1] Gábor Klaniczay, 'The Decline of Witches and the Rise of Vampires under the Eighteenth-century Habsburg Monarchy', in his *The Uses of Supernatural Power. The Transformation of Popular Religion in Medieval and Early Modern Europe* (Cambridge, 1990), pp. 168–88.

governed by the Habsburgs, and native princes ruling over Transylvania proper and over Hungarian counties east of the Tisza river, known as the Partium. This Transylvanian principality was surrounded on three sides by Ottoman-occupied territories, and princes elected by the local diet had to gain acceptance for their rule from the Porte and pay tribute to the Sultan. Elected princes, drawn in the late sixteenth century from the magnate Zápolyai and Báthori families, were nevertheless able to establish a semi-independent role for the principality between the Habsburgs and the Turks. Princes exercised effective authority over the three 'nations' represented in the Transylvanian diet of Hungarian nobles, Saxon towns and Szeklers. Catholic princes, however, had to recognise growing support in the diet for religious reform, and from 1568 four confessions received legal status in the principality. The Catholic Church was soon left marginalised with Lutherans dominating the Saxon community, the anti-Trinitarian Church gaining support in Hungarian towns and amongst Szeklers, and the Reformed Church strongly backed by many Hungarian nobles, especially in the Partium. During the 1590s Transylvania was plunged again into conflict against the Ottomans during the Fifteen Years War, and Rudolf II attempted to take advantage of the situation to reassert Habsburg sovereignty over Transylvania and to promote the cause of counter-reform across Hungary. In 1604 István Bocskai, a major Reformed landowner from the Partium, led a successful revolt against Rudolf and became the first of a series of Calvinist nobles to be elected as princes of Transylvania during the seventeenth century.[2]

Following the disruption caused by Bocskai's revolt and the devastation of the Fifteen Years War, Transylvania's Calvinist princes worked to consolidate the structure of government in the principality, and bring discipline and order to Transylvanian society. Bocskai, Gábor Bethlen and the Rákóczi princes also firmly advanced the interests of the Reformed Church against its confessional rivals, bolstering the distinct Protestant identity of the principality against Habsburg claims of sovereignty. Whilst Hungarian Protestantism had initially relied upon noble protection against royal and Catholic persecution, and Reformed ministers at the turn of the century had enthusiastically backed the cause of Bocskai's noble rebellion against monarchical authority, during the early seventeenth

---

[2] László Makkai, 'A Bocskai felkelés', in *Magyarország története*, ed. Pál Pach, (10 vols., Budapest, 1987), III, pp. 709–74; Kálmán Benda, 'A kálvini tanok hatása a magyar rendi ellenállás ideológiájára', *Helikon* 17 (1971), pp. 322–30; László Makkai, 'Nemesi köztár-saság és kálvinista teokrácia a 16. századi Lengyelországban és Magyarországon', *Ráday Gyűjtemény Évkönyve* 3 (1983), pp. 17–29.

century the Reformed Church in Transylvania became closely allied with princely power. Reformed religion acquired the status of public orthodoxy in Transylvania during this period, with Reformed clergy, nobles and princes dominating politics and society, and securing a relatively safe, if increasingly isolated, outpost for Calvinism in Eastern Europe.[3]

Princely commitment to the Reformed cause was not merely a public facade constructed for political advantage. György I Rákóczi and his wife Zsuzsanna Lórántffy were notably pious in their private devotions. Gábor Bethlen too, although perhaps more calculating, was at least widely believed to be 'a zealous Calvinist, seldome going without a Latine Testament in his pocket'.[4] Whilst formal connections between Church and state remained limited, very significant informal influence was exerted upon these princes and their families by chaplains and by the Transylvanian Reformed superintendent, who was normally resident at court in Gyulafehérvár (Alba Iulia). Reformed ministers encouraged princes to set high standards of personal morality and piety, to take care that God's word was preached effectively in parishes, to build up Protestant academies and schools, and to punish criminality and immorality. Transylvania's princes also promoted the implementation of the Church's programme of moral and social discipline, with Gábor Bethlen introducing a tough new law code in 1618 at the request of a Reformed synod. In response to this apparently godly rule, Reformed preachers portrayed their co-religionist princes as being divinely inspired guardians of true faith and justice in the principality, and Bocskai, Bethlen and the Rákóczis were frequently compared with biblical kings of the Old Testament. This typology of princes as Old Testament kings was followed across the continent, and indeed was far from unique to Calvinists. There was, however, a particularly powerful concentration on the motif of biblical Israel in Calvinist Transylvania, which drew upon Hungarians' origin myths, and was reinforced by the embattled position of the principality in close proximity to the non-Christian world.[5]

---

[3] Imre Révész, 'Bethlen Gábor, a kálvinista fejedelem', *Protestáns Szemle* 26 (1914), pp. 339–58; M. Tarnóc, *Erdély művelődése Bethlen Gábor és a két Rákóczi György korában* (Budapest, 1978); János Pokoly, 'Az erdélyi fejedelemek viszonya a protestáns egyházakhoz', *Protestáns Szemle* 8 (1896), pp. 546–61, 608–24.

[4] A comment by Péter Maksai Őse in Giovanni Botero, *The World, or an historicall description of the most famous kingdomes and commonweals therein* (1630). Rákóczi was described as a godly, Christian husband in Ferenc Szakály (ed.), *Szalárdi János és siralmas magyar krónikája* (Budapest, 1980), pp. 291–2.

[5] Szakály, *Szalárdi János krónikája*; M. Tarnoc, 'Szalárdi János történetszemlélete', *Irodalomtörténeti Közlemények* 74 (1970), pp. 89–96; P. Regan, 'Calvinism and the Dutch Israel

The death of a Reformed prince in Transylvania was a crucial moment both for the ruling noble family, anxious to secure a smooth transition of power and win the election of a nominated successor as prince, and also an opportunity for the Reformed Church to affirm divine sanction for continued Calvinist princely governance.[6] The funeral services conducted for Transylvania's princes, and particularly the funeral sermons given at these services by Reformed preachers, had important political and religious functions in this regard which I shall examine here. Funeral sermons shaped opinions about the dead, and the eulogies offered by Reformed clergy for dead princes idealised and even sanctified Reformed princely rule in Transylvania. Funeral sermons also proved to be lively instruments for Reformed preachers to instruct their living noble congregations on the need to follow the model characteristics of the deceased, and aimed to stimulate religious piety and moral behaviour. Some sermons indeed censured the lay elite for their moral failings, and demanded greater demonstrations of commitment to the Calvinist project of further Reformation, warning that continued disobedience might lead to divine judgement and punishment. From the 1630s one group of prominent Reformed clergy became particularly dissatisfied with the pace of adoption of moral reform within Transylvanian society, and began to view the deaths of princes and leading nobles as the fulfilment of prophetic words of judgement against the principality for its ungodliness and sinfulness. Reformed preachers indeed began to use funeral services to present the testimony of the godly dead as proof that judgement was at hand against the ungodly living, and I shall assess how these claims brought an apprehensive mood to the Transylvanian Church during the 1650s and placed a growing burden of responsibility upon the surviving leadership of the principality.

Funeral services in the Hungarian Reformed Church were simple affairs directed more towards the needs of surviving relatives and the congregation than towards the deceased. There was not much that Reformed ministers could do for the dead, except to grant them burial in a church graveyard and commend them to God's mercy. Services,

---

Thesis', in Bruce Gordon (ed.), *Protestant History and Identity in Sixteenth-Century Europe* (2 vols., Aldershot, 1996), II, pp. 91–107.

6 Compare with England where John Williams's two-hour funeral sermon for James I in 1625 was entitled 'Great Britain's Solomon'. Jennifer Woodward, *The Theatre of Death. The Ritual Management of Royal Funerals in Renaissance England, 1570–1625* (Woodbridge, 1997), pp. 175–203; P. S. Fritz, 'From "Public" to "Private": The Royal Funerals in England, 1500–1830', in Joachim Whaley (ed.), *Mirrors of Mortality. Studies in the Social History of Death* (London, 1981), pp. 61–79.

however, also remained pastoral failures in many ways, since clergy could not comfort friends and relatives with confidence that the deceased was assured of attaining salvation. Nor could ministers make recourse to the concept of Purgatory and invite the living to assist in speeding the souls of the dead to Heaven through intercessory masses, or by offering prayers and lighting candles. Reformed funeral services at least provided occasions for communities to pay their respects to the dead and formally mourn their loss. Not everyone though was even granted this privilege, since the Church reserved the right to refuse Christian burial to those who were considered to have died in sin. Anyone who failed to repent of an offence when asked to do so by their minister risked receiving a so-called ass's funeral. At these funerals the church bell was not rung, a traditional symbol of respect for the dead, which before the Reformation had also reminded the locality to pray for the deceased. Reformed ministers also regulated access to their graveyards, and ass's funerals ended with bodies being deposited outside consecrated ground, and in one northern Hungarian village bodies were even dumped at the foot of the local gallows.[7]

The focus of attention during Reformed funeral services fell upon the preacher and his sermon, with little other ceremony or decoration to assist the congregation to understand the lessons to be drawn from death. Funeral sermons were based upon a biblical text chosen by the minister, which mostly was somehow related to the life of the departed, and often contained stock phrases of praise for the qualities of the dead and glossed over their faults. Sermons also commonly aimed to prepare the living for their own deaths and attempted to supply ideals for future moral conduct, a tradition which had both Calvinist and humanist origins.[8] Leading ministers of the Hungarian Church devoted a good deal of attention during this period to the need to improve standards of preach-ing, including of sermons given during funerals. István Balog Selyei, court preacher to György II Rákóczi during the 1650s, for example, produced in 1655 his own collection of model funeral sermons for parish clergy to copy as a *Cemetery of Sermons for the*

---

[7] For such funerals (*szamár módon temettessék el*), see Hungarian State Archive, box 1907–8: 'Zempléni Egyházmegye Protocolluma' (1638–51), p. 148, and 'Zempléni Egyházmegye Protocolluma' (1653–72), pp. 31–2, 53–6, 112–113, 115; Jenő Zoványi, 'Miskolczi Csulyak István zempléni ref. esperes (1625–1645) egyházlátogatási jegyzőkönyvei', *Történelmi Tár* 7 (1906), pp. 58–9, 300, 304, 312; G. Németh (ed.), *Hegyaljai mezővárosok "törvényei" a xvii.–xviii. századból* (Budapest, 1990), pp. 29–42.

[8] Ralph Houlbrooke, 'Death, Church and Family in England between the Late Fifteenth and the Early Eighteenth Centuries', in his *Death, Ritual and Bereavement* (London, 1989), pp. 25–42; J. M. McManamon, *Funeral Oratory and the Cultural Ideals of Italian Humanism* (Chapel Hill, 1989).

Dead.[9] The Transylvanian superintendent István Geleji Katona also produced his own volumes of model sermons, with encouragement for preachers to be brief and to the point, which to Geleji meant preaching for around an hour. Geleji wrote that all sermons should aim to present orthodox theology and improve the religious knowledge of congregations. He offered a plan for ministers to follow when composing sermons, concentrating on developing a clear analysis of scripture passages in order to teach congregations more about God. Geleji was also anxious to prevent ministers from spending too much time on matters of individual conscience and morality, which he considered could weaken the faith of most peasant congregations, and make salvation seem an impossible goal for some.[10]

Geleji's concerns about moralistic preaching were directed primarily at colleagues such as Pál Medgyesi, who had studied at Dutch universities and in England between 1629 and 1631, and then served for many years as chaplain to Zsuzsanna Lórántffy, the wife of prince György I Rákóczi. Geleji charged that Medgyesi constantly nagged his congregations, and only tried to prick the consciences of his listeners to make them feel guilty about their faults. Medgyesi responded to this criticism by publishing his own ideas and advice about preaching, arguing that Geleji's approach of rehearsing knowledge about religion in sermons was useless, unless congregations were also encouraged to apply that knowledge to their daily lives. Quoting works by William Perkins and William Ames for support, Medgyesi argued that the 'testimony' of sermons must be devoted to the practical uses of God's word, and wrote that many of his colleagues' sermons failed to stress the need for congregations to improve their piety and morality. Whilst in the early decades of the seventeenth century some Reformed preachers certainly used funeral services to highlight the moral virtues of the dead and to suggest that the living ought to follow their example, ideas about moralistic preaching of practical theology had gained wider acceptance by the 1650s, especially since Medgyesi was then given the responsibility to provide many of the funeral sermons for members of the ruling family and leading nobles.[11]

9 István Balog Selyei, *Temetőkert, melyben . . . halotti alkalmatossággal való prédikáciok vannak* (Nagyvárad, 1655).
10 István Geleji Katona, *Praeconium Evangelicum* (2 vols., Gyulafehérvár, 1638–1640), I, introduction; István Geleji Katona, *Váltság-Titka* (3 vols., Nagyvárad, 1645–9), I, introduction; L. Gál, *Geleji Katona István igehirdetése* (Debrecen, 1939), pp. 211–17.
11 Pál Medgyesi, *Doce nos Orare et Praedicare* (Bártfa, 1650); István Bartók, 'Medgyesi Pál: Doce Praedicare', *Irodalomtörténeti Közlemények* 85 (1981), pp. 1–16; Dániel Borbáth,

In December 1606 István Bocskai died and the Transylvanian diet elected his ally Zsigmond Rákóczi to replace him. In 1608 Zsigmond resigned in favour of Gábor Báthori, but Báthori's efforts to play the different confessional parties in Transylvania off against one another robbed him of their trust. By 1613 Gábor Bethlen, another of Bocskai's old allies, had built up an alliance against Báthori, and gained sanction from the Porte to replace him as prince. With an Ottoman army marching towards Transylvania's south-western borders in support of Bethlen, Báthori was assassinated at Nagyvárad (Oradea) in October 1613 by the men of András Ghyczy, one of his own councillors, and the prince's body was thrown into a stream.[12] Reformed canons from the late sixteenth century had starkly warned that princes who failed to govern according to God's laws could expect to suffer such 'a hideous death because of indulgence and drunkenness like Balthasar, Darius, Alexander the Great and Attila', and for Reformed clergy the manner of Báthori's death provided final confirmation of his inconstant rule.[13]

Reformed ministers in Transylvania hoped that Gábor Bethlen would provide the principality with more godly leadership than Báthori had done. When Bethlen had been elected as prince in October 1613, a speech to the diet indeed suggested that he had not been chosen by the representatives of the three nations alone:

> Your Grace is given to us today by God, as he gave David after Saul, or Hezekiah after Ahaz, and we ask that as of old God blessed holy kings from amongst his people, David, Solomon and Hezekiah, he will bless and sanctify Your Grace with wisdom, truth and bravery.[14]

This language was not merely conventional flattery of Bethlen, but was precisely directed to the circumstances of his accession. With accusations raised against Bethlen that he had been involved in plotting Báthori's death, this imagery of the prince as a new David and of his predecessor as Saul, who had lost God's favour and been murdered, was developed to

---

'Medgyesi Pál homiletikája és Geleji Katona Istvánnal folytatott homiletikai vitája', in *Református Szemle* (1961), pp. 282–93. In 1637 János Iratosi translated William Perkins's piety tract on death *Salve for a Sickman, or a treatise containing the nature, differences, and kinds of death* (Cambridge, 1597) as *Patika szerszamos bolt, az az sok-fele halaloknak természetekröl, és azoknak nemeiröl. És ismét az jól és bódogúl való meg halásnak módgyáról való tanítás* (Löcse, 1637).

12 Reference to the funeral sermon for Bocskai is made in István Miskolczi Csulyak's diary, *Magyar Protestáns Egyháztörténeti Adattár* (14 vols., Budapest, 1902–30), xii, pp. 90–1; Lajos Demény, *Bethlen Gábor és kora* (Bucharest, 1982).

13 Antal Kiss, *A xvi. században tartott magyar református zsinatok végzései* (Budapest, 1881), pp. 175–80, 589, 607–11.

14 *Erdélyi Országgyűlési Emlékek 6*, iii, p. 55.

absolve Bethlen from any blame over Báthori's death. Indeed the identification of Bethlen with David, Solomon and Hezekiah suggested that he
had in fact inherited the mantle of István Bocskai, Transylvania's liberator,
or 'Moses of the Hungarians' as the Hungarian diet had described him in
April 1605. Bethlen's portrayal as a new David asserted that he was the
rightful and divinely appointed prince of Transylvania. Bethlen was
repeatedly depicted by Reformed ministers throughout his reign as a new
David, with a series of works aiming to enhance the status of princes in
Transylvania and to reveal how Bethlen embodied the virtues of Old
Testament kingship.[15] Meanwhile Gábor Báthori's remains were only
finally interred in 1628, with the sermon at this service given by Péter
Alvinczi, a long-standing adviser to Bethlen. Alvinczi's homily again outlined the relationship between David and Saul, describing how David's
love and compassion for Saul was shown by punishing those who
murdered him and by praising those who had given Saul a decent burial.
Alvinczi then paralleled this with Bethlen's generosity towards Báthori and
his execution of Báthori's murderers, and he praised Bethlen for the respect
which he had continued to show for Báthori after his death by arranging
his funeral.[16]

Bethlen proved successful not only in attracting positive portrayals of
himself as a godly prince by comparison with his dead predecessor, but
also in demonising his perceived opponents amongst Báthori's surviving
relatives. When Bethlen's wife Zsuzsanna Károlyi became gravely ill in
1618, Bethlen accused Anna Báthori, Gábor's sister, of causing the illness
and of involvement in witchcraft. Anna's reputation was certainly already
tainted by association with her cousin, Erzsébet Báthori, who had been
imprisoned in her castle in 1609 after charges of mass murder and
involvement in witchcraft were initiated by her own relatives. Bethlen
brought a prosecution against Anna Báthori on charges of witchcraft, and

---

[15] János Redmeczi, 'Az felséges Bethlen Gábornak öt rendbeli Isten anyaszentegyházával
cselekedett jótéteményéről', in László Makkai (ed.), *A fejedelem, 1613–1629*. *Erdély
öröksége 4* (Budapest, 1994), pp. 24–46; István Melotai Nyilas, *A szent Dávid XX.
zsoltárának magyarázatja* (Kassa, 1620); István Vásárhelyi Kerekes, *Epitaphion katastro-
phikon, azaz: szomoruságról örömre váltózó versek Bethlen Gábor erdélyi fejedelem tisztességére*
(Nagyszeben, 1618); Gáspár Bojti Veres, *Panegyris . . . Gabrielis Bethlen* (Heidelberg,
1617); György Szepsi Korocz, *Basilikon Doron. Az Angliai . . . elsö Jakab királynak . . . fia
tanitásáért irt királyi ajándék* (Oppenheim, 1612); László Makkai (ed.), *Bethlen Gábor
krónikásai, krónikák, emlékiratok, naplók a nagy fejedelemről* (Budapest, 1980).

[16] Péter Alvinczi, *Az néhai felséges Báthori Gábor . . . testének eltakarításakor tett intések*
(Gyulafehérvár, 1628); János Heltai, 'Bethlen Gábor és Báthori Gábor viszonya a kortársak
szemében', *Irodalomtörténet*, 65 (1983), pp. 685–708; L. Rácz, 'Főhatalom a xvi.–xvii.
századi erdélyben', in *Jogtudományi Közlöny* (1981), pp. 857–64.

death sentences were passed against Anna and other accused witches in 1621. The executions were however delayed because Bethlen seems to have believed in the power of the accused witches to reverse their magic and to cure his wife. When Zsuzsanna Károlyi finally died in 1622, Anna still managed to escape the death penalty, but her estates in Transylvania were confiscated, and she was banished from the principality along with two other aristocratic widows related to the Báthoris, Kata Török and Kata Iffju. Whether or not Bethlen actually believed that some truth lay behind his accusations, the interpretation placed upon the death of his first wife reinforced his claims to be a godly prince under attack from diabolic forces, and also in more practical terms bolstered his power through the acquisition of new lands in Transylvania.[17] The manner of Bethlen's own death and funeral in 1629 maintained to the last his image as a godly prince. In his will Bethlen left extensive provision to support the Reformed academy which he had founded at his capital, and Bethlen also expressed pious hopes that mutual respect between the various confessional communities of the principality would continue to flourish. Bethlen's counsellors, leading nobles and representatives from the Trans-ylvanian diet all attended his funeral service at the castle church in Gyulafehérvár. Whilst the sermon given at Bethlen's funeral remained unpublished, verses which lauded the character and achievements of the prince survive. These Hebrew, Greek and Latin verses were composed and read out by Johann Heinrich Alsted, Johann Heinrich Bisterfeld and Ludwig Piscator, the three new German teachers recently arrived from Herborn to teach at Bethlen's new academy.[18]

Bethlen had attempted to secure the succession before his death, and in 1626 the diet accepted the nomination of his second wife, Catherine of Brandenburg, to replace him. Catherine ruled until István Bethlen, Gábor's younger brother, was elected prince by the diet in 1630. However Bethlen was soon himself supplanted by György I Rákóczi, son of the former prince Zsigmond Rákóczi and the most extensive landowner in eastern Hungary. The Rákóczi family soon added further to their wealth by the marriage of the prince's eldest son György to the remaining Báthori heiress, Zsófia, and in 1642 the diet accepted that György would succeed his father as prince. György I Rákóczi strongly supported Reformed interests in Transylvania during his reign as prince, developing

---

[17]   Gábor Klaniczay, 'Witch-hunting in Hungary: Social or Cultural Tensions?', in *The Uses of Supernatural Power*, pp. 151–67.

[18]   Bethlen's will is in Makkai, *A fejedelem, 1613–1629*, pp. 125–37; Gyula Kristóf, 'Zsidó, görög és latin gyászversek Bethlen Gábor temetésére', *Erdélyi Múzeum* 36 (1931), pp. 90–7; Demény, *Bethlen Gábor és kora*, pp. 196–211.

local colleges and defending Protestants in Royal Hungary from attacks by the Habsburgs and Catholic magnates. Rákóczi however remained wary of reform proposals suggested by some clergy to alter the existing pattern of church government by introducing congregational presbyteries. Reform-minded clergy believed that the appointment of lay elders would assist parish clergy to exercise tighter control over the moral discipline of their congregations, and viewed the setting up of presbyteries as an essential step towards constructing the best form of Reformed Church. A national synod was called at Szatmár (Satu Mare) in 1646 to decide the question of church government, meeting in the presence of Rákóczi himself. The synod eventually resolved to uphold the existing clergy hierarchy of superintendents and archdeacons, and only allowed for presbyteries to be organised with the support of local lay patrons. This decision left reformers to consider the Church's failure in their terms to embrace the changes needed to bring about a true Reformation of religion and society in Transylvania.[19]

The anxious mood of many Reformed clergy about the state of the Church and the Transylvanian principality from the late 1640s was in part set by the response of reformers to this setback. Many other ministers however were also concerned about the progress of religious reform. The Hungarian Reformation had to a large extent been sponsored by the desire to purify a church and society discredited by the Ottoman invasions of the early sixteenth century. Protestants however could not explain why their programmes of reform had still not led to any reversal of Hungary's fortunes against the Ottomans. The tone of parallels between Transylvania and biblical Israel thus grew perceptibly more anxious from the 1640s, with scrutiny of Old Testament history providing graphic examples of the catastrophic results of incurring divine displeasure. Such concerns provided the context within which the deaths of princes, nobles and leading churchmen came to be widely understood as signs of impending divine judgement. In 1638, following the death of Johann Heinrich Alsted, the leading teacher at the Gyulafehérvár academy, superintendent István Geleji Katona wrote to György I Rákóczi revealing details of how Alsted had died. Geleji suggested that Alsted's death gave some intimation of his future salvation, writing that, 'no-one can have witnessed a better human death than his, which truly showed what a perfectly orthodox and knowledgeable theologian he was'. Geleji

---

[19] Imre Révész, *A szatmárnémeti nemzeti zsinat és az első magyar református ébredés* (Budapest, 1947); Jenő Zoványi, *Puritánus mozgalmak a magyar református egyházban* (Budapest, 1911); László Makkai, *A magyar puritánusok harca a feudálizmus ellen* (Budapest, 1952).

then continued that, 'I certainly cried my eyes out in bitterness at the death of poor Mr Alsted, and they have not yet dried, but to what use? I see that God was angry with us, and he will pour out some evil on us, before which he is selecting out his favoured people.'[20]

This theme of the godly dead as a testimony of God's anger and of impending judgement was powerfully taken up in the funeral sermons given by Pál Medgyesi from the late 1640s. Medgyesi was a leading supporter of presbyterial church government who became increasingly concerned at the slow pace of progress towards a Reformation of life in Hungarian congregations. When Gábor Bethlen's younger brother István died in January 1648, the princely branch of the Bethlen family died out with him. At his funeral service in March 1648, Medgyesi argued that Bethlen's death marked the removal of a major column of support from the Transylvanian principality, and urged his audience of leading nobles to repent of their sins if they wanted to remove the threat of imminent divine judgement. Medgyesi's chosen text for his sermon related the defeat and death of the pious king Josiah in battle against the Egyptian pharaoh, which led to the final collapse of the monarchy of Judah. Josiah's early death also fulfilled the prophecy given by Huldah that the king would be spared from witnessing the destruction of the temple at Jerusalem as a mark of God's favour upon him. Huldah also confirmed however that Josiah's piety was not sufficient to cover over the sins of previous generations and prevent righteous judgement from falling upon Judah. From his examination of this text, Medgyesi then offered his congregation a clear prophetic warning: 'When I think of the state of the nations of Israel and Judah, before their captivity in Assyria and Babylonia, I see as if in a mirror the frightening position of our own nation. Oh Lord, favour Your people.'[21]

In October 1648 prince György I Rákóczi died, his tomb at Gyulafehérvár marked by a commemorative tablet and marble sculptures of angels and people.[22] Medgyesi preached the sermon at Rákóczi's funeral on 10 January 1649, a year to the day after the death of István Bethlen. Medgyesi

---

[20] 'Én bizony, kgls uram, kisírhatnám mind a két szemeimet a szegény Alstedius uram halálán való keserüségemben, ugyan nem igen is száradtak még eddig meg, de mi haszna? Megharagudt as úr Isten reánk, látom, és valami nagy gonoszt szánt reánk, s az elött szedegeti ki ö kedvesebb emberit. Halált soha emberi állat szepbet az övénél nem láthatott, igazán megmútatá, hogy tökélletes orthodoxus és tudós theologus ember lött légyen.' Antal Beke, 'Geleji Katona István levelei Rákóczyhoz', *Irodalomtörténeti Közlemények* 4 (1894), pp. 336–46.

[21] Pál Medgyesi, *Erdély s egész magyar nép . . . hármas jajja* (Nagyvárad, 1653), pp. 58–9.

[22] Szakály, *Szalárdi János krónikája*, pp. 305–6.

first spoke of the qualities of the dead prince, as a God-fearing man whose value to the principality had been far greater than that of any army. Medgyesi dwelt on the faith, mercy and pious lifestyle of the dead prince, his renowned attention to reading the Bible and concern for the needs of the Church both in the Transylvanian principality and in Royal Hungary. Rákóczi was for Medgyesi, 'our sweet David, the shining light of our eyes . . . the ornate crown of our head'.[23] Whilst Medgyesi's sermon mostly struck a despondent tone, he retained some optimism for the future in the next generation of the Rákóczi family, through the newly elected prince György II Rákóczi and his younger brother, Zsigmond. High hopes were particularly placed upon Zsigmond as a potential candidate for the Polish crown, and as the chronicler János Szalárdi later enthused, Zsigmond was renowned as a most 'godly, devout and kind lord'.[24]

In June 1651 Zsigmond's prospects were further enhanced by his marriage to Maria Henrietta, daughter of Frederick V of the Palatinate. The marriage service was conducted at Sárospatak by the Bohemian Brethren leader, Jan Comenius, invited by the Rákóczis in 1650 to teach at Sárospatak College. Comenius shared in the expectation that Zsigmond was a potential saviour of Eastern Europe's persecuted and exiled Protestant communities. Comenius was further encouraged by the prophecies offered about Zsigmond by his fellow Brethren exile, Mikuláš Drabík, and addressed an appeal to Zsigmond in support of Drabík's prophecies as a 'Secret sermon of Nathan to David'. In this tract Comenius laid out the role which he foresaw for Zsigmond as the liberator of Central Europe who would spread light from Hungary into Moravia, Bohemia and Poland. Zsigmond was depicted as a new David who would free his people from the yoke of the Antichrist and Turkish oppression, and then move on to free neighbouring peoples from Austria to Poland.[25] However these extravagant plans quickly began to unravel in September 1651, when after only three months of marriage Maria Henrietta died. In December 1651 Henrietta was buried at Sárospatak, 'leaving her pious husband in unspeakably bitter and sad mourning'. Zsigmond seemed convinced by

---

23 'Sokáldásu édes Dávidunk, . . . szemünk ragyago világa, fejünk ékes Coronája.' Medgyesi, *Hármas jajja*, p. 25.
24 'Nagy reménységü, istenes, kegyes életü, kedves, méltóságos úr', Szakály, *Szalárdi János krónikája*, p. 312.
25 J. V. Kvacsala, 'Comenius irata Rákóczi Zsigmondhoz', *Magyar Protestáns Egyháztörténeti Adattár* 4 (1905), pp. 128–43; Comenius had Drabík's prophecies published in 1657 as *Lux in Tenebris* (Amsterdam), with further publications of Drabík's *Revelations* in 1659, 1663 and a complete edition in 1664 as *Lux e Tenebris* (Leiden); J. V. Kvacsala, 'Egy álpróféta a xvii–ik században', *Századok* 23 (1889), pp. 745–66.

Comenius's explanation that his new wife's sudden and unexpected death had been caused by his failure to act quickly enough upon Drabík's prophecies. Then in February 1652 Zsigmond too fell ill, and died aged only twenty-nine. György II Rákóczi also became seriously ill, but recovered in time to join his family at Zsigmond's burial in Gyulafehérvár in March 1652. Pál Medgyesi gave the funeral oration for Zsigmond, and by now was convinced that the recent deaths of leading members of princely families in Transylvania were a clear sign of judgement against the principality. Medgyesi again preached from a text on the death of Josiah, repeating his analysis that the deaths of such godly men as Zsigmond meant that the future would bring grave dangers for Transylvania, and argued that the people must quickly turn towards God and away from their corruption if they wanted to avoid an imminent catastrophe.[26]

In 1653 Medgyesi published his three funeral sermons as *The Three Woes of Transylvania and the whole Hungarian People*, with a forward addressed to György II Rákóczi. Medgyesi's depiction of the deaths of István Bethlen, György and Zsigmond Rákóczi as Transylvania's three woes linked contemporary events to Isaiah's prophecy about Israel's six laments. Isaiah had indicted Israel for her sinfulness, and for the arrogant confidence of her leaders to rebel against the Assyrians. Isaiah outlined six laments which would bring imminent judgement against Israel: the acquisitive grabbing of property by landowners, the debauched and drunken behaviour of nobles, the corruption of judges, widespread unbelief and contempt for God's commands, moral perversion and prideful conceit. The prophet foretold of a purifying judgement to fall upon the ruling elite as a result of their own behaviour, and because of general immorality amongst the people. Isaiah prophesied that the signs of this judgement would be seen in the removal of pillars from the established order. The deaths of judges and prophets, elders and councillors, political leaders and soldiers would deprive Israel of wise leadership and leave her vulnerable to external attack. Isaiah finally warned that complete military collapse would follow, with the only remaining hope that a remnant of the nation would survive to await a coming messianic saviour.[27]

Pál Medgyesi was convinced that the failure to bring about a true Reformation of religion and society in Transylvania, with widespread

---

[26] 'Mikor as illyen istenfélö, nagy reménységü használatos embereket látjuk hogy a' veszet idkben meghalnak, tudván hogy jövendö nagy veszedelemnek mutatoja az.' Medgyesi, *Hármas jajja*, pp. 25, 36, 41. Szakály, *Szalárdi János krónikája*, p. 312.

[27] R. E. Clements, *New Century Bible Commentary. Isaiah 1–39* (London, 1980); J. Mauchline, *Isaiah 1–39. Introduction and Commentary* (London, 1962).

sinfulness and immorality, had resulted in a similar divine judgement against 'Transylvania and the whole Hungarian people'. Medgyesi thought that more woes would soon afflict Transylvania with further deaths of leading nobles, and eventually result in military disaster. Medgyesi seemed to gain early confirmation of the accuracy of his prophecy, with the deaths of three of György I Rákóczi's most prominent councillors, Ferenc Bethlen, Zsigmond Barcsai and Mátyás Huszár.[28] In November 1656 Medgyesi again used the testimony of death as a sign of imminent judgement upon the living at the funeral at Szerdahely (Miercurea Sibiului) of Zsuzsanna Lónyai, the wife of the high sheriff of Zemplén county. Medgyesi's sermon, *The Fate of the Just in the World*, was filled with dark warnings that all God-fearing people of Transylvania should prepare for an imminent battle ahead.[29] Johann Heinrich Bisterfeld had also died in 1655, removing the Rákóczi family's most experienced diplomatic adviser. In 1656 Zsuzsanna Lórántffy reminded her son of just how much Bisterfeld's advice and loyalty had been missed during a crucial year of diplomatic manoeuvring between Transylvania and Sweden. Meanwhile, visionaries in the principality received credence for their claims that the mid-1650s would mark a turning point in Transylvania's destiny. A minister at Nagyvárad wrote in 1655 of the passing and changing times, and of the sun and moon prophesying in 'mourning clothes' that the final days were at hand.[30] Looking back from 1662, János Szalárdi's *Miserable Hungarian Chronicle* recalled the prophecy of Imre Szilvásújfalvi Anderkó that 1657 would be the year of destiny. Szalárdi also recorded bad omens from the year of György II Rákóczi's election as Transylvanian prince in 1648, with two lightning strikes on the castle at Nagyvárad, and the accidental death of a man when a church bell fell on him. Szalárdi wrote that such 'sad signs of the soon ensuing general great evil were seen as if shown by a finger'.[31]

This whirl of prophetic utterances in Transylvania during the 1650s mostly predicted imminent disaster for the principality, but some remained convinced that the Rákóczi house would soon liberate Eastern

---

[28] Szakály, *Szalárdi János krónikája*, p. 307.

[29] Pál Medgyesi, *Igazak sorsa a világon. Gyászbeszéd Bocskai István felesége Lónyai Zsuzsanna felett* (Sárospatak, 1657).

[30] 'Az üdök el multak, mindenek változnak, Még az csillagok, is egekben bujdosnak, Nap és hold egy más közt gyász ruhát hordoznak, Azok is minékünk ugyan praedicálnak.' 'Másodszor jelenti az világnak végét, Amaz rettenetes napnak el jövését, Az Chrisztus szinének hamar jelenését, Mind az egész földnek az ö vétkes terhét.' K. Szabó, 'Egy gúnyirat a váradi ref. esperesség presbyterianus papjai ellen, 1655–böl', *Magyar Protestáns Egyházi és Iskolai Figyelmező* 1 (1870), pp. 590–8.

[31] Szakály, *Szalárdi János krónikája*, pp. 197–8, 342–3, 349–50.

Europe from Catholic persecution and Ottoman oppression. This expectation was fuelled in January 1657 when György II Rákóczi embarked upon an invasion of Poland in alliance with Charles X of Sweden. Rákóczi acted without seeking prior approval from the Porte, and in the face of opposition from his mother and wife and from older advisers in his council. At first the army's advance went to plan and the Transylvanian and Swedish armies met in May 1657. However, Charles was then compelled to send back part of his army to face the Danes, and then withdrew completely from Poland in June 1657. Left bereft of allies, Rákóczi had no alternative but to sign a humiliating capitulation to the Polish king, Jan Casimir. Rákóczi's retreating army was then surprised by an attack from the Tatars, with those who survived taken prisoner to the Crimea, and the Poles took advantage of Rákóczi's weakness by launching an attack upon north-eastern Hungary.[32] Pál Medgyesi lost little time in asserting that this was the military calamity which he had prophesied and feared. In his *Fourth Woe and Lament of the True Hungarian People*, preached in response to the Polish capture of Munkács (Mukačevo) in June 1657, Medgyesi listed the sins of idolatry, drunkenness, blasphemous cursing, fornication, magical incantation, Sunday markets, lying and criminality as the causes of this traumatic invasion. Medgyesi suggested that Hungarians could not justifiably raise any complaints against God for judging and abandoning them, but rather ought to be astonished that God had been patient with the Hungarians for so long. Medgyesi compared the situation in Transylvania with the state of Israel under similar circumstances, and quoted from Hosea, inserting Hungarians into the place of the Israelites: 'Hear the word of the Lord, you Hungarians [sons of Israel], because the Lord has a charge to bring against you who live in the land.'[33]

In August 1657 Mehmed Khan of the Crimean Tatars was sanctioned by the Porte to sweep his army into the Szekler lands of eastern Transylvania. In September 1657 Medgyesi again proclaimed his message of sin, judgement and death in his *Fifth Woe and Lament of the Hungarians* in two sermons given at Sárospatak. Medgyesi preached from Lamentations on Israel's exile and the destruction of Jerusalem, equating the sins of Israel with the current sins of the Hungarians. Medgyesi exclaimed that 'glory has left our Israel', so 'woe, woe, unto us

---

[32] Robert Frost, *After the Deluge: Poland–Lithuania and the Second Northern War, 1655–1660* (Cambridge, 1993); S. Szilágyi (ed.), *Erdély és az északkeleti háború-levelek és okiratok* (2 vols., Budapest, 1890–1).

[33] Pál Medgyesi, *Igaz magyar nép negyedik jajja s-siralma* (Sárospatak, 1657), pp. 17–18, 20–1.

for we have sinned!' Medgyesi then outlined the 'bloody flags' which had signalled oncoming disaster in the deaths of good councillors, teachers and God-fearing people.[34] Medgyesi also warned of further perils ahead:

Verily, verily if we do not repent, it is to be feared, yes to be feared that with the passing of that thousand years, and because furious pagans are upon us, that the period of final judgement should not be drawn onto our heads. There are three great woes in the Apocalypse, the next more troublesome than the last: then the final level of the seventh trumpet. Oh, thus will our woes begin to flow over us!'[35]

The years between 1658 and 1660 brought chaos and war to Transylvania, with a bitter battle waged by Rákóczi to retain control against domestic rivals, and against the Ottomans who wanted the diet to depose him. With the main Transylvanian army still in the Crimea, in May 1658 an Ottoman invasion force quickly overran border fortresses, whilst the undefended Transylvanian capital was destroyed by Tatars. Medgyesi took the opportunity of a funeral at Sárospatak in July 1659 for Ferenc Ibrányi, a major landowner in Szabolcs county, to repeat his explanation for these disasters once again. In this sermon, *The Destruction of Joseph, or the Great Devastation of the Hungarian Nation in 1658*, Medgyesi accounted for Hungarian defeat through sin, and dramatically presented his audience with the image of the ground running red with the blood of Hungarian dead, as a testimony to the sins of the living.[36] Medgyesi then published his *Sixth Woe of the Hungarians* in 1660, repeating his message on the need for 'Magyar Judah' to turn away from sin and back to God. Medgyesi also reflected upon the funeral sermons which he had given since 1648, concluding that they marked the unfolding of a prophetic revelation about Transylvania's future. Medgyesi was fearful that these individual deaths might soon be followed by the universal death of the apocalypse and warned: 'Oh, Magyar Judah! Will you not learn from the example

---

[34] Pál Medgyesi, 'Ötödik jaj és siralom' in Szakály, *Szalárdi János krónikája*, pp. 686–719.

[35] 'Elment, elköltözött a dicsöség a mi Izraelünkböl, megszünék és nagy hirtelen elvágódék a mi szívünknek s állapotunknak koronája. Jaj, jaj! (méltán felvehetjük e szókat, sirathatjuk vele magunkat) jaj, jaj nekünk, mert vétkeztünk!' Pál Medgyesi, 'Ötödik jaj és siralom', in G. Szigethy (ed.), *Erdély romlásának okairól* (Budapest, 1984), p. 21.

[36] When many peasants on Ibrányi's land died of plague in 1646 he had blamed himself for their deaths: 'God for my sins has taken away to dark death one by one very many of the poor.' Pál Pach (ed.), *Magyarország története* (10 vols., Budapest, 1987), iii, p. 1001; Pál Medgyesi, *Joseph romlasa avagy magyar nemzet 1658 esztendöbéli nagy pusztulása* (Sárospatak, 1659).

of old Judah, in whose path you are walking, and believe that your payment will be the same.'[37]

In the summer of 1660 another Ottoman army made steady progress towards Transylvania, but before it arrived in the principality György II Rákóczi was injured in battle against the Buda Pasha at Gyalu (Gilău), later dying of his wounds at Nagyvárad in June 1660. Rákóczi's death at least meant that he was spared from witnessing the final Ottoman attack on Transylvania, with a 50,000-strong army besieging and capturing the crucial border fortress of Nagyvárad. The garrison at Nagyvárad was severely depleted by the time of the siege, with the remaining soldiers and a few hundred citizens coming under the direction of Máté Balogh, assisted by János Rácz, deputy sheriff of Bihar county, and by János Szalárdi.[38] Szalárdi survived the siege to provide his chronicle of how righteous judgement had been brought against Transylvania during these years, ending with the capture of even the apparently faithful city of Nagyvárad. János Rácz however died of wounds sustained during the siege and was buried at Debrecen in August 1660. György Komáromi Csipkés gave the funeral oration, later published as *A Mirror of Mournful Things*. Komáromi set out his purpose in the sermon to provide instruction on how sinfulness had resulted in the recent sorrowful events. He drew upon the story of Josiah's death and compared the siege of Nagyvárad with the fatal battle which Josiah had fought on the plain of Megiddo, and suggested that just as Josiah had been brought back wounded to Jerusalem after facing the Egyptian pharaoh, so János Rácz had been brought from Nagyvárad to Debrecen 'to give up his spirit peacefully and quietly'.[39]

The Rákóczi family was only finally able to conduct György's funeral at Sárospatak in April 1661, with Rákóczi's body prepared by his widow for the burial service. Zsuzsanna Lórántffy had suffered a fatal stroke in April 1660, ending Pál Medgyesi's connections with the Rákóczi family, and so it fell to István Czeglédi to give Rákóczi's funeral oration. An audience of magnates from Hungary and Transylvania heard Czeglédi claim that their inability to adhere to moral standards of behaviour had

---

[37] 'Félek mondom igen, hogy a végsö-is, oh ne résznyire (particulariter) már, hanem egészlen (universaliter) Temetö ne fogjon lenni.' Medgyesi, *Magyarok hatodik jajja*; Pál Medgyesi, 'Istenhez való igaz magtérés', pp. 35–6, in Medgyesi, *Sok Jajjokban* (Sárospatak, 1658), pp. 35–6.

[38] János Bethlen, *Innocentia Transylvaniae* (Kolozsvár, 1659). Szakály, *Szalárdi János krónikája*, pp. 322, 630–3.

[39] György Komáromi Csipkés, *Szomoru esetek tüköre. Gyászbeszéd Rácz János fölött* (Sárospatak, 1661).

brought judgement against the country. Czeglédi argued that sinfulness had destroyed 'our Israel's glory', and caused God to withdraw his support from the Transylvanian army. He however excluded Rákóczi from all responsibility for the military disaster. For Czeglédi, Rákóczi's glorious death in battle against the heathen army revealed that he had been 'Israel's illuminating candle', and he sadly wondered 'Are we looking at the closed eyes of you, who was the sweet light of our eyes?'[40]

During the early seventeenth century Reformed clergy became convinced that God had provided the Transylvanian principality with godly magistrates in István Bocskai, Gábor Bethlen and the Rákóczi princes. In different ways the deaths of Gábor Báthori, Zsuzsanna Károlyi and Gábor Bethlen were interpreted by Reformed ministers to confirm the claims of Reformed princely authority over Transylvania. For Reformed preachers, however, this authority had been established for the purpose of promoting religious and moral reform. When expected advances in standards of personal piety and morality failed to emerge in Transylvania, Reformed preachers' representations of the deaths of princes and nobles took on a completely different aspect. Comparisons with biblical Israel which had previously sanctified princely power began from the late 1640s to be vehicles for prophecies of judgement and destruction which could overwhelm the principality. The deaths of István Bethlen, György I Rákóczi, Zsigmond Rákóczi, Johann Heinrich Alsted, Johann Heinrich Bisterfeld and leading noble councillors were, however, seen by Reformed ministers to bear witness to those individuals' piety, with God showing his favour by removing them before his judgement fell upon the principality. György II Rákóczi's heroic death in battle against the Ottomans also brought him relief from blame for the military catastrophe which had engulfed Transylvania, and allowed him to join the ranks of the godly dead. The ungodly living meanwhile remained burdened with the stark choice presented to them by Reformed preachers, of either attempting to emulate the piety of the community of godly dead, or face further punishment and disaster, perhaps even final judgement.

---

[40] 'Tégedet, tégedet szemünk szép világa szem bé-hunyva nézzünké?' István Czeglédi, *Ama ritka példájú . . . II. Rákóczi György . . . testének földben tétele felett predikáció* (Kassa, 1661), sig. b3; István Czeglédi, *Az országok romlásáról irott könyv* (Kassa, 1659); Szakály, *Szalárdi János krónikája*, pp. 648–9.

12 Funeral sermons and orations as religious propaganda in sixteenth-century France

Larissa Juliet Taylor

The funeral oration had many incarnations before the sixteenth century. In ancient Greece it served as a celebration of state ideology and success in war;[1] by contrast, the Roman *laudatio funebris* focused on the historical individual, with a recounting of his or her virtues.[2] But with the decline of the Roman Empire, the 'living tradition of funeral oratory . . . vanished in the West'.[3] Funeral sermons began to reappear in the High Middle Ages, given on the occasion of the death of a king or other great figure, but were still rare at the end of the Middle Ages.[4] Much like saint's day sermons, which sometimes spent little time on the saint but provided an opportunity for a preacher to discuss contemporary problems,[5] this type was frequently used to promote moral reformation.[6] With the revival of classical and rhetorical values in the

---

An earlier version of this chapter was presented at the Sixteenth Century Studies Conference in Atlanta in October 1997. The research was supported by a grant from Colby College.

[1] John M. McManamon, *Funeral Oratory and the Cultural Ideals of Italian Humanism* (Chapel Hill, 1989), p. 6; and 'The Ideal Renaissance Pope: Funeral Oratory', *Archivum Historiae Pontificiae* 14 (1976), p. 20.

[2] McManamon, *Funeral Oratory*, p. 6; Verdun L. Saulnier, 'L'oraison funèbre au XVIe siècle', *Bibliothèque d'Humanisme et Renaissance* 10 (1948), p. 126.

[3] McManamon, *Funeral Oratory*, p. 7; David L. d'Avray, *Death and the Prince: Memorial Preaching before 1350* (Oxford, 1994), p. 20.

[4] In her study of the effect of model sermon collections on receptivity to the Reformation, Anne Thayer has found only two in sixty-six among printed sermon collections, 1450–1520, and only one funeral sermon in 276 manuscripts. Anne Thiel Thayer, 'Penitence and Preaching on the Eve of the Reformation: a Comparative Overview from Frequently Printed Model Sermon Collections, 1450–1520' (Harvard University PhD thesis, 1996), pp. 37–8.

[5] D'Avray, *Death and the Prince*, p. 20.

[6] David L. d'Avray, 'The Comparative Study of Memorial Preaching', *Transactions of the Royal Historical Society* 5th ser. 40 (1990), p. 34.

Renaissance the genre was truly rediscovered. Describing themselves as painters, Italian humanists 'sought to create an image that would impel the audience to imitate a person's excellence'.[7] The format of this 'praise and blame' sermon required an exordium in which the speaker expressed his inadequacy in light of the task, followed by a discussion of the subject's ancestry, birth, youth, pursuits in life and deeds, with comparisons and conclusions. It would usually include both lamentation and consolation.[8] Despite its characterisation by some scholars as narrow and 'more seriously restricted than other sermons',[9] the funeral sermon was actually quite adaptable to the needs of a preacher. Verdun Saulnier attributes the birth of the modern funeral sermon to the outbreak of religious war in the middle of the sixteenth century,[10] yet does not really explore how preachers used the genre in revolutionary ways. Instead he focuses on sermons delivered as part of the apotheosis of Henri IV, which offered a preview of the seventeenth-century classical funeral sermon.[11] This chapter will argue that funeral sermons in sixteenth-century France provided preachers with an unsurpassed vehicle for religious propaganda. Preachers could retain aspects of the Roman and Renaissance traditions as well as those of saint's day sermons, but in general their preaching more closely approximated the ancient Greek model. The life and death of the deceased – often an icon of Catholic culture in France – and the need to exhort others to imitate his or her example in the very real war that was being waged on the faith by heretics and even the king, spurred preachers to use the occasion for a strident brand of religious propaganda that could rouse people to action. If the goal of preachers since the time of Augustine had been to 'move, persuade and delight', during the Religious Wars a fourth element was introduced without apology by most preachers – the need to incite.

Early sixteenth-century sermons closely followed the Renaissance model. In his oration for Pierre duc de Bourbon, Laurent Bureau traced his subject's glorious ancestry far back into the royal house of France, and

---

[7] McManamon, *Funeral Oratory*, pp. 31–2.

[8] McManamon, 'Ideal Renaissance Pope', pp. 21–2.

[9] Susan Powell and Alan J. Fletcher, ' "In die Sepulture seu Trigintali": the Late Medieval Funeral and Memorial Sermon', *Leeds Studies in English* 12 (1981), p. 200.

[10] Saulnier, 'L'oraison funèbre', pp. 128–30.

[11] Significant work has been done on sermons given for Henri IV. While these 'sometimes rose to the level of great truths of Christian dogma, they were above all the reflection of a life and a reign, the portrait of a great, heroic prince'. Jacques Hennequin, *Henri IV dans ses oraisons funèbres ou la naissance d'une légende* (Paris, 1977), p. 225.

compared him to the apostle Peter.[12] Even as late as the 1540s and early 1550s, preachers often failed to realise the potential for religious propaganda. Étienne Paris delivered two funeral sermons in 1545 on the death of Charles de Valois, son of Francis I. In Renaissance style, he begins by lamenting that what should have been a marriage sermon had been changed by a turn of fortune into a funeral oration.[13] Paris praises Charles's distinguished ancestry, his pursuits, his deeds in arms and his good character. Gracious, kind and good-natured, Charles was 'a faithful man and good Christian'.[14] But nowhere does Paris contrast Charles's piety with the irreverence and heresy of his contemporaries, nor does he attribute any feelings on the subject to the dead prince. In short, the two sermons are a celebration of the life and lamentation of the death of a prince; they do not make the leap to a discussion of contemporary problems.

The death of Claude de Lorraine duc de Guise in 1550 offered more possibilities, which Claude Guilliaud tentatively explored. Into his discussion he introduced heretics, 'who believe in sexual freedom and communal property, and are now expanding everywhere, just like the Goths, the Gepids, the Alans, the Vandals, the Ostrogoths and other barbarians in order to ruin Christendom'.[15] The duke is portrayed as a man of piety, who heard mass devoutly in his chambers and 'kissed the holy host with great tears and devotion'.[16] He lived as the embodiment of faith, hope and charity,[17] praying frequently, showing his devotion to the true cross, and equalling the emperor Constantine in his piety.[18] Guilliaud briefly mentions the duke's efforts to repress heresy but does not really exploit the possibilities.[19] Pierre Doré, a doctor of the Faculty of Theology of Paris who had been imprisoned in 1540 for 'rebellion, disobedience, and contradiction . . . of the king and of injunctions of the court of Parlement',[20] and who served as chaplain to the duke, went further according

---

[12] Jean d'Auton, *Chroniques de Louis XII* (4 vols., Paris, 1889–95), III, p. 8.

[13] Etienne Paris, *Homélies suivant les matieres traictées ès principales festes & solennitez de l'année* (Paris, 1575), p. 132.

[14] *Ibid.*, p. 145.

[15] Claude Guilliaud, *L'oraison funebre declarative des gestes, meurs, vie & trespas du tresillustre prince, Claude de Lorraine, duc de Guyse, & d'Aumalle, Pair de France, Gouverneur & Lieutenant general pour le Roy en ses pays de Bourgogne: Prononcée a l'enterrement dudict Seigneur, par maistre Claude Guilliauld, docteur en theologie, Presens messieurs les Cardinaulx & Princes, assemblez a Iaynville pour le dict enterrement* (Paris, 1550), fol. 21.

[16] *Ibid.*, fol. 25.   [17] *Ibid.*, fol. 18.   [18] *Ibid.*, fol. 25.   [19] *Ibid.*, fol. 18.

[20] James Farge, *Biographical Register of Paris Doctors of Theology, 1500–1536* (Toronto, 1980), p. 138.

to Labitte, comparing his master to the king: 'People, you have reason to mourn for your lord [*ton seigneur*].'[21]

Not much earlier, in 1547, the most popular Parisian Catholic preacher of the time, François Le Picart, was showing his colleagues what they could do with a carefully constructed funeral sermon. His opportunity came upon the death of his friend, the Franciscan Pierre Descornes, a vociferous antagonist of heretics. Descornes had already gained notoriety in Book III of *Gargantua and Pantagruel*, in which Rabelais writes: 'Ho, ho, ho: our horny Pierre Cornu – except that fat Franciscan just has the name and you'll have the real thing – God keep and protect you! Give us a little Franciscan preaching, will you, and I'll go around begging for alms!'[22] Despite his fierce denunciations of heresy, Le Picart regularly filled his sermons with examples of God's goodness and mercy.[23] But he was one of the earliest preachers to understand how the death of a Catholic leader could be used to castigate heretics, console good Catholics and spur all to defend the faith. Discarding the Renaissance rhetorical form, Le Picart's basic theme in this sermon could be colloquially termed, 'Why do bad things happen to good people?' This must trouble his audience, who see 'that God allows wicked and iniquitous people, fighting against our faith, to live to sixty or eighty years'.[24] Such a beginning allows Le Picart to expostulate against heretics who abound more than ever before, so that 'we see the Church of God diminished, enduring tribulations and innumerable adversities in assaults by the Devil and the heretics'.[25] Using military language, he asks how at the height of this war, God could have taken a man who battled so valiantly for the faith.[26] Le Picart praises Descornes's virtues, punning on his name: 'This man was a truly good man, nourished on the milk of the gospels, who communicated his doctrine so well that there is not a street or corner [cornet] in the city of Paris that did not experience it. You know of his works, his fasting, his abstinence, and the labours that he undertook to demonstrate the honour of God.'[27] He compares Descornes to Moses,[28] and quickly returns to warlike imagery. 'We marvel therefore that God

---

[21] Pierre Doré, *Oraison panégyrique pour Claude de Lorraine*, quoted in Charles Labitte, *De la démocratie chez les prédicateurs de la Ligue* (1841, repr. Geneva, 1971), p. 14.

[22] François Rabelais, *Gargantua and Pantagruel*, tr. Burton Raffael (New York, 1990), p. 280.

[23] Larissa Juliet Taylor, 'The Good Shepherd: François Le Picart (1504–1556) and Preaching Reform from Within', *Sixteenth Century Journal* 28 (1997), pp. 793–810.

[24] François Le Picart, *Les sermons et instructions chrestiennes, pour tous les Dimenches & toutes les festes des saincts, depuis Pasques iusques à la Trinité* (Paris, 1566), fols. 201–2.

[25] *Ibid.*, fol. 202.   [26] *Ibid.*, fol. 203.   [27] *Ibid.*, fol. 204.   [28] *Ibid.*

has taken this man at such an important point in our affairs, a man who was like a tower, a fighting machine, and a fortress against the enemies of the faith who seek nothing else but to destroy the Church.'[29] In Paris, the heretics rejoice that their enemy is dead, but they are like 'the Egyptians and Pharaoh, who with his army persecuted the children of Israel. God said: "Unsheath your sword on them".'[30] Le Picart warns the heretics who look for salvation outside the Church that they will share the fate of Dinah, daughter of Leah, who was raped and defiled when she left her home.[31] So why has God called this man away now? He answers that this is a signal to his people to take up the fight and imitate the deceased.[32] When they do, the war will be won: 'Just as we see with big waves or strong rains, they do not last long, but pass quickly. So these wicked heretics will not endure, but will be destroyed and annihilated.'[33] Finally, Le Picart turns to Catholics, admonishing them to put their own house in order, for '[o]ur ambition and greed for honours and benefices is like a machine and mortar launched against the church . . . We are no better than heretics. We don't deny God with our mouths, but through our deeds and manner of living we renounce Him.'[34] The answer to Le Picart's original question is simple: God took a good man while letting the wicked prosper as a wake-up call that must not go unheeded. In its call to action, this may be the first real *Reveille-matin des françois.*[35]

Le Picart's own death nine years later, in 1556, brought from the pulpits numerous voices in praise of 'the pearl of our age'[36] and the 'hammer of heretics'.[37] His friend Gabriel Dupuiherbault offered a poem upon his death which also employed a fighting theme:

> Hercules the Theban overcame monsters
> Throughout the world. Our François Le Picart
> A man almost more than human, by grand and divine art
> As much as can be found here on earth, jousted against monsters.
> The French Hercules in speaking, offered so much

---

[29] *Ibid.*, fol. 205.   [30] *Ibid.*   [31] *Ibid.*, fol. 204.   [32] *Ibid.*, fol. 207.

[33] *Ibid.*, fol. 206.   [34] *Ibid.*, fol. 207.

[35] This is a reference to the 1573 *Reveille-matin des françois,* an anonymous work published first in Basle under the name of Eusèbe Philadelphe Cosmopolite.

[36] Barbier Aubusson de la Maisonneuve, *Deploration sur le trespas de noble & vénérable personne monsieur maistre François Picard, Docteur en Theologie, Doyen de sainct Germain de lauxerrois, qui mourut à Paris le dixseptiesme iour de Septembre, l'an mil cinq cens cinquante & six. Par un poete François* (Paris, 1556), fol. Aii.

[37] Artus Desiré, *Les regretz et complainctes de Passe partout et Bruictquicourt, sur la mémoire renouvellée du trespas et bout de l'an, de feu tres noble et venerable personne Maistre Françoys Picart, docteur en théologie et grand doyen de sainct Germain de l'Aucerroys* (Paris, 1557), fol. Aiiii.

That listeners were drawn to him.
Our François Le Picart, in hurling his tongue
Like a dart, conquered so many people for their God.
Hercules the Theban succumbed to his flesh.
Our François Le Picart surmounted the flesh and the world[38]

What Le Picart and his colleagues had started would reach its fullest expression after the beginning of the Religious Wars in 1562. The wave of assassinations that struck France in the second half of the century offered the perfect opportunity for polemic and demagoguery. After the murder of Francis duc de Guise in 1563, Jacques Le Hongre cried from the pulpit of Notre-Dame that his hero had died a martyr's death.[39]

Arnaud Sorbin, who would later praise the St Bartholomew's Day Massacre in his sermons,[40] had been called to court as preacher of the king in 1567.[41] Although in his homilies Sorbin argued that force was ineffective in winning over heretics,[42] his funeral sermons are considerably more strident. In 1568 he used the death of Anne de Montmorency as his battle cry. War had raised the stakes in the twenty-one years since Le Picart had issued his challenge, and Sorbin's sermon is decidedly pessimistic, even eschatological. He begins, 'It's late enough . . . that we lament in this miserable season, punished all over with wounds', adding that 'God has deprived us of the presence of prophets and the judges of the ancients.'[43] This was a sad contrast to the past:

Oh misery more than deplorable! Where is the Christian people? Who ever felt greater sorrow from a wound than the French nation does now? She had until now been embellished with an infinity of heroic people, of whom the piety, the virtues and the experience of affairs, both military and political, rendered her not only happy but admirable to her neighbours. But now the heroes are reduced to a tiny number, ever since heresy took hold. Tribulations and sorrow over these ills has so diminished their number through seduction and death in battle, that the whole people is excessively

---

[38] Gabriel Dupuiherbault, *De penitence, et des parties d'icelle, selon la verité de l'Eglise orthodoxe & catholique, & la necessité de salut . . . auquel sont adiouxtez les Epitaphes de feu Monsieur Picart* (Paris, 1557), no pagination.

[39] Labitte, *Démocratie*, p. 15.   [40] *Ibid.*, p. 19.

[41] Saulnier, 'L'oraison funèbre', p. 135.

[42] This can be seen especially in the prayers that end each sermon: Arnaud Sorbin, *Homelies de R.P. en Dieu M. Arnauld Sorbin, Evesque de Nevers, Predicateur du Roy, Sur les Evangiles des Dimanches de l'Advent. Ensemble les Homelies de la Canonique S. Iude, pour les Feries de l'Advent, & iour de Noel* (Paris, 1584).

[43] Arnaud Sorbin, *Second oraison funebre, prononcee au lieu de Montmorency le 16. de Febvrier, à la sepulture du corps de messire Anne de Montmorency, pair & Conestable de France* (Paris, 1568), fol. 8.

mournful. Oh what calamity! There remains what David said would happen to the Israelite people. This poor realm is menaced with irreparable ruin.[44]

The madness of these miserable heretics has deprived France of all of its heroes: 'Do we not cry without cease?'[45] In an ominous comparison, Sorbin tells his listeners:

> Console yourselves for the sorrow of Jerusalem, because you see that our holiness has been laid waste, our altar is demolished, our temple destroyed, our psalter humiliated, our hymns silenced, our merrymaking annihilated, our candles extinguished, the arch of our testament plundered, our saints profaned . . . Our priests have been burned, our clergy has been imprisoned, our virgins have been defiled, our wives have been raped, [and] . . . our fortresses have been weakened.[46]

He exclaims in rising desperation that there are 'so few Moses, who pray for the people, few Joshuas, who fight for them; rare are the Gideons who oppose the Midianites'. Suggestively, he goes on: 'and even fewer Samsons, who would love to die in order to crush the Philistines'.[47] Using the conditional, he says, 'the avenging hand of so sovereign a king would overcome the error of the Calvinists, as did the hand that subdued the rebellions and impieties of the Visigoths and Ostrogoths, who tried to suppress the newly implanted faith'.[48] Taking the theme further, he exclaims, 'Oh, precious bones of the invincible emperor Charlemagne! If only you could be put back together and for some time reunited with your vital form, would you accept the woes of this poor and almost devastated realm without pursuing those who have caused this and who work tirelessly to make things worse?'[49] He sighs, thinking of those who in the past had been willing to sacrifice their lives for the extirpation of rebels to God and country. Sorbin ends with a prayer to end the discords that are tearing France apart.[50] Anne de Montmorency may have been a true hero to Sorbin, but in this sermon his death is a mere pretext for calling on the king to be a king and for true Christians to eradicate heresy. Although the same man would later eulogise mignons of Henri III killed in a duel by members of the Guise faction,[51] his sermon of 1568 marks a clear step forward in the propaganda wars from the pulpit. If Le

---

[44] *Ibid.*, fol. 10.   [45] *Ibid.*, fol. 11.   [46] *Ibid.*   [47] *Ibid.*, fol. 12.
[48] *Ibid.*, fol. 13.   [49] *Ibid.*   [50] *Ibid.*, fol. 17.
[51] Arnaud Sorbin, *Oraison funebre de notable Iaques de Levis, fils de noble A. de Levis Comte de Kailus, Gentilhomme chambellan ordinaire du Roy, prononcee en l'Eglise S. Paul, en Paris, le dernier de May, 1578* (Paris, 1578). This gained him the bishopric of Nevers in 1578, but Sorbin used the appointment to serve as a model prelate. He later rallied to the cause of Henri IV. Saulnier, 'L'oraison funèbre', p. 136.

Picart had used military images, Sorbin was now calling not only for the strong hand of a righteous king but men willing to die in a just cause.[52]

In the same year, 1568, Simon Vigor pronounced the funeral sermon for Queen Elizabeth of Spain, sister of Charles IX, in the presence of princes, prelates and nobles. Vigor was a great preacher, the most famous in Paris during the 1560s.[53] In 1568, he was named as one of four *prédicateurs du roi*. Barbara Diefendorf believes Charles IX made this appointment in an effort to co-opt Vigor, who had spoken out only a few months earlier against royal policy.[54] In this sermon, he manages to combine the precepts of Renaissance rhetoric with a very skilful and subtle argument. He excuses his incompetence in the face of so daunting a task, saying that he is little practised in this genre of oratory,[55] but adds that because of the great virtues of his subject he has no need for the ornaments of rhetoric, which would only serve to obscure and obfuscate: 'The truth is like a good and honest lady who is content with her natural beauty.'[56] As in classical Roman and Renaissance Italian funeral orations, Vigor concentrates on the person Elizabeth and her virtues. But the sermon is interwoven with a number of overarching themes that involve politics, gender and religion. Elizabeth's sex is an issue from the beginning:

[W]e can celebrate the memories of such great ladies who have served as a mirror for all the virtues of their times, more so than many men and weak princes, who have left no illustrious reminders, yet who by nature and instruction ought in all good actions to surpass women . . . It is notable that many women excel a large part of men when they have been instructed with the same care and diligence as men.[57]

As he proceeds, Vigor mentions that it is normal to praise the dead with mention of their ancestors, but complains that this makes their renown contingent on that of others. Vigor says he has plenty to say without a recital of Elizabeth's ancestry.[58] But then he adds a 'passing word', praising

---

52 Overt attacks on kingship were rare before the 1580s. For the pamphlet literature, see James R. Smither, 'The St Bartholomew's Day Massacre and Images of Kingship in France: 1572–1574', *Sixteenth Century Journal* 22 (1991), pp. 27–46.

53 Barbara B. Diefendorf, 'Simon Vigor: a Radical Preacher in Sixteenth-Century Paris', *Sixteenth Century Journal* 18 (1987), p. 401.

54 *Ibid.*, p. 402. She adds that if this was the case, the king underestimated his man.

55 Simon Vigor, *Oraison funebre prononcee aux obseques, de treshaute, tres-puissante, & tres catholique Princesse, ma Dame Elizabeth de France, Royne des Espagnes, prononcee en l'Eglise nostre Dame de Paris, le xxv. du mois d'Octobre 1568, par M. S. Vigor chanoine theologal en ladite Eglise, & Predicateur du Roy* (Paris, 1568), p. 8.

56 *Ibid.*   57 *Ibid.*, pp. 6–7.   58 *Ibid.*, p. 9.

her grandparents, Francis I and Claude, and her parents, Henri II and Queen Catherine. 'If Jupiter had been of such parentage, he would have easily become a good Christian!'[59] Vigor lavishes praise on Catherine, still not unusual at this date, though Vigor's earlier attacks on royal policy certainly call his sincerity into question. She is 'a mother so wise and prudent . . . who always took such great care to have her children instructed in piety, religion, integrity, devotion, sanctity, and probity of life . . . [She is] one of the happiest queens in the world today, being rich with children so well brought up and instructed.'[60] Vigor then continues his gendered discourse by setting Elizabeth up as the model for royalty:

> '[S]he exhibited charity toward her parents, goodwill toward everyone, accompanied by a condemnation and contempt for the vanities of this world, with all its ostentation and pomp, a virtue rarely found among people at court, especially those of a great house, nourished in the delicacies of this world. The first care she had from childhood was to fear God, to serve Him and love Him, only taking pleasure when she heard talk of His Divine Majesty. She was extremely devout to hear the services of the Church and the Word of God . . . She was horrified whenever she heard lewd words, and fled from dishonest talk, even though many at court glorify such wickedness.[61]

Vigor soon reveals his main reason for describing Elizabeth's virtues in such great detail: '[S]he was put on this earth to one day be the cause of great good for the realm, and by consequence all of Christendom.'[62] Part of the grand design for Elizabeth was political, but with religious overtones. Vigor explains that by her marriage to the King of Spain, Elizabeth put an end to the enmity that had rent both kingdoms: '[W]ithout her these two great houses would have been menaced with impending ruin by the continuing wars as well as the seditions and factions of rebels and traitors to God and His Church.'[63] In at least the first part of this task she succeeded, making herself beloved of the people of Spain and rendering her husband kind and gentle.[64] Also employing biblical Egyptian themes, Vigor compares her to Joseph the Patriarch in Egypt.[65] After her arrival, Spain was spared contagious diseases, civil war and all the scourges of God.[66]

Vigor then extends his argument by making the general observation that 'religion is a means for binding and uniting two realms'.[67] So effective did the marriage prove in this regard that Vigor has no doubt

---

[59] *Ibid.*, p. 10.   [60] *Ibid.*, p. 12.   [61] *Ibid.*, p. 15.   [62] *Ibid.*
[63] *Ibid.*   [64] *Ibid.*, pp. 17, 21.   [65] *Ibid.*, p. 21.   [66] *Ibid.*, p. 22.
[67] *Ibid.*, p. 18.

that 'if the Most Catholic King were not so preoccupied today with the wars in his lands, especially in Flanders, he would in imitation of his ancestors, come to our aid with a powerful army to chase the traitors and enemies of God and the king from La Rochelle and the region of Poitou, which has been taken by the rebels'.[68] This would have been Elizabeth's wish, for as the fervent Catholic she was, she hated heretics with all her heart.[69]

The reader (and one assumes in its original form, the auditor) begins to apprehend Vigor's main point, as he expounds on how Elizabeth showed her devotion:

> [S]he had an oratory built adjoining her chamber . . . So reverent was she toward the holy and sacred eucharist that if by chance she was outside and the Holy Sacrament was being carried to a sick person, she abandoned her plans and descended from her litter with all of her ladies, prostrating herself devoutly on the ground to adore Our Lord. Then she would follow it on foot to its destination, and afterwards she would follow it back to the church along with her retinue. On those rare occasions when she was outside for recreation, she would visit all of the holy places, hospitals, and monasteries, especially those for poor girls .[70]

Her strength and devotion induce Vigor to compare her to another Queen of Spain, Isabella, who 'chased the Moors from Granada and provided the means for Christopher Columbus to discover the New World, even though he had been scorned by the other courts of Europe'.[71] Both women were horrified when they heard 'that the precious body of Jesus Christ is trampled upon, that grand and magnificent churches constructed by earlier kings and emperors are destroyed, ruined, and cast to the ground, that the bones and relics of the saints are thrown into the fire with great indignities, their images broken and burnt, that poor priests and ministers of God are killed with barbarous cruelty'.[72] What Vigor has done thus far is to create the image of a member of the royal house of France who is saintly in her devotion and her horror of heresy and impiety. He contrasts the freedom from disorder of the realm into which she married with the devastation of her native land. The implication is obvious, and Vigor makes it even more clear as he paints a vivid death-bed scene, which he says he learned about from the letters of those present. Elizabeth, speaking to the French ambassador, made three recommendations to her brother and mother. First, they should endure patiently the news of her death. Second, 'she recommends to them the

---

[68] *Ibid.*, p. 19.   [69] *Ibid.*   [70] *Ibid.*, p. 21.   [71] *Ibid.*, p. 22.
[72] *Ibid.*, p. 23.

234 Larissa Juliet Taylor

Catholic religion, praying they put their hand to the extermination of all false religion, especially the religion that pretends to be reformed, and praying that God will give them the means to put this work into execution'. Third, she asks that they conserve the peace between the two realms.[73] After making these requests, Elizabeth elaborated on her second point, the threat to the faith in France. Martial imagery is again present:

> Nearing death, and barely able to speak, she nevertheless battled against those who dishonour God and blaspheme against His name, desiring that after her death those who remain will avenge such impieties and wickedness. In her last letter, she exhorted her brother, the Most Christian King, to fight against them and never again permit God to be dishonoured and injured in his realm . . . He should make good and holy edicts. He should put his hand to their execution . . . He should take up the defence of God. He should sustain the Church, so afflicted and despoiled. He should only admit to his council wise and virtuous Catholics, and certainly no one who is suspect. He will not endure blasphemers or evil people to be around him, especially heretics and traitors to God . . . He will use with justice the sword God has given him for the salvation of the good against heretics.[74]

If Charles IX is left in any doubt about what she means, Elizabeth spells it out: 'you are no longer a child; that age has passed and you are now a man. It is up to you to command. Make yourself obeyed.'[75]

Speaking in his own voice, Vigor addresses Elizabeth directly, asking that in death she pray for her native land.[76] Returning to her voice, he has Elizabeth express a last wish: 'After my death I pray for vengeance for God, His Church, His king and the realm.'[77] Vigor has masterfully used a dead queen, who by her deeds and her words overcame the weakness of her sex, in order to shame her brother, an adult male, into following her lead in extirpating heresy. If he does not, not only his kingship but his virility will be called into question. This sermon displays an almost uncanny prescience for, after the death of the duc d'Anjou, last Catholic heir to the throne, in 1584, *ligueurs* promoted the candidacy of Elizabeth's daughter, the Spanish infanta, with the proviso that she be married to one of their leaders.

The death of Charles IX in 1574 once again provided Arnaud Sorbin with a chance to rouse his listeners to action. Two sermons, delivered consecutively on 13 and 14 August at Notre-Dame and Saint-Denis, were personally prepared for publication by the preacher, who affirmed that

---

[73] *Ibid.*, p. 27.   [74] *Ibid.*, p. 31.   [75] *Ibid.*, p. 32.   [76] *Ibid.*, p. 35.
[77] *Ibid.*, p. 36.

they closely followed what he actually said.[78] In the title of both sermons, Charles is described as *propugnateur* (fighter) for the faith. Addressing himself to the new king, Sorbin confides how many times Charles had lamented the physical distance between the brothers once Henri had become King of Poland.[79] Avid to hear the Word of God preached and to recount what he had heard to others, Charles one day 'responded to a man who was boasting of having changed his religion in old age, going from a Catholic to a heretic. "Truly", the king said, "you are an awfully old tree to be replanted", thus tacitly suggesting that he was useless and barren.'[80] Throughout, Sorbin speaks of *nostre miserable saison,* 'our wretched times', which began almost immediately after Charles came to the throne. Reprising themes used by other preachers, Sorbin asks,

> Where is the Clovis, who in seventeen years of his reign so rigorously pursued the Arians, enemies of his faith? Where is the Charles Martel, who in forty-three years of war, or the Pepin in seventeen years of his reign, or the Charlemagne, who in thirty of his, endured so many evils and obtained so many victories against miscreants, enemies of God? Because if Clovis, newly baptized, confirmed the faith in France, our king restored it when it was almost lost.[81]

In what is undoubtedly a reference to the recent St Bartholomew's Day Massacre, Sorbin thanks God for having miraculously given Charles the means to uncover and counteract the secret conspiracies that his enemies had planned.[82] For what Charles had to endure during his reign, the preacher characterises the heretics as 'parricides, not only of your father, but the father of your country'.[83] Almost certainly aware of Vigor's account of Elizabeth's last moments, Sorbin relates that 'in the words he spoke at the end of his life to his mother the queen, he prayed her to execute justice on the disturbers of the peace in the realm, in order to show his people the love he bore them.'[84] Sorbin ends the Saint-Denis sermon by admonishing good Christians to follow the example Charles had set, without letting wars, plots or treason keep them from professing their faith in Jesus Christ and the Catholic Church.[85]

---

[78] Arnaud Sorbin, *Oraison funebre du treshault, puissant et treschrestien Roy de France, Charles IX, piteux & debonnaire, propugnateur de la Foy, & amateur des bons esprits: prononcee en l'Eglise Nostre dame de Paris, le XII. de Iuillet, M.D.LXXIIII* (Paris, 1574), fol. 3.

[79] *Ibid.,* fol. 9.   [80] *Ibid.,* fol. 14.   [81] *Ibid.,* fol. 20.   [82] *Ibid.,* fol. 21.

[83] *Ibid.,* fol. 25.

[84] Arnaud Sorbin, *Seconde oraison funebre du treschrestien et puissant Roy de France, Charles IX, Prince debonnaire, propugnateur de la Foy, & amateur des bons esprits: prononcee en l'Eglise S. Denys en France, le treizieme iour du mois de Iuillet, M.D.LXXIIII* (Paris, 1574).

[85] *Ibid.,* fol. 12.

As we have seen, many of the preachers in the years after 1547 used the funeral sermon as a means to press for vigorous, even military, action against the heretics. But even after St Bartholomew's, not all preachers did so. The Jesuit Emond Auger delivered a funeral sermon of 1574 for the Cardinal of Lorraine, 'who died in his hands'.[86] This is a simple lamentation of death, in which Auger uses the occasion to praise the king. He relates that the king and queen came to see the cardinal the same day he had administered extreme unction. Auger says that 'he had never seen the king so afflicted'.[87] Similarly, in a bizarre funeral sermon given for the duc d'Anjou in 1584, the Franciscan Jacques Berson laments that the last of Catherine's sons had had to grow up 'in the midst of cruel and bloody civil wars'.[88] Although Berson refers to the catastrophe that has befallen France, he concentrates on the duke, speaking of how he profited from daily attendance at sermons.[89] What is so peculiar about this sermon is Berson's blow-by-blow account of the duke's final illness, recounted in graphic detail. Funeral and memorial orations could therefore *also* be used as royal propaganda or, in the hands of a less skilled preacher, could devolve into triviality. Ignoring the opportunity that an important death provided in itself made a political statement – an implicit plea to tone down the rhetoric of violence.

With the radicalisation of preaching in the 1580s, the funeral sermon was used increasingly as a call to arms in the wake of what was considered a martyrdom. The judicial murder of Mary Stuart by Elizabeth of England roused the fury of French Catholic preachers at the death of a Catholic symbol and France's former queen, herself a Guise. Renaud de Beaune, archbishop of Bourges, shouted from the pulpit of Notre-Dame, challenging Henri III to make war on this Jezebel: 'Marie accused! Accused of what crime? Accused of being Catholic! Happy crime! Desirable accusation! No one can therefore be innocent before you if they aren't guilty before God! Do not fabricate more testimony, she admits this crime, she publishes it, she preaches it!'[90] He continued: 'Christian princes! God calls you forth to vengeance

---

[86] Emond Auger, *Bref discours sus la mort de feu monsieur le cardinal de Lorraine, extret d'une lettre escripte d'Avignon le vingt-septiesme du moys passé par M. Maistre Emond Auger de la compagnée de Iesus envoyee à l'un de ses amys* (Paris, 1574), fol. Aii.

[87] *Ibid.*, fol. Aiii.

[88] Jacques Berson, *Regret funebre contenant les actions et derniers propos de Monseigneur, fils de France, frere unique du Roy, depuis sa maladie iusques à son trespas* (Paris, 1584), p. 7.

[89] *Ibid.*, p. 9.

[90] Renaud de Beaune, *Oraison funebre de Marie, royne d'Escosse*, quoted in Labitte, *Démocratie*, p. 32.

on this nation which has polluted churches, contaminated altars, and massacred priests. If you are negligent in avenging these injuries, He will add your injuries to His own!'[91] Yet only a few years later this same preacher was appointed royal almoner to Henri IV and was responsible for composing and announcing his conversion to Catholicism. As a result of his support for royalty during the late 1580s and 1590s, Renaud de Beaune was characterised as a Judas, a would-be antipope, and that worst of all epithets, a *politique*. [92]

The preachers of the League did not need the occasion of a funeral to propagandise in their sermons. The preacher Jean Guincestre announced on Ash Wednesday of 1589 that he would not preach the gospel of Lent, because everyone already knew it anyway; he would instead recount the life, deeds and abominable acts of the perfidious tyrant Henri de Valois.[93] The assassination of the duc de Guise by Henri III in 1588 had unleashed the wrath of *ligueur* preachers in both their regular preaching and funeral sermons. Guise became a popular saint and martyr to the cause, while Guincestre referred to the erstwhile king as a *vilain Herodes*, an anagram of Henri de Valois.[94] Another preacher at Notre-Dame, Jean-François Pigenat, questioned 'if one could not be found among them zealous enough to avenge the great Lorraine with the blood of the tyrant?'.[95] Funeral sermons for the duke and the cardinal were delivered in almost every town in France, most of them echoing Pigenat's words. It was not long before they bore fruit, and Henri III was stabbed by the dagger of a Catholic zealot, Jacques Clément. Not surprisingly, one of the few non-satirical funeral sermons delivered for the king at the time of his death was given by Auger, who was ostracised as a result.[96] A similar fate befell Jean de la Barrière, an austere Cistercian whom Henri III had befriended by building his order a house in Paris. After la Barrière pronounced his funeral oration at Bordeaux, his monks revolted, and he suffered persecution by *ligueurs* for more than a decade.[97] If Henri's death was the cause for rejoicing, that of Clément called for eulogies of the highest order. In Clément we see the fruit of decades of efforts by Catholic propagandists in the pulpit. The leaders of the *Seize* asked all preachers to cover three points in their next sermon: (1) to justify the action of the Dominican by

---

[91] *Ibid.*, p. 33.
[92] Frederic J. Baumgartner, 'Renaud de Beaune, Politique Prelate', *Sixteenth Century Journal* 9 (1978), pp. 99, 104.
[93] Labitte, *Démocratie*, p. 48.   [94] *Ibid.*, p. 43.   [95] *Ibid.*, p. 45.
[96] *Ibid.*, p. 60.
[97] *Ibid.* It was only after the abjuration of Henri IV and his entry into Paris that funeral sermons proper were given for Henri III. *Ibid.*, p. 265.

comparing him with Judith; (2) to state that Henri of Navarre could not succeed Henri de Valois; and (3) to tell all those who supported the king of Navarre that they would be excommunicated.[98] The preachers were happy to oblige. By the late 1580s, most preachers not only advocated, but also celebrated tyrannicide. Jean Boucher, curé of Saint Benoît, was among the most intemperate and vociferous critics of both Henri III and Henri IV. According to the memoirist Pierre de l'Estoile, 'Boucher preached "nothing but killing" . . . He excited his congregation in "words and gestures" to do away with the *"politiques"*; Estoile feared that he would descend from his pulpit and dismember someone before their eyes.'[99] Boucher extolled Clément's deed, claiming that 'a new David has killed Goliath; a new Judith has killed Holofernes'.[100] In August of 1593, shortly after Henri of Navarre's conversion, Boucher published his *Sermones de la simulée conversion*, arguing that as a heretic Henri could never ascend the French throne.

Contrary to the claim that the funeral sermon was a restricted genre, it proved in mid- and late sixteenth-century France to be a highly malleable form that could be adapted for propagandistic uses in times of religious crisis. The theme of death provided the perfect opportunity for a preacher to talk about heroes and martyrs, cowards and tyrants, all of whom were present in their world. Skilled preachers might continue to employ the elements of the Renaissance funeral oration, but many chose to discard the parts that did not directly serve their purpose. In most cases, the person whose death was being remembered was little more than a pretext for a diatribe that lamented the woes of the day, particularly the atrocious acts of the heretics, or that castigated a weak, irresolute or perfidious king. The funeral sermons of the *ligueurs* of the 1580s demonstrate this genre taken to its extreme form. Yet the sermons after 1547 bespeak an increasing awareness of crisis and the need for strong leadership in the fight against heresy. This usage can first be seen clearly in the sermon of François Le Picart for his fellow preacher Descornes in 1547. The life and death of a good Christian gave Le Picart the opportunity to issue a call to all Catholics to live as they should, and to fight heresy. His words and his choices of biblical passages focus on the idea of war – a war against the heretics. Arnaud Sorbin carries the theme further, asking where have all the heroes gone? Finally, Simon Vigor's

---

[98] *Ibid.*, p. 79.

[99] Quoted in Mark Greengrass, *France in the Age of Henri IV* (2nd edn, London and New York, 1995), p. 64.

[100] Quoted in R. J. Knecht, *The French Wars of Religion* (2nd edn, London and New York, 1996), p. 74.

eulogy of Elizabeth of France explores themes that would be fully developed by later preachers – an overt criticism of royal inaction and a suggestion of Spanish intervention. Just as Le Picart had threatened heretics with the fate of Dinah, Vigor adroitly yet diplomatically uses a reversal of gender imagery to vilify a weak king who will not carry out his duties as Most Christian King. Most of the preachers before the St Bartholomew's Day Massacre were either royal preachers or in the main-stream of Catholic preaching. That they broached such themes reflects a crisis they felt was getting out of hand, and in their sermons they set the tone for later *ligueur* preachers who instigated events. Before 1572, preachers knew what they were doing, but not necessarily where they were going – that would be left to the *ligueurs*. This was war, and, as in the Greek funeral oration, preachers were exalting an ideology – in this case that of militant Catholicism – and calling on their listeners to imitate and avenge the fallen heroes of war.

13 The worst death becomes a good death: the passion of Don Rodrigo Calderón

James M. Boyden

Exemplary and cautionary deaths

Philip II, King of Spain, died at the age of seventy-one in the Escorial on 13 September 1598, after a long illness. For nearly two months the king had been confined to bed, his mind lucid while he suffered the torments of racking fevers, gout, arthritis, fluid retention, blood poisoning and uncontrollable diarrhoea. Philip's pains were compounded by his physicians, who lanced the boils that erupted on his body, and doubtless also by the shame of lying in his own excrement. While Philip II's foreign enemies and hostile historians would point to his prolonged and agonising mortal illness as a scourge visited upon the king by an angry God, Spanish observers of the royal death-bed emphasised Philip's resignation and steadfast faith through his final ordeal. Always devout, once he knew that he was dying the king turned his remaining energies to pious exercises, 'never tiring – though many others became exhausted – of hearing, speaking and reading spiritual and heavenly things'. He bore extended suffering without complaint, displaying the faith, hope and charity proper to a Christian. 'The last words that he spoke', according to his chaplain, 'were that he was dying as a Catholic in the faith and obedience of the holy Roman Church.'[1]

---

[1] Carlos Eire provides a superb account and analysis of the king's death in *From Madrid to Purgatory: the Art and Craft of Dying in Sixteenth-Century Spain* (Cambridge, 1995). Quotations from Fray José de Sigüenza, *Fundación del monasterio de El Escorial* (1602), introduced by F. C. Sainz de Robles (Madrid, 1963), p. 188; and Fray Antonio Cervera de la Torre, *Testimonio auténtico y verdadero de las cosas notables que pasaron en la dichosa muerte del Rey N. S. don Felipe II, que Santa Gloria haya* (Madrid, 1600), excerpted in Rafael Vargas Hidalgo, 'Documentos inéditos sobre la muerte de Felipe II y la literatura fúnebre de los siglos XVI y XVII', *Boletín de la Real Academia de la Historia* 192 (1995), p. 399.

Reacting to the news of the king's decease his subjects donned mourning, spontaneously or at the order of municipal authorities. Memorial services were held in the principal towns of the Spanish monarchy. *Mortuus est Philippus Rex*, a motet composed by the music master of Valencia Cathedral, asserted that 'all people wept for him with a great moan, and they lamented for many days'. Philip's modern biographers proffer more equivocal assessments: for them, popular grief was tempered by criticism of the late king, and 'the praise was also accompanied by a sense of relief'.[2] In any case, a spate of publications commemorated the king's exemplary death. In the Mediterranean lands of the Spanish monarchy alone at least forty-one works appeared by 1610 narrating Philip II's final days, describing his exequies, or reproducing memorial sermons.[3]

Carlos Eire argues persuasively that the authors of this memorial literature discerned in the last days of the Prudent King 'a lesson in death and the art of dying and a convenient vehicle for religious and monarchical propaganda'.[4] Most obviously, the passing of a powerful ruler underscored the inevitability of death, providing a concrete illustration of the lesson symbolised by the dance of death or the Castilian proverb 'muerése el rey y el papa, y el que no tiene capa' (literally, death comes for the king and the pope, as well as for him who owns no cloak).[5] Moreover, the narrative of Philip's resolution and piety in his agony comprised as it were an individualised treatise of the *ars moriendi*. According to one observer, the king 'upheld a model of perfection in the way of dying that all Christians – prelates and kings, laymen and clerks, great and small – ought to imitate'.[6]

Convincing as well is Eire's demonstration that beyond providing pious instruction for other mortals, heralding the good death of Philip II served a number of intertwined interests of Church and state. The king's

---

[2] Geoffrey Parker, *Philip II* (Boston, 1978), pp. 198–9; Henry Kamen, *Philip of Spain* (New Haven, 1997), epilogue (quotation at p. 317). For text, translations and a performance of Ambrosio Cotes's 1598 motet, *Mortuus est Philippus Rex: Music for the Life and Death of the Spanish King* (London, Hyperion Records Ltd, compact disc CDA67046, 1998).

[3] See the list in Vargas Hidalgo, 'Documentos inéditos', pp. 454–60.

[4] Eire, *From Madrid to Purgatory*, p. 258.

[5] My summary of the lessons of Philip's death in this paragraph and the next is drawn from Eire's exegesis, *ibid.*, part II, chaps. 3–5; the proverb was collected by the seventeenth-century linguist Gonzalo Correas, in *Vocabulario de refranes y frases proverbiales y otras fórmulas comunes de la lengua castellana*, ed. Miguel Mir (Madrid, 1906), p. 471.

[6] Fray Diego de Yepes, 'Relación del confesor', in Vargas Hidalgo, 'Documentos inéditos', p. 379.

inspiring end offered validation of Catholic ritual and soteriology. In addition, the assertion that the king had died a holy death reinforced the legitimacy of Spanish monarchy and helped to smooth the succession of the young Philip III. To the same end, the Escorial, Philip II's emblematic construction and the place of his death and interment, was depicted as the sacred centre whence sprang the physical and spiritual renewal of the dynasty. The king had built the Escorial 'in the same way a silkworm constructs its cocoon, and lies dead within it, so that the new majesty of his son might emerge just as another silkworm springs from the cocoon to renew the days and works of the predecessor entombed therein'.[7] Furthermore, Eire links the laudation of Philip's good death to the central attitude he finds encapsulated in the proverb 'como vive muere' (as one lives, so one dies). 'Death', he argues, 'was a moment that summed up a lifetime of behaviour'; it 'was also commonly believed [that] a good death was the best possible indication of a good life'. An admirable Christian death validated the life of the deceased, and in Philip's case functioned as a refutation of criticism of his rule.[8]

If secular and ecclesiastical elites could and did laud exemplary deaths to encourage emulation and respect for established hierarchies – Eire cites, in addition to Philip, Charles V and Teresa of Avila, and the list of prominent figures praised for their deaths could be vastly extended – they were also in the business of staging *cautionary* deaths to discourage crime, rebellion and impiety. The life (and perhaps more to the point, afterlife) implications of a bad death were nowhere more baldly evident than in the public punishment of heretics in inquisitorial *autos de fe*. Maureen Flynn asserts that the rituals of ceremonial punishment constituted a 'mimesis of the Last Judgement'. For Flynn, the *auto de fe* was a 'theatre of penitence' presenting spectators with a representation of apocalyptic justice, and involving them in 'something like a religious bullfight', the struggle between errant belief and Catholic truth. For most of the sinners being penanced by the Inquisition, this drama ended in public recanta-tion of their errors and reconciliation with the Church, a cathartic outcome that stirred the emotions of the onlookers. The unrepentant, however, were 'relaxed' to the secular authorities and burned alive. For eyewitnesses these awful executions brought home the ultimate sanction that should compel obedience to the teaching of the Church: 'Watching a

---

[7] Baltasar Porreño, *Dichos y hechos del rey don Felipe II* (1628), ed. Angel González Palencia (Madrid, 1942), p. 18.

[8] Eire, *From Madrid to Purgatory*, pp. 524ff. for discussion of 'como vive muere'; for this meaning of Philip's good death, see pp. 361–2. Quoted passages at pp. 362 and 525.

recalcitrant heretic burn', Flynn observes, 'was like peering through a window into hell.'[9] The quintessentially bad death of a heretic at the stake taught an incomparable lesson in the temporal and eternal consequences of bad living and disobedience.

Another manifestation of the cautionary death was the public execution of criminals by the secular authorities. The laws of the Spanish kingdoms, in common with those of other early modern monarchies, decreed capital sanctions for a broad array of crimes. Assessing the actual incidence of executions and the trend in their number over the course of the Habsburg centuries is, however, difficult. Against José Antonio Maravall's contention that harsher repressive measures and the 'ruthless staging of cruelty' characterised Baroque regimes must be balanced evidence that death sentences were increasingly commuted to terms of service in the galleys.[10] Moreover murderers could be pardoned – usually in return for monetary compensation – by the relatives of their victims and go free or, at worst, into exile. Still, executions were common, and like the great urban *autos de fe* they drew large crowds of spectators (perhaps as many as 20,000 in Seville). Mary Elizabeth Perry states that 'scarcely a week went by without a public execution' in Seville; this is a very loose estimate, but we do know that a single Sevillian Jesuit accompanied 309 felons to the scaffold between 1578 and 1616.[11]

Public executions, of course, were meant to serve not just the judicial imperative of retribution but also administrative goals of edification and deterrence. Most of these spectacles were directed towards a local audience. Occasionally, though, an execution was a grand event of state, staged to make an impression on a wider public. One such execution took place in Seville in 1634, when Don Juan de Benavides was put to death in the Plaza de San Francisco. Benavides had enjoyed a distinguished military career, culminating with the command of the fleet returning from New Spain in 1628. To his great misfortune the entire fleet had been captured off the north coast of Cuba by a larger Dutch

---

[9] Maureen Flynn, 'Mimesis of the Last Judgement: the Spanish *Auto de fé*', *Sixteenth Century Journal* 22 (1991), pp. 281–97.

[10] José Antonio Maravall, *La cultura del barroco: análisis de una estructura histórica* (Barcelona, 1975), pp. 296–8, 338–42. The quotation is from the English version, *Culture of the Baroque: Analysis of a Historical Structure*, tr. Terry Cochran (Minneapolis, 1986), p. 164. For condemnation to the galleys, see Ruth Pike, *Penal Servitude in Early Modern Spain* (Madison, 1983), chap. 1.

[11] Antonio Domínguez Ortiz, 'Delitos y suplicios en la Sevilla imperial (La crónica negra de un misionero jesuita)', in *Crisis y decadencia de la España de los Austrias* (Barcelona, 1969), pp. 38–40; Mary Elizabeth Perry, *Crime and Society in Early Modern Seville* (Hanover NH, 1980), p. 139.

squadron. Back in Spain, Benavides languished in confinement until a royal death sentence was handed down in 1633. Carla Phillips concludes that Benavides was punished so harshly *pour encourager les autres,* since the loss of the fleet 'was due at least as much to bad luck as to any incompetence on his part'. Faced with protests from nobles angered by the perceived mistreatment of one of their own, the crown kept preparations for the execution under wraps until the last instant. Philip IV took a direct interest in the precautions intended to prevent aristocratic demonstrations or disruptions of the spectacle of justice. Nevertheless, a large crowd formed in the plaza to witness Benavides's death. No protest interrupted the spectacle, but aristocratic displeasure was made evident later in the elaborate funeral rites held at the expense of a leading nobleman.[12] Whether Benavides's cautionary end had the effect desired by its stage managers in Madrid remains an open question (though perhaps it did, since nearly three decades passed before another treasure fleet was lost). In any case it is interesting to note the care that was taken at the highest levels to maintain secrecy about the impending execution and to guard against untoward demonstrations. Philip IV and his leadership team knew from previous experience that state executions could misfire, and that audiences might draw unintended and even subversive lessons from a public spectacle of death.

'Living, he seemed to deserve death'

Rodrigo Calderón was born in Antwerp in the 1570s, the son of a Spanish captain, Francisco Calderón, and his half-Flemish wife María de Aranda y Sandelín. Rodrigo's mother died around 1582, and Francisco Calderón returned to Spain and his native town of Valladolid with his young son. After remarrying, in 1589 he settled his son Rodrigo as a page in the household of Don Francisco de Sandoval y Rojas, marquis of Denia and a grandee of Spain.[13] Over the next decade, the young servant formed close ties to his master the marquis. This relationship was the

---

[12] Carla Rahn Phillips, *Six Galleons for the King of Spain: Imperial Defense in the Early Seventeenth Century* (Baltimore, 1986), pp. 3–7.

[13] Julián Juderías, 'Un proceso político en tiempo de Felipe III. Don Rodrigo Calderón, marqués de Siete Iglesias, su vida, su proceso y su muerte', *Revista de archivos, bibliotecas y museos (RdeABM),* 3rd series, year IX (1905), vol. 13, pp. 336–8. This study was published in two instalments, the first in the issue of *RdeABM* cited above, pp. 334–65, and the continuation in *RdeABM,* 3rd series, year X (1906), vol. 14, pp. 1–31. Since the page numbers of the two instalments do not overlap, subsequent citations will include merely a short title and the page number(s).

making of Rodrigo Calderón, for in the same years when it was coalescing the marquis of Denia was establishing himself as the favourite of the young crown prince Philip, who succeeded Philip II in 1598. Over the objections of the old king's ministers, Denia had become *caballerizo mayor* (master of the horse) in the prince's household in August 1598. Once Philip II died, it became clear immediately that the marquis enjoyed paramount favour with the new king. On the day of his father's funeral, Philip III named his favourite to the Council of State. During the next year, Philip III and Denia shouldered aside most of the remaining collaborators of Philip II. The favourite's continued ascent was marked by his retention of the post of *caballerizo mayor* (but now in the king's household), by his appointment to head the privy chamber as *sumiller de corps*, and by the king's gift of the additional title of duke of Lerma in November 1599.[14]

The decision-making processes of the monarchy were restructured to reflect Lerma's supreme favour (*privanza* or *valimiento*) with the king. Then as now, critics of the reign have argued that Lerma exercised supremacy *over* the king. Certainly he was a very powerful chief minister, effectively controlling the flow of information between the royal councils and Philip III. Key positions in the court and councils were entrusted to Lerma's relatives, allies and creatures. Prominent among the latter was Rodrigo Calderón, who at Lerma's instance had gained a position within the privy chamber in 1599, and by the next year had been elevated to the office of *secretario de la cámara*, or patronage secretary. This post 'permitted him to control petitions for *mercedes* [favours] addressed to the king'.[15] Calderón's occupancy of this key position testifies to the duke's personal confidence in him, and indeed Antonio Feros asserts that:

> from 1598 to 1618, Calderón acted as *the* favourite of the Duke. In many ways the relationship between Lerma and Calderón parallels the association between Philip III and Lerma. Calderón maintained constant contact with Lerma and accompanied him everywhere. Calderón was also in charge of writing Lerma's responses to various royal ministers . . . But [his] most important role was as Lerma's private counsellor.[16]

His close collaboration with the duke brought Rodrigo Calderón power,

---

[14] Antonio Feros, 'The King's Favorite, the Duke of Lerma: Power, Wealth and Court Culture in the Reign of Philip III of Spain, 1598–1621' (Johns Hopkins University PhD diss., 1994), provides the best account of Lerma's rise and of his central role in the government of Philip III.
[15] Feros, 'The King's Favorite', p. 245.   [16] *Ibid.*

honours and riches, and along with them notoriety and bitter resentment; eventually his identification with the favourite would bring him to grief.

Contemporary accounts provide some glimpses of the role Calderón played in the administration of his master the duke. In a vivid biographical sketch of 1605, the Venetian ambassador Contarini portrayed Lerma as moody, oscillating between the affability of a great lord and bouts of deep melancholy. In the former mood he was expansive and 'agreeable to the highest degree; everyone comes away from conversing with him very satisfied'. Conversely, in the duke's periods of melancholy, 'there is no use trying to conduct business with him'. Given Lerma's nature, those with affairs to transact at court had to cultivate the men who were truly close to him. For the Venetian, the most influential among the duke's creatures was Pedro Franqueza, secretary to the Council of State. Despite his secretarial status, Franqueza 'is number one and all-important, since he and the duke of Lerma together resolve all affairs'. In Contarini's reckoning, Rodrigo Calderón acted as appointments secretary for the duke, 'reminding him of the affairs of those to whom he [Calderón] is well disposed' and advancing or withholding petitions as he saw fit. 'Therefore', the ambassador concluded, 'he is a bad man to have for an enemy.'[17]

As a Lerma partisan, Matías de Novoa did not dwell on the darker side of the duke's personality in his retrospective chronicle of the reign of Philip III. His depiction of the relationship between Lerma and Calderón is nonetheless very revealing:

> The duke remitted to Don Rodrigo the refusal of petitions that he would not venture to deny himself because of the gentility of his temperament; thus Don Rodrigo performed this function; and when only one in four of the requests submitted gained approval all those who had business with him came to believe either that he was blocking them from favour or that he was ill disposed toward them; it is a hard truth that the minister who performs this duty will have to bear the blame for it.[18]

Predictably, this role in the distribution of patronage made Calderón unpopular at court. By 1603 he, along with Franqueza, was the target of a denunciation addressed to the king's confessor by Íñigo Ibáñez, a minor functionary who had previously landed in trouble for a 1599 pamphlet criticising the government of the dead king Philip II. Then Ibáñez had

---

[17] In Luis Cabrera de Córdoba, *Relaciones de las cosas sucedidas en la córte de España, desde 1599 hasta 1614* (Madrid, 1857), pp. 569 (Lerma), 571 (Franqueza), 577 (Calderón).

[18] Matías de Novoa, 'Historia de Felipe III, rey de España', in *Colección de documentos inéditos para la historia de España* (112 vols., Madrid, 1842–95), LXI, p. 101.

likely been writing at the behest of Lerma's partisans; now, though, he demanded that both of the duke's favourites be barred from conducting official business. If not, he alleged, 'the government was headed for ruin, since they were selling offices and accepting bribes'. At Lerma's orders, the unfortunate Ibáñez was arrested and held incommunicado while talk that he was insane spread around the court. Julián Juderías remarked that 'the punishment imposed upon him reveals that he was not so mad after all'- Ibáñez was condemned to death, with the sentence later commuted to imprisonment in the castle of Simancas.[19] Another episode indicating Calderón's unpopularity occurred in September 1604. Coming home in a sedan chair from the palace in Valladolid, Calderón was accosted at the entrance to his house by an assassin wielding a pistol. This time good fortune protected him where the duke of Lerma could not; the gun misfired and the would-be assassin ran off, 'leaving Don Rodrigo exceedingly alarmed'.[20]

From its own time down to the present, the Lerma regime has been a byword for corruption and peculation.[21] Of the duke himself, Contarini wrote, accurately, that 'he is now [1605] very rich, where once he was very poor'. He summarised one means of this enrichment by alleging that when dealing 'with the duke of Lerma, it is not hard to give him presents'. According to the Venetian, 'it is public knowledge that he receives jewels, tapestries, and household ornaments [from abroad], and in Spain they regale him after the same fashion'. Where Lerma preferred luxury goods to cash, Contarini implied that his intimates were less discriminating. Franqueza 'is a man of low character, but very shrewd, and so exceedingly greedy that it is not necessary to seek any other means to transact business with him . . . you cannot negotiate with this one through words or queries but only by putting him in your debt'. Calderón came off slightly better – or worse, from one point of view, since Contarini deemed him too insignificant to bribe. 'He is a lad with a bad reputation', the

---

[19] Juderías, 'Un proceso político', pp. 342, 347; Cabrera de Córdoba, *Relaciones*, p. 173.

[20] Cabrera de Córdoba, *Relaciones*, p. 227.

[21] This judgement seems likely to stand, despite the vigorous and largely favourable reappraisal of the reign currently underway. For some of the best of this revisionist historiography, see Feros, 'The King's Favorite'; Bernardo García García, *La Pax Hispanica: Política exterior del Duque de Lerma* (Leuven, 1996); Magdalena S. Sánchez, *The Empress, the Queen, and the Nun: Women and Power at the Court of Philip III of Spain* (Baltimore, 1998); Paul Allen, 'The Strategy of Peace: Spanish Foreign Policy and the *Pax Hispanica*, 1598–1609' (Yale University PhD diss., 1995); Martha Hoffman-Strock, 'Carved on Rings and Painted in Pictures: the Education and Formation of the Spanish Royal Family, 1601–1634' (Yale University PhD diss., 1996).

ambassador wrote, 'but I have not given him anything, since he is not a minister of state nor does his power resound very far.'[22]

Contarini underestimated Rodrigo Calderón, who accumulated vast honours and riches while he performed his unpopular duties as Lerma's henchman. In 1602 Calderón made a good marriage with Inés de Vargas, heiress to the lordship of La Oliva near Plasencia and a relative of the powerful Mendoza clan. Later Philip III elevated the status of his wife's estate and made Rodrigo Calderón count of La Oliva. In the meantime Calderón acquired a number of lucrative municipal offices, as well as the postmastership of Valladolid and a sinecure on the *Chancillería* or high court of royal justice there. Besides the salaries and fees that came with these offices, Calderón secured the privileges of collecting a royalty on bulls of the Santa Cruzada printed in Valladolid and a share of the imposts charged on Brazil wood arriving at Lisbon. Reportedly, these privileges alone produced an income of 18,000 ducats per year. Royal beneficence touched Calderón's three sons as well; each of them was awarded an *hábito* in one of the Iberian military orders, while their father was made *comendador* of Ocaña in Santiago, the most prestigious of the orders. Calderón's ascent reached its peak when the king made him marquis of Siete Iglesias in June 1614; his recently minted title of count of La Oliva passed to his eldest son. The new marquis also became commander of the king's German guard, a post that entitled him to a military escort as he moved through the streets. An exhaustive list of Calderón's honours and holdings would include other lucrative privileges as well as such perquisites as private theatre boxes in Valladolid and Madrid. Juderías computes his income at its height at 200,000 ducats per year, a vast sum and almost certainly an overestimate. But there can be no disputing that Rodrigo Calderón grew rich during his period of favour at court.[23]

Outside their own charmed circle, Lerma and his men were disliked and resented for their accumulation of wealth and honours. Principled outrage accounted for some of the criticism, like that voiced by the Jesuit historian Juan de Mariana. 'We see ministers springing from the dust of the earth', he wrote, 'who in a moment are groaning under the weight of an income reckoned in thousands. Where has this wealth come from, if not from the lifeblood of the poor or wrenched from the guts of

---

[22] Cabrera de Córdoba, *Relaciones*, pp. 569, 571, 577.
[23] Juderías, 'Un proceso político', *passim*, esp. pp. 16, 352, 364. For the grant of the marquisate of Siete Iglesias and transfer of the title of La Oliva, Cabrera de Córdoba, *Relaciones*, p. 558.

businessmen and petitioners?'[24] Other attacks on the regime stemmed from the jealousy and ambitions of rival courtiers; there is much truth, for example, in Novoa's analysis, which sees envy and a desire to supplant the current favourites behind the opposition of the clerical clique around the queen or the faction associated with the count of Olivares. 'Even the most exalted positions', he wrote, 'are not so high that they cannot be nipped by the venomous tooth of envy. Those who rise the farthest attract the harshest rivalry and are the most battered by the fury and choler of diverse gales . . . For men do not conspire together for any other purpose than to overthrow he whom they perceive as most prosperous.'[25]

Doubtless Rodrigo Calderón was tarred by his close association with Lerma, disliked for his role in patronage, and envied for the wealth and honours he amassed. Some of his unpopularity, however, arose from his own personality and behaviour. As his power increased, so did his arrogance. According to a contemporary, 'the word got out of Don Rodrigo's favour and his great influence in everything, and this was no small cause of his growing haughty and pompous. Many gentlemen were aggrieved by the lack of respect that he showed them. He seldom returned visits and often placed obstacles in the paths of those who wanted to secure an audience.'[26] 'He was a better menial than lord', concluded a hostile chronicler. 'He served humbly but commanded superciliously, which endeared him to his master but rendered him detestable other-wise.'[27] Calderón was an upstart, and resented as such. 'Quite forgetting who he had been,' observed an early biographer, 'he was overbearing and arrogant with those who needed his help.'[28] Not surprisingly, Calderón was afflicted by another unlikeable trait of the parvenu, insecurity about his origins that led him to fabricate a more exalted lineage for himself. Returning from a state mission to France and the Spanish Netherlands in 1612, he astounded the court by claiming to have discovered in Flanders that he was actually a bastard of Don Fadrique Alvarez de Toledo, fourth duke of Alba, who had died in 1585. A court chronicler remarked drily that 'this bit of news provokes wonderment in many of those to whom he has chosen to confide it'. Francisco de Quevedo, writing a decade later, was characteristically sarcastic:

---

[24] Quoted in Juderías, 'Un proceso político', p. 348.
[25] Novoa, 'Historia de Felipe III', p. 100.
[26] Jerónimo Gascón de Torquemada, quoted in Juderías, 'Un proceso político', pp. 345–6.
[27] Virgilio Malvezzi, *Historia de los primeros años del reinado de Felipe IV*, ed. D. L. Shaw (London, 1968), p. 79.
[28] Gabriel de Narváez Aldana, *Próspera y adversa fortuna de Don Rodrigo Calderón* (1658), quoted in Juderías, 'Un proceso político', p. 345.

Don Rodrigo Calderón was the son of Francisco Calderón, an honourable and most virtuous man, and of a Flemish lady of rank. Nevertheless his haughty airs impelled him to seek out another father (in order to render his person commensurate with his fortune). And so part of the nonsense of his vanity and ambition was to re-father himself, now as the son of the old duke of Alba, preferring to be a careless by-blow of the duke rather than the fruit of holy wedlock. This delusion wasn't easily put across, however, and for lack of options he had to content himself with being the son of his father. [29]

The poet Luis de Góngora was scathing as well, although as an occasional client of Rodrigo Calderón he perhaps kept this verse to himself: 'Rivulet, where will this reaching and climbing end? With you becoming the Guadalquivir, and the Guadalquivir becoming the sea?'[30]

Calderón's haughty airs were most likely provocative at times, and perhaps explain the confrontation that erupted between the marquis of Siete Iglesias and one Lieutenant Verdugo of the king's Spanish guard in the Plaza Mayor of Madrid during the festivities marking the royal weddings in 1615. No clear evidence remains of the incident, but only a haunting premonitory couplet of the count of Villamediana:

> Pendencia con Verdugo, y en la plaza?
> Mala señal por cierto te amenaza.

The count's verse plays on the name Verdugo, which means executioner; thus, 'an affray with Verdugo, and in the plaza? / Surely a bad sign hangs over you.'[31]

The fall of Rodrigo Calderón, presaged by Villamediana, proceeded in three stages over a period of more than a decade. The first inkling of trouble came in 1605–7, when, in Juderías's phrase, a 'gust of morality' blew through the court. New initiatives to address the monarchy's fiscal crisis provoked scrutiny of the activities of some of Lerma's closest collaborators, including Pedro Franqueza. For a time Lerma attempted to protect his subordinates, but eventually the duke sacrificed them to preserve his own credit with the king. Franqueza was arrested in January 1607 and, after his property had been seized and inventoried, he was charged with 474 abuses of his official duties. His trial ended in 1609

---

[29] Cabrera de Córdoba, *Relaciones*, p. 497; Francisco de Quevedo y Villegas, 'Grandes anales de quince días', in *Obras*, vol. I, ed. A. Fernández-Guerra y Orbe, *Biblioteca de Autores Españoles (BAE)* 23 (Madrid, 1923), p. 206.

[30] Quevedo, 'Grandes anales', p. 206. Editor's note 'c' reproduces, purportedly from a manuscript in Góngora's hand, this variant of the celebrated *letrilla* 'A un fulano de arroio' in *Obras poéticas de D. Luis de Góngora*, vol. III (New York, 1921), pp. 50–2.

[31] Juan de Tassis y Peralta, count of Villamediana, in *Poetas líricos de los siglos XVI y XVII*, vol. II, ed. Adolfo de Castro, *BAE* 42 (Madrid, 1951), p. 161.

with a sentence that stripped Franqueza of all his offices, ordered him to pay fines of 1.4 million ducats into the treasury, and condemned him to perpetual house arrest away from the court. Franqueza died in these reduced circumstances in 1614.[32]

Rodrigo Calderón escaped direct implication, but 'a wave of public anger' against him led the king to order an audit of his affairs. Lerma remained loyal to his creature in this instance, though, and while Calderón was stripped of his title as *secretario de la cámara* he was compensated by an extraordinary *cédula* (warrant) of Philip III, 'pardoning him for all past deeds and forbidding anyone from publicly persecuting and criticising him'.[33] Unsurprisingly, this royal licence did nothing to curb the highhandedness that had earned him opprobrium around the court, nor did it save Calderón from the machinations of enemies close to the queen, Margaret of Austria. Urged by two of her spiritual advisers and concerned by the influence that Lerma and his men exercised over her husband, the pious queen spurred a secret investigation of Calderón's affairs in 1611. Under the pressure of this inquest, Calderón connived at murder to silence a shady associate, Francisco Juara. His responsibility for Juara's death was soon suspected at court; perhaps more alarming, when the queen died as a consequence of childbirth in October 1611, rumours began to circulate that Calderón had suborned her attendants to cause his regal enemy's death. This charge was incredible, the product, as Quevedo observed, of 'loose talk, which is broadcast widely and too easily believed . . . of crimes manufactured from whole cloth out of the detestation inspired by such great favour'.[34] But however far-fetched, the rumour that Calderón had arranged the queen's death would circulate for years.

No judicial proceedings were initiated and Lerma continued to support his protégé, but this imbroglio of 1611 cost Rodrigo Calderón the personal favour of Philip III. This loss of the king's approval inaugurated the first stage in Calderón's protracted fall from grace; he could no longer expect the sort of immunity that Philip III had been willing to extend in 1607. In the short run, Lerma contrived to protect Calderón by sending him on missions abroad, and even won for him a

---

[32] Feros, 'The King's Favorite', pp. 260–74; Julián Juderías, *Los favoritos de Felipe III: Don Pedro Franqueza, conde de Villalonga, secretario de Estado* (Madrid, 1909), esp. pp. 41–8.

[33] Feros, 'The King's Favorite', pp. 274–5; Juderías, 'Un proceso político', pp. 350–1, includes extensive excerpts from the *cédula*.

[34] Novoa, 'Historia de Felipe III', pp. 101–5, 110–14; Juderías, 'Un proceso político', pp. 353–6; Sánchez, *The Empress, the Queen, and the Nun*, pp. 24–5, 33–4; Feros, 'The King's Favorite', pp. 281–2; and Quevedo, 'Grandes anales', p. 206.

last round of royal *mercedes* (including the marquisate of Siete Iglesias) in 1614. But Lerma's own days of surpassing favour were numbered. The king's growing dissatisfaction, coupled with the intrigues of his enemies and the rival ambitions to *privanza* of his own son, the duke of Uceda, led to Lerma's dismissal from court in October 1618.[35]

The duke's fall from grace was a disaster for Rodrigo Calderón, who was left without protection from his many enemies in the court. This upheaval was the second milepost on his road to ruin. With Lerma gone, the king turned resolutely against Rodrigo Calderón and empanelled a tribunal to look into his alleged crimes. Philip III's instructions openly charged the magistrates to investigate the murder of Francisco Juara, while a secret addendum ordered them to determine whether Calderón had played a role in the queen's death. Advised about these proceedings, Calderón tried to hide some of his wealth, but rather curiously he made no attempt to flee.[36] Perhaps he remained arrogant enough to believe that he could weather this storm. In early 1619 the tribunal ordered Calderón's arrest, and he was taken without a struggle in his house in Valladolid on 20 February. He was conveyed to a prison in the city, while his residences there and in Madrid were searched, and his movable property seized and inventoried. En route to detention, crowds jeered him as a traitor. Calderón's many enemies were jubilant. Some doubtless hoped that he could be coerced to testify to the crimes of the duke of Lerma, while others brought forward new and increasingly wild charges, including that Don Rodrigo had resorted to witchcraft to impose his will on the king and other luminaries.[37]

As the investigation proceeded during 1619, Calderón was held in a variety of rural fortresses before being brought to Madrid for interrogation. In the capital, he was jailed in his own house near the Puerta de Fuencarral. His wife and children, penniless because of the sequestration that had accompanied Calderón's arrest, had taken refuge elsewhere. An observer found pathos in the prisoner's situation:

> In the great room that had been the stage for his pleasures, feasting, and rejoicing . . . three compartments had been fashioned; the one in the middle, very cramped and dark, was where he lived and slept, with the candles never extinguished and watched by two guards and a servant.

A second compartment served as a chapel, where Calderón heard mass

---

[35] For the best modern account of Lerma's fall, see Feros, 'The King's Favorite', pp. 292–7.

[36] Novoa, 'Historia de Felipe III', pp. 163–5.

[37] Juderías, 'Un proceso político', pp. 6–17, remains the most convenient account of the judicial process.

surrounded by guards, while his judges used the third enclosure as a head-
quarters for their inquiry.[38] Otherwise the house was empty; appraised by
the authorities at a value of 760,000 ducats, Calderón's household furnish-
ings, art objects and jewels now formed the basis of dozens of charges of
financial misconduct levelled against him. The investigators were
frustrated in other aspects of the case, especially by their inability to sub-
stantiate the rumours that Calderón had harmed the late queen. Thwarted
in that direction, they vigorously pursued charges of sorcery, even
admitting testimony that apparitions of the dead had appeared to accuse
Calderón of murder. At the end of the year the king had examined the
preliminary findings of the investigation, and authorised Calderón's interrogation under torture, which was carried out in January 1620. Calderón
withstood the torment, admitting nothing, and calling out for assistance to
the late Queen Margaret. Two weeks later, Luis de Góngora reported that
the judges were dissatisfied and might undertake a second interrogation
under torture once their prisoner recovered from the first session.[39]

Months passed before the tribunal presented its conclusive findings to
Philip III in September 1620. The report listed 244 counts of civil
misconduct in the king's service, most of them involving bribery and
financial swindles. As to the criminal case, the findings cleared Calderón
of involvement in the queen's death, but found him culpable in the
murder of Francisco Juara and a number of lesser offences.[40] Calderón's
attorneys were allowed to respond. Logically enough, they relied upon
the royal *cédula* of 1607 as a defence against the bulk of the civil findings.
It is not clear whether Calderón denied the criminal findings; Juderías
observes that the investigation's yield on this score 'was surprising in its
insignificance', when 'everyone had believed that Calderón would be
revealed for a monster of iniquity, or at least a regicide'. Since the
generally clement Philip III had reserved to himself the disposition of the
case, there was reason to hope for leniency.[41] And indeed by February
1621 the king may have formed the intention to release Calderón and
perhaps to restore his fortune. Before he could act, though, Philip III fell
ill, dying on 31 March 1621. For Rodrigo Calderón, this was the final
calamity that precipitated his utter ruin. A chronicler recorded that 'as

---

[38] Antonio de León Pinelo, *Anales de Madrid*, ed. P. Fernández Martín (Madrid, 1971),
    p. 222.
[39] Góngora to Francisco del Corral, 20 January 1620, in *Obras poéticas*, III, pp. 167–8.
[40] One source (*Noticias de Madrid, 1621–1627*, ed. A. González Palencia (Madrid, 1942),
    p. 4) reports 280 civil counts. See Novoa, 'Historia de Felipe III', pp. 313–15, for a full
    account of these findings, coloured by the author's sympathy for Calderón.
[41] Juderías, 'Un proceso político', p. 11.

soon as he learned of the death of King Philip III, he knew that his own demise was assured, and said so'.[42]

'Dying, he appeared worthy to live'

The men around the new king – most notably Baltasar de Zúñiga and the count of Olivares – had no love for his father's courtiers or favourites. More important, they meant to inaugurate a new era in the government of the Spanish monarchy. Blaming the old regime for laxity, irresolution and disastrous fiscal malfeasance, they were determined to make a clean break with the past.[43] In the first hours of his reign, Philip IV blocked an attempt by the duke of Lerma to return to court and designated Zúñiga his chief minister. More ominously, 'on the same day that his father died, the king requested the record of the trial of [the marquis of] Siete Iglesias'. Within a week he had met three times with Calderón's judges.[44] The king and his ministers pressed the tribunal to recommend a death sentence and, although one judge held out for clemency, in the end they got their way. John Elliott writes that 'Zúñiga and Olivares had clearly decided that they needed an exemplary victim': what better way to demonstrate that the reformers meant business?[45]

On 9 July 1621 one of the king's secretaries came to Calderón's house to inform the prisoner of his sentences. In the civil case, he was to lose all his titles and privileges and pay fines of 1.25 million ducats. As to the criminal charges, for the murder of Francisco Juara and for 'having obtained His Majesty's *cédulas* through foul means' he was condemned to public execution in the Plaza Mayor of Madrid, along with the confiscation of half his remaining goods. Reportedly, Calderón received the news calmly, indicated that he understood the sentence, and then addressed himself to a crucifix in the room: 'May God be praised! And blessed be Our Lady the Virgin.' Luis de Góngora reported this scene about ten days after the event, noting the sympathy Calderón's demeanour had evoked in the secretary and other eyewitnesses (including his own informant?). Subsequent accounts add to Calderón's response the phrase 'with me, Lord, may your will be done!'. This smacks of retrospective

---

[42] León Pinelo, *Anales de Madrid*, p. 236; see also Novoa, 'Historia de Felipe III', p. 373.

[43] For the definitive account of the agenda of the new regime, see John H. Elliott, *The Count-Duke of Olivares: the Statesman in an Age of Decline* (New Haven, 1986), part I.

[44] Luis de Góngora to Francisco del Corral, 6 April 1621, in *Obras poéticas*, III, p. 186.

[45] Elliott, *Count-Duke of Olivares*, pp. 107–8; Novoa, 'Historia de Felipe III', pp. 370–4; see also Juderías, 'Un proceso político', p. 13.

mythmaking but in drawing a parallel with Christ (Mark 14:36) reveals one facet of the later legend of Rodrigo Calderón.[46]

By some accounts, Calderón had long been pious and subordinated himself to the divine will from the outset of his trial. The evidence adduced in support of previous devotion is unconvincing. One chronicler asserted that Calderón had for years prayed the office of the Virgin and made a daily or even twice-daily examination of conscience; another contended that in order to avoid vain ostentation 'in the years of his prosperity' he had kept his generous almsgiving secret.[47] Novoa claimed that before his arrest in 1619, he had consulted a spiritual adviser in Valladolid, who 'said to him that if he wanted to risk his eternal salvation he should flee, but that if he wished to be saved he should stand his ground and suffer the travails that were in store for him'.[48] In any case, the resignation and pious exaltation with which he heard his sentence set the tone for the brief remainder of Rodrigo Calderón's life. He allowed an appeal to go forward only to ease the conscience of his attorney. The appeal failed, along with an attempt to recuse some of the judges on grounds of personal animosity. Notified on 1 October of this final legal setback, Calderón once again reacted only with thanks to God.[49]

With his long experience of the politics of the court, Calderón could not have held out much hope for the success of his appeals or for clemency from a young king surrounded by Zúñiga, Olivares and their allies. Meanwhile, the friends of his days of glory had little influence with the new rulers of Spain, and seem anyway to have been disinclined to intervene. In verse the count of Villamediana suggested, plausibly, that Calderón alive posed a threat to his former associates:

> The nightingale is in a cage
> With shackles that are stinging.
> And his friends at this stage
> Prefer him mute to singing.[50]

---

[46] *Noticias de Madrid*, pp. 4–5 provides a clear account of the sentence. For Calderón's response, Góngora to Francisco del Corral, 20 July 1621, *Obras poéticas*, III, p. 198. Two accounts including the additional phrase are Novoa, 'Historia de Felipe III', p. 374, and Gascón de Torquemada, quoted in Juderías, 'Un proceso político', p. 15. There is a discrepancy in the dating of this event, with Novoa stating that Calderón was notified on 14 July.

[47] Juderías, 'Un proceso político', pp. 18–19; Novoa, 'Historia de Felipe III', p. 378.

[48] Novoa, 'Historia de Felipe III', p. 165.

[49] *Ibid.*, pp. 375–6; Quevedo, 'Grandes anales', p. 208; Góngora to Francisco del Corral, 20 July 1621, *Obras poéticas*, III, p. 198.

[50] Juan de Tassis y Peralta, count of Villamediana, 'A don Rodrigo Calderón, estando preso', in *Poetas líricos*, p. 161.

256 *James M. Boyden*

Whether prompted by these considerations or from genuine piety, from the moment when he learned his sentence Don Rodrigo seems to have devoted his energies to Christian preparation for death and the afterlife. In Quevedo's words, 'he transcended the prospects of this life and began to commune with ultimate realities shorn of the veil of worldly vanities'.[51] Seeking a spiritual adviser, he sent a message to the famous Jesuit preacher Jerónimo de Florencia asking him to attend and console him in his prison. The Jesuit declined, a predictable response given that he had recently been chosen to serve on the Junta de Reformación; this commission, a pet project of the new regime, had been tasked to restore public morality and, in the king's words, 'to uproot vices and abuses and bribery'. Calderón's execution was part of this agenda, and easing his passage to the next life evidently was not.[52] After this rebuff, Calderón turned with greater success to Fray Gabriel del Santísimo Sacramento, the *procurador general* of the Discalced Carmelites, who agreed to act as his confessor. In the weeks leading up to Calderón's execution, other Discalced Carmelites would aid in his spiritual direction, joined after a time by Fray Gregorio de Pedrosa, a Hieronymite and royal preacher. Despite a longtime friendship with the condemned man, Pedrosa initially refused his plea for help. In the prevailing atmosphere, ambitious clerics might well have been reluctant to associate with Rodrigo Calderón.[53]

Under this primarily Carmelite direction, Calderón spent the late summer and early autumn in a devotional frenzy. To atone for the vanity and luxury of his earlier life, he quit trimming his hair and beard, and slept fully dressed on a leather pallet on the floor. To mortify the flesh, he wore hair cloth on his torso and arms and a crucifix pegged to his chest. He fasted three days a week, directing that his food should be distributed to the poor, and otherwise ate little besides broth and eggs. By day, he heard mass, made frequent confessions, and alternated between prayer, reading devotional books and discussing spiritual matters with attending clerics. By night, he slept for brief periods under his cloak, devoting most of the hours before morning to more devotional reading, physical 'disciplines' and silent prayer punctuated by exclamations of remorse for his sins. His preferred reading was a hagiography of Teresa of Avila, along with the saint's own writings, hardly a surprising choice under Carmelite tutelage. Reportedly he recited whole passages from memory, and was

---

51 Quevedo, 'Grandes anales', p. 208.
52 For Florencia's refusal, Góngora to Francisco del Corral, 20 July 1621, in *Obras poéticas*, III, p. 198; for the Junta and its mission, Elliott, *Count-Duke of Olivares*, pp. 104–5.
53 Góngora to Francisco del Corral, 20 July 1621, *Obras poéticas*, III, p. 198; Novoa, 'Historia de Felipe III', p. 375; Quevedo, 'Grandes anales', p. 208.

also much affected by Molina's *Oración*; Calderón could doubtless take comfort in a Molinist interpretation of his situation as a providential opportunity to accept divine grace.[54]

On the morning of 20 October 1621, the magistrate Pedro Fernández de Mansilla directed the constables under his command to stand ready to carry out Calderón's execution on the following day. He also ordered the clearing of commercial stalls from the Plaza Mayor and the erection of a scaffold. Evidently this notification had been conveyed to the Discalced Carmelites on the evening of 19 October, since Fray Pedro de la Concepción appeared at Calderón's house at midnight. He found the condemned man praying in silence. Calderón could have had little doubt about the meaning of this visit, particularly when the friar began a discourse on 'the miseries of human existence and the satisfactions of everlasting life'. Asked whether any sensible being would not gladly exchange his temporal being for eternal life, Calderón purportedly responded that 'I would gladly give up not just one, but a thousand lives for God.' The friar judged this the right moment to come forward with his news. Manifesting devotion, Calderón simply repeated three times: 'with me, Lord, may your will be done'. He spent the rest of the night in prayer and earnest spiritual colloquy with Fray Pedro.[55]

In the sources that have come down to us, Calderón's last thirty-six hours comprise a representation of the good death, intensified by references to martyrdom. Of course, the condemned man's circumstances diverged from those described in the *ars moriendi* literature, most obviously in that in his case a healthy man faced a certain hour of death. Otherwise the parallels are unmistakable. At least from the date of his sentencing, Calderón had put aside the illusory hopes of earthly existence to prepare himself for the climactic passage to the afterlife. 'They have taken from me my father, my wife, my sons, my wealth, my honour, and tomorrow they will take my life', he remarked on the evening of 20 October to the Carmelite Juan de la Madre de Dios. 'Of all this I have come to believe that it is very little in comparison to relinquishing God.' The friar added his gloss: 'loving Him more than anything he was no longer tormented by the memory of losing everything, but only concerned that his death should provide an example so that others might live

---

[54] For this devotional regimen, see Novoa, 'Historia de Felipe III', pp. 374ff., and the other near-contemporary accounts excerpted in Juderías, 'Un proceso político', pp. 17–19.

[55] 'Relación de lo sucedido en la ejecución de la sentencia que se dió a don Rodrigo Calderón, miércoles y jueves, veinte y veintiún del mes de octubre de 1621', in *La historia de España en sus documentos: el siglo XVII*, ed. Fernando Díaz-Plaja (Madrid, 1957), p. 96; Novoa, 'Historia de Felipe III', pp. 376–7.

in a way that would lead them to salvation'.[56] In his devotional regimen, he contemplated and grieved for his sins, and simultaneously reinforced his hope in Christ's redemptive grace. The Carmelites had offered the rather Molinist assurance that 'God reserves great rewards to those wise enough to make fruitful use of their sufferings, offering Him their travails in recognition of His holy Passion.'[57]

These were steps towards the good death, delineated for example in the influential Castilian *ars moriendi* treatise, the *Agonía del tránsito de la muerte* (1536) of Alejo Venegas (or Vanegas). On his way to death, Calderón also performed more concrete actions of the sort recommended by Venegas.[58] On the morning of 20 October, he confessed and drew up a testament disposing of 2,000 ducats, which by terms of his sentence had been left in his power for this purpose. The mandatory bequests to the poor and back wages for a page who had served him in prison nearly exhausted this sum, and Calderón had to commend the support of his family to his father.[59] Without property, Don Rodrigo could make few provisions for his soul, but Fray Juan de la Madre de Dios offered him various suffrages – masses, rosaries, fasts and prayers, until his release from Purgatory – on behalf of the Discalced Carmelites. Then he took communion – the *viaticum* – at the climax of 'a mass of the Holy Mother Teresa de Jesús' said for him by Fray Gabriel del Santísimo Sacramento. As he awaited the host, he exclaimed 'Lord, just as You come to me today I will go to You tomorrow.' Restlessly Calderón continued his devotions through the night, and even when pressed by the priests to lie down he continued to contemplate the crucifix and an image of Teresa of Avila. Towards morning, he asked one of the friars whether he would be given extreme unction and was told that 'it was not the custom of the Church to give [that sacrament] to those who die in this way'. This heartless doctrine was explained by Robert Bellarmine in a nearly contemporaneous tract as arising from the fact that extreme unction often acted to restore its beneficiaries to health, a manifestation of grace that would be inappropriate in the case of a condemned criminal. Calderón, unfazed, asked the friar to explain the last rites to him anyway.[60]

Venegas, like other writers in this genre, warned against the final

---

[56] Novoa, 'Historia de Felipe III', p. 379.   [57] *Ibid.*, p. 377.

[58] Full title: *Agonía del tránsito de la muerte con los avisos y consuelos que cerca della son provechosos*; the Alcalá de Henares edition of 1565 is reprinted in *Escritores místicos españoles*, ed. Miguel Mir (Madrid, 1911), i, pp. 105–318. For discussion of this text and its influence, see Eire, *From Madrid to Purgatory*, pp. 27–8 and *passim*.

[59] Juderías, 'Un proceso político', pp. 20–2.

[60] Novoa, 'Historia de Felipe III', pp. 377–80; Robert Bellarmine, 'The Art of Dying Well'

temptations facing the dying person, and Calderón seems to have striven to resist these occasions of sin. He steered a careful path between the twin shoals of despair and overconfidence regarding salvation. 'His fear [of the Lord] was no less than his confidence,' Novoa wrote, '[and these] sensations are equally ingratiating to God, since fear indicates humility and recognition of one's own wretchedness, while confidence signifies a glorious affirmation of His power and mercy.'[61] Don Rodrigo also evinced a concern lest he succumb to the temptation of vainglory by flaunting his devotions. Thus he concealed his fasting from his guards, and removed his hair shirts before leaving his prison on his final journey to the Plaza Mayor. Novoa intended no irony when he wrote that 'there was no better proof of his virtues than the dissimulation and circumspection with which he exercised them'.[62] At the very end on the scaffold, one of the priests counselled him against another temptation, saying 'calm yourself, for the demon is abroad here trying to disquiet you'.[63]

All of the narratives attest to the remarkable composure and gentle resignation that Calderón demonstrated throughout the grim procession to the Plaza Mayor and on the scaffold itself. When *alcalde* Fernández de Mansilla and the constables arrived at 11.30 a.m. on 21 October to take him from his prison to the place of execution, Don Rodrigo stepped to the street without hesitation and spoke to them in a strong voice, acquiescing in their requests for his pardon and asking them in turn to pardon him. Then the executioner brought him the black mule that he was to ride, and Calderón mounted 'in a manly and spirited fashion'. The former courtier's long unkempt beard and the untrimmed locks streaming from his cap made a powerful impression of humility (see Plate 13.1). Calderón gripped his crucifix as the procession set off to the sound of tolling bells and the criers' repeated proclamation of his crimes and the punishment assessed by the king's justice, ending with the chilling traditional formula: 'He who does such [deeds], thus shall he pay [their price] (*quien tal hace que tal pague*).' In Novoa's highly sympathetic account, at the sight of Calderón's bravery and devotion tears overcame the crowds that lined the way and the officers of the procession itself. Even the relatively dispassionate chronicler who drafted the contemporary

---

(1619), in *Spiritual Writings*, ed. and tr. J. P. Donnelly and R. J. Teske (New York, 1989), p. 350.

[61] Novoa, 'Historia de Felipe III', p. 377; for this temptation, Venegas, *Agonía*, pp. 147–9.

[62] Novoa, 'Historia de Felipe III', pp. 377, 380; for the temptation of vainglory, Venegas, *Agonía*, pp. 149–57.

[63] Quoted in Juderías, 'Un proceso político', p. 26; for demonic interference with the dying person, Venegas, *Agonía*, pp. 169–73.

Plate 13.1   *Rodrigo Calderón at the time of his execution. Artist unknown.*

relación of the event asserted that, as the procession approached the Plaza Mayor, 'great lamentations of grief and compassion' erupted from the 'numberless crowd' witnessing the spectacle.[64] Reacting to the compassion of the crowd, Calderón said to his confessor that far from feeling shamed by being paraded through the streets, 'this is following in the steps of my Lord Jesus Christ, better said, this is to go in triumph, since Christ was blasphemed by all while everyone is commending me to God'.[65]

In the Plaza Mayor the constables had to force a passage through the crush of onlookers to reach the scaffold. Once halted there, Calderón dismounted under the eyes of the crowd filling the balconies, and, holding his crucifix before him, resolutely climbed the steps to the platform. On the way, he remarked to the Hieronymite Pedrosa that 'since we are going to lose the body, let's save the soul'. Atop the scaffold

---

[64] 'Relación de lo sucedido', pp. 96–7; Novoa, 'Historia de Felipe III', pp. 381–3.
[65] Novoa, 'Historia de Felipe III', p. 383.

he made a final confession and upon being absolved prostrated himself and thrice kissed the floorboards. He arose, walked calmly to the chair where he would die, and sat down, all the while conversing with the priests 'about matters of his salvation'. The executioner approached, tied Calderón's arms, legs and torso to the chair, and asked his forgiveness. Don Rodrigo obliged, and kissed the executioner's cheek in token of peace.[66] Fray Gabriel reportedly observed 'that they had bound Christ as well, and with this he began to recite commemorations of the passion of Jesus Christ'.[67] Calderón's composure seems to have faltered only once, when after being blindfolded he reacted in fear that the executioner would slash his throat from behind, rather than face to face as befitted his status as a nobleman and knight of Santiago. Reassured on this point, he again objected in a firm voice when the executioner grasped the blindfold in his left hand to hold the prisoner's head up as he cut his throat with the knife in his right hand. 'Don't pull,' he said, 'I'll stay still.' Then the blow fell, 'and repeating the sweet name of Jesus, he gave up the ghost' at 12.30 p.m.[68]

Calderón's body was displayed on the scaffold until nightfall. At eight o'clock, with the assistance of a *beata*, the executioner stripped and shrouded the body, which was placed in a coffin and borne through the streets in a candlelit procession including a number of clerics and the members of three confraternities. According to one source, a number of lords and gentlemen wanted to assist in the burial but were forbidden by royal order, which stipulated as well that Calderón's body should be taken to the churchyard of San Ginés and deposited with the corpses of other executed criminals. The cortège, followed by 'many people of the lower sort, as well as coaches, with people in the streets to watch it pass', ended up at San Ginés only briefly, if at all. Then it was diverted to the Discalced Carmelite house, or at least Calderón's remains arrived there at some point during the evening. The coffin was placed in a vault in the chapel of the Chapter, 'where today may be seen a tomb draped in black cloth and the habit of Santiago'. The honours granted Calderón in defiance of express orders may have led to the arrest of the constables in charge of the funeral procession.[69]

---

[66] 'Relación de lo sucedido', pp. 97–8.
[67] Novoa, 'Historia de Felipe III', p. 386.
[68] *Ibid.*, p. 387; Juderías, 'Un proceso político', p. 27; 'Relación de lo sucedido', p. 98.
[69] 'Relación de lo sucedido', p. 98; León Pinelo, *Anales de Madrid*, p. 238; Quevedo, 'Grandes anales', p. 210.

Conclusions

Rodrigo Calderón's demeanour, and the reaction that it provoked, badly blurred the message that the government of Philip IV had hoped to convey through his execution. Olivares must have bristled at the message he received from the duke of Alba, asserting that at the Plaza Mayor he had seen 'not just a Roman dying, but a Roman and an Apostle combined'. The reform programme of the new regime included, besides its desire to expunge the misdeeds of the previous reign, the intention to reform customs and behaviour in the direction of the neo-Tacitean Christian stoicism of thinkers like Justus Lipsius.[70] Now on the scaffold where he was to pay for the misdeeds of a corrupt administration, the odious creature of the duke of Lerma had co-opted the virtues of the reformers. As John Elliott concludes, Zúñiga and Olivares had 'miscalculated badly' in their choice of a victim; 'the ritual murder planned by the new regime to serve as a symbol of cleansing and regeneration brought only a massive condemnation'.[71]

In death, Rodrigo Calderón attracted a level of admiration and approbation that he had never known in life. Great lords honoured the parvenu by endowing masses for his soul, while religious houses vied to donate additional suffrages.[72] The celebrated writers of the age – among them Lope de Vega, Luis de Góngora, the count of Villamediana, Francisco de Quevedo and Francisco López de Zárate – composed eulogies to honour the executed favourite.[73] Quevedo, while eulogising Calderón himself, had nothing but scorn for other poets whom he accused of castigating the dead man during his trial only to write fawning epitaphs after his death, 'crying like crocodiles for what they have

---

[70] For Alba's message, see Novoa, 'Historia de Felipe III', p. 390; for the influence of Lipsius on Olivares, see *Memoriales y cartas del Conde Duque de Olivares*, ed. John H. Elliott and José F. de la Peña (Madrid, 1978), I, pp. xlvii–xlix, and John H. Elliott, 'Quevedo and the Count-Duke of Olivares', in his *Spain and its World, 1500–1700: Selected Essays* (New Haven, 1989), pp. 199–200.

[71] Elliott, *Count-Duke of Olivares*, p. 108.

[72] Juderías, 'Un proceso político', p. 29.

[73] In addition to the specific poems cited below, see Lope de Vega y Carpio, 'A un cadahalso', in *Obras poéticas*, ed. José Manuel Blecua (Barcelona, 1969), I, pp. 1307–8; Luis de Góngora, 'En la muerte de don Rodrigo Calderón', and 'De las muertes de don Rodrigo Calderón, del conde de Villamediana y conde de Lemus', in *Sonetos completos*, ed. Bibuté Ciplijauskaité (Madrid, 1969), pp. 218, 221; Francisco de Quevedo, 'En la muerte de don Rodrigo Calderón', in *Obras en verso*, ed. Luis Astrana Marín (Madrid, 1932), p. 466; Francisco López de Zárate, 'Al marqués de Siete Iglesias don Rodrigo Calderón en su sepulcro', in José María Lope Toledo, *El poeta Francisco López de Zárate* (Logroño, 1954), p. 56.

eaten'.[74] As a blanket judgement this is unfair – López de Zárate for one had been loyal to his patron Calderón. Quevedo's comment does, however, suggest that the outpouring of poetic eulogies should be seen at least in part as a response to a post-mortem re-evaluation of Rodrigo Calderón and a perceived public taste for praise of the dead man. Beyond this, and beyond the rather imprecise evidence of grieving crowds at the execution or accompanying the cortège, the classic proof of the posthumous repute of Rodrigo Calderón is that his name entered the Castilian language in a variant pair of idiomatic expressions. 'To conduct oneself more honourably than Don Rodrigo on the scaffold (*andar más honrado que don Rodrigo en la horca*)', or 'to be prouder than Don Rodrigo on the gallows (*tener más orgullo que don Rodrigo en la horca*)' remained bywords long after Calderón himself had been forgotten.[75]

These expressions encapsulate one aspect of the posthumous adulation accorded Rodrigo Calderón. Those who saw or heard about his conduct on the day of execution were impressed by Calderón's bravery, by the concern for honour he had displayed in insisting upon receiving the death blow from the front, and by his spirit and self-control throughout the ordeal. His comportment had reflected some of the key secular values of an aristocratic culture. It seems, however, that Calderón's enactment of the good death sanctioned by Catholic doctrine and tradition was no less impressive to those who honoured his memory. Villamediana's incisive memorial sonnet, for example, focuses on Don Rodrigo's transformation by virtue of a good death:

> . . . Living, he seemed deserving of death
> dying, he appeared worthy to live . . .
> If his glories brought him to grief
> His griefs restored him to Glory.[76]

One of Góngora's sonnets uses the metaphor of the phoenix, with its obvious Christian implications, to eulogise Calderón. Like Villamediana, Góngora sees Calderón's death as the supreme validation of his life:

> Lacking a flame, the knife purged your former being.
> Gloriously reborn in your spurting blood, donning wings

---

[74] Quevedo, 'Grandes anales', p. 210.

[75] *Ibid.*, editor's note 'b', p. 209; and Bartolomé Bennassar, *The Spanish Character: Attitudes and Mentalities from the Sixteenth to the Nineteenth Century*, tr. Benjamin Keen (Berkeley, 1979), pp. 11–12.

[76] Juan de Tassis y Peralta, count of Villamediana, 'A la muerte de don Rodrigo Calderón', in *Obras*, ed. Juan Manuel Rozas (Madrid, 1980), p. 378.

Not of vulgar fame but of Christian valour and burning faith;
For this you will thank your tomb more than life's abodes.[77]

Much of Novoa's narrative is of course couched in the rhetoric of the good death; he refers specifically to Calderón's acceptance 'that to die well is the greatest happiness' and even asserts, as some eulogists of Philip II had done in celebrating the king's exemplary death, that Calderón's end could instruct the world in the truth of Catholicism.[78]

Ironically, it is likely that public knowledge of Calderón's intense devotion owed much to the efforts of Discalced Carmelites in a cause warmly supported by the count-duke of Olivares. As Calderón prepared for death under the supervision of a Discalced Carmelite confessor and spiritual advisers, canonisation proceedings were underway in Rome for Teresa of Avila, the order's greatest figure. She would be canonised by Gregory XV on 12 March 1622. More significantly, the Discalced Carmelites were determined that Teresa should become patron saint of Spain in place of Santiago. First steps in that process had followed closely upon Teresa's beatification by Paul V in 1614. Under Carmelite influence, Philip III had prevailed upon the pope in 1618 to designate her as co-patron with Santiago. According to Américo Castro, Santiago retained the support of the bulk of the population, while 'the salons favoured Theresa [*sic*]'. This distinction is too facile, given that Quevedo was among the most outspoken advocates of the traditional Apostle, but it is true that Teresian sentiment was strong at the highest levels of the court. The Discalced Carmelites hoped to take advantage of this situation to have Teresa made sole national patron. The count-duke himself enthusiastically endorsed the 1626 decision of the *cortes* of Castile to support Teresa's cause. Rivalry between the partisans of the two saints, quite sharp throughout the 1620s, intensified after the apparent victory of the Teresians in 1627, when Urban VIII adjudicated the patronage to the Avilan saint. The ensuing controversy ended only with a papal compromise ensuring a sort of local option co-patronage in 1630.[79]

As the story of Rodrigo Calderón's spiritual journey has come down to us, primarily in Novoa's detailed reconstruction, Teresa of Avila played a very prominent role in his preparation for a good death. He found great solace in her hagiography and her devotional writings, prayed before her

---

[77] Luis de Góngora, 'Al mismo' (1621), in *Sonetos completos*, p. 219.
[78] Novoa, 'Historia de Felipe III', pp. 380, 388.
[79] Américo Castro, *The Spaniards: an Introduction to their History*, tr. W. F. King and S. Margaretten (Berkeley, 1971), pp. 456–66 (quotation at p. 463); Elliott, *Count-Duke of Olivares*, pp. 323–4.

comforting image, and received his final communion during a mass in her honour. On his last morning, according to Novoa, Calderón asked a Discalced Carmelite who was about to say mass for him to remember, when he immersed part of the host in the chalice, 'that he should place his soul [in the chalice] along with it and soak it in His precious blood'. 'This', Novoa continued, 'was a most glorious imitation of the Holy Mother Teresa of Jesus', who had done the same and been miraculously rewarded with a mouthful of blood as sweet as nectar.[80] As the friars might have seen it, the conversion of a hard case like Calderón into a model of Christian resignation could only enhance Teresa's reputation as a powerful friend to Spanish souls. It would be surprising if Calderón's Discalced Carmelite advisers had not publicised his devotions and the details of his good death.[81]

Finally, the good death and posthumous commemoration of Rodrigo Calderón perhaps speaks to the strength of ingrained cultural models relative to the power of activist rulers to shape public opinion. Concluding his analysis of the exemplary death of Philip II, Carlos Eire asserts that 'what I hope to have shown here is the way in which structures of meaning and structures of power are dynamically interrelated, how the mythopoeic process surrounding Philip's death *both* expressed and shaped the collective mentality'.[82] Enacting his good death, Philip had worked from a cultural script that was second nature for the king and his subjects alike. The laudation of his death as exemplary reaffirmed the authority of this script while it enlisted a strong cultural sanction for a favourable retrospective assessment of the king's actions in life. A generation later, the government of Philip IV set out to portray Rodrigo Calderón as the criminal embodiment of all that had been wrong with the previous reign, and to stage his cautionary death to dramatise a clean break with the past and as a warning to similar malefactors. In the event, though, this hideous theatre of state power could not impose its message on a populace that saw instead a convincing representation of behaviours long endorsed in the culture of Catholic and aristocratic Castile. Despite powerful prompting, the audience witnessed, not the king's righteous justice, but instead the heroism of a brave and honourable hidalgo who traversed a Madrilenian *via dolorosa* to its terminus in an exemplary Christian death.

---

[80] Novoa, 'Historia de Felipe III', p. 381.
[81] It is possible that the Carmelite Fray Pedro de la Madre de Dios identified by Quevedo as an active advocate for Teresa's designation as patron could be the Fray Juan de la Madre de Dios who figured among Calderón's advisers. Francisco de Quevedo, 'Memorial por el patronato de Santiago, y por todos los santos naturales de España, en favor de la elección de Cristo nuestro Señor', in *Obras*, I, p. 234.
[82] Eire, *From Madrid to Purgatory*, p. 367.

14 Tokens of innocence: infant baptism, death and burial in early modern England

Will Coster

The function of a rite of passage, as envisaged by Arnold van Gennep in the opening decade of the twentieth century, was to facilitate and mark the life-course transformations between the different rooms that made up the house of community.[1] But these rites were not as independent from each other as this model of ritual implies. Under pre-industrial demographic conditions, death all too often travelled close behind birth. In such circumstances, the idealised fabric of ritual separation, purification and incorporation could be distorted and potential conflicts and dilemmas created. Furthermore, these rites cannot be separated from the beliefs that underpinned and accompanied them.[2] When these rituals and ideas underwent a process of transformation, or attack, these distortions were all the more acute. The focus of this investigation is one such dilemma, the fate of children who died before baptism, in an era of religious change and debate, the Reformation in England.

If ritual can be seen as the place within the profane where individuals experience the sacred, it is also true that the ceremonials of the Church are the point at which the historiography of the social meets that of the religious.[3] The seismic shift in the study of late medieval and early modern religion over the last twenty years has brought these two historiographies closer together, and has emphasised the integration of society with religious practice, particularly in the pre-Reformation

I am grateful to Professor Claire Cross, Dr Ralph Houlbrooke and Dr Peter Marshall for reading and commenting on earlier drafts of this paper.

[1] A. van Gennep, *The Rites of Passage* (Chicago, 1960).
[2] See the important comments in R. Horton, *Ritual Man in Africa* (London, 1964), p. 655.
[3] R. Scribner, 'Cosmic Order and Daily Life: Sacred and Secular in Pre-Industrial German Society', in his *Popular Culture and Popular Movements in Reformation Germany* (London and Ronceverte, 1987), p. 2.

period.[4] This in turn raises questions about the means by which change was achieved, whether, in Christopher Haigh's phraseology, 'from above' or 'from below', and also about the speed with which such transformations were accomplished.[5] Increasingly, historians have begun to look to the concept of the 'Long Reformation' to explain the process of religious metamorphosis that was arguably still underway in the seventeenth century.[6] The transformation of rites of passage may have touched the laity more closely than any of the theological and ritual changes brought about by the Reformation in England. It is the contention of this chapter that attempting to trace reactions to perhaps the most intimate and poignant of these changes, the status and commemoration of dead infants, can take us some way towards an understanding of the speed with which reformation permeated society, between the break with Rome and the restoration of the Stuart monarchy in 1660.

The study of rites of passage is also part of the burgeoning historiography of the family. One of the major methodological approaches to this aspect of social history, concentrating on biographical and literary sources to gain an impression of the emotional world of individuals in pre-industrial England, has been closely associated with a view of family relationships which can be summarised as pessimistic.[7] In particular, the vicissitudes of pre-industrial demography, especially high infant mortality, have been seen as creating circumstances in which, to quote Lawrence Stone, 'it was very rash for parents to get too emotionally concerned about creatures whose expectation of life was so very low'.[8] This thesis has been firmly rejected by many historians working in the field, who have uncovered evidence of the frequent warmth of such relationships.[9] However, it remains generally accepted, even by these revisionists, that it took time for affection to develop between parent and child and that very young children were not the subjects of extended mourning or a deep sense of loss.[10]

---

[4] Most effectively in E. Duffy, *The Stripping of the Altars: Traditional Religion in England 1400–1580* (New Haven, 1992), pp. 11–52.

[5] C. Haigh, 'The Recent Historiography of the English Reformation', in Haigh (ed.), *The English Reformation Revised* (Cambridge, 1987), pp. 19–33.

[6] N. Tyacke (ed.), *England's Long Reformation, 1500–1800* (London, 1998).

[7] M. Anderson, *Approaches to the History of the European Family 1500–1914* (London, 1980), pp. 39–45.

[8] L. Stone, *The Family, Sex and Marriage in England, 1500–1800* (London, 1977), p. 70. See also P. Ariès, *Centuries of Childhood* (London, 1962).

[9] Particularly by L. Pollock, *Forgotten Children: Parent–Child Relationships from 1500 to 1900* (Cambridge, 1983).

[10] R. Houlbrooke, *The English Family 1450–1700* (London, 1984), p. 136; and C. Gittings, *Death, Burial and the Individual in Early Modern England* (London, 1984), p. 81.

Nonetheless, reactions to the loss of newborn children among the people of the past remains an under-researched topic, partly because the diaries and letters of early modern individuals, already confined largely to the middling sort and the higher orders, are so often silent on the subject.

An alternative means of entering this world of private emotion is through an investigation of responses to the 'economy of the sacred' evidenced in the rituals that defined social and familial structures.[11] While the constancy of human psychology can be debated, what the historian can illuminate are the specific circumstances in which individuals in the past found themselves, and their ability to reject, accept and adapt to them. To this end, this chapter will examine the theological debates surrounding the fate of infants, the associated symbolism of baptism, its use in the iconography of memorials, the changing meanings of terms applied to children and the reasons for and significance of these changes. Much effort has been spent investigating the magical properties of, and participation in, these rites, but there has been little interest in reactions to this fundamental change in the soteriology of early modern England, and the redrawing of the lines between salvation and damnation, purity and corruption.

It is hardly surprising that pioneering historians of the family were pessimistic about attitudes to children in the past, given the teaching of the medieval church on the fate of unbaptised infants.[12] Nevertheless, despite the widespread acceptance of St Augustine's emphasis on the necessity of baptism to expunge original sin, in both the eastern and western medieval churches, its logical corollary, that many infants were doomed to eternal torment, was a concept that some struggled to accept.[13] More commonly, in the scheme of late medieval Catholicism they were assigned not to Hell, but to Limbo.[14] However, it is debatable to what degree the common people of early modern Europe understood the finer points of late medieval eschatology. Certainly, the rulings of church councils suggest that the interval between birth and baptism shortened between the twelfth and fifteenth centuries, perhaps as a result

---

[11] Scribner, 'Cosmic Order and Daily Life', p. 1.

[12] G. G. Coulton, *Infant Perdition in the Middle Ages* (London, 1922). R. De Simon, 'Modern Research on Saint Augustine's Doctrine of Original Sin', *Augustinian Studies* 11 (1980), pp. 205–28, provides a useful survey of the debates.

[13] J. Baun, 'The Fate of Babies Dying before Baptism in Byzantium', in D. Wood (ed.), *The Church and Childhood*, Studies in Church History, 31 (Oxford, 1994), pp. 115–25.

[14] St Thomas Aquinas, *Summa Theologica* (55 vols., London, 1963), LII, 3a, q52, 7, pp. 173–7. See Peter Marshall's chapter in this volume.

of growing popular concerns over the fate of unbaptised children.[15] Moreover, some elements of the baptismal rite, most obviously the exorcism of the child, indicated an extreme view of original sin. In the Sarum Use, the priest addressed the Devil directly, saying, 'I exorcise thee, unclean spirit, in the name of God the Father, and of the Son, and of the Holy Ghost, that thou come out and depart from this servant of God.'[16] The implication of demonic possession, or bewitchment of the newborn, can hardly have eased anxieties about the post-mortem fate of children or the need for baptism.[17] References to unbaptised infants being buried away from the general community, outside of the church; or only in the north aisle; outside of the churchyard; or in a separate corner, all point to concerns over their spiritual status.[18]

Despite the elaborately formed nature of the late medieval rites, all that was actually necessary for baptism was for a child to be touched with water in the name of the Father, Son and Holy Ghost. John Mirk's *Instructions for Parish Priests*, written in the fourteenth century, and widely used in the fifteenth, urged midwives to have clean water ready in case the life of the child was in danger and such baptism became necessary.[19] On the eve of the Reformation, dislike of delay is evident in complaints against members of the clergy. For example, around 1535, one of the laments of the parishioners of Wembury in Devon was that, when a priest was summoned from the Prior of Plympton to baptise a sick child, a delay of eight hours meant the child had already died before he arrived.[20]

The beginnings of disintegration in this theology can be seen in the years following Henry VIII's break with Rome. The *Bishops' Book*, issued in 1537, underlined the doctrine of original sin, stressing the efficacy of baptism in salvation, 'inasmuch as infants and children dying in their infancy shall undoubtedly be saved thereby, and else not'.[21] However, the final clause of this sentence was notable by its absence from the generally more conservative *King's Book*, issued six years later, leaving open the

---

[15] J. D. C. Fisher, *Christian Initiation: Baptism in the Medieval West. A Study of the Disintegration of the Primitive Rite of Initiation* (London, 1965), pp. 109–12.

[16] *Ibid.*, p. 162.

[17] J. Bossy, *Christianity in the West, 1400–1700* (Oxford, 1985), p. 14.

[18] J. Schmitt, *Ghosts in the Middle Ages: the Living and the Dead in Medieval Society*, tr. T. L. Fagan (Chicago and London, 1998), p. 183; C. Daniell, *Death and Burial in Medieval England 1066–1550* (London, 1997), pp. 103–9.

[19] G. Kristenson (ed.), *John Mirk's Instructions for Parish Priests* (London, 1974), p. 209. See also K. Thomas, *Religion and the Decline of Magic: Studies in Popular Beliefs in Sixteenth- and Seventeenth-Century England* (London, 1971), p. 41.

[20] J. Youings, *The Dissolution of the Monasteries* (London, 1971), p. 140.

[21] J. D. C. Fisher, *Christian Initiation, the Reformation Period* (London, 1970), p. 74.

possibility that unbaptised children could be saved.[22] This was taken slightly further in the first Edwardian Prayer Book of 1549. At the beginning of the baptismal ceremony, the priest was to stress that 'all men bee conceyved and borne in sinne, and that no manne borne in sinne, can enter the kingdom of God (except that he be regenerate, and borne anewe of water, and the holy ghost)'.[23] But there was also a somewhat contra-dictory emphasis on the public nature of baptism, 'wherfore the people are to be admonished, that it is moste conveniente that baptisme shoulde not be ministered but upon Sondayes and other holy dayes, when the most number of people maye come together'.[24] This emphasis introduced the potential for delay, and thus undermined the imperative nature of the rite. To a population still being taught the necessity of baptism, this must have been an alarming development. The point was not lost on the western rebels of 1549, one of whose articles stated that 'we will that our curates shall minister the sacrament of baptism at all times as well in the week-day as the holy-day'.[25]

This rubric was maintained in the 1552 and 1559 Prayer Books, but the theological formula eventually settled upon by the established church further played down the significance of the sacrament. The *Thirty-nine Articles* argued, along Calvinist lines, that the sacrament of baptism was not 'absolutely', but only 'formally' necessary for salvation, conceiving it as a means by which 'faith is confirmed and grace increased'.[26] Confusingly, the liturgy of the Church retained a ceremony of private baptism 'in tyme of necessitie', and the canons of 1604 set out a penalty of suspension for three weeks if a cleric was responsible for a child dying without baptism.[27] Yet, in a cosmology shorn of Purgatory and Limbo, those few individuals who continued to take the concept of original sin to its logical conclusion were preaching a hard gospel indeed. It is scarcely surprising that the vicar of Ashford in Kent, who asserted in 1569 that children dying without baptism were 'firebrands of Hell', was reported by his churchwardens.[28]

---

22   *Ibid.*, p. 77.
23   *The First and Second Prayer Books of Edward VI* (London, 1952), p. 236.
24   *Ibid.*
25   J. E. Cox (ed.), *Miscellaneous Writings and Letters of Thomas Cranmer* (Cambridge, 1846), p. 175. For commentary, see A. R. Greenwood, 'A Study of the Rebel Petitions of 1549' (University of Manchester PhD thesis, 1990), pp. 77–9.
26   *The Constitutions and Canons Ecclesiastical (made in the year 1603, and amended in the year 1865), to which are added the Thirty-nine Articles of the Church of England* (London, 1908), pp. 38–9; and G. W. Bromily, *Baptism and the Anglican Reformers* (Bristol, 1953), pp. 58–60.
27   *Constitutions and Canons*, p. 38.
28   A. Hussey, 'Archbishop Parker's Visitation', *Home Counties Magazine* 5 (1903), p. 286.

Similarly, when Richard Baxter at Kidderminster in Worcestershire, in the early 1640s, stated 'that infants before regeneration had so much guilt and corruption as made them loathsome in the eyes of God', he was verbally abused in the street by his parishioners.[29] But such arguments were rarely advanced, and the implication given by the Church of England was that salvation was not imparted by baptism, or as Richard Hooker put it, 'grace is not absolutely tied unto the sacraments'.[30] Although not accepted by all, this marked a fundamental shift in the meaning and significance of the baptismal rite and in the perceived nature of infants.

This transformation can be seen encapsulated in the symbolism of the white baptismal cloth. Changes in the employment of this emblem provide a touchstone for understanding the negotiation between the shifting theological concepts of the period and the hopes and aspirations of the people for their young. This cloth had originally been a strip of material tied on to protect the chrism oil, with which the child was anointed in the medieval baptismal rite. In the ceremony of confirmation, this remained simply a band, but by the fifteenth century, across Europe, in baptism it had become a white sheet or robe. In England this was referred to as the chrisom cloth.[31] In the rite contained in the Sarum Use, it was placed on the child after the final anointing, the priest saying, 'receive a white robe, holy and unstained, which thou must bring before the tribunal of our Lord Jesus Christ that thou mayest have eternal life and live for ever and ever. Amen.'[32] The implications of dressing a child in a white cloth after baptism were made explicit in the 1549 Prayer Book, which instructed the priest to say 'take this white vesture for a token of innocence, which by God's grace in this holy sacrament of baptism is given to thee'.[33]

Whereas the Sarum Use had only observed that the cloth could be

---

[29]   N. H. Keeble (ed.), *The Autobiography of Richard Baxter* (London, 1931), p. 28.

[30]   Richard Hooker, *Of the Laws of Ecclesiastical Polity, the Fifth Book*, ed. R. Bayne (London, 1902), pp. 290–1. For a general discussion, see David Cressy, *Birth, Marriage, and Death: Ritual, Religion, and the Life-cycle in Tudor and Stuart England* (Oxford, 1997), pp. 114–16.

[31]   This must be distinguished from the sheets used to wrap the chrismatory (containing the oil and chrisom) and those used to cover the font after it had been blessed. This was probably what was being referred to in the churchwardens' accounts of Prescot, Lancashire for 1603 where 1d was paid for 'the christening cloth' to be washed. See *The Church-wardens' Accounts of Prescot, Lancashire 1523–1607*, ed. F. A. Bailey, Lancashire and Cheshire Record Society, 104 (1953), p. 60. See also J. C. Cox, *Churchwardens' Accounts, from the Fourteenth to the Close of the Seventeenth Century* (London, 1913), pp. 132, 152–3.

[32]   Fisher, *Baptism in the Medieval West*, p. 174.

[33]   *Prayer Books of Edward VI*, p. 241.

reused and should be brought back to the church, more revealingly the Prayer Book of 1549 instructed 'that the chrisoms be brought to the church and delivered to the priests after the accustomed manner at the purification of the mother of every child'.[34] It is clear from parish registers and churchwardens' accounts that the delay between birth of a child and the ceremony of purification, popularly known as the churching of women, was very close to twenty-eight days.[35] This time period, during which the women enjoyed, or endured, a degree of ritual separation from church and community, is crucial in understanding the significance of this cloth. In a case before the Court of Arches in 1636, it was asserted that at Basingstoke in Hampshire, 'it was an ancient custom . . . that women coming to be churched brought with them a piece of linen cloth which was offered and given to the vicar, but if any child died before the mother's churching it was buried in the said chrisom'.[36] If the linear progression of ritual, from baptism to purification and distant burial, was reordered by the death of the child, the chrisom cloth became the child's shroud, marking it out as destined for Heaven, despite any contagion attached to the mother.

Such a custom throws interesting light on perhaps the most famous English *cause célèbre* of the early sixteenth century, that of Richard Hunne, the merchant tailor and freeman of the city of London, found hanged in the Lollard's Tower in 1514. His earliest known legal entanglement with the church authorities was over the failure to deliver his infant son's winding sheet, which according to Polydore Vergil was 'the linen cloth in which the baby had been wrapped at his baptism', as a mortuary offering after the child's death.[37] Most recent historians have judged Hunne to have been at fault in this matter, and have generally been puzzled by his refusal to surrender an item of little value.[38] One possibility is that, in this case, resentment of clerical exactions was exacerbated by a dislike of the breaking of customs of interment for infants. Whether or not the clergy were entitled to such cloths as

---

[34] Fisher, *Baptism in the Medieval West*, p. 174; *Prayer Books of Edward VI*, pp. 240–1.

[35] W. Coster, 'Purity, Profanity and Puritanism: the Churching of Women 1500–1700', in W. Sheils and D. Woods (eds.), *Women in the Church*, Studies in Church History, 29 (Oxford, 1990), pp. 377–87; J. Boulton, *Neighbourhood and Society: a London Suburb in the Seventeenth Century* (Cambridge, 1987), pp. 276–7.

[36] *Calendar of State Papers, Domestic Series, in the Reign of Charles I, 1636–37*, ed. J. Bruce (London, 1867), p. 274.

[37] Quotation from *The Anglica Historia of Polydore Vergil, AD 1485–1537*, ed. Denys Hay, Camden Society, third series, 74 (1955), p. 74. For the case proceedings see S. F. C. Milsom, 'Richard Hunne's "Praemunire"', *English Historical Review* 76 (1961), p. 80.

[38] S. Brigden, *London and the Reformation* (Oxford, 1989), p. 98.

mortuaries, they clearly did not usually claim them.[39] This may have been because the cloth had a greater significance as an indicator of the removal of original sin through baptism. What this case may demonstrate is not antagonism between custom and self-interest, but between two rival customs.

Antiquarians (and in their wake many historians), with the 1549 Prayer Book in mind, have asserted that such infants, buried after baptism, but before churching, became known as 'chrisom children'.[40] However, others have stated that a chrisom child was one buried before baptism.[41] The term occurs from time to time in English parish registers, particularly in the seventeenth century. Examples, from the burial register of St Martin's, Coney Street, York, for May 1677, are of 'a chrisom child born and buried of Mr Whitekerr, pipemaker, the 27th day', and 'a chrisom child of Mr Lewis Etherington, born and buried the 29th'.[42] In neither case is there a corresponding baptismal entry. The brevity of these lives and the very wording of the entries seems to indicate that these children had not been baptised. Therefore, it seems there are two contradictory views on what a chrisom child was, both with evidence to support their cases. This debate has some significance for students of early modern demography, particularly those interested in infant mortality, but the understanding of the term can also be seen as a means of investigating change in popular religion, in the aftermath of alterations to the baptismal ceremony. An obvious solution to these apparently contradictory views presents itself in the possibility that the term changed its meaning between the publication of the 1549 Prayer Book and the widespread appearance of 'chrisom children' in burial registers of the seventeenth century.

While Luther and Zwingli had preserved the cloth in their baptismal

---

[39] A suggestion made by S. M. Jack, 'The Conflict of Common Law and Canon Law in Sixteenth-Century England: Richard Hunne Revisited', *Parergon*, new series, 3 (1985), pp. 131 and 133.

[40] For antiquarians, see J. C. Cox, *The Parish Registers of England* (London, 1910), p. 59; and T. F. Thiselton-Dyer, *English Social Life as told by Parish Registers* (London, 1895). For historians, see C. Gittings, *Death, Burial and the Individual*, p. 84; J. Litten, *The English Way of Death, the Common Funeral since 1450* (London, 1991), p. 61; Cressy, *Birth, Marriage, and Death*, p. 163.

[41] M. Drake, 'Introduction', in *Population Studies from Parish Registers: a Selection of Readings from Local Population Studies* (Matlock, 1982), p. xxii. For a debate sparked by this article, see E. Morrisson, 'Comment' and note from the editor in *Local Population Studies* 32 (Spring, 1984), pp. 61–2; and a letter from J. J. Greenwood in *Local Population Studies* 33 (Autumn, 1984), p. 71.

[42] *The Parish Register of St Martin Coney Street, York, 1557–1812*, ed. R. B. Cook, Yorkshire Parish Register Society, 36 (1909), p. 116. I am grateful to Dr Chris Galley for drawing these examples to my attention.

rites, Martin Bucer removed it from his ceremony in use in Strasbourg from 1525.[43] He also objected to its survival in the first Edwardian Prayer Book. While careful not to criticise the implication he saw in it of maternal affection for a child, and without a fundamental theological objection, he stressed his fear that the Catholic Church spread superstition through such signs.[44] That Bucer's advice was taken, and all reference to chrisom cloths was dropped from the 1552 Prayer Book (and subsequent Books of Common Prayer), suggests the possibility of change. But the use of such cloths was not forbidden, and, as Bucer's assessment indicates, was not considered a matter of fundamental principle among most reformers. That mothers being churched at Dutton in Essex brought handkerchiefs to the minister in the nineteenth century argues for continuity of custom, but it also demonstrates that the offering could be disassociated from the baptismal ceremony.[45] The evidence concerning the custom in Basingstoke implies that practices had not changed by the 1630s, but this case needs to be examined against the background of the disputes between Puritan and Laudian tendencies within the Church, which were particularly acute over the churching of women. Whether the use of chrisom cloths had been continuous in this parish, or whether the vicar, Ambrose Webb, restored a lapsed custom among other 'irregularities' alleged by his parishioner, one George Baynard, is uncertain.[46] It should also be noted that this amounted to an important source of income for parish clergy and a considerable expense for parishioners. Thus, like tithes, the custom was likely to become a point of tension between pastors and people where it survived. The note in the parish register of Winckenby, Lincolnshire, stating that the chrisom cloth was to be 'half a yeard of fine linen long and a full yard in width', may have been to prevent cloths of lesser value being used.[47] Such difficulties were almost certainly behind the item in the *Interpretation of the Bishops* of 1560–1, which instructed that, 'to avoid contention, let the curate have the value of the chrisom, not under the value of four pence and above, as they can agree, and as the state of the parents may require'.[48]

---

[43] H. T. Lehmann (ed.), *Luther Works* (55 vols., Philadelphia, 1965), LV, p. 109; Fisher, *Christian Initiation, the Reformation Period*, pp. 126–31; H. O. Old, *The Shaping of the Reformed Baptismal Rite in the Sixteenth Century* (Grand Rapids, MI, 1992), pp. 65–6.

[44] E. C. Whitaker, *Martin Bucer and the Book of Common Prayer* (Great Wakering, Essex, 1974), p. 99.

[45] Cox, *Parish Registers*, p. 62.

[46] Bruce, *State Papers, Domestic Series, in the Reign of Charles I*, p. 274.

[47] Cox, *Parish Registers*, p. 60.

[48] W. H. Frere and W. W. Kennedy (eds.), *Visitation Articles and Injunctions of the Period of the Reformation* (3 vols., London, 1910), III, pp. 62 and 71.

As this instruction indicates, by the mid-sixteenth century in many parishes women were bringing a 'chrisom' of money, rather than of cloth, to their churching. This practice ended at Hatherleigh and Crediton in Devon, probably in the 1560s.[49] However, the 'chrisom book' kept at the parish of St Thomas in New Sarum, Wiltshire, between 1569 and 1592 indicates the continuity of this custom and its separation from the offering given for a woman's churching.[50] The sums left varied between 1d and 1s, but were most commonly 6d. Differences in value did appear to reflect the wealth of the families concerned. This can be seen in a few cases, like those for 1571, which included an offering of 10d from Mistress Tycheborne, 'for her chysam', but only 4d from 'goddwyf Knight a pore woman'.[51] The average value of payments rose very slightly over the period, from a mean of 5.2d in the year 1569–70 to 5.8d in 1591–2, a rise slightly behind overall inflation. But in contrast, the value of offerings at churchings fell, from a mean of 2.7d in the first year of the book, to 2d in the last. In early modern England a payment that kept pace with inflation was usually tied to goods; this, and the graduated nature of the 'chrisom' in this parish, both suggest that it was based on the value of the chrisom sheet employed. This is underlined by four cases where we are explicitly told that the chrisom had been given in cloth, suggesting that very occasionally the old custom was still fully used.[52] It is also interesting that in the many instances where the scribe noted that the child was dead or buried, no payment was given. It seems evident that in this parish, the cloth was still being used in baptism into the late sixteenth century, and that although a payment in money had normally been substituted at the mother's churching, children dying before this point were probably still being buried in chrisom cloths.

One reason for, or consequence of, the substitution of payments may have been a desire to pass particular cloths between generations. This helps in part to explain the references to chrisom and christening cloths in wills and household accounts, like that in the will of Elizabeth Payne of Cranbrook, Kent in 1611, who left 'half my great christening sheet'

[49] R. Whiting, *The Blind Devotion of the People: Popular Religion and the English Reformation* (Cambridge, 1989), p. 135.

[50] E. R. Neville, 'The Chrysom Book of St Thomas New Sarum', *Wiltshire Notes and Queries* 5 (1907), pp. 462–8, 512–14, 561–6; 6 (1908), pp. 19–25, 57–60, 107–10, 208–11; 7 (1909), pp. 302–5, 344–8; 8 (1910), pp. 391–5, 455–9, 492–8, 547–50.

[51] *Ibid.*, 5 (1907), p. 467.

[52] *Ibid.*, 7 (1909), pp. 345, 346; 8 (1910), pp. 391 and 457. Two of these were by the same couple.

among other items to her son.[53] It may also allow us to see the origins of modern christening robes, which are also often handed down through families. The mention of a christening sheet 'with buttons' in the household accounts of Henry Best in 1640 implies that the plain white cloth was evolving into a more complex and valuable object.[54]

'Chrisom children' were not merely recorded in parish registers, they are also represented iconographically on some of the stone and brass church memorials that fill English parish churches. Yet, here too there is uncertainty over the meaning of the term. Distinctions should be (but often have not been) drawn between images of children wrapped in single sheets (secured with strips of material or rope, which may have been chrisom cloths); the handful of infants depicted in shrouds; and the much larger numbers of children depicted as wrapped in swaddling bands (often with hoods, ruffs and secured with pins).[55] The first category can be seen in the image of a child pictured with its father, probably Thomas Scheffe, on a brass from Cranbrook in Kent made around 1520 (see Plate 14.1); the second form on a monument from 1455 to Richard Manfeld, his sister and brother, from Taplow in Buckinghamshire (see Plate 14.2); and the final category can be seen in the sketch of a brass made in 1587, now lost, depicting Peter Best, from Mertsham in Surrey (see Plate 14.3).

There are as many as fifty-seven such images on brasses from the late medieval and early modern periods of which evidence has survived.[56] However, once images of children in swaddling bands have been excluded, the number of monuments that may show children in chrisom cloths becomes quite small, with only four depicting them in unsecured cloths or shrouds and seventeen with children in single cloths secured with cords. The depiction of crosses on the foreheads of a number of these children, like that of Elyn Bray of Stoke D'Abernon, Surrey from

---

[53] J. de Launay (ed.), *Abstracts of Cranbrook Wills Proved in the Courts of Canterbury, and now preserved in Kent Archives Office, Maidstone, Kent 1396–1640* (Canterbury, 1984), p. 242.

[54] *The Farming and Memorandum Books of Henry Best of Elmswell, 1642*, ed. D. Woodward (London, 1984), p. 200.

[55] Those failing to make this distinction include J. Franklin, *Brasses* (London, 1978), pp. 101–2; J. Page-Phillips, *Children on Brasses* (London, 1970), pp. 52–3; and J. Page-Phillips (ed.), *Macklin's Monumental Brasses* (London, 1907, repr. 1978), pp. 81–2. Among those clearly distinguishing is J. Bertram, *Brasses and Brass Rubbing in England* (Newton Abbot, 1972), p. 111. All of these works have been used as source material for this investigation with the addition of M. Clayton, *Catalogue of Rubbings and Incised Slabs* (London, 1915, repr. 1979) and R. Le Strange, *A Complete Descriptive Guide to British Monumental Brasses* (London, 1972).

[56] Larger numbers survive on stone memorials, but these are less comprehensively catalogued.

Plate 14.1   *Brass, probably of Thomas and John Scheffe, Cranbrook in Kent,* c. *1520.*

1516 (see Plate 14.4), suggests that these children had died after baptism, indicating that the definition implied in the Sarum and 1549 rites applied here.[57] Naming was a major function of the baptismal ceremony and that inscriptions give names for many of these children may also indicate that they were baptised.

It should, however, be noted that most of these monuments were not to children, but primarily dedicated to parents, and that their offspring appear on them somewhat incidentally. For example, the two infants, probably twins, pictured in the arms of Anne Asteley, from Blickling in Norfolk, who died in 1512, are clearly designed to indicate her death in or close after childbirth, and it is unclear whether or not the children survived (see Plate 14.5). There are only fourteen brasses of children in single cloths that were not primarily dedicated to adults.

An assessment of the iconography of infant burial is also made

---

[57] H. Monckton, 'Notes from the Parish Registers of Maidstone', *Archaeologica Cantiana* 29 (1911), p. 320, makes this observation. I am grateful to Peter Marshall for drawing this reference to my attention.

Plate 14.2   *Brass of Richard, Isabella and John Manfeld, Taplow in Buckinghamshire, 1455.*

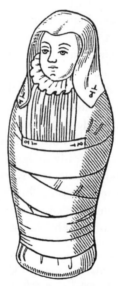

Plate 14.3   *Sketch of lost brass of Peter Best, Mertsham in Surrey, 1587.*

Plate 14.4   *Brass of Elyn Bray, Stoke D'Abernon, Surrey, 1516.*

problematic by the apparent lack of any such monuments for the period between 1533 and 1580. This is probably the result of the nadir in brass production that occurred in this period.[58] However, towards the end of the sixteenth century, brasses were rehabilitated as suitable memorials to the godly.[59] Very few brasses of infants from this period of revival portray them as wrapped in single sheets of cloth. This could be taken to indicate that the practice of using chrisom cloths had died out in the mid-sixteenth century. However, it seems unlikely that these children were being buried in swaddling bands. It is far from clear that any of these children are depicted as ready for burial, and what these images may show are different fashions in swaddling among the social elite, fashions that changed in the late sixteenth century, as they began to echo those of adults.

---

[58] J. Bertram, *Lost Brasses* (Newton Abbot, 1976), pp. 116–24.
[59] R. Rex, 'Monumental Brasses and the Reformation', *Transactions of the Monumental Brass Society* 14 (1990), pp. 376–94.

Plate 14.5   *Brass of Anne á Wode, wife of Thomas Asteley, Blickling in Norfolk, 1512.*

Nevertheless, that even a few individuals went to the expense of creating monuments for very young children is significant. Such memorials provided a reminder of the transitory nature of human life, but they may also suggest that there could be considerable affection even for the newborn. These two motivations can both be discerned in the brass to Anne Consant, commemorated in Upper Deal, Kent. She was the only child of the headmaster of King's School, Rochester, after a marriage of thirteen years. She died, aged only thirty-one days, as the inscription reveals, 'suddenly' on 20 July 1606. Her epitaph translates as, 'I who so soon departed this life have so soon begun to live, and I who but now was as nothing, have become one of heaven's company.'[60] Given the age of the child she was almost certainly baptised and it is more than likely the mother had been churched; yet this child appears wrapped in a single sheet, secured with bindings.

It seems then that what many of these 'chrisom' brasses actually depict

---

[60] S. Beedell, *Brasses and Brass Rubbing* (Edinburgh, 1973), p. 49.

are young children, who were swaddled or buried in the only sort of clothes they were likely to wear at that age, single sheets of cloth. Since children with crosses may be older than a month and those without younger, there is simply no means of telling whether they were chrisom children in either of the two possible senses.

If memorials do not provide a reliable guide to continuity and change in infant burial practices, then it becomes necessary to look elsewhere for evidence of definitions of what a chrisom child was. The parish register of Kirkburton in the West Riding of Yorkshire, supplies an opportunity to analyse this phenomenon, as it recorded the burials of 'chrisom children' between 1568 and 1710.[61] Kirkburton was a large upland parish, in the pastoral and clothworking Pennine hinterland of Huddersfield. The parish register contains a number of gaps, one, between 1618 and 1627, is of major significance, but together the other five (all between 1568 and 1660) total less than nine years. Of five scribes in this period only Roger Nauson, the curate from 1567 to 1575 (recording from 1573), failed completely to note such burials. On average from 1568 to 1659, there were just over four burials of chrisom children a year, a total of 388.

It is immediately evident from the entries themselves that some of the infants designated as chrisom children in the burial register had been baptised. For example, the first case in the register is that of Margery Kay, baptised 31 October 1568 and buried 'Margery Kay a chrisom child', 26 November that same year.[62] However, it is equally clear that some children were unbaptised, as in the entry for January 1655, concerning 'a chisom child of George Killner borne and buried the first day'.[63] As with memorial brasses, one means of establishing whether these children were baptised before death is to determine whether they were named. Twenty-six named and two unnamed chrisom children were registered as buried in the period from 1568 to 1583. From that point until the end of the period under study (with only one exception) they were entered anonymously by the name of their father. Particularly as it does not correspond to a change of scribe, this pattern seems to suggest that a change of meaning of the term, from baptised to unbaptised children, occurred during the 1580s.

This possibility can be tested by a more detailed analysis, cross-

---

[61] *The Parish Registers of the Parish of Kirkburton, co. York*, ed. F. A. Collins (2 vols., Exeter, 1887, 1889).

[62] *Ibid.*, I, p. 65.

[63] *Ibid.*, II, p. 23.

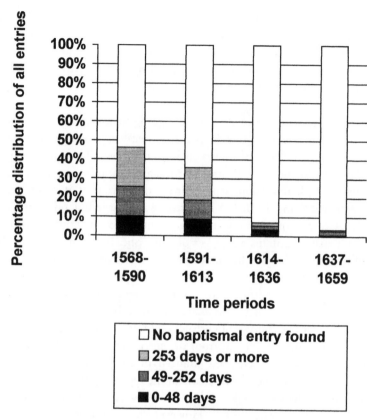

Figure 14.1   *Time between baptismal and burial entries of chrisom children in the parish register of Kirkburton, Yorkshire, 1568–1659.*

referencing these burial entries with the baptismal register. There are a number of problems with such an investigation. The apparent number of correspondences may have been inflated by instances of persons sharing the same names. After the 1580s, it is also difficult to be certain whether baptismal and burial entries referring to the same parents were dealing with the same children. Conversely, it seems likely that there was considerable under-recording of baptisms in the register, or that children were baptised in other parishes. Nevertheless, with these problems in mind, these figures do give an indication of changing definitions of what a chrisom child was at least to scribes in one Yorkshire parish.

As can be seen in Figure 14.1, in the overwhelming majority of cases, 308 out of the 388 (79.4 per cent), there was no corresponding baptismal entry for the reference in the burial register. However, it is also clear that the proportion of instances in which this term was used to describe baptised children was much higher at the beginning of the period for which the register is relevant. In the period 1568–90, in 18 out of 39 instances (46.2 per cent) there were corresponding baptismal entries. This figure fell steadily to 53 out of 148 cases (35.8 per cent) in the period 1591–1613; 4 out of 56 instances (7.1 per cent) in the period 1614–36; and only 5 out of 145 (3.4 per cent) in the period 1637–59. This indicates that the term 'chrisom child', which was used for both those children baptised and those unbaptised in the late sixteenth century, was exclusively used to describe unbaptised children by the mid-seventeenth century, with the last instance for which a baptism was evident being for 1645.

However, these figures also reveal a considerable amount of additional information. It is clear that the term was only very rarely used in the sense implied in the 1549 Prayer Book by the late sixteenth century. It is probable that most women were churched within thirty days of the birth of their children, and the overwhelming majority within forty-eight days of their baptism, in the sixteenth and seventeenth centuries.[64] However, even in the period 1568–90, only four children (10.3 per cent) described as chrisoms in the Kirkburton register had a corresponding baptismal entry within the previous forty-eight days. There were, somewhat surprisingly, more children described as chrisoms at burial that had been baptised over forty-nine days previously, and therefore whose mothers had almost certainly already been churched. In the period 1568–90, there were six children (15.4 per cent) with corresponding baptismal entries between forty-nine days and nine months, and eight (20.5 per cent) with such entries after a gap of over nine months. That these figures cannot simply be put down to problems with the accuracy of the registers is suggested by the fact that entries with corresponding recorded baptisms in this period fell in line with those for the period under forty-nine days. Instead, it seems that, by the late sixteenth century, the term 'chrisom child' was used to describe not only unbaptised children and those baptised and buried before churching, but also to delineate those buried over a year after their baptism.

It seems then that if the definition of a chrisom child in the early sixteenth century had been, as logic suggests, those children buried between baptism and their mother's churching, that already by the late sixteenth century it had changed to include unbaptised children and those over one month old. But it also seems in the period covered by the Kirkburton register that the term was increasingly being used only to

---

[64] Coster, 'Purity, Profanity and Puritanism', p. 382.

refer to unbaptised children. This can be seen most clearly in the period between 1653 and 1660, when births were recorded as well as baptisms. Eighteen instances of chrisom burials were given in the register and, although births were noted for all, for none was a baptism recorded. Fourteen were born and buried the same day, three the next and one after a week. This sample cannot be treated as typical, not only because of its size, but because birth and burial were more likely to be recorded if on the same day. Yet, it does suggest that these were very young children, usually only a few days old and therefore, by the mid-seventeenth century, unlikely to have been baptised.

Whether these findings from one Yorkshire parish can be extrapolated on a wider geographical basis is debatable. It is likely that the chronology of change varied from parish to parish. Language would also have been affected by dialect, and regional differences in usage. Nevertheless, this evidence does appear to fit into the pattern of national changes to religious practice that began in the middle of the sixteenth century and reached their apogee in the mid-seventeenth century. What remains is to explain this change and to examine its implications.

One cause of this transformation of meaning may have been the lengthening gap between birth and baptism. Sixteenth-century parish registers that allow the effects of this change to be explored, by a comparison of dates of both births and baptisms, are rare, but the analysis of the baptismal register of St Peter's, Cornhill in London, undertaken by B. M. Berry and R. S. Schofield, indicates an interesting pattern. In the period 1574–8, 75 per cent of all children were baptised within five days, but this delay gradually lengthened until the same proportions were not baptised until fourteen days by the period 1655–6.[65] In addition, while 65 per cent of baptisms were on Sundays in the period 1574–8, this rose to 84 and 82 per cent in the periods 1585–9 and 1596–8, respectively.[66] While the authors rightly remind us of the danger of basing a national hypothesis on one parish register, this information suggests a gradual deterioration of the imperative of rapid baptism. This appears to have begun with successful attempts by the church authorities in the late sixteenth century to re-order baptism as a part of public Sunday worship.[67]

---

[65] B. M. Berry, and R. S. Schofield, 'Age at Baptism in Pre-Industrial England', *Population Studies* 25 (1971), pp. 462–3.

[66] *Ibid.*

[67] In Kirkburton, in the period 1653–60, cumulatively, one-quarter of the 111 children registered born were baptised within five days, half within a week, three-quarters within eleven days.

Infant mortality remained relatively high throughout the sixteenth and seventeenth centuries. Around 13 per cent of children died in the first year of life, around 9 per cent within the first month, 4 per cent in the first week, and 2 per cent within a day.[68] Although David Cressy has stated that 'very few of these children escaped baptism', as the delay in the rite increased in the late sixteenth and early seventeenth centuries an increasing proportion of these children would have died unbaptised.[69] If we accept that there was a widespread belief in the late medieval period in the need for infants to undergo the rite in order to be saved, then parents must have adjusted to a belief system where baptism was not a necessity for salvation, or faced a situation where an increasing proportion of their children were denied the chance to enter Heaven.

Such a change would have affected the definition of the chrisom child because of the accompanying symbolism of the chrisom cloth as a token of innocence. There is additional evidence that the idea of innocence was closely associated with that of the chrisom child. Thus Shakespeare had the death of Falstaff reported as 'a finer end, and went away an it had been any christom child'.[70] Similarly, Bunyan used it to describe Mr Badman, who appeared to have died peacefully: 'so stilly, so quietly, so like a lamb or a chrisom child'.[71] Connotations of the broader meaning of an innocent, as one who was simple minded, can be seen from a burial entry for 1567 in the register of Herne, Kent, concerning 'Old Arnold, a chrysomer', unlikely to be a child under any definition.[72] In the Kirkburton area, the word chrisom continued to retain this meaning into the eighteenth century.[73]

If a chrisom child was an infant in a state of innocence, then the inclusion and cultural identification of unbaptised children with this term would imply that they too were considered free from the stigma and consequences of original sin. There is some evidence from folklore that such a view was not universal. From one end of the country, there is the

---

[68] R. S. Schofield and E. A. Wrigley, 'Infant and Child Mortality in England in the Late Tudor and Early Stuart Period', in C. Webster (ed.), *Health, Medicine and Mortality in the Sixteenth Century* (Cambridge, 1979), p. 75, and their *The Population History of England 1541–1871. A Reconstruction* (Cambridge, 1981), p. 249.

[69] Cressy, *Birth, Marriage, and Death*, p. 117.

[70] W. Shakespeare, *Henry V* ii.iii.11.

[71] J. Bunyan, *Grace Abounding and the Life and Death of Mr Badman* (London, 1938), p. 302.

[72] J. A. Simpson and E. S. C. Werner (eds.), *The Oxford English Dictionary* (2nd edn, 20 vols., Oxford, 1989), iii, p. 177.

[73] J. D. Halliwell, *A Dictionary of Archaic and Provincial Words* (2 vols., London, 1838), i, p. 249.

image of Dartmoor stalked by the 'Whisht' hounds, tracking the wandering souls of chrisom children, suggesting they were not expected to enter Heaven.[74] Similarly, in the nineteenth-century northern borders, it may have been thought unfortunate to tread on the graves of unbaptised children, indicating a fear of supernatural contagion. However, one Devonport man claimed that, in his youth, 'it was thought lucky to have a stillborn child put into an open grave, as it was considered a sure passport to heaven for the next person buried there'.[75] It seems then that in some quarters newborn children were no longer considered as spiritually impure, marking a fundamental change in popular perceptions about the nature of infants.

The desire for rapid baptism in late medieval England shows not only the prevalence of the idea of original sin, but also concern over the fate of newborn children. Recent medical research has begun to stress the very real grief felt by modern parents at the death of very young children.[76] Although it is undoubtedly true that it took time for relationships to develop, and was greater in proportion to the length of the pregnancy, this grief is closely associated with the hopes and aspirations of parenthood, pressures that also applied to adults in the sixteenth and seventeenth centuries. In the medieval period, parents evidently found some solace in the assurance of salvation brought about by rapid baptism. The English Reformation removed the availability of this solution and eroded the idea that made it an imperative. The reaction of the population was to extend the period in which children were seen as innocent. If this change in popular belief was a consequence of institutionalised reform, it cannot have begun before the 1540s. The evidence of the parish register of Kirkburton suggests that by the late 1560s this process was already far advanced. Possibly, the term chrisom child came to embrace all children under a month old. Thus, a calf slaughtered after less than one month old was referred to in some areas as a chrisom calf.[77] But the Kirkburton register indicates that this was an intermediate stage in a process by which the meaning of the term changed to signify almost exclusively those

---

[74] T. Brown, *The Fate of the Dead, a Study in Folk-Eschatology in the West Country after the Reformation* (Ipswich, 1979), p. 37.

[75] W. Henderson, *The Folklore of the Northern Counties of England and the Borders* (London, 1838, repr. Wakefield, 1973), p. 6.

[76] For example, C. M. Lemmer, 'Mothers' and Fathers' Experiences of Perinatal Bereavement' (University of Utah PhD thesis, 1988); S. K. Theut *et al.*, 'Perinatal Loss and Parental Bereavement', *American Journal of Psychiatry* 146 (5) (1989), pp. 635–9; and R. Harrigan *et al.*, 'Perinatal Grief: Responses to the Loss of an Infant', *Journal of Neonatal Nursing* 12 (5) (1993), pp. 25–31. I owe these references to Mrs Julie Lewis.

[77] Halliwell, *Archaic and Provincial Words*, I, p. 249.

children who had died before baptism, a process seemingly complete by the mid-seventeenth century. Under this new definition, the emphasis was even more centred on the innocence of infants at birth.

As an example of the impact of the Reformation on the English people, this pattern indicates that some changes that influenced the fundamental perceptions of the population were brought about with surprising speed. Nevertheless, the full consequences of these transformations were not resolved until almost a century later. Thus, concerning the fate of children, the English Reformation was both quick and slow in its effects, both short and long. There was a high degree of adaptability among ministers and people, but also a degree of confusion and diversity, problems seemingly all the more acute on the fringes of the English kingdom.

Nevertheless, in the shift from the view of the newborn as tainted, demonically possessed or even damned, to regarding them as innocent vessels, perhaps inevitably to be corrupted by the world, the recurrent themes of the pollution and contagion associated with childbirth were considerably downplayed. This view was not universally accepted in early modern England, but perhaps in its growth we can see the beginnings of a 'modern' view of innate childhood innocence emerging from the negotiation between theological change and the emotions and desires of the people.

15 The afterlives of monstrous infants in Reformation Germany

Philip M. Soergel

'They say they are called monsters, because they de-monstrate or signify something', St Augustine observed in Book xxi of *The City of God*. 'But let their diviners see', he continued, 'how they are either deceived, or even when they do predict true things, it is because they are inspired by spirits, who are intent upon entangling the minds of men . . . in the meshes of a hurtful curiosity.'[1] Human inquisitiveness, Augustine counselled, would do better to ponder the ways in which the monster, an infant or animal born severely deformed, displayed God's power to transform Creation. Its birth and certain death was not a revelation of the earthly future. Instead its appearance might be the result of inherently natural processes the divinity had hidden in the physical world, processes the human mind might never comprehend. For Christians, however, its importance lay in hinting at the far-off, heavenly perfection God would bestow on the body at the end of time.

When they came to consider deformed infants, medieval intellectuals often agreed with the fifth-century bishop. Like Augustine, most denied that *monstra* could be divined for reliable clues to future military, political or social events, and instead they often fixed the meaning of deformed birth in eschatology.[2] At the same time scholastic philosophers were fascinated by the hidden, yet natural causes of deformities and their

---

[1] Saint Augustine, *The City of God*, tr. Marcus Dods (New York, 1950), p. 778.
[2] Caroline Bynum, *The Resurrection of the Body in Western Christianity, 200–1336* (New York, 1995), pp. 98–9; 123–4, 189–90 and 265–6; Valerie Flint, 'Monsters and the Antipodes in the Early Middle Ages and Enlightenment', in her *Ideas in the Medieval West: Texts and Their Contexts* (London, 1988), pp. 65–80. Besides the works of scholastic philosophers, the medieval bestiaries were one place in which the discussion about the natural and moral causes of the 'monstrous races' was kept alive throughout the Middle Ages. See Jerome B. Friedman, *The Monstrous Races in Medieval Art and Thought* (Cambridge, MA, 1981).

works resonated with frequent speculation about the physical processes that produced monsters. Quite often, their explanations turned to blame parents, either for conceiving children at prohibited times or for performing the sexual act in positions that damaged the seeds. Another compelling explanation indicted the porous imagination of mothers, which might deform the unborn child in the weeks following conception.

The medieval study of *monstra*, then, concentrated on deformed birth as a problem of nature, a nature that was understood as complex and filled with unseen potentialities. Certainly, these tactics made deformed birth less fearsome and more routine for medieval scholars. But in all likelihood, the unschooled probably continued to interpret the appearance of the seriously deformed with the very strategies Augustine had condemned in late antiquity. Monstrous births were portents, events charged with dread and wonder that could be used for predicting the future.

Renaissance men and women, both learned and unlearned, often came to view monstrous births in this way, too.[3] Fuelled by rising apocalyptic expectation and a renewed knowledge of antique systems of divination, early modern intellectuals placed monstrous births within a system of signs and prophecy. In a brilliant work of historical detection, Ottavia Niccoli has traced the origins of the rising early modern interest in the prophetic meaning of monsters to late fifteenth-century Italy.[4] In the midst of the political and military misfortunes of the Italian Wars (1494–1530) the peninsula's urban populations avidly traded scores of texts that treated specific cases of deformed birth. Those who commented on these events, from cultivated members of the papal curia to street-corner preachers, were unconcerned with their natural causes. Instead they broadcast these monsters as prophetic and apocalyptic signs. In this watchful climate, seriously deformed infants, like the Monster of Ravenna born in that city in 1506, were variously interpreted by the belligerent parties in the wars. Did the child signal coming catastrophe for the Ravennese, the Florentines, the French or the Spanish? On the shifting sands of Italy's political chaos, the deformed infant could be

---

[3] Aby Warburg, *Die Erneuerung der heidnischen Antike, kulturwissenschaftliche Beiträge der Europäischen Renaissance*, in Fritz Rougement and Gertrud Bing (eds.), *Gesammelte Schriften* (2 vols., Liechtenstein, 1969), I and II; Jean Céard, *La Nature et les prodiges. L'insolite au XVIe siècle en France* (Geneva, 1977); Rudolf Wittkower, 'Marvels of the East: the Study of Monsters in Early Modern Europe', *Journal of the Warburg and Courtauld Institutes* 5 (1942), pp. 159–97.

[4] Ottavia Niccoli, *Prophecy and People in Renaissance Italy*, tr. Lydia G. Cochrane (Princeton, 1990).

subjected to an almost infinite series of readings and re-readings, and prophetic commentary could grant the child, who had long since died, a dubious afterlife.

The lineage of 'monstrous' prophecies that Niccoli has unearthed in Italy was spectacular but brief; by 1530, censorship and political repression had moved to stamp out the uninhibited prophetic culture that had flourished in the previous generation. As a result, deformed infants and animals retreated from public view to be housed in the curiosity cabinets of Italy's learned and politically empowered elite. Had it not been for the outbreak of the Protestant Reformations in Northern Europe, the monster might have remained there like some discarded political and cultural artefact. But in Germany, the early evangelical reformers and their artistic disciples came to rely on monsters and deformed births to campaign against a corrupt Rome. In 1523, both Martin Luther and Philip Melanchthon wrote tracts popularising cases of monstrosities. Luther, for his part, treated the recent birth of a deformed calf, the 'Monk Calf of Freyberg', using it to condemn degenerate monasticism and the Roman Church generally. Melanchthon, on the other hand, considered the famous but mythical case of the so-called 'Papal Ass', a fantastic hybrid creature allegedly pulled from the Tiber at Rome in 1496. In Melanchthon's treatment that creature became a divine pronouncement about the papacy's nature as Antichrist and a sign of the nearness of the Apocalypse.[5]

In the generations that followed evangelicals avidly imitated Melanchthon's and Luther's early efforts. As the Reformation matured, though, the deformed infant became more than just a polemical tool to be deployed against a corrupt Rome. Gradually, polemic deepened to become evangelical piety. Heightened interest in the prophetic and portentous meanings of deformed infants now came to grant these children a new importance in sixteenth-century life and religion. Evangelical pastors, theologians and church officials all came to promote deformed infants they observed on the domestic scene as apocalyptic signs, as testimonies to the enormous deforming power of sin, and as natural curiosities that demonstrated God's terrifying lordship over Creation.

---

[5] Both pieces were published separately, but also in a single edition: Martin Luther and Philip Melanchthon, *Deuttung der czwo grewlichen Figuren, Bapstesels czu Rom und Munchkalbs zu Freijberg ijnn Meijsszen funden* (Wittenberg, 1523); Martin Luther, *Werke* (58 vols., Weimar, 1883–1948), XI, pp. 370–85; also reprinted in Konrad Lange, *Der Papstesel. Ein Beitrag zur Kultur- und Kunstgeschichte des Reformationszeitalters* (Göttingen, 1891), pp. 106–16.

Dieser Hase hierunder conterfeyt ist im Jar M. D .lxxxiij.
zu Türckheim an der Hardt im 28. Aprillen gefangen/ vnd dem Durchleuchtigen/ Hochgebornen
Fürsten vnd Herrn/ Herrn Johan Casimirn/ Pfaltzgraffen bey Rheyn/vnd Hertzogen in Beyern/zc.
gehn Fridelsheim vberschickt worden.

A ls es tausent fünff hundert Jar
Drey vnd achtzig gezehlet war/
Das sich ein gewächs eines Hasen/
Indem Aprillen sehen lassen/
Welches zu Türckheim an der Hart/
Uff der Jag ghetzt vnd gfangen ward/
... das sihet an dem gesehen werden/
Vernsehen sehen gegen der Erden/
... ein aber vbersich thun stehen/
Vnd/ wie man kan fur augen sehen/

Thüt sich am födbern theile finden
Eyn eynger Hass. jedoch dahinden/
Sich der Leib thut vnderschiedlich
In zweytheil strecken wunderlich/
Nach Fridelsheim geschicket was/
Wie man mich bericht dieser Hass/
Dem Durchleuchten Fürst vnd Herrn/
Johan Casimir gross von Ehrn
Uberschendet/daruber sich
Verwundern thete menniglich.

Diss wunderbare Monstrum hie/
So zuner ist gesehen nie
Soll auch ein massen jederman/
Dass Gottes wlialio sehen lahn/
Ein zorn vnd seinen grossen Gwalt/
Den er erzeigt vat manigfalt/
An Menschen Kindern vnd Vich/
Uff das ein jeder bessere sich/
Vnd Gott als ein Schöpffern vnd Herrn/
Erkennen vnd auch fordten lehrn.

Gedruckt zu Heydelberg bey Jacob Müller.

Plate 15.1   *A typical prodigy broadside printed at Heidelberg in 1583.*
The account told of the birth of non-separated twin hares from the town.
The hares were sent to the Count Palatine Johann Casimir, who may have
used them to stock his curiosity cabinet.

In some cases the fantastic images of monstrous births that circulated
in Reformation Germany, and which were to be imitated somewhat later
in France and England, were concocted out of whole cloth. More often,
though, a real infant, verified by observations in the text about the time,
date and place of its birth and death, is treated in the tracts and broadsides
that issued from both the penny press and elite theological circles. In
Germany, moreover, this intensified concern about deformities developed
unevenly, for while commentary about monsters was present everywhere
in the empire (see Plate 15.1), it was largely in Lutheran towns and
territories that monstrous infants were most vigorously publicised and
subjected to complex patterns of interpretation. There the attention to
human and animal deformities was only a part of a swelling interest in
nature's marvels and prodigies, an interest that had been touched off by

the Reformation. In Lutheran regions, an active trade in prophecies about comets, celestial visions, earthquakes, floods, together with monstrous births satisfied a desire for divine confirmation inherited from the medieval world. While early modern Catholics turned to the saints to search for these signs, Lutherans trained their eyes intently upon nature. And there they found the subject for a lush marvel literature that entertained theories about the meanings behind God's stunning violations of the natural order. This 'prodigy culture' became a common 'safe' way for evangelicals to indulge an appetite for events in which God's hand was made brilliantly evident. Prodigies and marvels were 'safe' because they elicited wide-eyed, pious amazement, but did not inspire a false faith in works or the mediation of the saints.

But other, often overlooked, stimuli also helped generate the relatively greater proliferation of interest in monstrously deformed infants among sixteenth-century Lutherans. One of these factors was certainly the series of theological disputes that occurred within the new religion in the wake of Luther's death in 1546 and the political turmoil of the 1550s and 1560s. In this byzantine series of controversies, supporters of the moral synergism of Philip Melanchthon, or the Philippists as they came to be known, fought vigorously against 'Gnesio-Lutherans', the party who desired to enforce a strict interpretation of Luther's doctrines of human depravity and utter helplessness in the process of salvation. One key issue in these decades-long debates focused on the nature of sin and its effects on humankind.[6] In the 1550s, for instance, the combative, polemical theologian Matthias Flacius Illyricus had dubbed sin the very essence (*Wesen*) of human nature. The effects of the Fall, Flacius argued in extreme moments, had been so severe as to alter the very substance of human nature, creating a kind of kinship between humans and the Devil.[7] It was a scholastic definition of sin – that it was a force accidental and external to human nature, a profound stain that clung to the soul – that eventually prevailed. Yet a long-standing debate continued around these issues even after the evangelical Formula of Concord (1577) decisively outlawed the Flacian position. Flacius's extreme rhetoric and his conceptualisation of sin as the very stuff of human nature continued to draw support from some Gnesio-Lutheran extremists during the last quarter of the sixteenth century. And echoes of this debate can be seen in

---

[6]   A recent and concise summary of these disputes is to be found in Irene Dingel, 'The Echo of Controversy: Caspar Fuger's Attempt to Propagate the Formula of Concord among the Common People', *Sixteenth Century Journal* 26 (1995), pp. 515–31.

[7]   These controversies are considered at greater length in Wilhelm Preger, *Matthias Flacius Illyricus und seine Zeit* (2 vols., Erlangen, 1859–61).

the ongoing theological discussions of monsters, as some Lutheran
theologians came to interpret monstrous births as divine proof for their
dismal assessments of human nature.

While these intricate disputes concerning Original Sin may have
played a role in elite, theological discussions of monsters, they are rarely
mentioned in the cheap, broadly addressed broadsides and pamphlets
that poured from German presses in the second half of the sixteenth
century. Still, these texts do reveal important connections to the learned,
theological culture of the later Reformation. Their authors relied upon
monsters as an important tool to teach certain key tenets of Lutheran
orthodoxy, particularly human depravity and the inability of human
beings to participate in their salvation. As evangelical orthodoxy took
shape in the second half of the sixteenth century, its leaders may have
moved to eradicate both the extremes of the Flacian and Philippist
positions. At the same time, Lutheran ideas concerning sin and human
nature remained profoundly different from those notions espoused by the
other magisterial Reformations. Like Calvinism, Lutheranism continually
reiterated that human beings were utterly depraved, helpless before an
omnipotent God. But unlike Calvinism, Anglicanism or Catholicism,
Lutheran theology persisted in denying that there was any possible
sanctification, any remediation for the human species. Instead, it usually
warned that humankind was becoming more wicked, more helplessly
enslaved to sin with each passing generation.

In other parts of Europe tales of monstrous birth might function as
parables to remind men and women of the dangers of sexual licence and
impropriety. But in the monstrous birth texts printed in Reformation
Germany, parental and, more particularly, maternal guilt was usually
denied. Instead blame was transposed to the level of social estates,
communities and nations. In the birth and death of a monstrous child,
evangelical commentators reminded their audience, God was proclaiming
the faults and errors of the entire species. These texts were the product of
a new technology of guilt that aimed to create a profound sense of
unworthiness in readers and to remind them that mere piety alone could
not influence God, nor hold back the course of human degeneration He
had initiated.

This heightened reliance on the deformed infant arose at the same
time as new attitudes towards death and the dead were also reshaping
evangelical life. Scholars have long pointed to sixteenth-century Protestant changes – the denial of Purgatory and the sacrificial character of the
mass, the attacks on the corruption and abuse of the indulgence trade, the
abolition of the veneration of the saints, and the embrace of extramural

burial – as changes that helped to curb the intercourse between the dead and the living that was a common feature of life in medieval times. These were, to be sure, fundamental alterations that would eventually transform the ways in which people related to the departed. More recent research, though, has tended to call attention to the ways in which a cult of the dead could seep back into the new religions. If Luther and other reformers advocated that the deceased be taken without fanfare and display from their homes to the place of burial, the evangelical funeral sermon came to be the place at which the deceased's life and demeanor could be celebrated.[8] In the tens of thousands of printed copies of these sermons that circulated in the late sixteenth and seventeenth centuries, Lutherans kept alive memories of the dead, taking pious lessons from the *curriculum vitae* their pastors carefully constructed for the departed.[9] The Reformers, too, may have attacked the cult of the saints as a 'false' and 'deceiving' superstition, but they could not prevent themselves from becoming objects of the very same kind of veneration. Luther's birth place, Eisleben, was celebrated as Germany's 'New Bethlehem', and was the destination for pious pilgrimages until at least the eighteenth century.[10] In this and countless other developments, the new religion came face to face with the continuing affection of the people for ancestral worship.

The massive popularity of monstrous birth accounts in the second half of the sixteenth century presents us, too, with certain seeming paradoxes. Generally, Lutheranism laboured to lengthen the distance between the living and the dead. But in scores of both cheap and imposing texts, Lutheran pastors and theologians seized upon the deformed infant, transforming its brief life and its corpse into a morality lesson for their lay audience. The illustrations contained in the numerous texts that circulated about these children were effigies, since the infants these texts treated were almost always stillborn, or they died in the hours

---

[8] Craig M. Koslofsky, 'Death and Ritual in Reformation Germany' (University of Michigan PhD thesis, 1994).

[9] Jill Bepler, 'Women in German Funeral Sermons: Models of Virtue or Slice of Life?', *German Life and Letters* 44 (October 1991), pp. 392–403; Rudolf Lenz (ed.), *Leichenpredigten als Quelle historischer Wissenschaften* (3 vols., Coburg, 1979 and 1984); Eileen T. Dugan, 'The Funeral Sermons as a Key to Familial Values in Early Modern Nördlingen', *Sixteenth Century Journal* 20 (1989), pp. 631–44; and Rudolf Lenz, *De mortuis nil nisi bene? Leichenpredigten als multidisziplinäre Quelle unter besonderer Berücksichtigung der Historischen Familienforschung der Bildungsgeschichte und der Literaturgeschichte* (Sigmaringen, 1990).

[10] Robert Scribner's classic article, 'Incombustible Luther' treats these themes. It is reproduced in his *Popular Culture and Popular Movements in Reformation Germany* (London and Ronceverte, 1987).

Warhafftige Contrafactur einer erschrecklichen Wundergeburt
eines Knäbleins/welches recht am newen Jarstage dieses jetzlauffenden 1578. Jars
von aller alten Frawen in Euringa Terra,del nous,iele,ist geboren worden.

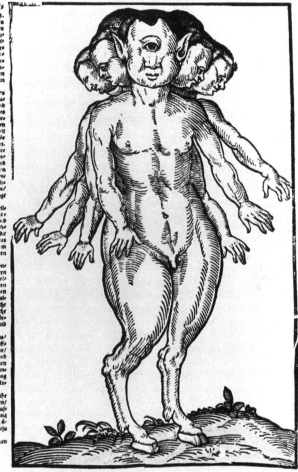

Plate 15.2 *A 1578 broadside announcing the abnormal birth of a child to an old woman in the Netherlands.*

just after delivery. The printed text, then, opened up an afterlife for the monstrous infant, an afterlife in which the messages observers construed from the child's body continued to shape the experience of the living. These messages often squarely attacked lingering notions of human improvement, even as they transformed the deformed corpse into a dark inversion of traditional notions about human sanctity. The deformed corpse became an embodiment of human wickedness, or as many writers counselled, a view of human nature through the very eyes of God. (See Plate 15.2).

These jeremiads, though, did not always enter a milieu prepared to receive such dim pronouncements. In Germany's villages and towns, intense curiosity about nature's marvels seems to have mingled uneasily alongside pious fervour. Everywhere in Europe, for example, parents seem to have displayed the corpses of their deformed infants to those willing to pay the price of admission.[11] The numerous monstrous birth accounts printed in late-Reformation Germany frequently make note of these displays. In fact, the public viewing of these children is mentioned in so many of these texts that we are led to conclude that it was standard practice in the days and weeks following the deformed child's birth and speedy death.[12] Evangelical texts usually fashioned these displays into pious pilgrimages, and authors observed that the faithful flocked to view the child's corpse as an object directly formed by the hand of God. At the same time these texts made no mention of the grimmer, commercial

---

[11] Niccoli, *Prophecy and People*, pp. 33–5.

[12] *Zu wissen. Ein wunderparlichs unnd erschrockeliches ding das dyser zeyt in Welschen Landen. Als man Zalt nach Christi unsers herren gepurt funfftzehenhundert unnd Zwelff Jar* [incipit] (1512); *Diese gegenwertig wunderlich Kindsgepurt mit zweyen leiblin vnter einem Haupt* (Nuremberg, 1547); Johann Müller, *Eine Seltzame und wunderliche gebert newlich zu Herbsleben in Düringen geschehen* (Magdeburg, 1553); *Warhaffte Abconterfectur der Erschrocklichen wundergeburt so dises 1560. Jar im Marckt zu Zusmerhausen am 21. tag Aprillis von ainer Frawen geborn ist* (1560); *Ware abcontrafactur und bericht eines kindes . . . Denn vierden december . . . geborn ist worden zu Breslaw* (Breslau, 1551); Johannes Göltz, *Ein erschreckliche Geburt Und augenscheinlich Wunderzeichen des Allmechtigen Gottes so sich auff den 4. tag des Christmonats des 1563. Jhars* (Schmalkalden, Strasbourg, Erfurt, 1563); *Ein neuwe seltzam Warhafftige wundergeburt die dise yetzlauffenden 1565 Jhars an ort und enden gleich nachbenennet sich hat sehen lassen* (1565); *Warhafftige Beschreibung einer wunderbarlichen seltzamen und erschroecklichen Geburt so in disem M.D.Lxix. Jar geschehen ist* (Augsburg, 1569); *Warhafftige Beschreibung einer Wunderbarer unnd Seltzamen Geburt so in disem LXXI. Jar allhier zu Querfurt gebracht hat* (Eisleben, 1571); *Von einer Warhafftigen, doch erschrecklichen . . . Geburt* (Königsberg (?), 1581); *Ein ware Abcontrafactur oder beschreibung einer seltzamen unnd wunderbarlichen Geburt* (Frankfurt-am-Main, 1580); *Eigentliche Abcontrafetung einer seltzamen erschrecklichen Wundergeburt zu Rhena, vier Meilen von Schwerin* (1590); *Grundtliche und Warhafftige Newe Zeittung von einer unerhoerten Mißgeburt so zur Liben in Ober Laußnitz eines armen Hirten Weib geboren* (Nuremberg, 1599); *Zwey warhafftige newe Zeitung von einer schrecklichen Mißgeburt* (Stettin, 1628); *Warhafftiges Abcontrafayt und Beschreibung der vor augen stehenden erschröcklichen Mißgeburt so von Ehrlichen Eltern Mit Name Hans Philipp Burger und Schneider und seriner Haußfrawen Agnes in der Stadt Winenenden 2 Meil von der Fürstl. Hauptstatt Stuttgart auff die Welt geboren worden* (Stuttgart, 1640). Reprints of many of these works are to be found in Walter L. Strauss, *The German Single-Leaf Woodcut, 1500–1550* (4 vols., New York, 1974) and *The German Single-Leaf Woodcut, 1550–1600* (3 vols., New York, 1975); and Walter L. Strauss and Dorothy Alexander, *The German Single-Leaf Woodcut, 1600–1700* (2 vols., New York, 1977).

realities that surrounded these events. In an account printed at Erfurt in 1563, for instance, a country pastor, Johannes Göltz, told of a terrifying sign that had recently occurred in his village, Werringschleben: a child had been born without bones and with sculpted skin that resembled the ruffles and frippery typical of contemporary styles. At the conclusion of his poetic text calling for repentance, Göltz listed the villages that had made pilgrimage to see the child, together with the guarantee that these viewers numbered 'more than a thousand' people.[13]

But if Göltz's work extolled piety, humility and repentance as the properly devout responses, sheer gawking curiosity seems often to have reigned in the high streets and markets of German towns. Those born with serious abnormalities who survived to maturity, or those who developed debilitating conditions that distorted their bodies, might look forward to a lifetime spent displaying themselves. Such was the career on which the enterprising Hans de Moer embarked in the 1540s and his life presents us with what may be the first recorded freak shows in European history. Born in Brabant, de Moer toured the continent for over twenty years showing himself on feast and market days. An illustrated handbill survives from one of his expositions that described his oddities as follows. He had a goitre-like growth that began at his ear and stretched all the way to his stomach and he could manipulate this growth to look like a Spanish cape or the gobbler of a New World turkey! Although the brief text to his handbill concluded that the meaning of his deformities was 'known only to God', the religious invocation at de Moer's displays seems to ring hollow.[14] The sheer peculiarity of his abnormalities probably inspired most of his viewers to plunk down their admissions, and sheer curiosity could always threaten to overwhelm pious sentiment.

De Moer was only one of the first in a long line of sixteenth- and seventeenth-century freaks, some of whom eventually made their way into the polite, and elevated company of kings and princes.[15] The display

13 Johannes Göltz, *Ein erschreckliche Geburt*, reprinted in Strauss, *German Single-Leaf Woodcut, 1550–1600*, I, p. 111.

14 *Hans de Moer geboren aus Brabant* [incipit] (1566), reprinted with commentary in Wolfgang Harms (ed.), *Die Sammlung der Herzog August Bibliothek in Wolfenbüttel* (2 vols., Tübingen, 1985), I, p. 230.

15 *Abconterfetung der Wunderbaren gestalt so Hans Kaltenbrunn mit jme an die Welt Geboren* (1566), reprinted in Strauss, *German Single-Leaf Woodcut, 1550–1600*, III, p. 1329; *Eine rechte warhaffte Abcontrofactur unnd Wunderbarlichen Geschöpff Von einer Jungfrawen welche in Ostfriessland dem 12. Novemb. 1596 geboren* (Prague, 1616), reprinted in Strauss and Alexander, *German Single-Leaf Woodcut, 1600–1700*, II, p. 730; *Kundt und zuwissen sey Jedermaenniglich* [incipit] (1616), reprinted in Strauss and Alexander, *German Single-Leaf Woodcut, 1600–1700*, II, p. 751; *Newe Zeitung von einere Frantzosen Wunderbarliche*

of these unfortunates seems to have satisfied a strong craving, felt by many, to view the macabre possibilities nature had to offer. Most infants born 'monstrous', though, were not so lucky as a Hans de Moer. They succumbed quite quickly to their infirmities, and their deaths seem to have touched off a relatively predictable series of events that led ultimately to their exploitation in print. The illustrations found in almost all texts frequently point to certain recognisable and fatal birth defects: severe spina bifida, Siamese twins and extreme prematurity are just a few of the many kinds of medical conditions that can be identified in these prints. The authors of the accompanying texts, though, were little concerned with the medical and natural forces that had resulted in the child's death. Rather they treated these events as divinely produced spectacles, and they packed their accounts with details, like the pilgrimage of locals, to enhance the events' dramatic effect.

Besides small pilgrimages from the vicinity, many accounts recount the visits of local officials and nobles to inspect the child. A 'terrifying birth' that occurred on 21 April 1560 at Zusmerhausen near Augsburg, for instance, was viewed by the local count, Joergen von Schwangau, who arrived with his court, other nobles and several 'Christian people'.[16] Impressed by what he had seen, Von Schwangau summoned an Augsburg illuminator to draw the child. A number of broadsides and pamphlets reveal in similar fashion the process through which nobles and officials came to learn of the event, and the ways in which the child's appearance came to be recorded by artists for posterity. Certainly, these observations helped to lend veracity to the account: high-ranking notables had witnessed the event, and had even supervised the child's faithful artistic rendering. Yet a darker purpose also stands behind the inclusion of this information. Throughout the sixteenth century, early modern urban and state officials were becoming more suspicious of midwives and mothers. The fear that mothers or midwives might use the diagnosis of monstrous birth to hide the killing of an infant with only mild deformities was real. In some places, ordinances came to prescribe that local officials should investigate all cases of strange birth and inspect the child to rule out suspicions of infanticide.[17] References to the viewing of a child by local

Mißgeburt eines Kindes so sich begeben und zugetragen hat (Görlitz, 1638), reprinted in Strauss and Alexander, *German Single-Leaf Woodcut, 1600–1700*, I, p. 446.

[16] *Warhaffte Abconterfectur der Erschrocklichen wundergeburt so dises 1560. Jar im Marckt zu Zusmerhausen am 21. Tag Aprillis von ainer Frawen geborn ist* (Augsburg, 1560), reprinted in Strauss, *German Single-Leaf Woodcut, 1550–1600*, III, p. 1093.

[17] Merry Wiesner, 'The Midwives of South Germany and the Public/Private Dichotomy', in Hilary Marland (ed.), *The Art of Midwifery* (London, 1993), pp. 77–94.

officials, then, helped to dispel any lingering suspicions in readers' minds about fraud or deceit. One late account of a monstrous birth that occurred near Stuttgart in 1640, for instance, records the exhumation of a child by local officials. The child had been immediately buried, but when local authorities learned of the event, they demanded that the body be disinterred for inspection. Impressed by the child's deformities, the officials commissioned a local artist to draw the corpse before its reburial.[18]

Several accounts refer to the transfer of a child after its death. Locals sought out experts in the surrounding vicinity to help make sense of the infant's abnormalities. In these cases the officials they identified were usually neighbouring pastors or Church officials, rather than medics or magistrates. In 1566, for example, village officials at Broderode in Thuringia brought a stillborn boy with an open skull to Christoph Vischer, who was likely a pastor in nearby Schmalkalden.[19] Impressed by what he saw, he promptly published a text interpreting the deformities he inspected on the child's corpse. In an account of a monstrous birth published in 1579, Andreas Celichius, President of the Evangelical Church at Magdeburg, explained that a local pastor from Pleetze had brought the infant's body to have it inspected by religious authorities. Celichius recounts his inspection, which occurred together with several of 'his colleagues'.[20] This search for authorities who might better illuminate a child's meaning is mentioned elsewhere.[21] And one text even refers to the sale of infants' corpses. A Nuremberg broadside from 1547 explains the lineage of Siamese twins recently displayed in that city. A local burgher had purchased the infants from their parents in Louvain. On his

---

[18] *Warhafftiges Abcontrafayt und Beschreibung der vor augen stehenden erschröcklichen Mißgeburt* (Stuttgart, 1640).

[19] Christoph Vischer, *Ware Abcontrafactur einer missgeburt so zu Brott Roda den 8. Augusti dieses 1566. Jhars Tod auff diese Welt geboren ist* (Schmalkalden, 1566), reprinted in Strauss, *German Single-Leaf Woodcut, 1550–1600*, III, p. 917.

[20] Andreas Celichius, *Historia von einer hesslichen wunder Miss Geburt in der alten Marcke Brandenburgk* (Magdeburg, 1579), fol. Aiir.

[21] Some examples include Johannes Gambstadt, *Warhafftige Beschreibung einer Wunderbarer unnd Seltzamen Geburt so in disem LXXI. Jar allhier zu Querfurt gebracht hat* (Eisleben, 1571), reprinted in Strauss, *German Single-Leaf Woodcut, 1550–1600*, I, p. 236; *Warhafftige Beschreibung einer wunderbarlichen seltzamen und erschroecklichen Geburt so in disem M.D.Lxix. Jar geschehen ist* (Augsburg, 1569), reprinted in Strauss, *German Single-Leaf Woodcut, 1550–1600*, II, p. 664; *Ein neuewe seltzam Warhafftige wundergeburt die dise yetzlauffenden 1565 Jhars an ort und enden gleich nachbenennet sich hat sehen lassen* (Strasbourg, 1565), reprinted in Strauss, *German Single-Leaf Woodcut, 1550–1600*, III, p. 1206; Jacob Faustus, *Eine Warhafftige Erschreckliche und wunderliche Kinder Geburt . . . dieses 1564. Jahrs im Dorff Dachwich* (Erfurt, 1564); Paul Langen, *Von einer erschrecklichen Mißgeburt eines Kindes so da ist geboren worden in diesem 1629 Jahr* (Hof, 1629).

return to Franconia, the merchant set them up in his house for people to view, presumably for the cost of an admission. But also, as the text tells us, 'to spark the fear of God' in the locals.[22]

Details like these helped to make the printed exploitation of monstrous births appear as the product of a series of social exchanges. Social experiences like the child's inspection and viewing by officials, the pilgrimages that developed to its body, and the infant's subsequent travels into the households of more distant experts – all these factors helped authorise the printed description. But the printed text and its accompanying image was intended to function, not as mere journalistic reportage of the sensational, but as a direct iconic replacement for the experience of having seen the infant or animal personally. To evoke the emotions of fear, wonder and dread that these spectacles were reported to have inspired, both the artists who depicted the child and the authors who related the event moved to mask and sometimes even obliterate ties to a human family. Mothers frequently remain unnamed, or if they are referred to, they are denoted only as their husband's housewife. The words 'birth' or 'was born' are similarly repressed in some accounts and are not even used to describe the process that has brought such an 'abhorrent' child into the world.[23]

A common visual rhetoric prevailed as well. This rhetoric aimed to capture the monstrous infant's strange, 'detestable' nature by removing the child from the normal social settings in which newborns were usually depicted. Most images of sixteenth-century childbirth depicted the arrival of a live, whole child as an undeniably social event that occurred within the confines of a house, usually the bedchamber, and among a circle of female relatives, friends and attendants. When they turned to depict a monstrous birth, though, artists suppressed these same architectural and familial references. Although the infants they depicted were usually dead by the time they arrived on the scene, many illustrators presented the monster as a living, breathing specimen, standing in the open air before the sparest of landscapes. Or at other times, the child's corpse was shown lying in the sleep of death, but like a relic intended for display. Through both styles of depiction, artists took their audience into a close-up

---

[22] *Diese gegenwertig wunderberlich Kindsgepurt mit zweyen leiblin vnter einem Haupt* (Nuremberg, 1547), reprinted in Eugen Holländer, *Wunder, Wundergeburt und Wundergestalt. Eine kulturhistorischen Studie in Einblattdrucken des 15. bis 18. Jahrhunderts* (Stuttgart, 1922), p. 79.

[23] A broadside from 1531, for example, describes monstrous triplets born at Augsburg as merely 'coming out' of a woman. *Anzeygung wunderbarlicher geschichten und geburt dises xxxi. Jars zu Augspurg geschichten/zc.* (Augsburg, 1531).

Ein sehr schröckliche vnd abscheuliche Wunderge=
burt/ so auff nechst vergangnem Donnerstag/den XXI. tag Aprilis dises
M. D. LXIX. jars/ zu Renchen/ nie weit von Offenburg/ vnd
drey meil wegs von Straszburg oder Röcin gelegen/
lebendig in die Welt geborn ist.

¶ Getruckt zu Straszburg/bey Thebolt Berger
am Weinmarckt zum Treübel.

Plate 15.3 *Illustration of the account of an abnormal birth of a child at Renchen near Strasbourg on 21 April 1569.*

position where they might carefully consider each of the infant's abnormalities.

Let us turn to a typical example, a 1569 broadside relating the birth of a 'terrifying and abhorrent' child in an Alsatian village named Renchen, not far from Strasbourg.[24] (See Plate 15.3.) Its image relies on the typical conventions of 'close-up' depiction. The child is shown standing, alive,

[24] *Ein sehr schröckliche und abscheulich Wundergeburt . . . dises M.D. LXIX jars zu Renchen*

before a meagre landscape. The text tells us that the infant had been born on 21 April with two heads, one on top of the other, a rare, but universally fatal condition recognised by modern medical science. The event is not explained according to any natural philosophical or medical wisdom available to sixteenth-century people. As in most accounts, there is little faith in natural explanations of deformities, because they fail to explain why the event has occurred specifically to these parents at this particular place and time. The anonymous author, moreover, seems concerned to exclude causes like improper coitus or flawed maternal imagining, since he concludes that the parents, Anna Giblerin and Hans Gannser, were 'fine' and 'honest' married people. Their misfortune was not, in other words, of their own making, but was a sign worked upon their infant directly by God. He did so, the commentator theorises, to convince the 'children of this world' of the necessity of repentance. The author styles the child a 'living mirror of God's anger', and argues that the impact of the event was greater than a sermon, since its stunning visual nature could speak to those whose hearts were hardened to words.

Following this prologue the author turns to relate the circumstances of the event. At the birth the mother was accompanied by 'several honourable women', and, following a painful delivery, she brought forth a live child who survived long enough to be baptised. The text relates these details straightforwardly, while refusing to give the child's name or to comment on how long it lived. But when the author comes to describe the child's anatomy, he expends enormous energy to amass details about its bodily deformities. The infant's body, he observes, is 'beautiful and fully formed, the same as any other child'. But on this whole body, intrusive, frightening pronouncements accrue with meanings that demand explanation. The text narrates these abnormalities in great detail, describing the precise relationship between the two heads and theorising about how the child received its life breath. Of the four orifices for eyes, for example, only one appeared to have an eyeball that functioned normally. With this kind of highly specific attention, the text roamed over the infant's body until it reached the right hand. There, it observed, the child looked as if it was bound at the wrist with a bracelet that made the hand 'blue and swollen'.

The conclusion to this broadside makes clear both the reason for this intense attention to anatomical detail and the solitary concentration on the figure of the monster itself. Such 'unusual, detestable births' do not

---

geborn ist (Strasbourg, 1569), reprinted in Strauss, *German Single-Leaf Woodcut, 1550–1600*, i, p. 116.

occur by chance. Rather they are sent by God to pronounce something, and these pronouncements are not intended for individuals, but for the collectivity. What they usually pronounce, the text warns, is some terrifying metamorphosis. Here the presence of two heads – one above the other – signifies that both political authorities and subjects will be affected by these changes. As in many cases, the child's deformities are projected out, revealing a general discord in the world, a cacophony of sinful disease that will soon be expunged. But a merciful patriarch is using this child as a reminder to give the unrepentant and the faithful, the politically empowered and the subjected, one more chance to set things right. The text thus concludes with a formulaic call to repentance.

This account of the Renchen birth related the story of a child who had survived for a time before succumbing to its deformities. In most cases, though, texts related an infant's or animal's birth and speedy death. It is not surprising, then, that many interpretations link the event to plagues, war and other events that will soon unleash an increase of mortality upon the world.[25] At other times the child's death is transformed into a symbol of the spiritual and earthly deaths of humankind, the inexorable punishment for Adam and Eve's disobedience.[26] And still other authors draw upon the ancient natural philosopher, Pliny, to remind their readers that the births and deaths of monsters are often connected to change, change in the worldly and spiritual regiments.[27]

To discern the precise nature of these changes, many texts rely on

---

[25] *Zwey warhafftige newe Zeitung von einer schrecklichen Mißgeburt* (Stettin, 1628); *Ein wunderbarliche seltzsame erschroecklich Geburt so zu Lauterbrunnen drey meyl von Augspurg hat zugetragen in disem 61. Jar den 18. tag Decembris* (1561); Celichius, *Historia von einer hesslichen wunder und Miss Geburt; Eigentliche Abcontrafetung einer seltzamen erschrecklichen Wundergeburt zu Rhena, vier Meilen von Schwerin* (1590); *Gründtliche und Warhafftige Newe Zeittung von einer unerhoerten Mißgeburt so zur Liben in Ober Laußnitz eines armen Hirten Weib geboren* (Nuremberg, 1599); Langen, *Von einer erschrecklichen Mißgeburt.*

[26] Simon Paul, *Bildnis unnd Gestalt einer erschrecklichen unnatuerlichen und ungewohnlichen Geburt einer Kindes welches Anno 1577. Den 20. Decembris zu grevesmuelen im Land zu Meckelnburg von eines Schneiders M.B. ehelichen hausfrauwen geboren ist* (Rostock, 1578); Simon Paul, *Bildnis und Gestalt einer erschrecklichen unnatuerlichen und ungewoehnlichen Geburdt einer Kindlins welches Anno 1578. Den 15. Decembris zu Rostock geboren ist* (Rostock, 1579); Celichius, *Historia von einer hesslichen wunder unt Miss Geburt.*

[27] Through his oft-reprinted collection of monstrous births and prodigies the Lutheran natural philosopher Job Fincel seems to have popularised this Plinian interpretation. See especially Job Fincel, *Wunderzeichen. Der dritte Theil* (Jena, 1562), fol. biv v. On Job Fincel, see the authoritative article of Heinz Schilling, 'Job Fincel und die Zeichen der Endzeit', in Wolfgang Brückner (ed.), *Volkserzählung und Reformation. Ein Handbuch zur Tradierung und Funktion von Erzählstoffen und Erzählliteratur im Protestantismus* (Berlin, 1972), pp. 325–92.

allegory as their dominant hermeneutic. Here these late-Reformation commentaries actively imitated the approaches that Martin Luther and Philip Melanchthon had once used in their by-now famous tracts on monsters. Both those works had roamed over the bodies of the monstrosities they treated to conduct a kind of spiritual autopsy. The abnormalities that they discerned on the bodies of these creatures had then been related to other estates and orders in contemporary society. In his *On the Meaning of the Monk Calf at Freyberg* of 1523, Luther had scrutinised the dead calf's body, making it into a microcosmic pronouncement about the degeneration sin had worked over the centuries on the monastic estate. For several pages, Luther treated the animal's corpse in intricate detail, dissecting its deformities to reveal a running divine commentary on monasticism and the Church. The animal's small, misshapen ears, for instance, were a sign of the tyranny of auricular confession. The calf had had a growth-like deformity on its back that resembled a monastic cowl, and this cowl had been torn, signs of the many human deviations and schisms that had crept into the monastic estate over the centuries. That this cowl-like growth had been torn at the animal's back and that the animal had been stillborn were proofs of the approaching dissolution of the monastic estate.[28]

This same concentrated, allegorical scrutiny of the deformed infant's corpse came to dominate in many monstrous birth texts in the second half of the century. In this approach the monstrous infant's corpse became an emblem, and its many abnormalities were related to the macrocosm of contemporary German society. The terse and cheap account published by the pastor Johannes Göltz in 1563 shows the adaptability of this tactic.[29] Among the deformities that Göltz identified on a girl stillborn in his parish were a head shaped like a helmet with a cow's snout, skin sculpted to look like contemporary clothing, and bird's claws at the hands and feet. In explaining these abnormalities he reminded his readers that they had occurred on the body at four places: the head, arms, legs and feet. Each site corresponded to one of society's four estates: the head referred to political authority; the arms to nobility and patricians; the legs to the common man; and the feet to the clergy. The shape of each deformity, Göltz counselled his readers, revealed a specific divine pronouncement about its particular sin. The snout-like nose and misshapen head, for instance, pointed to the vainglorious life to which many in Germany's

---

[28] Martin Luther, *Deuttung des Munchkalbs zu Freyberg jnn Meijsszen funden* (Wittenberg, 1523), reprinted in Lange, *Der Papstesel*, pp. 111–16.

[29] Göltz, *Ein erschreckliche Geburt.*

courts had abandoned themselves, a life filled with boozing and gluttony. The arms, draped in sculpted forms of skins that resembled the wasteful puffs of contemporary clothing, were an indictment of the vanities of fine people, both nobles and patricians, who spent more on a 'single skirt, blouse, or bodice', than one did in the 'old days to celebrate an entire wedding'. As he turned to the child's torso and legs, he observed them draped with the wasteful, and oft-prohibited style of Turkish pants (*Pluderhosen*), then popular among peasants in the empire. The Devil himself had 'unleashed' these pants on the world, Göltz charged, and their appearance on the deformed infant's body was ample proof that God was less than pleased with the style. Finally, Göltz arrived at the child's feet, where bird's claws rather than toes were present, a sign that revealed the 'false teaching' that had crept into the preacher's vocation and which was tearing at Christians' 'soul and blood'.

Underlying this account, as in so many of these evangelical texts, was a profound sense of despair. The Evangel, crystalline in its clarity at its inception, had been clouded over through the vices of human pride, deceit and vanity. In his conclusion, Göltz reminded his readers that the lectionary reading for the day on which the birth occurred had been Luke 21, Christ's warning of eschatological tribulation, a sign that further pointed to the apocalyptic nature of this monstrous birth. Repentance, both for the wicked and the pious, was the only sane response to such an event.

Göltz's text was brief. It was published in three cities in both broadside and pamphlet formats, but even the pamphlet edition was only five folio pages long. As attention to monstrous births grew at the end of the century, more complex and learned 'sacred autopsies' flourished too. In his *History of a Detestable Miracle and Misbirth in the Old Mark Branden-burg* (1579), Andreas Celichius dissected the body of a child born at Pleetze, not far from Stendhal.[30] Among the numerous abnormalities that Celichius had spotted on the infant's skinless body were a helmet-like form atop the head, crystal-like eyes, and again, capacious folds of skin at the legs that resembled Turkish trousers and bird's claws at the hands and feet. Celichius began by cataloguing each and every one of this stillbirth's abnormalities before proceeding to discuss for more than thirty pages the messages they bore for contemporary Germans. For the Magdeburg church official, the infant was a kind of icon of sin, an icon in the original sense of that word, since Celichius believed the child was a divinely inscribed pronouncement. As such, he argued, the child's body revealed

---

[30] Celichius, *Historia von einer hesslichen wunder und Miss Geburt.*

to observers the full scope of contemporary moral degeneration. As he considered each of its abnormalities, he was moved to make ever more dismal pronouncements about human sinfulness. 'We are all children of iniquity, degenerated devil's spawn,' he summarised in one particularly bleak passage, 'and we carry the worm of Adam's apple in our bones, blood, and marrow.'[31] To view a child like this, Celichius concluded, was to see human nature laid bare. Through the birth, God was, in other words, holding up a mirror to human beings, a mirror intended for their wide-eyed, pious gaze.

The utter helplessness of human beings in their fallen state may have been the primary message Celichius drew from the corpse of an abnormal birth. At the same time, he moved to identify with hairsplitting precision the specific shortcomings God was making obvious in the 'detestable' infant. These faults ranged from love of luxury, to avarice, pride, diabolically inspired heresies and sexual depravity. And these specific shortcomings were revealed in the very shapes of the child's body. Contemporary Germans' love of luxury, for instance, was evidenced in the folds of skins upon the child's legs, folds that resembled the prohibited 'Turkish' trousers. The infant's bird-like claws pointed, not to the clergy, but to the robbing, 'raven-like' behaviour of contemporaries, the search after mammon to which many had abandoned themselves. Celichius, a church official, fixed the meaning of the helmet-like form atop the child's head in theological terms. It was a sign of God's displeasure with the currents of theological discord among evangelicals, strife introduced by those who wished to corrupt and dim the clarity of Luther's truth. In this way Celichius progressed over the child's corpse from head to toe, relating each and every physical infirmity to the macrocosmic degeneration he observed in his own times.

With his dissection complete the evangelical author arrived at the destination that had captivated many western commentators since Augustine's time: the Last Judgement and its longed-for dissolution of human suffering. Like many before him, Celichius saw the child as an eschatological signpost that pointed to the nearing end of history. In a world in which both physical and moral degeneration appeared increasingly common, in which daily testimonies to both human wickedness and reproductive abnormality were rife, divine judgement must surely be at hand. The route that Celichius followed to establish this certainty, however, differs strikingly from Augustine and medieval theological traditions. From the shape of a deformed infant's body, the greatest

---

[31]   *Ibid.*, fol. Aiiii v.

sureties led, not to an understanding of God's mysterious, yet merciful ordering of nature, but backward into the Garden of Eden and the stain of Original Sin. Through a kind of involuted logic, his interpretation of the monster's body began with human shortcomings, and it continually led the reader back to the Fall and the decay it continued to reproduce in all human beings. That that disobedience would soon be judged and punished appeared to him to be indisputable. But for Celichius, no attempt to understand the birth and death of this horrifically deformed child could be separated from its central signification: to make obvious the enormous weight of humankind's disobedience and the hideous deformations that sin was continually working on men's and women's natures. Like many other writers of similar texts, he insisted that the true purpose of the sign was as a visual sermon of repentance, a *Bußpredigt*, calling both the pious and the wicked to constant amendment of their lives.

Celichius's work was unusual by virtue of its length and intricate exposition. It was not a cheap, sensationalistic text like Göltz's or the anonymous 1569 account of the two-headed Renchen monster. Instead, it was a carefully wrought theological exposition of the complexities of meanings that reposed in a particular infant's abnormalities. While such accounts were always rarer than the lurid texts that flowed from the penny press, many similar works still appeared around the same time.[32] Johannes Cuno's *Pride's Weal*, published at Magdeburg in 1594, is likely the last of these elite, theological expositions on a monstrous infant's corpse. It broadcast the birth of a son to a local woman, Anna Meinecken.[33] Cuno, a Lutheran minister from the vicinity, transformed a gruesome birth into an event that captured, then inverted older hagiographical topoi, enlisting them to serve his dismal judgements on human nature. His tract was long and imposing, filled with numerous observations, details and moralisms that were frequently missing in other shorter accounts of monstrous births. Like almost all texts, however, he dismissed the details of Anna Meinecken's five-day labour in a single sentence as

---

[32] The works by Paul, and Cuno fall into this category, as well as the many compendia published by members of the theological elite. Bibliographical references to these collected editions of prodigies and monstrous births can be found in Rudolf Schenda, 'Die deutschen Prodigiensammlungen des 16 und 17 Jahrhunderts', *Archiv für Geschichte des Buchwesens* 4 (1961), pp. 638–98. The most complete evangelical work on monstrous birth was written during this period by a Flacian disciple: Christoph Irenaeus, *De Monstris. Von seltzamen Wundergeburten* (Ursel, 1583).

[33] Johannes Cuno, *Hoffartswohlstand. Nach der geblendeten Weltkinder art zu reden* (Magdeburg, 1594).

mere matter-of-fact happenstance. After struggling to deliver her child from Saturday until the following Wednesday, Cuno observed, Anna Meinecken gave up the ghost and was sewn into her shroud.

Cuno's gaze fell instead upon the truly dramatic way in which God had used Anna's dead body to reveal His pronouncements about monstrous human nature. In the morning after her death, the women attending Anna's body were wakened by a loud noise emanating from her corpse like some rumbling from the tomb. Terrified, they sent for the midwife, who arrived and ripped open Anna's shroud to find her body palpitating. Her corpse, which had been 'brown and black-coloured like a snake upon its death', now was snow white. Immediately, the midwife performed a Caesarian to deliver Anna's dead boy, who looked about a year old and was covered with stylish bands, rings and bracelets. This miraculous revelation thus provided Cuno with the ammunition he needed to condemn a degenerate human nature. For more than a hundred pages, he minutely catalogued the divine pronouncements God had made on this child's body, exhausting their meanings to a point of baroque complexity.

The topoi included in Cuno's narrative relied on older stories about saintly autopsies. Cut open after their death, the bodies of the saints had long revealed sacred hieroglyphs inscribed on their hearts and internal organs, physical signs that could be said to confirm sanctity.[34] Here, however, the midwife's knife had opened up a woman's body to expose divine pronouncements, not about sanctity, but about human evil. God had intervened in the mundane exercise of a woman's funeral to ensure that the condemning texts he had inscribed on the body of a monstrous child would be made known. And Cuno proceeded to decode those hieroglyphs using the conventions of the now time-honoured practices of sacred autopsy.

Cuno's work provides a fitting conclusion to our consideration of the various roles that the monstrous infant's corpse played in the religious culture of late sixteenth-century Lutheranism. While allegory survived as a framework in which to interpret the deformed corpse long after the publication of Cuno's *Pride's Weal*, no member of the religion's theological elite seems to have turned again to treat monstrous birth with his sheer verve, intensity or complexity. At the same time, urgent, cheap

---

[34] Piero Camporesi, *The Incorruptible Flesh: Bodily Mutation and Mortification in Religion and Folklore*, tr. Tania Croft-Murray (Cambridge, 1988), pp. 3–7; Katharine Park, 'The Criminal and the Saintly Body: Autopsy and Dissection in Renaissance Italy', *Renaissance Quarterly* 47 (1994), pp. 1–33; Giulia Calvi, *Histories of a Plague Year. The Social and Imaginary in Baroque Florence*, tr. Dario Biocca and Brant T. Ragan Jr (Berkeley, 1986), pp. 212–26.

prophecies about the births and deaths of monsters continued to appear in Lutheran towns and territories until the second half of the seventeenth century. But when members of the learned elite came to consider monsters in the seventeenth century, it was often natural philosophers and medics, not theologians, who conducted the discussion. They considered the problem of monstrosity as an issue of a divinely created nature, a nature that again resembled the notions of Augustine and the scholastics, including their emphasis on nature's complexity and its unseen, latent forces and possibilities. The gradual triumph of this sensibility was to be accompanied by a steady evaporation of the immediacy and extremes of the late-Reformation sense of sin. In the space opened up by the rejection of the notion that human beings could only understand nature through the lens of sin, new modes of thought and expression could flourish, modes that stressed the human ability to comprehend and master the environment.

The genesis of these habits of thought, though, can be traced back to the religious culture of the later Reformation and a time in which both elites and people had perceived the monstrous infant to be a source of spiritual insight and theological authority. That society had pictured the nameless monster, a highly unusual member of the dead, as a still-living mirror in which human misdeeds could be viewed. Or they had looked upon the deformed corpse as an iconic embodiment of the race's wickedness. These strategies were, to be sure, ways that dispensed with frightening, morally troubling events and found a deeper purpose in human suffering. But they were also perceived by pastors, theologians and church officials as ways to inculcate new religious ideas, like the utter helplessness of human beings outside of a gratuitous, divine infusion of faith. To drive this point home to towns and villages where sheer voyeurism competed side by side with pious devotion, these same authors went to extraordinary lengths to capture the curiosity of their audience, transforming the deformed corpse into a grim inversion of traditional sanctity. The rhetoric they fashioned was not lost in subsequent centuries; the flaws of human reproduction remained marks of Cain, signs of Original Sin, and symbols of human alienation outside Eden's perfection. But in adopting the deformed infant's corpse as a didactic tool for teaching religious principles, the sixteenth-century Reformation also came to rely on the purely human taste for marvels and oddities. And for many, sheer fascination with the medium – the monstrous infant's corpse – may have always overshadowed the message.

Index